3RD EDITION

D0589460

3

internet commerce
Digital Models for Business

internet commerce

Digital Models for Business

3RD EDITION

Elaine **LAWRENCE**   John **LAWRENCE**

Stephen **NEWTON**   Stephen **DANN**

Brian **CORBITT**   Theerasak **THANASANKIT**

John Wiley & Sons Australia, Ltd

Third edition published 2003 by
John Wiley & Sons Australia, Ltd
33 Park Road, Milton, Qld 4064

Offices also in Sydney and Melbourne

Typeset in 10.5/12.5 pt Rotis Serif

First edition 1998
Second edition 2000

© E. Lawrence, S. Newton, B. Corbitt, J. Lawrence,
   S. Dann and T. Thanasankit 2003

National Library of Australia
Cataloguing-in-publication data

Internet commerce: digital models for business.

3rd ed.
Includes index.
For tertiary students
ISBN 0 470 80235 9.

1. Electronic commerce.   2. Business enterprises —
Computer networks. I. Lawrence, Elaine.

658.054678

Cover image and images used in internal design:
© 2002 Digital Vision and © 2002 Digital Vision/
Simon Osborne

Printed in Singapore by
Markono Print Media Pte Ltd

10 9 8 7 6 5 4 3 2 1

BRIEF CONTENTS

CONTENTS

CHAPTER 03 **TECHNOLOGY BASICS**   51

PREFACE

We were very thrilled with the success of the first and second editions of this textbook and thank our readers for their kind words of encouragement. The first edition won the Australian Publishers Award for Excellence in the Tertiary Technology Section in 1999.

Electronic business over the Internet has undergone exponential growth during the past seven years. Information technology is driving this economic growth, yet from early 2000 many companies began to experience difficulties as organisations shifted to the Internet's high-change/high-speed environment. It has been a heady ride and many e-businesses have fallen by the wayside. Nonetheless, three start-up dot.com companies, Amazon, eBay and Yahoo!, are now among the world's best-known brands. These three pioneers have software at their core — they innovate with it, they buy out other software companies to obtain exclusive use and they use software to replace people. Many large corporations now recognise that the Web can assist them to realise efficiency improvements, cost reductions and increased business opportunities leading to improved profits. This textbook examines how the e-commerce market has matured over the years.

This burgeoning use of the Internet demands that employees and managers understand and be skilled in Internet commerce practices in order for their businesses to gain a competitive advantage. The third edition of *Internet Commerce: Digital Models for Business* has updated the material for the rapidly emerging field of Internet/electronic commerce. This new edition places the study of Internet commerce within an international and national framework. It includes new, more detailed end-of-chapter case studies to illustrate the emerging trends and features. The multidisciplinary team of authors has covered the business, management, technical and legal aspects of this exciting area of commerce on the Internet.

Objectives of the book

After completing the book, students will:

- have received a thorough grounding in electronic commerce on the Internet
- know the stakeholders in electronic commerce and their capabilities and limitations in the strategic convergence of technology and business
- understand the rapid changes taking place in electronic commerce
- be aware of the new technologies of importance to electronic commerce
- have been exposed to important research and development trends in the area

John Wiley & Sons Australia will maintain a web site (see www.johnwiley. com.au/highered/internet-commerce) to keep readers abreast of recent changes with timely updates.

The authors hope that lecturers and students will find this new edition, web site and supplements useful and valuable adjuncts to their study of Internet commerce.

Special thanks go to Ms Roma Simmonds, an IT consultant at Qantas, for her contributions to chapters 3, 5 and 9. Special thanks are also extended to Katina Michael (University of Wollongong), Amanda Toshack (University of Wollongong), Jeff Chamberlain (Deakin University), John Paul Sargent (University of Wollongong), Bruce Howarth and Theerasak Thanasankit (Monash University) for preparing the end-of-chapter case studies. We would also like to thank our colleagues who reviewed the text throughout the development of the new edition.

Elaine Lawrence
Stephen Newton
Brian Corbitt
John Lawrence
Stephen Dann
Theerasak Thanasankit
November 2002

ABOUT THE AUTHORS

Elaine LAWRENCE

Elaine Lawrence, DTech, MBIT, GradDip Commercial Computing, BA, CCNA, CCAI, MACS, is a senior lecturer in Computer Systems in the Faculty of Information Technology, University of Technology, Sydney. She is the Program Leader for the graduate courses in Internetworking. Her research interests are in Internet commerce, Internet networking and flexible learning strategies, in particular in cooperation with Cisco. Elaine is a founding member of the Internet/intranet consulting business, Cyber.Consult. She has designed and delivered seminars on electronic commerce in the United States, South Africa, Europe, Malaysia and Australia. Elaine is the lead author of *Technology of Internet Business* (John Wiley & Sons, 2002) and has written two books for the CCH Hands-On Solutions series on electronic commerce, namely *Setting up a Shopfront* (1998) and *Virtual Tax Reform* (1999).

Stephen NEWTON

Stephen Newton is a principal consultant with eStrategies, a private consulting firm that specialises in providing Internet business strategic advice and software development services to a corporate and government client base. He has completed a Master's degree in Computing Science, specialising in e-commerce, and is the co-author of *Technology of Internet Business* (John Wiley & Sons, 2002).

Brian CORBITT

Brian Corbitt is Professor of Information Systems and Head of School in the School of Information Systems at Deakin University, Melbourne. He specialises in IS in developing countries; ICT and electronic commerce policy development, analysis and implementation; business modelling and electronic commerce trade relationships; and knowledge management in tertiary institutions. Brian is currently responsible for the development of e-learning and knowledge management initiatives at Deakin University as Pro Vice-Chancellor.

John LAWRENCE

John Lawrence, LLB, BSc (Hons), MBA, is a barrister practising in the areas of electronic commerce, environmental and planning laws, construction and building disputes, and contract law. He is a Registered Legal Practitioner,

New South Wales, and is a member of the New South Wales Bar Association, the Institution of Engineers, Australia and the Institute of Arbitrators and Mediators, Australia.

Stephen Dann

Stephen Dann, PhD, BCom (Hons), AMAMI, is a Senior Consultant, Marketing and Research, with Sparten. He is a strategic marketing trainer and consultant specialising in consumer behaviour and new technology adoptions. Prior to branching out as a consultant, Stephen was a lecturer in the School of Marketing, Griffith University. He has spoken at national and international conferences on his research, including a personal invitation to the Princess Diana Memorial Conference in London to present his research on the potential use of the Princess's death in road safety campaigns. Stephen has lectured internationally on communications theory and practice and has spent some time as a visiting Professor at Emerson College in Boston. Stephen's areas of specialisation are Internet marketing strategy, communications and consumer behaviour. Stephen is co-author of *Strategic Internet Marketing* (John Wiley & Sons, 2001).

Theerasak THANASANKIT

Theerasak Thanasankit, BSocSciInfoMgt, MBusSys, PhD, is a Senior Lecturer in the School of Information Management and Systems at Monash University. Theerasak previously worked at the University of Melbourne in both the Department of Accounting and the Department of Information Systems. He has also worked at Victoria University in Wellington, New Zealand. Theerasak's research focuses on the role of national culture on e-commerce, IT/IS adoption in Southeast Asia and requirements engineering.

ACKNOWLEDGEMENTS

Images

Pp. 18, 39, 119 (left): Reproduced with permission from Telstra; p. 31: Reproduced with permission from Ozemail; p. 40: Reproduced with permission from Yahoo! Australia & NZ; p. 59: Reproduced with permission from Autobytel Inc.; p. 61: © ASX Ltd. All rights reserved. This material is reproduced with permission of ASX. This material should not be reproduced, stored in a retrieval system or transmitted in any form whether in whole or in part without the prior written permission of ASX; pp. 66, 67 (middle): Netscape website © 2002 Netscape Communications Corporation. Screenshot used with permission; p. 67 (bottom): Screen shot reprinted by permission from Microsoft Corporation; p. 85: Screen shot of ABC online reproduced with permission of the Australian Broadcasting Corporation; p. 88: Reproduced with permission from Greg Norman Interactive; p. 109: © Australian Information Industry Association Ltd 1999; p. 110: Reproduced with permission from Trintech; p. 112: Reproduced with permission from Discovercard.com; p. 119 (top): Reproduced with permission from Hertz Australia Pty Limited; p. 119 (right): Reproduced with permission from dpunkt.verlag; p. 120 (top left): Reproduced with permission from Queensland Transport; p. 120 (above right): Reproduced with permission from National Australia Bank and MasterCard International; p. 120 (below right): Reproduced with permission from National Australia Bank; p. 120 (below left): Reproduced with permission of Medical Benefits Fund of Australia Ltd; p. 131: Australian Picture Library/Bettmann/Corbis; p. 132: iCube Solutions; p. 155: Reproduced with permission from Wiley Publishing Inc.; p. 168: Reproduced with permission from DoubleClick Inc.; p. 172: Reproduced with permission from Qantas; p. 179: Reproduced with permission from Dell Computer; p. 194 (below): Reproduced with the permission of Ford Motor Company; p. 194 (top): Reproduced with permission from Woolworths Limited; p. 196: Reproduced with permission from News Interactive; p. 212: National Office for the Information Economy; p. 213: National Office for the Information Economy; p. 271: Culture and recreation page, from www.cultureandrecreation.gov.au. Copyright Commonwealth of Australia. Reproduced with permission; p. 276: Reproduced with permission from FishNet Security; p. 285: Reproduced with permission from the Business Entry Point, Department of Industry, Tourism and Resources; p. 292: Reproduced with permission from Eurotechnology Japan K.K.

Text
Pp. 4–5: Reproduced with permission from The Economist Intelligence Unit; pp. 22–3: Reproduced with permission from Internet Corporation for Assigned Names and Numbers (ICANN) www.internic.net/faqs/new-tlds.html; pp. 24–5: Reprinted with the kind permission of Optus; pp. 45–9: Jason Sargent, University of Wollongong; p. 64: Adapted from *Electronic Commerce*, by R. Kalakota & A. Whinston, 1997, Addison Wesley, p. 55. Reprinted by permission of Pearson Education, Inc., Upper Saddle River, NJ; p. 92: Reproduced with permission from Netcraft; p. 172: Adapted from *E-Business: Roadmap for Success*, by R. Kalakota & M. Robinson, 1999, Addison Wesley Longman, pp. 111–12 © Adapted by permission of Pearson Education, Inc., Upper Saddle River, NJ; p. 186: *Global Software Teams: Collaborating across borders and time zones*, by Erran Carmel, © Reprinted by permission of Pearson Education, Inc., Upper Saddle River, NJ; pp. 209–10: Reproduced with permission from Joint Venture: Silicon Valley Network; p. 215: Adapted from 'Examples of payment systems on the Internet'. Reproduced with permission from Daon Security & Accountability Systems; p. 219: Taxable Importations, from www.customs.gov.au/taxref/issues.htm. Copyright Commonwealth of Australia. Reproduced with permission; p. 221: Reproduced with permission from the Australian Senate; p. 242: Republished with permission from The Fast Company, from *Life of crime*, Christine Canabou, Fast Company, 1 April, 2001, p 60. Permission conveyed through Copyright Clearance Center, Inc.; p. 280: Adapted from, Durlacher Research 1999, 'Mobile commerce report', www.durlacher.com/downloads/mcomreport.pdf. Reproduced with permission.

Introduction to Internet commerce

LEARNING outcomes

You will have mastered the material in this chapter when you can:

- understand the difference between the Internet and the World Wide Web
- understand and define electronic commerce and Internet commerce
- appreciate the reasons for the dot.bombs and learn from past mistakes
- give practical examples to illustrate the theory of creative destruction
- understand the underlying technologies of the Internet
- know the main Internet commerce players and their capabilities and limitations in the strategic convergence of technology and business.

'Every new successful commercial invention, from electricity to the Internet, was built upon the back of financial mania.'

Roger McNamee of Integral Capital Partners, in A. Perkins 2001, 'The angler: seeing the future in real time', *Red Herring*, 15 June, p. 21.

INTRODUCTION

There have been enormous changes in the world of Internet commerce since the publication of the first edition of this book in 1998. Excitement about the new way of conducting business was reaching fever pitch in this year and **dot.com** businesses were multiplying exponentially. New ways of doing business online were being developed. For example, the company Priceline.com came up with the radical idea of empowering the customer. Customers could set their price for items such as airline tickets and hotel rooms, and sellers could then decide whether or not to accept their offers. However, in April 2000, the situation changed radically – many dot.coms (often referred to as dot.bombs) failed and the investment frenzy abated.[1] The new online economy will be different and this edition highlights the changes that have occurred since the second edition was published in 2000.

THE GROWTH OF INTERNET COMMERCE

The exponential growth in the use of the **Internet** underpins the fact that it is growing faster than any other technology in history. For individuals and companies alike, the Internet presents a new and highly effective avenue for communicating and conducting business online. Not only has the Web introduced a cheaper way of doing business, it presents new opportunities to expand existing markets; facilitates market globalisation; and promotes open trade. The technology also encourages new uses of information and stimulates exploration of as-yet untapped virtual supply chains.

The Economist Intelligence Unit and Pyramid Research have conducted research to determine the e-readiness rankings of various countries. E-readiness is a term used to describe how conducive a country's business industry is to Internet commerce and covers areas such as the computer literacy of the population, the security of Internet transactions and the level of sophistication of the country's telecommunications infrastructure.[2] The Economist Intelligence Unit and Pyramid Research have investigated the world's 60 largest economies and rated each using the following categories:

- *E-business leaders*: countries that are almost 'e-ready' but are subject to concerns about a lack of regulation.
- *E-business contenders*: countries whose infrastructure and business environments are ready, but that still need to work on the other factors of e-readiness.
- *E-business followers*: countries that have begun to work towards e-readiness. This category holds the largest number of countries.
- *E-business laggards*: countries that have major problems, especially connectivity, to address before the move to e-readiness and that risk being left behind.[3]

Table 1.1 highlights some of the findings.

TABLE 1.1	SELECTED E-READINESS RANKINGS
E-READINESS RANKING (OUT OF 60)	**COUNTRY**
E-business leaders	
1	United States
2	Australia
3	United Kingdom
4	Canada
5	Norway
6	Sweden
7	Singapore
8	Finland
9	Denmark
E-business contenders	
14	Ireland
15	France
16 (tie)	Austria
16 (tie)	Taiwan
18	Japan
19	Belgium
20	New Zealand
21	South Korea
22	Italy
E-business followers	
26	Greece
27	Czech Republic
28	Hungary
29	Chile
30	Poland
31	Argentina
32	Slovakia
33	Malaysia
34	Mexico
	(*continued*)

TABLE 1.1	SELECTED E-READINESS RANKINGS *(continued)*
E-READINESS RANKING (OUT OF 60)	**COUNTRY**
E-business laggards	
48	Bulgaria
49	China
50 (tie)	Ecuador
50 (tie)	Iran
52 (tie)	Romania
52 (tie)	Ukraine
54 (tie)	Algeria
54 (tie)	Indonesia
56	Nigeria

SOURCE: Economist Intelligence Unit 2001, 'The Economist Intelligence Unit/Pyramid Research e-readiness rankings', 8 May, accessed July 2002, www.ebusinessforum.com/index.asp?layout=rich_story&doc_id=367.

DEFINITIONS OF ELECTRONIC COMMERCE AND INTERNET COMMERCE

There has been an explosion of names to identify doing business electronically, such as electronic commerce, e-tailing, B2C, B2B, e-commerce, iCommerce, Internet commerce and digital commerce. In this book, we use the terms 'electronic commerce' and 'Internet commerce' interchangeably. Electronic commerce can be defined as the buying and selling of information, products and services via computer networks today and in the future, using any one of the myriad of networks that make up the Internet.[4]

One area that this book will be concentrating on is business-to-consumer (B2C) e-commerce, where products, services or information are purchased by consumers acting for themselves rather than for a business. This B2C e-commerce also includes other new (non-traditional) channels such as mobile devices like phones and personal digital assistants (PDAs). Once a purchase has been made via one of these new channels, the products or services may then be delivered over the Internet (e.g. music, software), via a third-party service directly to the consumer's nominated address or picked up from a physical outlet, such as a petrol station. B2C e-commerce is commonly thought of as only retailing via an Internet channel (e-tailing) and while this is the largest portion of the B2C market it also encompasses segments such as share brokerage, insurance, online magazines and the rapidly expanding auction market (e.g. www.ebay.com).[5]

While the Internet was established in the 1960s in the United States, it was not until the 1990s that its commercial potential started to be realised. Prior to that, the Internet was an academic and research tool for government, educational and non-profit organisations that was subsidised by the government and kept strictly out of reach of the business community. In the mid-1980s the National Science Foundation (NSF) created a high-speed, long-distance telecommunications network into which other networks could be linked. (Other organisations now support this link.) By 1991 NSF had dropped its restrictive usage policy and allowed in many commercial sites.[6] This development, along with the arrival of the **World Wide Web**, caused the business community to take notice of the Internet. The Web is a graphical **hypertext** environment that operates within the Internet. It supports multimedia presentations, which include audio, video, text and graphics. The protocol (a set of rules, procedures and standards) that underpins the Web is **hypertext transfer protocol (HTTP)** and the protocol for doing business on the Web is secure hypertext transfer protocol (HTTPs), which provides a basis for secure communications, authentication, digital signatures and encryption.

WEB BROWSERS, INTERNET COMMERCE AND SECURITY

A web **browser** is a piece of software that allows the user to access information in the form of sound, text, graphics and video clips on the Internet. Browsers such as Netscape Navigator and Microsoft's Internet Explorer (combined with supporting software) provide an interface to the Web via hypertext transfer protocol or other types of Internet tool, such as **file transfer protocol (FTP)**.

The secure hypertext transfer protocol enables:

- browsers to encrypt information being sent to a **server**, digitally sign requests and authenticate the identity of a server
- servers to encrypt replies, to digitally sign replies and authenticate the identity of browsers.

Prior to the establishment of the Web, the Internet was text-based, command-driven and user-unfriendly. Once multimedia became part of the scenario, businesses started to see the potential in using it. Two features are encouraging businesses to use the Internet: codification and distribution. Codification refers to the organised storage of information in a computer system (e.g. ASCII text and standards for storing photographs, videos and audio). Distribution refers to the ability to use **hypertext markup language (HTML)**, a programming language used to create a web page that allows codified information to be shared globally (as well as **email**), no matter whether the information is text, photographs or embedded web pages.[7] Entrepreneurs quickly saw the real business possibilities that the Web offered. A new standard called **extensible markup language (XML)** allows developers to develop custom tags such as <item-number>, <item-name>

and <item-price>. Such a language enables browsers and web servers to implement transaction-processing tasks. In fact, just as HTML allows for open text publishing, so XML allows for open database publishing.[8]

Uniform resource locators and business significance

Uniform resource locators (URLs), also known as universal resource locators, are addresses for web resources on the Internet. Users are able to enter these addresses into their browser software and make direct connections with the relevant web pages. Table 1.2 shows some URL examples and table 1.3 explains the meanings and uses of these protocols. For further examples on how to understand the Internet visit the site www.learnthenet.com.

TABLE 1.2	UNIFORM RESOURCE LOCATOR (URL) EXAMPLES	
PROTOCOL	**WEB SERVER OR COMPUTER NAME**	**DIRECTORY NAME AND/OR FILENAME**
file://	/CI/Digital Commerce/	INTRO/index.htm
telnet://	138.25.78.8	(login library)
gopher://	info.anu.edu.au:70	/11/OtherSites/othergophers
news:	news.newusers.questions	
http://	www.ssw.com.au	/index.htm
https://	www.davidjones.com.au	
ftp://	ftp.deakin.edu.au	/pub/pc-net/

TABLE 1.3	PROTOCOL MEANINGS AND USES	
PROTOCOL	**ACTION**	**PURPOSE**
file://	Retrieve local HTML and multimedia files	Useful for editing purposes
telnet://	Log onto and work on a remote computer	Useful for checking out external libraries' resources
gopher://	Access text-based menu system	Useful for searching and receiving documents
news:	Read messages from discussion groups	Communicating with wide range of people on topics of mutual interest
http://	Retrieve text and multimedia to a local computer	Linking a user's browser client to a web server
https://	To secure transactions	Encrypting credit card transactions
ftp://	Download files from remote computer	E.g. downloading software

THE GROWTH OF COMMERCIAL DOMAIN NAMES

The Internet commercial domain (indicated on a URL by '.com') was the fastest growing segment over the last two years. In Australia there are now so many commercial domains registered that some companies are going offshore to Norfolk Island to register their domain names. Many Australian companies are also registering their business names in the United States where it is cheaper and where a country code (e.g. Australia's country code is '.au') is not added. Some Australian cyber businesses believe that having '.au' on their **domain name** could deter overseas shoppers from dealing with them. In 2001 two new domain names were released: .biz and .info. An unusual method of applying for a .biz domain was set up. First, interested parties could file an IP claim in which they declared some intellectual property ('IP') in a registered or unregistered trademark. This step was designed to help businesses to protect their valuable IP before '.biz' registration began and to notify other applicants of that claim. Second, requests for a particular domain (which could include business or company names, as well as registered or unregistered trademarks) were submitted prior to the '.biz' launch in October 2001. Finally, a lottery took place in which one of the registered applicants received the .biz name. A similar procedure existed for the .info domain. (See case study 1 at the end of this chapter for more information on the different domain names.)

Obviously, it is important for businesses to have a URL that reflects their business name. For example, an Internet/**intranet** consulting and training business called Cyber.Consult has a registered domain name and virtual server at www.cyberconsult.com.au. Thus, it is easy for people to quickly work out what a business address is, whether it is for BHP, David Jones or Cyber.Consult. It is vitally important for companies to register their Internet address as there have been cases of people registering well-known brand or company names and then asking the legitimate company for money to buy the 'Net' name. Registration of commercial domain names in Australia and elsewhere has been characterised by some problems, such as domain name squatting and misspelling popular names to catch browsers who mistype the name they are searching for.

HISTORY OF ELECTRONIC COMMERCE

Electronic data interchange (EDI) and email have been used for years in workflow and re-engineering applications. By October 1999 America Online had over 20 million subscribers. Many large businesses and government departments in Australia have insisted that their suppliers use EDI if they wish to continue trading with them. As a result, some companies who could not afford such expensive hardware and software lost contracts. However, the Internet combined with EDI offers businesses the opportunity to become part of the digital commerce phenomenon in the twenty-first century. Harris Technology in Sydney has a successful web site and also uses EDI to communicate with its supplier.

Automation in the financial services industry began with back-office functions (e.g. cheque processing in the 1960s), followed by new systems for credit card processing and wire transfers. Next, teller stations in local branches were automated to allow direct entry of particular transactions and direct access to customer account information. In the 1980s automation went from behind the counter to the customers via automatic teller machines (ATMs). In Australia customer acceptance of ATMs was not particularly fast, but ATM-style banking is now very popular. The concept of digitally transferring funds (electronic funds transfer or EFT) between banking institutions has expanded to personal banking with ATMs, ATM cards and point-of-sale machines. In the 1990s the personal computer moved from the office to the home, and financial institutions are extending their technology to bring services to customers' personal computers (or telephones) at home and at work. The institutions have found such facilities lower the cost of servicing customer transactions, while increasing revenue sources. These facilities also make the institutions more competitive in customer service, which leads to increased customer loyalty.[9]

'A paradigm shift is driving new business practices within the financial services industry. Financial institutions desire to build new computer systems across an open platform to handle the shift to secure digital transactions. Four critical issues are impacting the speed of the evolution:
- the need for improved technology to ensure the security of the transaction
- the availability of a variety of payment protocols
- system reliability for twenty-four hours a day times seven days a week operations
- the flexibility of the platform to add new capabilities as they become available.'[10]

BUSINESS REVOLUTION AND INTERNET COMMERCE

Just as the banks have seen how computer networks improve their viability, so businesses have started to recognise that the Internet allows:
- company and consumer transactions over public networks for home shopping and banking
- transactions with trading partners using EDI
- information-gathering, such as market research
- information distribution transactions.[11]

THE THEORY OF CREATIVE DESTRUCTION

Ways of doing business have been dramatically changed by the use of information technology — old ways of dealing with customers, suppliers and employees have been destroyed and replaced by radical new ways. Harvard economist Joseph Schumpeter calls this creative destruction. He believes that what has been destroyed is more important than what has been retained and that only by destroying old ways of doing business can new ways be created.[12] Let us consider an example that is very common in Australia. With the restructuring of businesses in Australia, many middle managers found themselves without jobs. These were often people in their late forties who had identified closely with the firms for which they had worked over the past 20 years. Many of these people had to destroy their way of marketing themselves as potential loyal employees and become sole practitioners. They could no longer find positions that would enable them to have secretaries, assistants and various support mechanisms to get them through the working day. For such people to survive, they had to reinvent themselves and become proficient in the use of information technology. If they obtained a private consulting job, they had to do all the parts of the job themselves, such as typing the report, preparing the invoices, doing their own research and running the modelling software.

Old business practices had to be thrown out and new information technology practices brought in. For example, the company Encyclopaedia Britannica, now also known as Britannica.com, had to reinvent the way it presented and sold its encyclopaedic database. At first the company resisted the move to digital media; however, continued growth of technology forced it to re-evaluate its business strategy. In 1994 it decided to market its encyclopaedia as a CD-ROM and as a subscription-based Internet service. The CD-ROM entered the market at a retail price of more than A$1200. This high price did not attract the expected business and the company was forced to reduce the price to A$199, which has proved to be a much more attractive proposition for buyers. The CD-ROM includes the entire text version of the *Encyclopaedia Britannica*, plus other helpful tools to assist students with homework. The encyclopaedia is also available on DVD (digital video disc). To further add value to its product, Encyclopaedia Britannica offers *Britannica Online* (www.eb.com), a subscription-based Internet service featuring the entire *Encyclopaedia Britannica* and other special features and tools, including an encyclopaedia for students. Encyclopaedia Britannica continues to reposition itself from a traditional publishing company into a twenty-first century media company. In October 1999 Encyclopaedia Britannica launched an online information service at www.britannica.com. The service contains the entire encyclopaedic database as well as current information such as news, weather, markets and sport, content from leading category magazines, books and links to 130 000 web sites classified and rated by Britannica's editorial team. *Encyclopaedia Britannica* is still available in print form, but is now also packaged with the CD-ROM version.

THE DIGITAL ECONOMY

The entire Internet is accessible to users on what is essentially an unrestricted and equal basis — known as *ubiquity*. The user can go anywhere on the Internet with a minimum of effort; there is no real technological reason for the user to start at a specific spot or web site. Because the Internet is interactive, exciting new forms of interactivity have developed. Software is distributed and tested online, information is exchanged and modified more easily, data is stored online – for example, using docSpace (www.docspace.com, now owned by Critical Path) – and virtual organisations can operate more effectively through interacting globally at any hour of the day or night. The speed at which businesses can be established on the Internet places a great deal of emphasis on being first in a particular market category. Further, many Internet-based businesses have been developed as overlays of existing infrastructure, which has reduced start-up costs and time of deployment.[13] However, early in 2000 many so-called dot.com companies collapsed, prompting journalists and commentators to come up with such names as dot.coma, dot.bomb and tech wreck economy. In Australia, well-known failures included LibertyOne, dstore and eisa. The Gartner Group, however, believes that for many corporations, the rise and fall of pure dot.coms will be seen as a 'phase' passed over in favour of long-term spending on improving connectivity and capturing revenue streams on the Web.[14]

Some larger older companies were judged too slow and too concerned with their histories to compete effectively in the dot.com economy. The classic illustration of this was the slow reaction of Barnes and Noble to the rise of online bookseller Amazon. However, Barnes and Noble is now the second largest online bookshop on the Web. Older companies are now snapping up many of the failing dot.com companies. The media giant Bertelsmann AG, for example, bought out an ailing CDNow for $141 million in 2000 and, by the end of that year, CDNow was the number three e-tailer in terms of the number of visitors.[15]

In fact, an economic revolution is occurring in every industry – from banking to selling groceries or cars, from planning weddings and birthday parties to managing farms and web servers, from routing container ships to making steel or selling postage stamps.

M-commerce

Increasingly, digital business is being carried out using mobile phones and **personal digital assistants (PDAs)** such as Palm Pilots. This business has been christened *m-commerce* or *w-commerce*, for mobile e-commerce and wireless e-commerce. M-commerce or w-commerce is the buying and selling of goods and services through wireless hand-held devices such as mobile phones and PDAs.[16] The widespread use of mobile phones and PDAs, particularly among the younger generation and mobile workers, should ensure a large market. **Wireless application protocol (WAP)** is an emerging technology behind m-commerce that is common in Europe, where mobile devices are equipped with web-ready micro-browsers. WAP is a specification for a set of communication protocols to standardise the way that wireless devices, such as mobile phones and radio transceivers, can be used for Internet access, including email and the Web.[17] In addition, smart phones, using **Bluetooth** technology, offer fax, email and phone capabilities all in one, to make m-commerce acceptable to an increasingly mobile workforce. Bluetooth is a computing and telecommunications industry specification that describes how mobile phones, computers and PDAs can interconnect easily with each other and with home and business phones and computers using a short-range wireless connection.[18]

The following areas are already utilising m-commerce:

- *Financial services*: mobile banking for customers who use their hand-held devices to access their accounts and pay their bills – for example, Swedish Postal Bank (PostBanken), Citibank (Singapore); also brokerage services, in which stock quotes can be displayed and trading conducted from the same hand-held device.[19]
- *Telecommunications*: service changes, bill payments and account reviews can all be conducted from the same hand-held device – for example, 50 per cent of Portuguese mobile phone customers are anonymous prepaid subscribers – they use ATM bill-payment facilities to reload their mobile phones for more talk time.[20]
- *Service/retail*: gives consumers the ability to place – and pay for – orders 'on-the-fly'; pilot schemes in Scandinavia allow consumers to use their mobile phones to pay for unattended car parking, soft drinks in vending machines and car washes.[21]
- *Information services*: delivery of financial news, sports information and traffic updates to a single mobile device; for example, Dagens Industri has a pilot scheme allowing subscribers to receive financial data and trade on the Stockholm Exchange using Ericsson PDAs.[22]

TYPES OF ELECTRONIC COMMERCE

There are nine segments of e-commerce: business to consumer (B2C), business to business (B2B), business to government (B2G), consumer to consumer (C2C), consumer to business (C2B), consumer to government (C2G), government to government (G2G), government to business (G2B) and government to consumer (G2C). The e-commerce matrix is set out in table 1.4. Although an organisation may implement a solution in one segment of e-commerce, the same solution also may be applicable to other segments. For example, initially a business might create an online catalogue to fulfil an urgent business-to-business need, but later the business can expand or retool the same application to service other segments of its business, such as business to consumer and/or government to business.[23] B2B exchanges are looking to shift to **peer-to-peer (P2P) networks**,[24] where participants exchange information directly with one another, bypassing central exchanges. The basic technology for this paradigm shift is already available, as seen in Napster.com, Gnutella and other file trading systems, but it remains to be seen how quickly business embraces this technological change. Some software developers believe that if Gnutella can become more user-friendly, the network will grow bigger than the Web. A file-swapping program called Gnucleus is one open source project currently under development.[25]

TABLE 1.4	THE E-COMMERCE MATRIX		
	BUSINESS	**CONSUMER**	**GOVERNMENT**
Business	B2B — GM/Ford, EDI networks	B2C — Amazon, Dell	B2G — tenders online, eProcurement
Consumer	C2B — Priceline, Accompany	C2C — eBay, QXL	C2G/G2C — online voting
Government	Online tenders	Paying traffic fines, Victorian government: (www.maxi.com.au)	G2G — state governments to federal government

SOURCE: Based on 'The e-commerce matrix', in 'The e-commerce survey', *The Economist*, 26 February 2000, p. 6.

Business-to-consumer (B2C)

This segment is growing rapidly, as demonstrated by the rise in online trading sites such as Schwab and eTrade and virtual bookstores such as Amazon. The growth of this section has been extremely fast, and once it assumes critical mass, real-world traders will find themselves experiencing problems. In the travel industry, margins are so thin that a loss of only 3 to 5 per cent of the market to the Internet would push large numbers of bricks-and-mortar travel firms out of business.[26] However, online travel agents may also face the same fate because of oversupply. A study by Bear Stearns of 1000 online travel sites predicts that only 20 per cent will survive in the longer term, principally the large and financially sound companies such as Travelocity.com and Expedia.[27]

Business-to-business (B2B)

Businesses are becoming networked enterprises using the Web to hook up with suppliers, distributors, resellers, consultants and contractors. These collaborative networks called **extranets** have revolutionised how many companies, such as Cisco, Coles Myer and General Electric, do business.

Business-to-government (B2G)

The B2G model of e-commerce generally involves electronic interaction between business and a government body in the form of electronic tendering and procurement. This model can involve a number of procurement activities such as:

- tendering, where the government provides requests for proposals (RFP) on the Web that businesses can download
- electronic negotiations, whereby businesses and the government may use the Internet (e.g. email) to negotiate conditions, contracts and other details
- supplier sourcing, where business suppliers register online to be added to the government's vendor source list so that they might be invited to bid for closed tenders
- online procurement systems, where government personnel can browse a web-based database of products that are offered by preferred suppliers.

The Victorian Government Purchasing Board (www.vgpb.vic.gov.au/) is an example of an organisation that advertises tender opportunities on its web site. Suppliers can download an RFP (for instance, as a PDF file or a Word for Windows document) and prepare a bid based on the RFP requirements. Most public organisations using this approach still require the bids to be delivered on paper to a locked box.

Consumer-to-consumer (C2C)

Originally, online auctions were used as a way for computer manufacturers to offload surplus material quickly. In the United States it was collectors of memorabilia and items such as 'Beanie Babies' and back issues of the *Saturday Evening Post* that propelled the growth of online auctions using the Auction model, such as eBay.com. Table 1.5 outlines some popular types of online auctions.

TABLE 1.5	TYPES OF AUCTIONS	
AUCTION TYPE	**HOW IT WORKS**	**EXAMPLE**
Classic	The starting bid represents the lowest price a seller will accept	www.sold.com.au
Reserve	The seller enters a low starting price to encourage bids, but requires a sale when the reserve price is met	www.eBay.com
Dutch	The seller lists several items; bidders may bid for the entire lot or choose any quantity	www.stuff.com.au
Robobid	Uses a proxy agent that automatically bids on the user's behalf up to a specified maximum named by the bidder	www.sold.com.au (auction agent)

SOURCE: Based on T. Sarno 1999, 'Going, going, gone online', *Icon*, *Sydney Morning Herald*, 17 July, p. 6.

Consumer-to-business (C2B)

This type of e-commerce is epitomised by the web site www.priceline.com, which developed the Reverse Auction model, where bidders set their price for items such as airline tickets or hotel rooms and a seller decides whether to supply them.[28]

Government-to-government (G2G)

In Australia, with its system of a federal government and state governments, the use of the Internet to communicate between governments is particularly relevant. The federal government web site (www.fed.gov.au) contains links to all the state government sites. In 1999, the federal government released its plan to encourage its departments and agencies to procure electronically by participating in existing electronic trading communities and encouraging the development of new ones. In a discussion paper entitled 'Moving to an electronic marketplace', the Office for Government Online (OGO) proposed supplementing the existing agency-based financial management systems that support procurement with a system in which 'the majority of agency purchases will be transacted from the desktop through electronic marketplaces on the Internet'.[29]

Government-to-business (G2B), government-to-consumer (G2C) and consumer-to-government (C2G)

During the transition to the goods and services tax (GST) in July 2000 the Australian Taxation Office (ATO) relied heavily on the Internet. News about the changeover was available at the ATO's web site (www.ato.gov.au) and citizens and small businesses were able to apply for their Australian Business Number (ABN) over the Web.

Speeding tickets and traffic fines may be paid online using the NSW Police Service's ePayments system for the Infringements Processing Bureau. The security of the payment system is supported by 128-bit encryption. ePayments is part of the first stage of the Infringements Management and Processing System (IMPS) Project, which includes a telephone-based, interactive voice response (IVR) service.[30] Over the next two years, subsequent releases of IMPS will see the replacement of the existing Traffic Penalties System with the establishment of an e-commerce portal for the Infringements Processing Bureau (IPB) and the creation of new B2C and B2B projects. For details, visit www.infringements.nsw.gov.au.

WHAT THE INTERNET MEANS FOR BUSINESSES IN AUSTRALIA

It is important for businesses to have an idea of what Internet commerce can offer before they try the Internet. Below are some of the key points of what Internet commerce can mean for businesses.[31]

Strategic competitive advantage

The Internet and intranets give businesses the opportunity to improve their internal business processes and customer interfaces to create a sustainable, competitive advantage. If businesses take up the challenge quickly, they have the opportunity to leapfrog over the competition. Many Australian employment agencies have been quick to see the potential of listing job vacancies online. Morgan and Banks encourages online résumé applications. This has led, in turn, to a radical rethink about how to write résumés and to specialists setting up businesses to advise on résumé construction for the Web. Such résumés should contain key words that will be picked up by web search engines. This is further explored in chapter 8.

Managers need to be aware of the potential

Managers must be educated so that they can see the possibilities of the Internet. In Australia, managers are often technically illiterate and proud of it. If this is the case, it is difficult for them to see the advantages that are offered by the Internet. It is important that executive education on the Internet be put in place to ensure that opportunities are not lost.

As the new digital economy grows, more and more people are becoming connected and sharing data between desktops while collaborating on projects. An interesting management tool that allows employees to flourish in an innovative and creative environment is the Business-of-One program. In such a model employees see themselves not as workers but as a business of one where they can contribute business opportunities. Employees thus run their work in an entrepreneurial way and are encouraged to own their duties. It is apparent that as downsizing occurs, the idea of the business of one (as an Internet business) becomes attractive.[32]

Different companies in Australia have undertaken different tactics to ensure that their staff become aware of the potential of the Internet. Sydney Water and Australian Water Technologies embarked on an Internet Awareness Program in early 1995. Cyber.Consult was engaged to run seminars for all staff, from top management down to support staff, to alert them to the potential of the Internet. After a series of seminars, a Vocational Education Training Accreditation Board (VETAB) accredited introductory course on the Internet and the Web was offered to all members of the corporations. This course forms part of the corporations' strategy of upgrading their staff's information technology skills. Cyber.Consult has developed a course in electronic commerce on the Internet as the corporations are interested in exploring the possibility of using the Internet commercially. Sydney Water customers are able to pay their water rates via the St George Bank web page.

Sydney-based company Internet Training and Support designed its course 'Untangle the Web' specifically for businesspeople who are apprehensive about using the Web and need to gain confidence and competence quickly. The company uses games, music and advanced learning techniques to convert fear into fun in its Internet courses.

In Australia, some organisations have merely set up a web site to demonstrate that they are technically 'with it'. This was a reasonable strategy in 1995, but in the twenty-first century it is vital to be more than a mere presence. Organisations should be transforming themselves into new digital commerce centres and be prepared to open digital markets. This digital marketing opportunity provides sellers with the opportunity to personalise their goods and services to one consumer at a time — the antithesis of mass marketing. Browser **cookies** (files that a web server stores on a user's computer) allow companies to create a more personalised web interaction for consumers, but this is fraught with danger if companies do not ask users for permission first.

Some Australian companies have shied away from the Internet because they have security fears, but at least they have seen the value of the intranet within the organisation. Use of intranets to enable employees to carry out tasks such as ordering hardware or software or requesting leave demonstrates the value of such a user-friendly interface. It can also pave the way for the organisation to communicate with the outside world on the Internet and communicate with suppliers and customers via intranets and extranets.

The term 'extranet' refers to a specialised and customised online information service provided by a company to its valued clients (either individuals or organisations). These can be suppliers (upstream) and other business partners (e.g. legal advisers, side-stream), rather than just the customers (downstream). It uses Internet connectivity and web technology as its platform. The differences (between the Internet and an extranet) are that an extranet has a specific audience and therefore is designed to satisfy the information needs of that audience.[33]

Email is another facility that can make doing business easier. Once companies see the value of email they generally realise that it is a truly valuable business tool for their organisation. Now that HTML-enhanced email is available, businesses can save lots of money by using email rather than normal post (known as 'snail mail') or faxes. Collaboration with others is the great advantage of doing business on the Internet. Team-building is made easier by the nature of the collaborative development aspect of the Internet. **Netscape** launched its 1997 product under the name 'Netscape Communicator' to underscore the value of the Internet in terms of communication. Lotus' product Domino builds on the background of **groupware**, which is an application that is networked to allow users to share data and maximise human interaction. Microsoft is now offering voice email.

One great advantage of the Internet is its potential for real-time training and **conferences**. Businesses are able to utilise **Internet protocol television (IP/TV)** and videoconferencing to deliver training right to the employee's desktop. Groups of people and individuals in different locations can hold interactive meetings. Using inexpensive software such as Microsoft's Net-Meeting, employees can see one another on screen and even collaborate using electronic whiteboard software, which can be used interactively.

POSSIBLE RISKS IN INTERNET COMMERCE

Security issues

Businesses are cautious because they fear that hackers will break into their networks and steal valuable information. It must be remembered that security issues have always been associated with computer networks. There are many techniques that have been developed over the years to combat security problems and these are addressed in chapter 6. Netscape produces the Secure Server and Secure Sockets Layer protocol to combat security problems, while Microsoft has produced the Microsoft Commerce Server and IBM has SecureWay. Microsoft has launched an e-commerce framework called .Net, which is a platform for XML Web services. XML Web services allow applications to communicate and share data over the Internet, regardless of the operating system or programming language.[34]

Shopping experience issues

Many people believe that shopping via computer will not take off because people view shopping as an entertainment or social event. This may have been so when women were not so widely represented in the workforce. Working women often find shopping, especially grocery shopping, a chore. In 1997 retail sales in large shopping centres slumped and research in the United States points to the fact that women are not keen on going to large shopping centres once a week to do their shopping. The St George Bank used an effective advertisement aimed at working women for its Internet banking facilities. It pointed out that while the woman in the advertisement did not have time to get through her various chores during her lunchbreak, at least she could do all her banking from the comfort of her own home. Advertisements for Internet shopping concentrate on the 'Wouldn't you rather be at home!' theme.

Micropayments or microtransactions issues

Critics have stated that until micropayments (small payments using, for example, digital cash) and microtransactions (small fee transactions down to 10 cents) are available, online shopping will fail. Electronic payment systems that allow for such transactions are covered in chapter 5.

Lack of standards issues

Internet commerce shows how technological advances leapfrog legal and government regulations and standards. Some attempts to set up standards include Secure Electronic Transactions (SET), a secure communication standard that could be used for handling credit cards over the Internet. In June 1998, SET (www.setco.org) awarded the right to use the SET trademark to the first four vendors of SET compliant software, namely Globeset Inc, Spyrus/ Terisa Systems, Trintech and Verifone Inc. Other standards include Open Buying on the Internet (OBI), which can be found at www.openbuy.org. These and others are addressed in more detail in chapters 5 and 6.

Lack of bandwidth

It takes a lot of transmission capacity, or bandwidth, on the Internet to transmit graphics, audio and video. The bandwidth of the communication channels that hook up computers to the Internet are measured in bits per second (bps). Businesses claim that lack of bandwidth will kill opportunities on the Internet. Telstra's Big Pond Cable web site allows download speeds of nearly 3 megabytes per second (Mbps) but this service is mainly restricted to residential districts in metropolitan areas. However, in May 1999 Telstra's Carrier Services group introduced a new low-cost, asymmetric satellite service for all of the 40 Big Pond direct points of presence (POPs) in Australia and will utilise high-quality international satellite transmission on multiple 45 Mbps links from the United States. In addition, Telstra is introducing a proxy cache service for capturing and storing frequently visited web sites locally in order to reduce the costs and time involved in downloading web sites from overseas and interstate. Web information will be stored in local cache farms in each capital city of Australia. Other communications companies are building their technology infrastructure by investing in similar projects. Cable & Wireless Optus owns 40 per cent of the Southern Cross cable network that links Australia and New Zealand to the United States via high-speed fibre optic cable.[35]

Wideband IP is a flexible, high-speed data networking solution that allows customers to change bandwidth from 4 Mbps to 1 Gbps by a click of the mouse, as shown in figure 1.1. Telstra Wideband IP is based on the international standard, Internet Protocol (IP). Through a Wideband IP Solution users can connect to other Telstra IP Solutions access services including an extensive range of permanent data and dial-up products, creating their own advanced 'virtual private network' (VPN). Telstra teamed with Cisco to develop this service.[36]

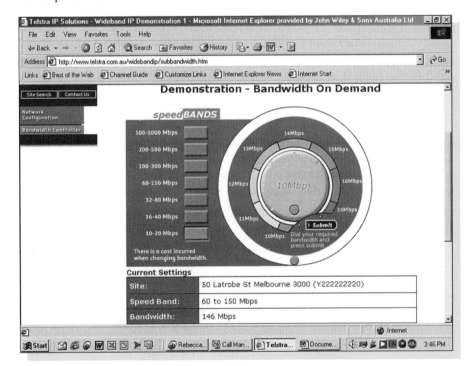

FIGURE 1.1: Telstra bandwith

STAKEHOLDERS IN INTERNET COMMERCE

One of the exciting possibilities with Internet commerce is the fact that a single person can start doing business on the Internet. Below are listed some of the companies and areas that have profited as a result of the rise of the Internet and its commercialisation:

- software developers, such as Superior Software for Windows
- hardware companies, such as Cisco and Dell
- access providers, such as Ozemail and BigPond
- telephone companies, such as Telstra, AAPT and Cable & Wireless Optus
- system integrators, such as JavaSoft
- consultants and trainers, such as Cyber.Consult (www.cyberconsult.com.au), Apt Strategies (www.aptstrategies.com.au) and Internet Training and Support
- buyer and seller services, such as search engines and portals (e.g. Yahoo!, Dogpile, MetaCrawler, WebCrawler, anzwers.com.au, Wombat search engine, ozsearch.com.au)
- information publishing engines, such as Adobe
- shopping malls, such as Malls.com
- home users, who use the Internet for banking and bill payments
- students (it is New South Wales government policy that every school has an Internet connection)
- employees, who may use intranets such as that at Sydney University
- business-to-business opportunities (see Cisco Systems at www.cisco.com).

INFORMATION SYSTEMS AND INTERNET COMMERCE

The connection between information systems and Internet commerce, whether it be B2C, B2B, C2C, G2B or G2C can be explained by examining the following definitions:

> IS (information system) is the collection of technical and human resources that provide the storage, computing, distribution, and communication for the information required by all or some part of an enterprise. A special form of IS is a management information system (MIS), which provides information for managing an enterprise.
>
> IS (information services) is a common name for an organisation within an enterprise that is responsible for its data processing and information system or systems.[37]

Managing the change to electronic business models is a vital part of the process and many information technology methodologies need to be invoked. In this text we consider the use of traditional systems development life-cycle methodologies (these are outlined in figure 1.2). As well, new methodologies such as rapid application development (RAD), joint application development

(JAD), extreme programming and prototyping are investigated as aids to assisting in this change. In the following chapters the information technology and project management requirements for setting up e-commerce web sites are examined.

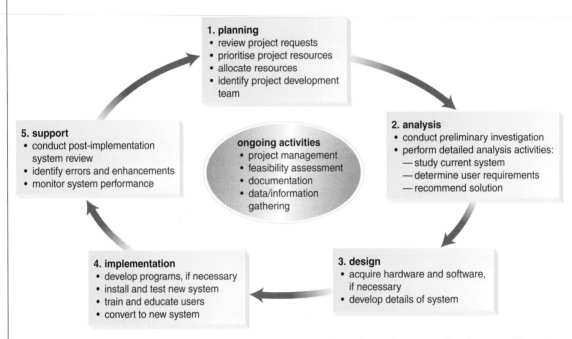

FIGURE 1.2: Traditional systems development life cycle

SOURCE: G. Shelly, T. Cashman and M. Vermatt 2000, *Discovering Computers 2001: Concepts for a Connected World*, Course Technology, Cambridge, MA.

ELECTRONIC COMMERCE AS A MANAGEMENT TOOL

Unfortunately, many managers are not technically literate and some of the rules that work in the real world do not necessarily work in cyberspace. Good managers traditionally look for measurable return on investment, protect revenue streams and try to enhance the cost of entry into their market to keep the wolves at bay.[38] The Internet changes cost of entry and revenue streams; strategic online development is a matter of portfolio management, risk assessment and management.

Organisations need to develop and adopt strategies that enable them to cope with rapid change and the accelerating nature of information flows. Becoming an e-business means the organisation must adopt an ethos of perpetual transformation, which is often traumatic. Deborah Nelson, vice-president of marketing for support services at Hewlett Packard illustrates the scale of the task when she comments that 'turning around a freighter is not easy'.[39]

In fact, internal business bureaucracies are the natural enemy of e-commerce; if left unchecked, bureaucracy may stifle competition. E-commerce cuts today's bureaucracy out of the loop as routine transactions are automated.[40] According to Prins Ralston, ex-president of the Australian Computing Society, big companies should form an e-commerce subsidiary under separate management and draw people from both the parent company and outside sources. He calls this a new wineskin model.

Electronic business over the Internet has had exponential growth over the past seven years. Information technology is driving economic growth and many companies are experiencing difficulties as organisations shift to the Internet's high-change/high-speed environment.[41] It has been a heady ride, with many e-businesses falling by the wayside en route. The fact remains, however, that three start-up dot.com companies, Amazon, eBay and Yahoo!, are now among the world's best-known brands.[42] These three pioneers have software at their core — they innovate with it, they buy out other software companies to obtain exclusive use and they use software to replace people.[43] In this textbook we examine how the e-commerce market has changed over the past seven years.

SUMMARY

This chapter has covered the history of electronic commerce. It has shown how electronic commerce started in the financial area and is now spreading to cover all aspects of commercial transactions over the Web. Businesses will have to reinvent themselves, change some business processes and even destroy some of their usual ways of doing business. Strategies for new business planning and implementation have been introduced and are covered in more depth in chapter 2. The growth of the Internet and intranets has provided new job opportunities and new ways of applying for jobs have developed. Businesses that want to stay competitive and viable must embrace the opportunities of setting up digital markets if they wish to survive in the twenty-first century.

Key terms

Bluetooth (p. 10)
browser (p. 5)
conferences (p. 16)
cookies (p. 15)
domain name (p. 7)
dot.com (p. 2)
email (p. 5)
extensible markup
    language (XML) (p. 5)
extranet (p. 12)
file transfer protocol
    (FTP) (p. 5)

groupware (p. 16)
hypertext (p. 5)
hypertext markup
    language (HTML)
    (p. 5)
hypertext transfer
    protocol (HTTP)
    (p. 5)
Internet (p. 2)
Internet protocol
    television (IP/TV)
    (p. 16)

intranet (p. 7)
Netscape (p. 16)
peer-to-peer (P2P)
    networks (p. 11)
personal digital assistants
    (PDAs) (p. 10)
server (p. 5)
uniform resource
    locators (URLs) (p. 6)
wireless application
    protocol (WAP) (p. 10)
World Wide Web (p. 5)

InterNIC FAQS ON NEW TOP-LEVEL DOMAINS

By Bruce Howarth

The following is a list of frequently asked questions (FAQs) about the new top-level domains (TLDs) that are being introduced to the Internet. This list will be updated frequently; please check back often.

WHAT IS THE STATUS OF ICANN'S NEW TLD PROGRAM?

ICANN is working to add seven new TLDs to the Internet's domain-name system. In November 2000, after extensive discussions throughout the global Internet community, the ICANN Board selected seven TLD proposals to be included in the first addition of a global TLD to the Internet since the 1980s. The selected TLDs are: .aero (for the air-transport industry), .biz (for businesses), .coop (for cooperatives), .info (for all uses), .museum (for museums), .name (for individuals) and .pro (for professions).

- .biz is already fully operational and accepting live registrations. For more information on these .biz, please visit the web site of NeuLevel, Inc., the company selected to operate this new TLD, at www.nic.biz/.

- .info is also fully operational and accepting live registrations. More info on .info registration is available at the web site of the .info registry operator, Afilias Limited, at www.nic.info/.

- .name is fully operational and accepting live registrations. The company selected to operate .name, Global Name Registry, has posted an informational page at www.nic.name/.

- .museum is also operational. The .museum TLD is sponsored by Museum Domain Management Association (MuseDoma). Muse-Doma's informational site can be located at www.nic.museum.

- .coop is operational. The .coop TLD is sponsored by the National Cooperative Business Association (NCBA). An informational site for .coop is available at www. nic.coop/.

- .aero is operational and is sponsored by Société Internationale de Telecommunications Aéronautiques SC (SITA). For more information on .aero, please visit www.nic.aero.

- The .pro registry agreement is still under negotiation. More information on .pro is available at the web site of the registry operator, RegistryPro, Ltd., at www.registrypro.com.

WHERE DO I REGISTER A .BIZ, .INFO OR .NAME DOMAIN NAME?

Domain names in .biz, .info and .name can only be registered through ICANN-accredited registrars and their resellers. Over 100 registrars have already signed new accreditation agreements making them eligible to register in the .biz, .info and .name TLDs. A list of accredited registrars is on the InterNIC web site at www.internic.net/regist.html.

HOW CAN I PROTECT MY TRADEMARK IN THE NEW TLDs?

You should consult your attorneys for advice regarding intellectual property issues in the new TLDs. All of the new TLDs are subject to ICANN's *Uniform Domain-Name Dispute-Resolution Policy* (often referred to as the 'UDRP'). Also, each new TLD has established procedures to minimise customer confusion and cybersquatting by allowing trademark holders to assert rights to their trademarks in the new TLDs before registrations are opened to the general public.

- *.biz*: Neulevel's start-up plan included an Intellectual Property Claim service, which provides notification to prospective .biz applicants of conflicts with intellectual property claims, and allows claimants to challenge any start-up registrations made in conflict with pre-existing trademark rights.

- *.info*: Afilias implemented a 'sunrise' period during which trademark holders were able to register their exact trademark as a second-level domain in .info. A 'sunrise challenge' period is currently underway in which anyone can challenge unqualified sunrise registrations.

- *.name*: The Global Name Registry has implemented a 'NameWatch Service' and 'Defensive Registrations' in order to prevent consumer confusion and protect intellectual property holders. These protections are subject to challenge by persons seeking to register their own personal name.

For more detailed information about intellectual property protections in the new TLDs, please visit the registry operators' web sites (above.)

SOURCE: InterNIC 2002, 'FAQs on new top-level domains', 24 January, accessed July 2002, www.internic.net/faqs/new-tlds.html.

QUESTIONS

1. Visit the new TLD .biz web site outlined above and prepare a report on the way in which a new Internet business might register its .biz name.

2. Research how to register a .com, a .com.au or a .au.com Internet business and prepare a short report.

3. Debate the proposition: 'A .biz web business name is more meaningful than a .com business name'.

4. What have been some of the most significant achievements of the National Office of the Information Economy? (See www.noie.gov.au.)

5. In Australia, the registration of commercial domain names has had a turbulent history. Do some research and write a report outlining the history of commercial domain names in Australia from 1994 onwards.

SATELLITE TECHNOLOGY WILL TRAIN COUNTRY DOCTORS

By Bruce Howarth

Rural doctors in New South Wales (NSW) can now access the latest in medical training and professional information with ease and speed — beamed direct to their homes via satellite.

In a deal with the NSW Rural Doctors Network (NSW RDN), Optus and The Health Channel will supply and install broadband satellite Internet and television receivers in over 70 doctors' homes in the state's outback.

Participating doctors will be supplied with a satellite dish, decoder box and modem, enabling them to receive regular Health Channel TV continuing medical education programs at home, as well as high-speed Internet access.

Bob Murray, General Manager Satellite for Optus, said satellite technology is the natural choice for communications in rural and remote areas.

'Using satellite technology, outback doctors can access professional information where and when they need it.

'The combination of The Health Channel's broadband TV content and high-speed Internet from the Optus satellites means that doctors can now stay up to date with medical information and techniques', Mr Murray said.

NSW Rural Doctors Network's Chief Executive Officer, Dr Ian Cameron, said remote doctors would now have dramatically improved access to information.

'For many years, poor communication services have contributed to the frustration and isolation often felt by doctors living and working in rural and remote areas. This service can change that — it will enable practitioners to foster communication with colleagues, greatly reducing their sense of professional isolation.

'Doctors' families will benefit too — they can now use TV and Internet services at speeds comparable with, or greater than, those enjoyed by their city counterparts', Dr Cameron said.

Director of The Health Channel, Andrew Ricker, said The Health Channel and Optus already broadcast educational programs to NSW RDN members via satellite TV.

'The new agreement furthers this existing relationship — and now The Health Channel and NSW RDN are able to explore new educational formats offered by the Optus service.

'Rural and remote doctors often work long hours with unpredictable schedules, making it important to deliver educational material in the most flexible manner possible. The service provided by The Health Channel and Optus will create new opportunities to deliver education programs directly to the doctors' personal computers', Mr Ricker said.

The Optus SatWeb one-way broadband product will be used to deliver Internet access, allowing download speeds comparable to cable connections — up to 400 Kbps. The Health Channel's educational broadcasts will continue to use Optus Aurora Business TV.

These services will be provided to doctors' homes in remote NSW towns like Bourke, Condobolin, Lightning Ridge, Warren and West Wyalong.

The program has been supported by the General Practice Branch of the Commonwealth Department of Health and Ageing.

SOURCE: Optus 2001, 'Satellite technology will train country doctors', 13 December, accessed July 2002, www3.optus.com.au/newsroom/.

QUESTIONS

1. Research the pros and cons of using satellite access to the Internet and prepare a chart listing your findings.
2. Research other examples of Internet technology being useful in the medical arena and prepare a short report.

Questions

1. In this chapter you have been given two examples of the theory of creative destruction. Find examples of how this theory might apply in any one of the following: travel industry, car industry, banking industry and leisure industry.

2. After carrying out some research, write a short paper on the history of the Internet in Australia or your choice of country.

3. Debate the following statement: 'Internet shopping will fail as it does not allow for a social shopping experience'.

4. Debate the following statement: 'Australian managers are technically illiterate and keyboard phobic'.

5. Do some research on how companies are using email and inexpensive software such as Microsoft's NetMeeting to enhance both inter- and intra-organisational communication.

6. Can a business register a business name that is a common dictionary word? For example, if a company were named Hills Hoist, could it register as www.hills.com.au?

7. The Norfolk Island computer guru, Robert Ryan, managed to get a .nf country code for the island despite the fact that it is not a separate country from Australia. This has meant that companies are able to register as www.mycompanyname.com.nf without having to follow the dictionary rule or other rules. Do a search of the Internet and see how many .com.nf entities you can find.

8. Do some research on the site NetRegistry (www.netregistry.com.au). How does its philosophy, method of registrations, cost and speed of registration differ from Internet Names Australia (www.ina.com.au)?

Suggested | reading

Fingar, P., Aronica, R. and Maizlish, B. 2001, *The Death of 'e' and the Birth of the Real Economy*, Meghan-Kitter Press, United States.

Gates, B. 1999, *Business @ The Speed of Thought: Using a Digital Nervous System*, Microsoft Press, United States.

Kalakota, R. and Whinston, A. 1996, *Frontiers of Electronic Commerce*, Addison-Wesley, United States.

McKeown, P. and Watson, R. 1996, *Metamorphosis − A Guide to the World Wide Web and Electronic Commerce*, John Wiley & Sons, New York.

Mougayer, W. 1997, *Opening Digital Markets*, CyberManagement, Canada.

Phillips, M. 1998, *Successful E-commerce*, Bookman, Australia.

Schneider, G. and Perry, J. 2001, *Electronic Commerce*, 2nd annual edn, Course Technology, Thomson Learning, Cambridge, MA.

Weill, P. and Vitale, M. 2001, *Place to Space: Migrating to Ebusiness Models*, Harvard Business School Press, United States.

End | notes

1. Silverstein, M., Stanger, P. and Abdelmessih, N. 2001, *The Next Chapter in Business-to-Consumer E-Commerce: Advantage Incumbent*, www.bcg.com/media_center/media.press.release_subpage42.asp

2. Economist Intelligence Unit 2001, *'Doing eBusiness'* in The Economist Intelligence Unit/Pyramid Research e-readiness rankings, 8 May 2001, www.ebusinessforum.com/index.asp?layout=rich_story&doc_id=367.

3. Ibid.

4. Kalakota, R. and Whinston, A. 1996, *Frontiers of Electronic Commerce*, Addison-Wesley, United States, p. 5.

5. PriceWaterhouseCoopers 2001, notes supplied for Week 1 of the course 'B2C Fundamental Principles and Technologies' at the University of Technology, Sydney.

6. McKeown, P. and Watson, R. 1996, *Metamorphosis: A Guide to the World Wide Web and Electronic Commerce*, John Wiley & Sons, New York, p. 6.

7. Ibid., p. 14.

8. Panko, R. 1999, *Business Data Communications and Networking*, 2nd edn, Prentice Hall, p. 413, www.prenhall.com/panko.

9. Flanagan, P. 1997, Internet Funds Transfer, University of Technology, Sydney, Masters Project, June 1997, p. 27.

10. Coleman, A. 1997, *Java Commerce: A Business Perspective*, JavaSoft, www.javasoft.com/products/commerce/bizper.html.

11. Kalakota and Whinston, op. cit., p. 2.

12. McKeown and Watson, op. cit., p. 2.

13. Adam, N. et al. 1999, *Electronic Commerce: Technical, Business and Legal Issues*, 2nd edn, Prentice Hall, New Jersey, Chapter 11.

14. Regan, K. 2000, 'Report: high-speed net set to transform e-commerce', *E-Commerce Times*, 17 October, www.ecommercetimes.com/news/articles2000/001017-5.shtml.

15. Mahoney, M. 2001, 'Where is CDNow, now?', *E-Commerce Times*, 18 January, www.ecommercetimes.com/perl/story/6804.html.

16. Definition from www.whatis.com.

17. Definition from www.whatis.com.

18. Definition from www.whatis.com.

19. Birch, D. 1999, *Mobile Financial Services: The Internet is Not the Only Digital Channel*, World Markets Research Centre, Business Briefing on Electronic Commerce, August, pp. 98–9, www.wmrc.com.

20. Ibid.

21. Ibid.
22. Ibid.
23. From the report *Mechanics of Becoming an Electronic Merchant* by Aseem Prakash, CEO of Interactive Knowledge On-Line, 10 August 1998, www.iko.com.au.
24. McAfee, A. 2001, 'P2P: fairer exchange', *Harvard Business Review*, as reported in *Business Review Weekly*, 9 February 2001, p. 78.
25. Angus, F. 2001, 'The GNU Web' in 'In search of the lost tribes of Napster', October, apcmag.com.
26. 'E-commerce – shopping around the Web', *The Economist*, 26 February 2000, p. 4.
27. 'Glut of online travel companies', *Computimes New Strait Times*, 24 April 2000, p. 23.
28. Sarno, T. 1999, 'Going, going, gone online', *Icon, Sydney Morning Herald*, 17 July, p. 6.
29. 'Federal government reveals eProcurement plan', *Ecommercetoday*, Issue 57, 26 August 2000, www.ecommercetoday.com.au.
30. 'NSW's online fines payment takes off', *Ecommercetoday*, Issue 100, 28 July 2000, www.ecommercetoday.com.au.
31. Mougayer, W. 1997, *Opening Digital Markets*, CyberManagement, Canada, pp. 113–18.
32. Harrison, L. G. 1997, 'Harrison on leadership', July 1997, www.altika.com/leadership.
33. Tjhai, P. 1996, '1997 will be the year of the "extranet"', *Computers Section, Australian*, 18 June, p. 34, and Payne, C. 1999, Extranet – The Quiet Business Communication Revolution, MA thesis for Science (Computing), University of Technology, Sydney.
34. .Net is defined at www.microsoft.com/net/whatis.asp.
35. Cable & Wireless OptusNetAccess Direct brochure at optusbusiness.com.au/00/01/00/000100fb.asp?spid=433.
36. www.telstra.com.au/widebandip/.
37. Definitions from www.whatis.com.
38. Birmingham, A. 1999, 'Dispatches: trick or treat?', *Information Age: Australia's IT News Trends Monthly*, November, www.acs.org.au/infoage.html, p. 6.
39. Newton, S. 1999, 'Electronic business: critical success factors for implementation – a case study of a manufacturer of electronic parts', Graduate Student Symposium, Collecter99, Wellington, November.
40. 'The hand on the bulldozer controls', *Rewire, Eric Wilson's E-commerce Manual, Sydney Morning Herald*, 27 April 1999, p. 3.
41. Raths, D. 2000/2001, 'Agent of e-change: IT management 2000', *Information Age*, December/January, p. 46.
42. 'Internet pioneers: we have lift off', *The Economist*, 3 February 2001, p. 73.
43. Ibid., p. 75.

CHAPTER 2

Business models for Internet commerce

LEARNING outcomes

You will have mastered the material in this chapter when you can:

- understand the various models that can be applied to B2C and B2B Internet commerce
- discuss the pros and cons of each model
- use strategic planning principles for Internet commerce.

'The bigger point is that the markets are sending traditional companies two useful signals. One is that they ignore the Internet at their peril. The second is that merely adding a web site onto an existing business is not enough; the whole business needs to be redesigned around the cost saving, communication easing properties of the Net.'

Leader in *The Economist*, 3 July 2000, in M. Allen 2002, *E-business, the Law and You*, Pearson, Sydney, p. 1.

INTRODUCTION

When the World Wide Web caught the imagination of marketing and businesspeople, it was only a matter of time before commercialisation of the Web became a reality. Even before the Web made its appearance in the early 1990s, some far-sighted people had seen the potential of doing business online. However, because the Internet had its roots in academia and research, commercialisation was usually frowned upon until the early 1990s.

Remember that there is no 'cookbook' approach to Internet commerce. If you look at the success stories (and failures!) over the past few years, it is interesting to note that those who have been successful have devised their own models, or have employed a combination of models to achieve their goals. They have often been young, entrepreneurial, risk-taking individuals.

In this chapter we examine some of the successful business models that have been used to establish businesses on the Internet. We examine these models from both a **business-to-consumer (B2C)** and a **business-to-business (B2B)** perspective, highlighting the subtle differences between the two forms of Internet commerce.

BUSINESS MODELS

No matter what business model the fledgling electronic business adopts, it is possible to adapt essential disciplines of successful management techniques to participate in online business on the Internet.[1] The key strategies that are put forward as being essential for establishing a successful presence on the Internet are:

- planning
- controlling
- monitoring
- adjusting
- managing quality (see figure 2.1).

Each of these strategies is dealt with in the context of providing advice for businesses wishing to maximise their cyber potential. Methods for building a commercial presence on the Internet include the following models:

- Fundamental models
  - Online Yellow Pages model
  - Subscription model
  - Advertising model
  - 3.5.7 model
  - Auction/Reverse Auction models
  - Affiliation model
  - Portal model.
- Buy/Sell Fulfilment models
  - Virtual Storefront model
  - eProcurement model.

- e-Marketplace models
  - Procurement Marketplace model
  - Vertical Marketplace model
  - Horizontal Marketplace model
  - Peer-to-Peer Networking model (see figure 2.1).

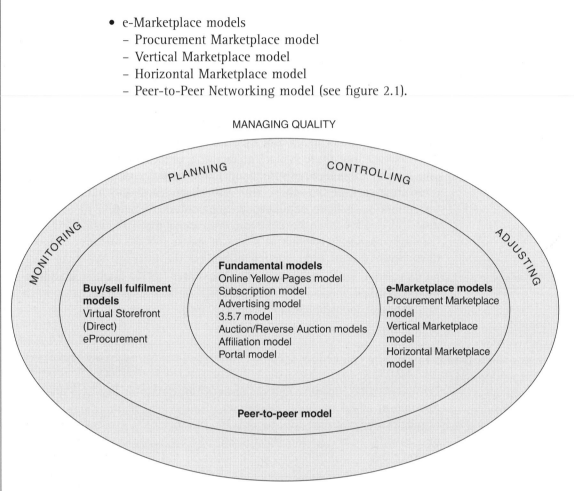

FIGURE 2.1: Strategies and models for a successful Internet presence

FUNDAMENTAL MODELS

Online Yellow Pages model

Businesses using the **Online Yellow Pages model**[2] create a hyperlink menu (or directory), with each item on the menu pointing towards related resources and providing further information on the particular topic. These menus can be created on **Gopher** servers, bulletin boards, the Web and a wide area information server (WAIS). This model creates a higher profile for businesses. A user or customer (or indeed a business, in terms of B2B e-commerce) is able to access business information by conducting a search either by name or by industry and business type. A site location identified by either a map or photograph may be used. When accessed, the site will contain such information as products or services and prices, any special offers and methods of payment.

Subscription model

Use of the **Subscription model**[3] has been borrowed from the publishing industry. Just as a consumer might subscribe to a monthly or weekly magazine, so a consumer is able to subscribe to an online version of a magazine or any product with updated versions offered on an ongoing basis. This model is becoming increasingly prevalent among businesses whose products can be delivered online, as can be seen by the practice of selling software by subscription in order to facilitate the timely dissemination of version upgrades to customers. This model has been used successfully by Netscape to allow users to upgrade to new versions of the browser.

Advertising model

The **Advertising model**[4] has been used by web sites such as search engine web pages (see figure 2.2). They offer advertising space on their web pages to obtain revenue. They use targeted advertising so that when a consumer goes to a search engine, such as Lycos, to search for cars for sale, for instance, advertisements for Holden or Ford might appear as banner advertisements on the search results page. Such one-to-one targeted marketing has excited many business entrepreneurs. Obviously, the web site has to be able to attract large numbers of people (of an appropriate demographic) if it is to sell advertising space.

FIGURE 2.2: ANZWERS — an online search engine specifically for Australian and New Zealand users (www.anzwers.com.au)

The Advertising model is appropriate primarily for service-oriented, online businesses. However, a site could lose business by advertising another company's business products in the online environment. Cross-marketing, the sale of complementary goods in conjunction with another good, is the major exemption. For example, a surfboard manufacturer might accept advertising from a supplier of 'surfie'-type clothing or accessories. In Australia, the earthmover and civil contractor company RP Equipment runs an online guide (www.rpdata.net.au/equip/) to new and used heavy equipment on the Internet. It also advertises a huge range of cars, utilities, light commercial vehicles, four-wheel drives and motorbikes online. If the cyber business offers valid opportunities for advertisers to convey their messages to an appropriate demographic, it may have a chance in attracting advertisers to contribute to the success of the new business.[5]

The 3.5.7 model

The **3.5.7 model**[6] lays the foundation for commercial success by using the Internet as a business communication tool. The 3.5.7 model can be used to plan a new web presence or rework an existing one. The model can essentially be broken down into three areas: three steps to a better focus, five strategies to evaluate the potential of a web presence and seven tactics to be used as a framework for building specific plans.

Three steps to a better focus

These three points outline why businesses on the Internet have not yet made millions of dollars and why they should still maintain their presence.

1. The Internet is not a sales transaction tool — yet. Its acceptance may parallel consumers' acceptance of ATMs and take a few years.
2. Communication is where the money is. Most companies should realise that the real potential for Internet commerce lies in its cheap communication costs.
3. You need new thinking, new strategies and a new approach — lateral, adventurous thinking is required.

Five-dimensional strategy

These five strategies each point to a key element of doing business online. Businesses should evaluate how each of these strategies could be better served through an online web presence.

1. communicating with existing customers
2. providing service and support
3. communicating with prospects
4. augmenting traditional business communication (what could be done on the Internet that is not being done now because of time or money constraints?)
5. internal communications.

Seven-point tactical guide

The following points provide tactics that can be improved using the Internet. Each tactic is a general framework on which to build specific plans.

1. building brand awareness and loyalty
2. direct-response promotions
3. education of the marketplace
4. product demonstration and distribution
5. public relations/press relations
6. research and product development
7. service and support.

Auction and Reverse Auction models

Originally, online auctions were used as a way for computer manufacturers to offload surplus material quickly. In the United States, collectors of items and memorabilia such as 'Beanie Babies' propelled the growth of online auctions using the **Auction model**. The Auction model depicts a web site that conducts an online auction for sellers — possibly individuals or companies. A brokerage is charged for the service, typically proportional to the cost of the auctioned item. Popular B2C auction sites include www.eBay.com.au and www.sold.com.au.

The web site www.priceline.com developed the **Reverse Auction model** (also known as the 'Name-Your-Price' model), where bidders set their price for items such as airline tickets and a seller decides whether to supply them.[7] Other well-known reverse auction model web sites include www.respond.com and www.lowestbid.com.au. In the case of www.lowestbid.com.au, businesses register their requirements on the web site and suppliers then compete in an 'underbid' process to secure the business with the buyer. Typically, this B2B auction scenario is best suited to certain commodities markets, including energy, mining and resources.

Affiliation model

The **Affiliation model** (also known as the 'Pay-for-Performance' model) encourages web-site owners to sign up under what is known as an associate or affiliate program. For example, Amazon.com invites web-site owners to sign up to sell the bookseller's inventory. Once approved, the affiliate is sent an email with instructions on how to set up links and banner ads. These affiliates do not directly sell but merely direct web surfers to the online store, which takes and fills the order. The merchant then pays the affiliate a small set fee for playing the rainmaker.[8]

Variations on the Affiliation model include pay-per-click and banner exchange programs. In the near future there may be potential issues for the development and operation of affiliate programs due to the granting of a patent of the idea to Amazon.com.

Portal model

A **Portal model** web site is designed to offer a variety of Internet services from a single convenient location and to drive high volume traffic.[9] The goal of the portal model is to become designated as the customer's browser's start-up page.

Most portals offer certain free services such as a search engine; local, national and worldwide news; sports and weather; references such as directories and maps; shopping malls; and email and chat rooms. In Australia, users of the popular web email service Hotmail are directed automatically to the Channel 9 Television and Microsoft portal www.ninemsn.com.au when they log out of the email screen. Other portal sites include major search engines such as AltaVista, Excite and Yahoo!

B2B portals offer services to businesses rather than individuals, tailoring news and other resources to a company focus. Examples of B2B portals include www.line56.com, which supplies information on B2B technology, and www.retailtrade.net, which connects retail suppliers and purchasers.

In the ever-increasing search for customer loyalty, personalised portals that allow customisation of interface and content features have become popular in recent years. Users are asked to personalise their portal, thus investing time and valuable personal information in the site. In return, users receive relevant, personalised information. Popular personalised portals include My.Yahoo! and My.Netscape.

Another derivation of the Portal model is the vertical portal or the Vortal. This specialised portal generally focuses on a single (or vertical) interest, rather than supplying information on a broad (or horizontal) spectrum of topics. The Vortal model emphasises 'quality' of market as opposed to 'quantity' of market, typically demonstrated with the Standard Portal model. In the B2B arena, www.b2btoday.com is an example of a Vortal providing news and marketing information for the B2B community.

BUY/SELL FULFILMENT MODELS

Virtual Storefront model

The **Virtual Storefront model**,[10] also known as the Direct or **Sell-Side model**, is a full information and transaction service designed to include the marketing of a business's services and products and/or online purchasing and customer support. Typically, this model has a B2C focus and may be used to reduce the costs associated with order entry and fulfilment while increasing global awareness and operating on a 24 × 7 basis. In cyberspace such transactions are increasingly being conducted entirely online through encrypted two-way data traffic between the consumer and the 'virtual store'. The product or merchandise purchased through either of these methods is then generally delivered to the purchaser at a later date by mail. In the case of information, software or entertainment products, however, the goods may simply be downloaded to the consumer's hard drive through the network connection. Examples of this model include www.amazon.com, www.dell.com and www.shopfast.com.au.

eProcurement model

The **eProcurement model**, also known as the **Buy-Side model**, enables indirect and internal operational costs within an organisation to be reduced by adopting an electronic approach to procurement. By 'electronifying' catalogues, deploying self-service requisitioning and order processing systems, and automating maintenance and repair operations (MRO) buying, organisations may reduce costs on the 'buy-side' of the supply chain. Typically, this model describes interactions between companies and has a B2B focus.

An early eProcurement (buy-side) adopter, Raytheon Systems Company, has employed this model and has reportedly reduced its cost per purchase order from more than US$100 to less than US$3.[11] General Electric is another such pioneer, establishing various buying modes including catalogue-based buying, spot purchases and requests for quotes (RFQs).

E-MARKETPLACE MODELS

Procurement Marketplace model

As a natural extension of the eProcurement model, which is in essence a 'one buyer to many suppliers' structure, the **Procurement Marketplace model** represents a 'many buyers to many suppliers' structure. This model allows company departments, business units and strategic partners to forge independent buying processes and relationships with suppliers. Thus, the model allows for consolidation and aggregation of product catalogues and MRO expenditures while simultaneously allowing business units to establish independent buying processes, relationships and work flows with their chosen suppliers.

In Australia, www.corprocure.com.au is an example of an independent, Internet-based B2B procurement marketplace.[12] The company represents a joint venture between 14 Australian companies including AMP, BHP and Coles Myer, and aims to deliver value to its trading partners by application of eProcurement techniques.

Vertical Marketplace model

The **Vertical Marketplace** (or exchange) aims to bring industry-specific buyers and sellers together to trade. Possibly the most popular of the e-Marketplace models, the Vertical Marketplace model operates in a particular vertical industry such as pharmaceuticals or steel production. By leveraging the buying power of participants, the vertical marketplace can be used to overcome inefficiencies often found in traditional distribution and sales channels. Furthermore, by combining technology with expertise in the industry, vertical marketplaces can be used to eliminate industry-specific problems associated with logistics and inventory management.

Generally, these buyers' markets are based upon a 'many-to-few' business model — a few large buyers purchase goods from many smaller buyers. The web site www.covisint.com is a famous example of the Vertical Marketplace model. In the pharmaceutical industry, the marketplace www.chemdex.com has been established to assist buyers in searching for and purchasing pharmaceuticals in a one-stop, online comparison marketplace. The marketplace creates efficiencies by drastically reducing search time for buyers while simultaneously reducing vendors' costs in reaching these buyers.

Private consortiums versus independent marketplaces

Vertical marketplaces may be private consortiums or they may be independently owned and operated. Independent vertical marketplaces bring multiple buyers and sellers together with the independent intermediary acting as the central node. This model is often referred to as the 'Butterfly' model (or Butterfly market), since the buyers and sellers represent the wings of a butterfly and the independent enabler as the body. An example of an independent industry-specific exchange serving the financial services industry in Australia is www.yieldbroker.com. The exchange provides fixed-income securities trading and research information for institutional and professional banking clients.

Horizontal Marketplace model

The marketplace that provides products and services across industries is commonly called a **Horizontal Marketplace** (or eBusiness portal). These marketplaces are operated by independent, third-party intermediaries and typically serve many clients, all known and registered with the marketplace. By facilitating e-commerce across the supply chain and the various industries involved, the horizontal marketplace streamlines the search and order process for clients. Typically, horizontal marketplaces are used effectively in the financial and travel services industries, where a client's needs may involve traversing many companies in many industries. Examples of horizontal marketplaces include www.commerceone.net and www.tradehub.net.

PEER-TO-PEER NETWORKING MODEL

In the models presented above we have seen how information and e-commerce transactions flow though a central hub or exchange. Whether it is in the form of a Yellow Pages web site or a vertical exchange, these central servers perform two vital functions: aggregation of trading partners and facilitation of trade between these partners.

The **Peer-to-Peer Networking model** is emerging as a new and powerful model in Internet business. Unlike the previous models, peer-to-peer networking operates without the need for a centralised server or exchange, trading partners finding each other and completing transactions in real time.

The Peer-to-Peer Networking model has been described as 'Napsterisation of the supply chain',[13] attributed to the Napster web site (www.napster.com) that enabled peer computers to find each other and exchange music without the need for centralised management. In terms of B2C and B2B e-commerce, the Peer-to-Peer Networking model bypasses the need for a central e-commerce exchange. Peers (or trading partners) operate independently and openly, finding each other by matching their individual needs. The peers then exchange relevant information and complete transactions, securely and efficiently, without the intervention of an intermediary service.

STRATEGIC PLANNING: IMPLEMENTING THE BUSINESS MODELS

Regardless of what type of business presence you wish to establish on the Internet, it is vital to carry out the five strategies of planning, controlling, monitoring, adjusting and managing quality.[14] Obviously, the size of the business will restrict the number of personnel involved in the operation, but the disciplines can be adapted for any business wishing to establish an electronic commercial presence.

Planning

The potential Internet business user should devise an effective plan outlined in a business/user requirements document, which covers strategies and schedules. This document should establish the baseline for the establishment of a presence on the Internet. For example, if the business is going to use the Online Yellow Pages, Advertising or Virtual Storefront models, particularly on the Web, it will need to plan a vibrant home page so that potential customers will stay longer at the site and/or continue to return to the site. It might be necessary to hire a professional firm to design the entire commercial site, particularly if the business is intending to link up a database to the home page or if it needs help designing attractive graphics.

Controlling

The cyber business should have a documented and well-defined structure that covers all the people involved (including the potential customers), duties, job descriptions and responsibilities. The customers must keep returning regardless of what model the business chooses. For example, added incentives may be attached to the home page to ensure return visits. If the business uses an outside consultant, it might be beneficial to be attached to that consultant's home page, particularly if that consultant can provide lots of return business to the site. The business should develop a budget and work out costs for every aspect of the business, such as creating web documents, storage costs, **firewalls**, credit card transaction costs, download charges and consulting charges.[15]

Monitoring

During the setting up of the business presence on the Internet, it is vital to keep close checks on time and money expenditure. If using an outside consultant, it is necessary to get competitive quotes from designers and to budget for software, hardware and design upgrades. Service providers often upgrade their special deals, so the Internet business must monitor these as well. If the business is using an already established web site, it should ask about the kind of traffic the site receives on a daily, weekly or monthly basis. This will help the business to judge the value of the advertising and promotion being conducted by the server service.[16]

Adjusting

Because the Internet is not a standard medium, the establishment of a presence will be ongoing. If the business chooses the Online Yellow Pages, Advertising or Virtual Storefront model, it must rely on a combination of stunning graphics, audio clips, video clips, **Java applets** and continually refreshed content to enable it to attract **bookmarking** – that is, subscribers who save and revisit the address of an interesting page.[17] Obviously, it is vital that such visually interesting pages do not take too long to load or the potential consumer will not bother to wait. It is also appropriate for businesses to move through the models as their needs change.

Managing quality

The cyber business must also have a commitment to quality. To be able to deliver quality it is essential to have a quality management system and it is the responsibility of the person in charge of quality to meet customer requirements. Publicity on the Internet costs a fraction of the price of the print medium, so it is vital to ensure that only top-quality information goes out to customers. Quality management should be seen as an integral part of each of the other four strategies. Listserv software enables worker groups to communicate and can act as a total quality management tool. This can help team members to keep in touch and involved, even when travelling. Group members can get hold of the most up-to-date versions of collaborative work and provide current versions and comments to all members simultaneously.[18] Australian businesses have used a combination of the business models to set up shop on the Internet with some excellent results. It is vital that users are not presented with error messages such as 'JavaScript Error: www.mycompany.com, line 20. Start glide is not defined'. This shows a lack of quality control.

USING THE ONLINE YELLOW PAGES MODEL

The advantages of the Online Yellow Pages model can be realised by remembering how effective the paper-based *Yellow Pages* are in advertising a firm's goods. If you take the concept online, the added attractions involved include being able to:

- search for a business by type or name (see figure 2.3)
- see the location of the business on a map.

Obviously, the key point about this model is the fact that you are able to communicate cheaply and effectively with existing and potential clients.

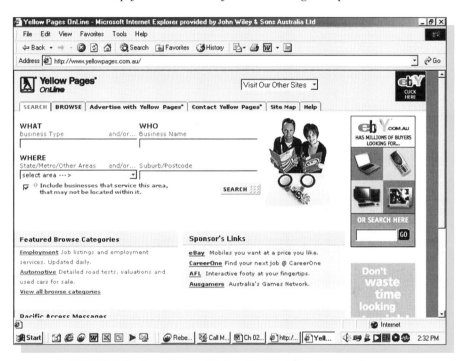

FIGURE 2.3: Home page of Yellow Pages Online (www.yellowpages.com.au)

USING THE VIRTUAL STOREFRONT MODEL

A virtual storefront is a full information service with online purchasing and customer support. This is a popular way of selling on the Internet and nowadays there are providers, such as Yahoo! Store, that streamline the process of setting up a virtual storefront (see figure 2.4). Potential clients are guided through the intricacies of setting up a commercial web site via the use of **wizards**. Clients are then able to design their own site and evaluate its impact before 'going live'. For more information, see chapter 4.

Another example of this model in Australia is the grocery chain, Woolworths, which provides an online shopping channel at www.woolworths.com.au. Potential purchasers register online before any trading is permitted. Once registered the purchaser is able to use a login name and password to access the site and select goods to place into a 'shopping basket'. The total is then added up and submitted. The online shopper is able to nominate a time for delivery and the method of payment – for example, via portable EFTPOS or credit card at the time of delivery. There is a charge for picking the order and a charge for delivery. As the shopper returns to the site a master list of groceries is presented to the online shopper, thus making the shopping easier as the weeks go by. The important advantage from the customer's perspective is that the order-processing time is greatly reduced because the traditional paper trail is significantly shorter and there is less human intervention in processing the order as there is no need to re-key the purchase order information. As the customer is able to make purchase choices from an electronic catalogue there are likely to be fewer ordering errors.

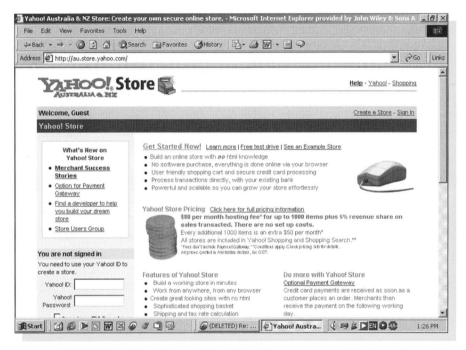

FIGURE 2.4: Yahoo! Store. Yahoo! helps firms to set up virtual storefront sites (www.au.store.yahoo.com)

USING THE VERTICAL MARKETPLACE MODEL

The uptake of B2B models and technology has been exceptional over the past two years, particularly in the Asia–Pacific region, with activity expected to expand considerably by 2004. Gartner Research predicts that the Asian B2B market (including Australia, China, Hong Kong, India, Singapore and Taiwan) will be worth nearly $1000 billion by 2004. On the global market, Gartner predicts $2700 billion in goods and services will be bought, sold and traded through e-marketplaces.[19]

Why is the Vertical Marketplace model proving to be so popular? Essentially, the vertical e-marketplace, or exchange, aims to support more business functionality than just online purchasing and negotiation. Additional benefits of B2B marketplaces include:

- lowering the operational costs and risks for suppliers and buyers
- supporting the entire supply chain by providing a contiguous web platform for collaboration and interaction; this also means better access to product information for supply-chain participants
- incorporating electronic catalogues, procurement and other B2B trading technologies, which lowers the cost of software and maintenance for participants while automating order processing and fulfilment
- reducing inventory levels throughout the supply chain by better matching supply and demand levels
- creating new marketing and distribution channels to customers
- increasing service levels and hence improving customer service and satisfaction.

Large companies have achieved success by leveraging the advantages provided by the Vertical Marketplace model. Ford, DaimlerChrysler and GM have collaborated to bring to the motor-vehicle supply chain the vertical marketplace www.covisint.com. This B2B exchange was created as a merger between the GM TradeXchange and the Ford AutoXchange. The exchange utilises a centralised inventory of auto parts and auto components to service the customer base. The technology for the exchange is provided by CommerceOne and Oracle and allows buyers and sellers to talk to each other in confidence and trade securely and, most importantly, in real time.

So, how have exchanges such as Covisint become successful? Fundamentally, the key to success for the e-marketplace is liquidity – the ability to achieve critical mass. Without sizing the market carefully, analysing the revenue in distribution and operational sales, and reaching a critical trading partner mass, potential e-marketplace developers are doomed to fail. In terms of the e-marketplace technical solution, table 2.1 provides several success factors that are key to designing and constructing a successful e-marketplace.

TABLE 2.1	E-MARKETPLACE DESIGN SUCCESS FACTORS
DESIGN SUCCESS FACTOR	**REQUIREMENTS OVERVIEW**
Performance and scalability	*Network performance* The solution must be capable of deployment across multiple networks to remote users over dial-up connections with a minimum speed of 28.8 Kbps. The network must cater for secure, reliable access across HTTP public networks and utilise true thin-client technology, meaning that no software other than a standard web browser should reside on the customer's machine. The application should employ dynamic HTML-based solutions to reduce the amount of data being transmitted across the network. *Scalability and reliability* Unlike a standard client-server solution that may service hundreds or thousands of concurrent users, the e-marketplace application demands a greater level of scalability and must be able to support tens of thousands of concurrent users, while also providing rapid response times and 24 × 7 reliability. In general, the design should incorporate **load-balancing techniques**, which allow the application to scale effectively by running across a number of processors and machines. Examples of load-balancing application technologies include BEA's WebLogic and IBM's WebSphere. *(continued)*

TABLE 2.1	E-MARKETPLACE DESIGN SUCCESS FACTORS (*continued*)
DESIGN SUCCESS FACTOR	**REQUIREMENTS OVERVIEW**
Application functionality	The e-marketplace must support both buy- and sell-side processes to support the entire supply chain. Application functionality must include the following: • simple, usable transaction software • catalogue-management and search facilities • cross-enterprise communication using XML or EDI • dynamic trade functionality including online quoting and dynamic auctions • comprehensive reporting and analysis tools.
Flexibility and manageability	The e-marketplace must be capable of managing the complex hierarchies and relationships that exist within the online trading community. This management may include administration of customers, suppliers, market administrators and their respective profiles. Management functionality must include: • user registration and administration • process and work-flow management • relationship management — managing discreet pricing and contractual relationships • usage tracking and billing.
Customisability and extensibility	The e-marketplace solution must be capable of meeting the changing needs of the supply chain. Customisation functionality must include: • customisation of core objects — utilisation of **COM/DCOM** or JavaBeans technology • branding and localisation — different countries and cultures demand branding and language customisation • best-of-breed integration — the solution must be open, extensible and plug-and-play.

SOURCE: W. Raisch 2001, *The E-Marketplace: Strategies for Success in B2B Ecommerce*, McGraw-Hill, New York, pp. 215–23.

PEER-TO-PEER NETWORKING: FROM MP3 TO B2P

The Peer-to-Peer (P2P) Networking model promises to radically change the way B2C and B2B transactions take place in Internet business and yet, in its most basic form, it is not a new concept. P2P enables computers (peers) to communicate with each other directly, with little or no intervention from a central server. Participants (individuals or companies) exchange information directly with one another over networks – a concept that dates back to the beginnings of the Apple operating system and Microsoft's Windows for Workgroups.

The difference, however, between peer-to-peer networking and traditional client-server networking is symmetry. With P2P networking, the concept of client-server no longer exists, because each computer or peer on the network simultaneously acts as a client and a server. To achieve this, the P2P architecture must consist of three main components:[20]

1. discovery mechanism – functionality that enables the peer to store and list all known peers on the network and the ability to discover new ones
2. server function – functionality that enables the listing of available files and the delivery of these files to peers
3. client function – complementing the server function.

Consumer versions of the P2P model are already available and are being used by companies such as Napster (www.napster.com), Gnutella and OpenNap (opennap.sourceforge.net) to share files of differing types including text, music (the MP3 format is popular) and video.

As with all emerging technologies, the P2P model offers both advantages and disadvantages to subscribers, as described in figure 2.5.

Advantages
High availability: many files (and services) distributed and replicated throughout the network mean resources are always available to P2P customers
Minimal disruption: the distributed nature of machines on P2P networks means that they are harder to locate and attack
Lower costs: infrastructure costs associated with central exchanges are reduced or eliminated
Reduced complexity: the complexity and expense of networks is reduced – the integration of one P2P software program is more cost-efficient than the integration of multiple exchanges
Open membership: P2P membership is completely open – opportunities exist to meet new partners, forge new relationships and create better deals
Standard formats: P2P architecture suits standard formats such as MP3 and XML

Disadvantages
Transactions: P2P is currently only used in simple transactions such as music file exchanges. Complex business-to-peer (B2P) transactions are nominally larger and much more complex in nature
Search functions: current search and download functions are simple; migration of these functions to multiple buyer/seller configurations with extensive product catalogue information becomes complex
Legalities: difficulties arise when material transmitted between peers is copyrighted; currently, swapping of copyrighted material (as in music files) between peers is against the law, as has been publicly demonstrated in the RIAA versus Napster court case

FIGURE 2.5: Advantages and disadvantages of the P2P model

Applications of P2P and B2P

There are many new and developing applications for P2P and business-to-peer (B2P) technology. These include:

- *Peering portals*: these allow companies to share their lists of products and services with one another. They link with companies' internal inventories to ensure listings are always up to date. Combined on the P2P network, company 'peering portals' will create a universal catalogue or 'shop window' of products and services for peers to utilise.[21]
- *C publish/subscribe (pub/sub) systems*: these support dynamic, many-to-many communication in a distributed environment. Often implemented as a P2P infrastructure, they enable information dissemination from information producers (publishers) to consumers (subscribers). Gnutella is a current example of a pub/sub system. Other potential uses of the pub/sub

architecture include stock quote dissemination, where subscribers specify stock quote symbols to receive and a basis for timing of receipt of quotes, and human resource résumé circulation, where publishers post their résumés to interested subscribers.[22]

- *Help desks*: the company Starbase has created a P2P system for help desks. Upon identification of a new help-desk problem, the receiving peer circulates the problem to all help-desk peers on the network. Once the problem is resolved, the solution is returned to the initial peer and then forwarded to the customer. The solution is recorded for later use.

Secrets of success

As we have seen, the P2P model has various uses and the scope for future applications is limitless. Regardless of structure and complexity, several basic key factors for success exist:

- The business must provide something that people want.
- The system must be easy to use.
- Consumers must come first.[23]

SUMMARY

In this chapter we have studied the various business models that are appropriate to B2C and B2B Internet commerce. As this is a developing field, it is vital to remain alert and be aware as new models make their appearance. The models described in this chapter were the Online Yellow Pages model, the Subscription model, the Advertising model, the 3.5.7 model, the Auction/ Reverse Auction models, the Affiliation model, the Portal model, the Virtual Storefront model, the eProcurement model, the e-Marketplace models and the Peer-to-Peer Networking model.

It is important to realise that as a web site evolves, business models will have to be adapted to suit the changing needs of the business. Whatever model(s) is adopted, it is important to plan, control, monitor, adjust and manage quality.

Key terms

Advertising model (p. 31)	firewalls (p. 38)	Procurement Marketplace model (p. 35)
Affiliation model (p. 33)	Gopher (p. 30)	Reverse Auction model (p. 33)
Auction model (p. 33)	Horizontal Marketplace (p. 36)	
bookmarking (p. 38)	Java applets (p. 38)	Sell-Side model (p. 34)
business-to-business (B2B) (p. 29)	load-balancing techniques (p. 41)	Subscription model (p. 31) 3.5.7 model (p. 32)
business-to-consumer (B2C) (p. 29)	Online Yellow Pages model (p. 30)	Vertical Marketplace (p. 35)
Buy-Side model (p. 35)	Peer-to-Peer Networking model (p. 37)	Virtual Storefront model (p. 34)
COM/DCOM (p. 42)		
eProcurement model (p. 35)	Portal model (p. 34)	wizards (p. 39)

Case study

ROYAL & SUNALLIANCE INSURANCE GROUP'S ONLINE BUSINESS MODEL

By Jason Sargent, University of Wollongong

The pace of advancing techno-logical change, evidenced by the increasing adoption of the Internet as a business and communications tool, has implications for companies attempting to compete both locally and globally. Strategies that were applicable for a business in the traditional sense may no longer be suitable. New strategies and business models need to be considered. How companies deal with the opportunities presented to them by this technology, their ability to merge and enhance their current traditional business processes with the technology, and their willingness to take advantage of e-commerce functionality made possible through web sites will determine just how successful companies become in the *new economy*.

One company that has taken on the challenges of implementing an online business model through the use of an online presence is the Fortune 500 company Royal & SunAlliance Insurance Group, which is positioned in the global insurance/reinsurance sector. Royal & Sun, based in the United Kingdom, was ranked number 172 by Fortune.com[24] in the Global 500 company list in 2002. Revenues generated in 2001 totalled US$25.570 billion. Royal & Sun-Alliance Insurance Group, as the business is known today, grew out of the alliance forged between SunAlliance (a merged entity between *Sun Fire Office*, established in 1710, and *Alliance*, established in 1824) and Royal Insurance (*Royal*, established in 1845). Royal & Sun-Alliance Insurance Group took its name in 1996[25] and is the world's oldest continually traded insurance company. Royal & Sun's web site, which was being updated at the time of publication, is shown in figure C2.1.

As part of its overall business strategy, Royal & Sun has implemented an online business model to succeed on the Web. The 3.5.7 online business model might best describe the most appropriate type of model employed by Royal & Sun. However, as is the case with many large corporations, several other models may at first seem equally appropriate. For instance, the Virtual Storefront model could also quite easily apply to Royal & Sun.

This scenario highlights the often-difficult task of classifying a company's online business model based on first impressions. The situation can become more ambiguous when, as is commonly the case, the nature of the business lends itself to the adoption of a hybrid amalgamation of suitable models, with features chosen from a combination. There is no steadfast rule that dictates that a business must implement one model or another, and hybrid models are becoming more evident as the sophistication of e-commerce evolves.

FIGURE C2.1: Royal & SunAlliance's web site (www.royalsunalliance.com)

By adopting the 3.5.7 online business model, Royal & Sun can differentiate its products, services and culture from its myriad competitors. In contrast to two other Fortune 500 companies positioned within the same global insurance market, Swiss Re26 and CNA Financial Corporation (CNA[27] being incorporated under the umbrella of American-based holding conglomerate Loews Corporation), Royal & Sun has taken a slightly different approach to deciding on and implementing its chosen online business model.

Once again, this indicates that not all models are suitable for all companies and that the decision-making process for choosing the appropriate online business model should not be taken lightly by a company.

Making an incorrect choice about any business model, especially an online business model, can quickly destroy consumer confidence, because the online impression of the business may not match the traditional corporate impression that the business has strived to achieve over many years. For instance, Royal & Sun has been nurturing part of its business persona since 1710.

There is also the recognition on Royal & Sun's behalf that the Internet is increasingly being applied as a business communication tool. By implementing the 3.5.7 model, Royal & Sun is in a position to take advantage of what this model offers, particularly the way the model allows for better planning by breaking down large tasks into more manageable smaller tasks. Features of this model that make it particularly relevant to Royal & Sun are the separation of the company's online presence into areas of focus, strategic planning and tactics. The model accomplishes this by providing greater clarity in the definition of tasks required by Royal & Sun as part of the company's business strategy for online success.

The 3.5.7 model also helps meet the sophistication and expectations criteria that Royal & Sun has for its online presence supplementing the company's traditional business. As the traditional business model evolves, by following the 3.5.7 model, the online portion of the business evolves in tandem.

This aspect reinforces the appropriateness of Royal & Sun's chosen model, because the 3.5.7 model is beneficial to businesses requiring reworking of their existing web site. This reworking of a company's existing site can also be achieved subtly through the 3.5.7 model with some simple techniques.

To enhance and support other aspects relating to the tactics and strategies of the 3.5.7 model, Royal & Sun has incorporated several functionalities into its web site, including foreign language accessibility, avenues allowing for customer contact by online means (e.g. email enquiries) and advanced search capabilities. The web site has menus linking to information sheets and brochures (outlining company policy and consumer- and business-related insurance products). This functionality directly addresses step two of the model's three steps to a better focus.

Royal & Sun's home page does not directly cater for customers from non-English speaking backgrounds by offering different language versions of www.royalsun.com/. Rather, the company incorporates the ability to link to country-specific home pages. So Chinese customers, for example, can choose from a country selector drop-down menu listing approximately 50 countries and from there be directed to links to the Royal & Sun site in their chosen country and language.

Royal & Sun primarily uses email programs for answering customer enquiries, handling public relations requests and general careers and investor issues. This illustrates that Royal & Sun is continuing to use its web presence as a business communications tool and this fits into the company's strategy of adopting the 3.5.7 model. The company has not incorporated any web-based forms, instead relying on a less formal approach, possibly realising that to appeal to a broader range of customers (who have varied IT skills and familiarity), email is the most appropriate medium.

To allow customers to find specific information located within the many pages of the web site in a timely manner, Royal & Sun uses the e-commerce functionality of search/advanced search facilities – a functionality adopted by most large businesses with substantial amounts of information posted on web pages throughout a site.

As Royal & Sun is not directly involved in selling services over the web, in the sense of online shopping mall transactions, the company has limited e-commerce-specific transactions. Those transactions that the company makes available are invariably in the form of client policy detail viewing and interaction areas, available through country/location-specific web sites.

Royal & Sun uses encryption as one of its e-commerce functionalities. This is currently limited to client login information. The encryption method used is Secure Socket Layer (SSL) 128-bit encryption of information sent over the Web. The only other security issue incorporated into the company's e-commerce functionality appears to be limited protection of its web pages and overall site. Any cascading style sheets and Java applets are hidden from the novice hacker viewing the pages' source code.

Royal & Sun has details readily available on privacy policies concerning acceptable use of information received and disseminated online. This is particularly important information for any commercial operation to disseminate to current and potential users of any associated pages of its web site.

Combined, these functionalities employed by Royal & Sun as part of its online strategy address the components of providing service and support, public relations and augmenting traditional business communication, as outlined within the structure of the 3.5.7 online business model.

The widespread adoption of the Internet by individuals came about as a result of utilising the possibilities of the new technology, primarily as a communications tool. Businesses, realising the possibilities of strengthening their market share by having an online presence, have been just as swift in the uptake of web technologies. Today's uncertain economic climate requires a business to implement a complete strategy, incorporating the traditional strategy plus the online strategy. Those who are specifically tasked with selecting the most appropriate online business model must consider issues such as matching the online impression of their company with that of its well-established traditional impression, maintaining customer confidence when migrating to online business processes and the vital online issues of security.

With these issues and the company's aims and objectives in place, businesses adopting online models such as the 3.5.7 model chosen by Royal & Sun position themselves for the greatest chance of success in markets that are becoming increasingly global in nature. Royal & Sun has managed to accomplish these tasks and looks set to continue its success from being a traditional insurance/reinsurance company to becoming a fully integrated market leader in the worldwide insurance/reinsurance marketplace.

QUESTIONS

1. How does an online business model allow businesses to supplement their current traditional business practices?

2. By visiting www.royalsunalliance.com, give examples of how the 3.5.7 model was appropriate for Royal & Sun.

3. Compare the two insurance companies CNA Financial Corporation and Swiss Re. What online business models are these companies using? How does their approach to implementing business models differ from Royal & Sun's?

4. What is Royal & Sun's intention by going online? Consider issues such as brand recognition and information dissemination.

5. How does the image used on Royal & Sun's web site fit with the features of the 3.5.7 model?

1. Explore the P2P file-sharing networks Morpheus (www.musiccity.com) and Aimster (www.aimster.com). How do these applications differ from Napster (www.napster.com)?

2. Locate a publish-subscribe system in operation. Research the performance, scalability and security issues associated with this system.

3. Sun Microsystems has released a P2P development infrastructure called JXTA. Compare and contrast this technology with Microsoft's P2P initiative, which forms part of the .NET architecture.

Suggested | reading

Butler, M., Power, T. and Richmond, C. 1999, *The E-Business Advantage*, The Ecademy, www.ecademy.com.

Kalakota, R. and Robinson, M. 1999, *E-Business: Roadmap for Success*, Addison-Wesley Longman, United States.

Kosiur, D. 1997, *Understanding Electronic Commerce: How Online Transactions Can Grow Your Business*, Microsoft Press, United States.

Lawrence, E. et al. 2002, *Technology of Internet Business*, John Wiley & Sons, Brisbane.

Power, T. and Jerjian, G. 1999, *The Battle of the Portals*, The Ecademy, www.ecademy.com.

Raisch, W. 2001, *The E-Marketplace: Strategies for Success in B2B Ecommerce*, McGraw-Hill, New York.

End | notes

1. De Marco, A. 1994, 'The five essential disciplines for successful projects', *The Source*, Australian Computer Society, Queensland, July, pp. 6–8.

2. Ellsworth, J. H. and Ellsworth, M. V. 1994, *The Internet Book*, John Wiley & Sons, New York, p. 66.

3. Fedewa, S. 1996, *Business Models for 'Internetpreneurs'*, Internet Entrepreneurs Support Service, Los Angeles, www.entrepreneurs.net/iess/articles/art4.html.

4. Ibid.

5. Ibid.

6. Settles, C. 1996, *The 3.5.7 for Maximising Your Business On-Line*, www.successful.com/357artic.html.

7. Sarno, T. 1999, 'Going, going, gone online', *Icon*, *Sydney Morning Herald*, 17 July, p. 6.

8. Rowe, C. 1999, 'Top sites pay you for sales! Read how', *Biz.Com*, *Sydney Morning Herald*, 6 September, p. 41.

9. Shelly, G., Cashman, T., Vermaat, M. and Walker, T. 1999, *Discovering Computers 2000*, Shelly Cashman Series, Course Technology, Cambridge, MA.

10. Ellsworth and Ellsworth, op. cit., p. 66.

11. Raisch, W. 2001, *The E-Marketplace: Strategies for Success in B2B Ecommerce*, McGraw-Hill, New York, p. 208.

12. Lawrence, E. et al. 2001, *Technology of Internet Business*, John Wiley & Sons, Brisbane.

13. White, A. G. 2000, 'Convergence of P2P and B2B: new economy business models', *Logility*, www.cpfr.org/WhitePapers/ConverganceofP2PandB2B.pdf.

14. De Marco, op. cit., pp. 6–8.

15. Angell, D. and Heslop, B. 1995, *The Internet Business Companion – Growing Your Business in the Electronic Age*, Addison-Wesley, United States.

16. Ibid., p. 144.

17. Robotham, J. 1995, 'On the Internet: firms say it pays to advertise', *Sydney Morning Herald*, 29 January, p. 9.

18. Ellsworth and Ellsworth, op. cit., p. 32.

19. Sweeny, J. 2001, *E-Business: Reality Bytes 2001*, Gartner Inc, 2/424 Upper Roma St, PO Box 487 Brisbane, Qld.

20. Withers, S. 2001, 'Peer, there and everywhere', *APC Magazine*, May, p. 92.

21. McAfee, A. 2001, 'P2P: A fairer exchange', *Business Review Weekly*, vol. 23, no. 5, 9 February, p. 2.

22. Wang, C. et al. 2002, *Security Issues and Requirements for Internet-Scale Publish-Subscribe Systems*, Proceedings of the 35th Hawaiian International Conference on System Sciences.

23. Withers, op. cit., p. 99.

24. www.fortune.com/.

25. www.royalsunalliance.com/wgo/about_us/corporate_history.jsp.

26. www.swissre.com/.

27. www.cna.com/.

Technology basics

LEARNING outcomes

You will have mastered the material in this chapter when you can:

- distinguish between the Internet, an intranet and an extranet
- describe the communications infrastructure supporting electronic commerce
- explain the various methods of Internet connection
- define and explain the meaning of the protocols used in electronic commerce
- explain why the Web is popular for personal use, commerce and trade
- explain client-server computing
- distinguish between fat client and thin client systems
- describe examples of commercial solutions using the Web.

'Millions of consumers are forming peer-to-peer networks', says StreamCast CEO Steve Griffin. 'They are not going to stop.'

E. Schonfeld 2002, 'Future Boy: Goodbye Napster, Hello Morpheus (and Audiogalaxy and Kazaa and Grokster...', *Business 2.0*, 15 March, accessed July 2002, www.business2.com/articles/web/print/0,1650,38874,FF.html.

INTRODUCTION

Electronic commerce is concerned with electronic ways of doing business. However, there is a need to also understand how various technologies support electronic commerce. These technologies can be used to speed up the trading and communication process between businesses, between businesses and consumers, and between businesses and their employees.

The technology basics that need to be understood include:
- the architecture of the Internet
- the communications infrastructure that allows electronic transmission of data
- the structure and role of the Web
- the enablers for electronic commerce.

This chapter focuses on these technology basics. Two key themes are discussed: the Internet and how it works, and the technologies that make electronic commerce work.

ALL THE NETS

The Internet, **intranets**, **extranets** and the Web dominate media reports about telecommunications, B2B electronic trading, B2C commerce and the accelerating use of electronic commerce throughout the world. It is the Internet that has made electronic commerce and the ability to trade globally commercially viable, even for small businesses.

The Internet

The Internet is a linkage of many small computer networks throughout the world. These links are created through physical networks, of either metallic wires or optical fibres, and these physical networks can be complemented by wireless links to end users. The Internet works because there are globally agreed rules, or **protocols**, about how information is exchanged.

The Internet has been adopted as a tool that assists business transactions, promotes products, allows interactive news broadcasts (e.g. CNN), provides news in text and visual form (e.g. Sydney City Information web sites), supports causes and activities to address social injustice, entertains, enables research and acts as an alternative publishing house (e.g. *MISQ* and *Information Systems Journal* at www.blackwell-science.com/products/journals/isj.htm). The Internet presents information not just as text but also with graphics, photos, audio and video transmission. It has the ability to support interactive visual and audio communication. The Internet is a globally available vehicle for immediate knowledge, information and communication.

Intranets

Intranets are computer networks that are privately developed and operated within an organisation. They rely on the standards and protocols of the Internet to operate, and are protected by various forms of security to guard the internal operations of the user organisation. Intranets operate as separate networks within the operations of the Internet (see figure 3.1). Intranets allow businesses to make information available instantaneously to all employees and help employees to share knowledge with each other — even if they are in different countries. For a business with operations around the world, its intranet brings employees a sense of belonging to one global team.

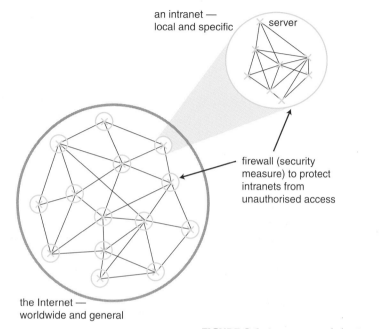

FIGURE 3.1: Intranets and the Internet

Extranets

An extranet is a collaborative network that uses Internet technology to link businesses with their suppliers, key customers or other businesses that share common goals. Extranets can be linked to business intranets where information is either accessible through a password system or through links that are established collaboratively. They can also be private worldwide networks that operate on protocols that are either the same as the Internet or specifically developed for those networks. Each of these networks is, unlike the Internet, not usually in the public domain. SITA (Société Internationale Telecommunications et Aéronautique) is a company that runs a private network that operates throughout the world supporting the booking systems of most international airline systems and companies. This system is totally owned by the users and protected from public use by various security systems.

Other users of extranets include newsgroups, where new ideas or information are shared between companies or groups of companies. Training programs also can be shared and operated through extranets. SITA provides online training to customers and its own employees using Lotus Notes software. Other companies use software that they have developed, called groupware. Sometimes this extends to shared catalogues that list all component parts or products that are of use to both suppliers and customers. Suppliers of aircraft parts, for example, would value being able to access Boeing's catalogues. However, the possibility of catalogues, booking systems and shared groupware being exposed to public access, or to capture by computer hackers, demands that attention be paid to appropriate security measures. Details of various security systems used to protect intranets and extranets are outlined in chapter 6.

These various networks, the Internet, intranet and extranet, perform different functions in electronic commerce (see figure 3.2). These functions are explained below.

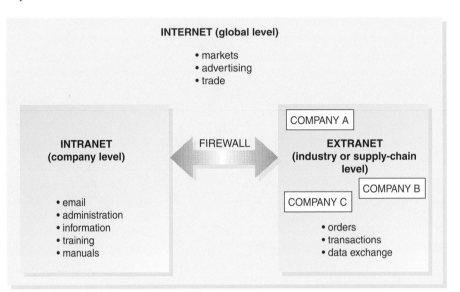

FIGURE 3.2: The role of different networks in electronic commerce

HOW THE INTERNET WORKS

The Internet operates within a structure that has existed to support other technologies, including telecommunications, and uses agreed standards and protocols. The Internet operates by taking data (such as an email message, a file, a document or a request for information), dividing it into separate parts called packets and transmitting those packets along the best available route to the destination computer. Packet switching allows data to be broken up into packets and sent over different routes to their destination. Once there, they are reassembled into meaningful information. The software used for packet switching on the Internet is the communications protocol called **transmission control protocol/Internet protocol (TCP/IP)**.

The Internet works on an infrastructure that covers all of the media necessary for moving information. The infrastructure that works with and complements the Internet includes private corporate networks, cable and satellite television, and telecommunication networks (see figure 3.3).

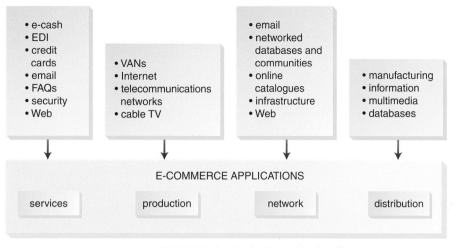

FIGURE 3.3: The building blocks of electronic commerce

Telecommunication infrastructure of the Internet

A number of existing telecommunication technologies support the Internet and facilitate electronic commerce. Technologies for telephone connections form a worldwide network of cables, satellites and microwave dishes, which allows the transmission of signals. The Internet transmits digital signals, which can readily use these existing telecommunication systems. In the last decade additional networks have been established throughout the world to provide many areas with access to cable television, while mobile communications networks have increased their data-carrying capacity. The transmissions that flow over the Internet can also use these networks.

To gain access to the Internet, either in the workplace or at home, consumers, businesses or individuals need to be able to connect to one of these physical or wireless telecommunication systems. The physical part of the Internet includes networks and communication lines owned and operated by many different companies and organisations. An Internet service provider (ISP), such as Telstra Bigpond or OptusNet, is an organisation that has a permanent connection to the Internet and sells temporary connections to others for a fee. Such local ISPs connect to regional host computers operated by national service providers, such as Telstra or Optus. Regional host computers are connected to the major networks that carry most of the Internet communication traffic by high-speed communication lines called backbones, which could be compared to highways that connect major cities across the country.

Connecting to the Internet

ISPs operate web-hosting facilities through which businesses and consumers can access the Internet. However, web users still have to connect to their ISP. Different users require different types of connection to the Internet. Large organisations such as universities and global companies often provide permanent,

24-hours-a-day, seven-days-a-week access for students and employees. On the other hand, individuals might connect to the Internet only occasionally, say, via an online service such as America Online.

There are two basic ways that businesses and individuals can connect to the Internet via their ISP: through a permanent connection or through a dial-up connection. The choice depends on the quantity of data being sent and received and the budget available for the connection.

Permanent connection

Direct online connection to the Internet can be via a **local area network (LAN)** (e.g. an **ethernet** LAN) or a cable modem or an asynchronous digital subscriber line (ADSL). An ethernet LAN allows a transmission speed of either 10 Mbps or 100 Mbps, and a cable modem or ADSL can transmit at speeds of between 500 Kbps and 2 Mbps. Businesses or individuals requiring 24-hours-a-day, seven-days-a-week access would normally be permanently connected to the Internet.

Dial-up connection

If the use of the Internet does not warrant a permanent connection, then a dial-up connection via a PC modem or via an Internet-enabled mobile device can be used. Typical PC modem connection speeds are between 28.8 Kbps and 56.0 Kbps; typical mobile device connection speeds are only 9.6 Kbps, but this will rapidly increase as mobile technologies take advantage of available mobile spectrums. There are two modes of operating the Internet: in an online mode or in an offline mode.

- *Online mode*: An online application operates on current data and can usefully be used only when the user is connected to the Internet. For example, stock exchange prices for different shares or airline ticket pricing and seat availability provide useful data to the user only when they are operating in near real time. For these applications users view and interact with data only when they are connected to the Internet.
- *Offline mode*: An 'offline' enabled application connection allows information to be downloaded and stored on a hard disk either by a user or by a user's agent when connected to the Internet. This downloaded information from the hard disk is then available for the user to access at any time. Special software is loaded onto a computer that when connected to the Internet will allow material to be downloaded. This could be data transferred from one company to another or email messages sent in different time zones. This special software allows replies written or sent in the offline period to be sent automatically once the machine is reconnected online to the Internet.

For the Internet to be accessible there needs to be a common set of traffic rules for the transfer of data between end users and the web servers. These traffic rules are the transmission protocols, which are discussed in the next section.

What is a protocol?

A protocol is a set of rules, procedures and standards for data transmission and manipulation. Network protocols are designed to allow a standard transmission of data and information. For successful transmission these rules have to be accepted by all computers involved in the transmission. Before the Internet came into common use, globally recognised protocols were already taken for granted. For example, it was expected that public telephone networks would provide a global point-to-point connection for voice or data, and in B2B data transactions over private networks **electronic data interchange (EDI)** had been established as a simple data transfer protocol.

In the early days of Internet development most research institutions, government agencies and businesses used small LANs within their organisation. The most common connection was via ethernet. There were few, if any, point-to-point links. One of the reasons for the lack of these simple point-to-point connections was the lack of a standard or protocol. **Point-to-point protocol (PPP)** was developed to provide that standard and to manage **Internet protocol (IP)** addresses at a host server for the Internet.[1] PPP permits a computer connected to a server via a serial line (such as a modem) to become an actual node on the Internet and enables anyone to connect from home, a business or any location through a telephone connection. This link allows individuals or businesses to receive, send and store email, browse the Web, and so on. PPP has been further developed by many of the Internet service providers running commercial access to the Internet for individuals and small businesses. PPP can enable the ISP developers to establish an automatic login that provides the user with a password and automatic dialling of a telephone number to gain access to the Internet.

Within organisations today users still connect to their LAN using an ethernet protocol — for example, CSMA/CD 802.3 — and the connection between their organisation's server and the Web uses PPP. PPP is also used when a single user, say, at home uses a dial-up connection to the Internet.

On top of PPP is the TCP/IP protocol stack. IP relays or routes packets of information over a network and TCP organises the session (e.g. the transfer of all the packets in a file download).

In addition to basic protocols, there are numerous protocols associated with specific applications. For example, POP3 (post office protocol)[2] and IMAP (Internet message access protocol) are protocols for sending email. POP3 allows users to log into the electronic host, download messages to their computer and upload messages to the host for delivery over the network. In businesses, or through a service provider, there is a computer that receives all incoming email messages. A **post office protocol (POP)** email program (such as Netscape Mail, Pegasus Mail or Eudora) downloads email from the POP server to a local mailbox. IMAP is similar but retains mailboxes on the host server.

Mobile protocols

Mobile technologies have changed rapidly in recent years. First-generation mobile phones used analogue technology. Second-generation mobile phones used digital technology with a data rate of 9.6 or 14.4 Kbps. The biggest second-generation technology is GSM; another second-generation technology used in Australia is CDMAONE. A two-and-a-half generation service being used is GPRS, which allows a data rate of up to 114 Kbps. Because the bandwidth of

GPRS varies, the call charging model is on a per-packet basis rather than per second, as for the second-generation services. Third-generation services will provide even higher bandwidths, eventually reaching 2 Mbps. Most third-generation services will be based on CDMA or a variation of CDMA.

Wireless application protocol (WAP)

Wireless application protocol (WAP) allows users with a WAP-enabled mobile phone to search for information on the Internet using a micro-browser in the phone. The pages on the Internet need to be written in wireless markup language (WML). A WAP service is provided by the mobile phone operator, but the user can browse WML pages all over the Internet. WAP has not been as successful as i-Mode, which is a service provided by NTT-DoCoMo in Japan. i-Mode uses different protocols to provide a similar service to WAP, but the real difference is in i-Mode's business model. This is based on sharing revenue with content providers, which encourages a wide range of content to be available to users.

Figure 3.4 shows how some of the protocols are used within the Internet network architecture.

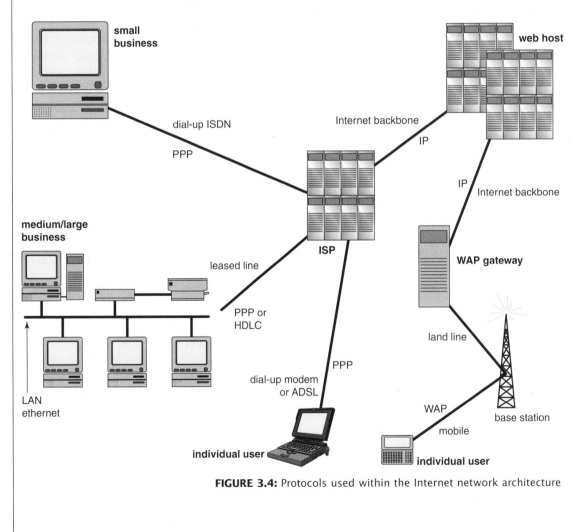

FIGURE 3.4: Protocols used within the Internet network architecture

The Web[3] was an improvement in the attributes of the Internet and was a huge leap forward in document storage, management and formatting. The Web allows the user to interchange and interconnect documents creating an interactive process whereby one document retrieved from the Internet can be used to establish a link to another document. This link is activated when the user clicks on a **hotlink** or hyperlink (a word, picture or feature highlighted within a document), which triggers the link to another document located on another computer in some other location in the world. Figure 3.5 shows some examples of hotlinks or hyperlinks embedded in the text of a web page.

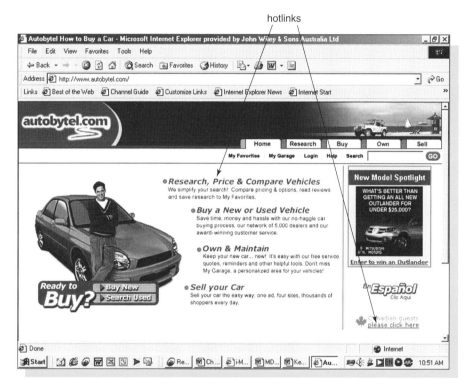

FIGURE 3.5: Hotlinks on the Autobytel web page (www.autobytel.com/)

Global hypertext publishing with HTML and HTTP

In the 1980s the International Standards Organisation released the specifications of a **standard generalised markup language (SGML)**. This protocol defined documents in a plain text but with tags that were embedded in the text. Hypertext markup language (HTML) is a form of SGML and contains commands such as 'top of page', 'bold', 'underline', and so on as embedded tags in text, which control how the text is presented to the user. A web browser (e.g. Netscape Navigator or Microsoft's Internet Explorer) understands HTML and will display a text file retrieved from a server[4] in line with the formatting as defined by the tags. HTML allows the developer of a web page to define hyperlinks between that document and any others that the developer thinks are important to link together. In addition, HTML allows the developer to define any multimedia objects, photos, video clips, audio clips and so on to be included in the document. To enable consistent transmission of documents on the Web, hypertext transfer protocol (HTTP) was developed and adopted. This is a multimedia transport protocol. It does not process the packages of data it transmits, but it is a mechanism that allows users to search for information or data on the Web.

HTTP defines computer links to the Web. The computers providing the links are called web servers. HTTP, and the ability of servers to support it, is what defines the Web and differentiates it from other networks. This protocol also defines the Web within the Internet. Web servers have become the places where home pages of all sorts have been developed and stored. The transmission of data within these pages relies on the simplicity and speed of HTTP.

In addition to the TCP/IP and HTTP protocols, the Internet uses other protocols for the transmission of information:

- **file transfer protocol (FTP)** to allow the transfer of files between computers
- **simple mail transfer protocol (SMTP)** to enable mail transfer between computers within the organisation
- **multipurpose Internet mail extensions (MIME)** to enable mail transfer in complex organisations.

Web servers are computers that run the HTTP process and that are connected to a TCP/IP network.

The **extensible markup language (XML)** is a data format for structured document interchange on the Web. A markup language is a mechanism to identify structures in a document. XML is a markup language for documents that contain structured information. Structured information is common in most documents and has two elements:

1. content (e.g. pictures, graphics, text, etc.)
2. the role that the content plays in the document — where the content is located in the document influences the meaning given to it (e.g. a statement in a footnote is an addendum or an explanation; text in the document is usually structured by headings that indicate what is to come).

XML specification defines a standard way to add markup to documents, but it is different to HTML. In HTML, the tag sets and tag semantics are fixed by protocols established by the World Wide Web Consortium (W3C) and are firmly established within existing browsers such as Internet Explorer. XML does not fix the tag sets or the semantics used. It really enables the user to define tags and the structured relationships between them. Like SGML, it supports structured documentation, but XML is designed for applications, especially richly structured documents, using the Web.

Active server pages (from Microsoft) allow for the creation of dynamic Internet sites by putting databases on the Internet. Customers can search company databases to retrieve updated information.

JavaScript is an interpreted scripting language that allows developers to add scrolling messages and data input forms to web pages.

Uniform resource locators

The HTML document that forms a web site is defined by a URL. This URL is a standard that gives the address or location of any web site. Each URL defines the Internet protocol being used, the server on which the web site is stored or located, and the path that will transmit the document.

In the web site shown in figure 3.6:

- the protocol is http:// (hypertext transfer protocol)
- the server address is www.asx.com.au – this address specifies the server where the site is stored and then the country where the server is located (in this case, it is in Australia).

The location of the two servers listed below is defined in their URLs. The protocol of each of these two URLs is not defined, so the web browser will assume that the protocol is http.

- .bradford.ac.uk (United Kingdom)
- .mail.bdg.co.th (Thailand).

However, in the following URL the protocol, server and path of each resource are all specified: http://www-cec.buseco.monash.edu.au/info/ecdefn.htm. The protocol of the resource is hypertext transfer protocol, the server is www-cec.buseco.monash.edu.au and the path of the resource is /info/ecdfn.htm.

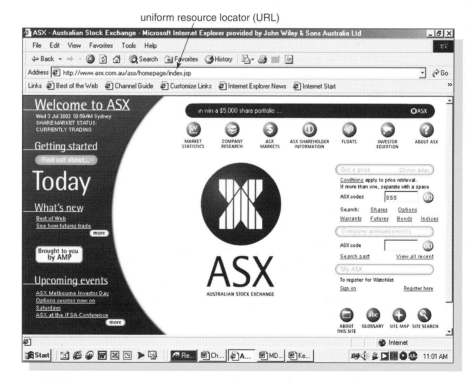

FIGURE 3.6: Web page showing the uniform resource locator of the Australian Stock Exchange (www.asx.com.au) © Australian Stock Exchange Ltd 2002

Architecture of the Web

The architects of the Web wanted to ensure that HTTP could be used to move information and data around the Web — that is, it would perform as the transfer protocol. HTTP and XML were not designed to process the data being transported. This is the role of a **common gateway interface (CGI)**. A CGI script provides a standard way for a web server to communicate with a translation program that negotiates the movement of data between a web server and an outside application, such as a database. CGI can be developed using several languages, including the following:

- Visual BASIC, Visual C++ and PowerBuilder, which are used on NT-based servers
- C, C++, Tcl and Perl, the most commonly used languages on Unix servers.

The client environment is independent of the CGI environment, although CGI scripts are not necessarily platform-independent. Scripts written in Visual BASIC, Delphi and Visual C++ can run only on Windows platforms (such as Windows 95 or NT), whereas scripts based on Unix shell scripts will run only on Unix servers. However, CGI's performance is somewhat limited in that there has to be an individual program started for each CGI request. The way CGI works is shown in figure 3.7.

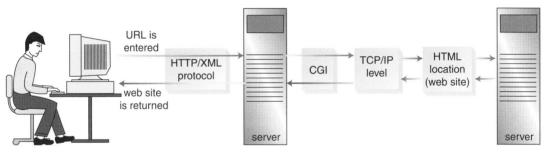

FIGURE 3.7: How CGI works

The Web is based on a three-part architecture:

- Hypertext markup language describes the contents of web pages on the Internet.
- Hypertext transfer protocol provides the language that allows servers and browsers to communicate.
- CGI is used by a web server to run a separate program that contains dynamic information, format it into HTML and send it on to the web server. For example, a web user at a virtual bookstore might enter some data, such as a book title, into HTML form on a web site. This data is sent to the web server, which uses the CGI interface to get the appropriate book title from the database and return the information, formatted appropriately, back to the user.

The modern Internet results from the interaction of a number of levels of providers and individuals. As can be seen from figure 3.8, individuals can connect (directly or via an intranet) to an ISP. The ISP is connected to an Internet access provider, which is connected to a national access provider. The national access provider is connected to a **very-high-speed backbone** (or spine) **network service (VBNS)**, the fastest communication lines on the Internet.

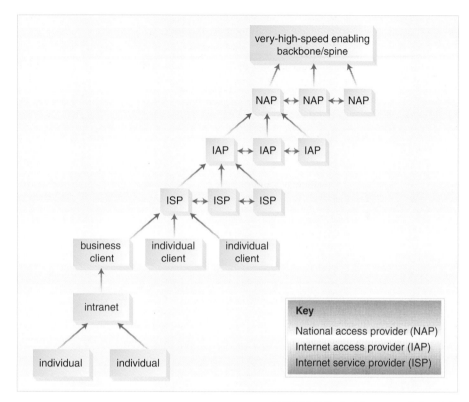

FIGURE 3.8: Architecture of the Web

These links use passwords and security protocols to allow access to the Internet. Access can be achieved in a number of ways, as shown in table 3.1.

The structure of the Web allows a user to interact with various databases, collect information, and search for identity-specific and defined knowledge and information (see figure 3.9). This structure enables users to access the Web for recreation purposes, for communication and for electronic commerce. This structure can support B2B e-commerce, B2C e-commerce and C2C e-commerce through:

- marketplaces and auctions facilitating the buying from other businesses of cost-effective supplies
- banks encouraging consumers to use the Web to access their account information and to perform banking transactions
- airlines encouraging consumers to access their web sites to search for availability of seats and to purchase 'e-tickets'
- consumers finding special interest groups to communicate with and to trade with people with similar interests.

TABLE 3.1	COMMON INTERNET ACCESS TECHNOLOGIES	
TYPE OF INTERNET ACCESS	**PROTOCOL**	**SPEED**
Dial-up terminal emulation (not a graphical interface)	Terminal emulation	Up to 56 Kbps
Dial-up IP: full access to Internet, but more complex to configure and set up	PPP	Up to 56 Kbps
Digital dial-up (ISDN)	PPP	64 Kbps, 128 Kbps
Leased line: high-speed dedicated link, but can be expensive if not used frequently	IP	1.54 Mbps (T1 US) 2 Mbps (E1)
Cable modems	—	Up to 10 Mbps (customers share so throughput will be lower)
Satellite (e.g. Satnet)	—	128 Kbps — may go up to 4000 Kbps
DSL (digital subscriber line) and ADSL (asynchronous digital subscriber line)	—	Up to 2 Mbps (high bitrate DSL)
Wireless (e.g. Bluetooth, Airport)	—	720 Kbps – 1 Mbps

SOURCE: Adapted from R. Kalakota and A. Whinston 1997, *Electronic Commerce: A Manager's Guide*, Addison-Wesley, United States, p. 55. © Reprinted with permission of Pearson Education, Inc., Upper Saddle River, New Jersey.

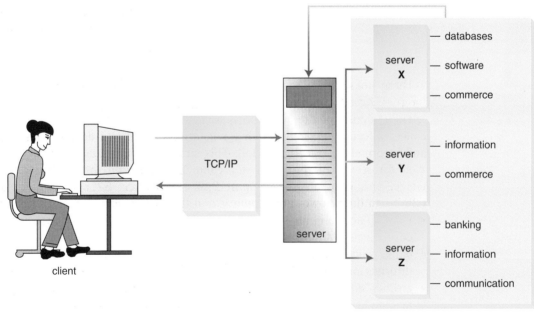

FIGURE 3.9: Structure of the Web

The major attraction of the Web for business and consumers is the ease of access and low start-up costs. For small businesses it is relatively cheap to establish a web site and ensure that it will be found by **search engines**. This gives the businesses entry to a global market for relatively little investment. In this way, the Web has supported many rural industries in Australia, allowing them to export their products all over the world. For the consumer the purchase of a modem and a relatively cheap contract with an ISP enables electronic commerce to begin.

WHY HAS THE WEB BECOME SO POPULAR?

The Web has become popular as a medium for communication and commerce for a number of interrelated reasons, including:

- protocols and standards have been agreed worldwide
- hardware, software and telecommunication links are affordable
- the Web has an intuitive, user-friendly interface
- easy-to-use tools are available for developing content for the Web
- search engines enable the easier location of items
- there are a high number of connected businesses and consumers
- security has been recognised as necessary for commercial transactions.

Protocols

Worldwide acceptance of common protocols such as the transmission protocols TCP/IP, POP3 and SMTP, document formatting protocols such as HTML and the transmission of documents using HTTP has given the Web a global foundation on which it can expand.

Affordable hardware, software and telecommunication links

PCs have become affordable household items for many consumers and standard equipment for businesses. Internet browsers are usually supplied with a PC's operating system and web page development software is relatively cheap. In addition, the cost of web servers has been decreasing, especially relative to their power and memory, and the cost of telecommunication links has been falling.

User-friendly interface

The development of simple hypertext protocols has allowed those people who are connected to the Internet to use it easily. The interface between the user and the information on the Internet is one that encourages extended use.

Content development

The hypertext protocols allow the content located at the various sites on the Internet to be easily developed and enhanced and specialist applications such as Microsoft's 'Front Page' make the development of multimedia web pages extremely easy. This results in a huge range of visually attractive and up-to-date content being available on the Web.

Search engines

Search engines are available that allow users to work through the Internet and find the information or data they require (see figure 3.10). These engines enable businesses or individual users to enter a key word or phrase that defines the information being sought. Search engines include Netscape Search, Yahoo!, Metacrawler, AltaVista Excite, Google and Ask Jeeves.

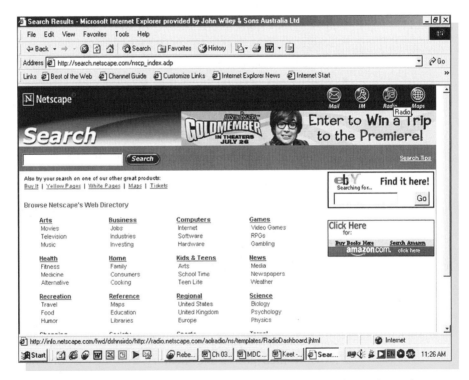

FIGURE 3.10: Netscape Search, one of the most commonly used search engines (http://search.netscape.com/)

Large corporations have developed sites that provide 'front door' access to the Internet. They include the attributes of search engines and focus the activities of the user within their corporate environment. The two largest of these providers are Netscape (see figure 3.11) and Microsoft (see figure 3.12).

FIGURE 3.11: Netscape's web page provides links to information and support for its various products (http://home.netscape.com/)

FIGURE 3.12: Microsoft's web site has links to product information and free demonstrations (www.microsoft.com) © Microsoft

Search engines have evolved into large sites offering long lists of free services such as email, personalisation features, chat rooms and a variety of content such as stock quotes, local news and weather. These directories have now further evolved into Internet '**portals**' — communication centres, service centres, virtual shopping malls, town centres and news hubs all rolled into one. The NineMSN home page (www.ninemsn.com.au/) is a portal into a large number of other services and products (see figure 3.13). How many can you find? What products can be found on this site?

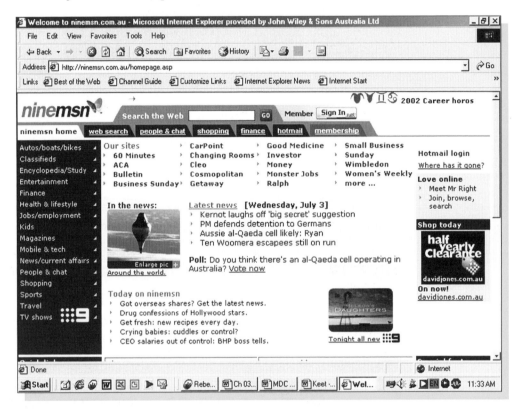

FIGURE 3.13: The NineMSN portal (www.ninemsn.com.au)

Portals have attracted a great deal of attention in terms of advertising revenue and were one of the driving forces behind the boom in Internet stocks on the New York Stock Exchange. Portal site companies were injecting millions of dollars into marketing efforts hoping to attract new Internet users needing direction and guidance in cyberspace. The intention of a portal is to capture the users and take them to a vast range of products and services. The intent is to keep the web user online as long as possible, increasing exposure to the sponsors working through and linked to the portal. Portals then are linking deals with Internet service providers. For example, web access provider and telecommunications giant AT&T has signed deals with three portal sites: Lycos, Excite and Infoseek. Yahoo! and MCI Communications have joined forces to provide a web-based online service.

High number of connected businesses and consumers

ISPs were established to provide businesses and individuals with access to the Internet. They link computers in a business or in the home to the Web for a small cost on a 'user-pays' system (see figure 3.14).

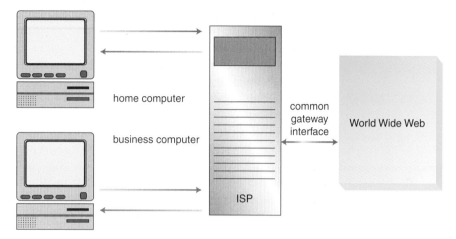

home computer

business computer

common gateway interface

World Wide Web

ISP

FIGURE 3.14: How an ISP links home and business computers to the Internet

Given the ease of use and low cost of access, the Web has become increasingly popular as potential business uses become apparent. These include:

- selling gifts (see www.violet.com)
- electronic publishing (see www.ibooks.com and www.infocus.com)
- banking and establishing digital cash and modes of exchange (see BankOne at www.bankone.com/)
- selling pharmaceuticals (www.tradegate.org.au/).

The Web is also popular because there are now millions of people and businesses throughout the world who own computers. Most of these computers have been sold with web-enabling software and inducements to link with commercial ISPs.

Security

A computer that is connected to the Internet needs to be protected from attacks. These attacks come from software that infiltrates a user's computer to either destroy its applications or spy on the contents of the computer and send information, such as bank account details, without the user's knowledge. There are two main forms of protection against these attacks — anti-virus software and firewalls.

A virus is a software program that takes control of the client machine to do something that the user does not want. The problem the virus causes can have a minimal effect — for example, it might simply flash a message on the screen — or it can have a disastrous effect — for example, it might start to destroy files on the computer. Viruses spread to other computers by being sent by other applications, typically by email. Some viruses even make copies of themselves and automatically send themselves to everyone in an email address book. In this way very damaging viruses such as 'Code Red' can quickly spread around the world.

Trojans are programs that trick people into loading them onto their computer. For example, a Trojan may be hidden in a free screen saver. You may not be aware of the Trojan, but it opens a back door in your computer and allows someone else to connect to your computer without your knowledge. In this way, data such as passwords can be read from your machine.

Worms are similar to viruses, but a worm spreads over a network from computer to computer. Unlike viruses, worms do not need to attach themselves to another program to spread; instead, a worm infects physically connected computers.

Anti-virus software inspects incoming messages, whether email or downloaded files, to see whether it can detect a virus. To do this it needs to do a comparison with virus signatures, which are code patterns that recognise viruses. The signature files are downloaded from the web site of the anti-virus software provider. These days, this is usually done automatically by the anti-virus software rather than relying on people to do a regular update.

The second form of virus protection is a firewall. A firewall allows you to define what applications you will use to connect to the Internet and what applications you will allow from the Internet. You can define incoming and outgoing filters differently. For example, you can program a firewall so that your computer does not respond to any application trying to see your computer, essentially making your computer invisible. Similarly, if a Trojan has infiltrated your computer, you can prevent it from sending out information.

For businesses, e-commerce payments must be secure. In addition to firewalls and anti-virus software, better encryption languages and processes (coding information in ways that make translation and capture very difficult) allow businesses to feel more secure about doing business electronically. The development of a standard or protocol for electronic payments, Secure Electronic Transaction (SET),[5] has ensured that further protection in a standardised form is available for businesses, yet it has not proved popular.

From this discussion it is obvious that there are a number of specific technologies that affect the operations of the Internet and the Web. In the next section, the most important technologies are discussed separately.

BUSINESS TECHNOLOGIES FOR THE WEB

The technologies that allow business use of the Internet to be more effective include databases, client-server architecture, new programming languages designed for the Internet, multimedia manipulation and transmitting voice traffic over the Internet. It is important to note that the following discussion is simply an introduction to this subject.

Databases

In traditional interbusiness online commerce, databases are shared in structured formats. EDI is an example of how databases can be linked. On the Web it is difficult to maintain the capture and sharing of data derived from existing databases. The protocols that drive the Web exchange data in semi-structured forms. This has the effect of making the transmission of transactional-type data very difficult using traditional databases. This data includes items as diverse as invoicing, stock levels and employee personal details. The Web operates systems that are designed to distribute complex material such as software or illustrated product catalogues that are more correctly designated as semi-structured.

On the Web the interaction of databases can be facilitated with **middleware**. This form of software acts as a middle operations gateway between the client and the servers operating the web sites. Middleware operates as the translator of structured data, enabling structured data to be reprocessed and then transmitted in a semi-structured format via the Web. At this time there are a number of software/middleware packages that permit the exchange of structured data, such as inventory systems, between databases. These include packages such as Oracle and mSQL (DBperl).[6] One of the most effective middleware packages is Sybase, which accepts **structured query language (SQL)**[7] commands, embedded within HTML forms. This enables structured data to be exchanged through a CGI system and then displayed in HTML form at the client end. The way these processes occur is shown in figure 3.15.

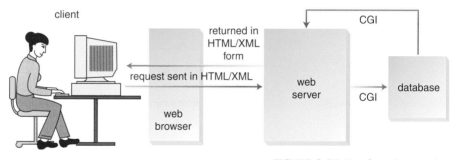

FIGURE 3.15: Database integration

Further developments in database integration and use on the Internet include object request brokering (ORB). This software acts as a broker that finds, retrieves and delivers data and information. (See www.corba.org for details.)

Client–server architecture

One of the key structures of the Internet is the client-server architecture, which is at its very foundations. During the 1980s basic computer architecture to run big software applications relied on a big central computer that held all the required software and data and that users connected to using dumb terminals. The terminals did no intelligent processing. As applications came to depend more and more on interacting with users, a new architecture emerged where some of the application processing and data manipulation was spread out away from the central computer to the user terminals. This architecture is based on a server at the centre, which holds the master copy of the data and is in control of the overall system, and a number of clients attached to the server that carry out some of the application processing and store some of the data files for their own local processing. Client-server technologies tend to be split into two classifications – thin clients and fat clients.

The **thin client system** is a PC where some application files are stored and run, but the vast majority of the processing takes place on the central file server. A **fat client system**, on the other hand, stores many applications and files for local processing by the PC.

Thin client systems may operate in a more cost-effective way depending on the user organisation's requirements. In the thin client architecture the server is the one location where software upgrades are performed, where all processing is done and where all files are stored. There does not have to be a powerful PC for each user. Security should be easier as there is only one access point to be protected and only the server has to be upgraded with new releases of software. All these factors can contribute to cost savings when a thin client architecture is adopted.

However, where users will be performing a high level of transactions there can be some performance advantages for adopting a fat client architecture to enable some application processing to be done locally. A fat client architecture also relieves the load on the network between the client and the server.

An application of client-server technologies has been developed by Citrix in the United States. Citrix is a server-based computing system with software for Microsoft Windows NT Server 4.0, and there is also a Terminal Server edition. Citrix has also developed WinFrame®. This integrated server-based software is a commercially developed solution for deploying, managing and accessing business applications across the enterprise and provides access to virtually any application, across any type of network connection to any type of client.

New programming languages for the Internet

JavaBeans is a portable, platform-independent component model written in the **Java** programming language. JavaBeans was developed in collaboration with industry. JavaBeans technology allows Internet software developers to write reusable web components and run them anywhere because of the platform-independent power of Java technology. JavaBeans' components are reusable software components that can be manipulated visually in a builder tool. JavaBeans can be combined to create traditional applications or their related smaller web-oriented relatives, applets.

JavaBeans is becoming very popular with web developers to free them from large, slow and inflexible software applications. JavaBeans is used to build up a portable, reusable code base. These application/components allow developers to quickly meet new market opportunities. JavaBeans-based products include Corel, EnterpriseSoft, Gemstone, IBM, K&A Software, KL Group, Lotus development, Novell, ProtoView Development, Rogue Wave and Stingray Software among many others.

Multimedia manipulation

Further development of the Internet and the Web has encompassed more than new programming languages such as Java. The Web enables transmission that utilises both audio and video. This attribute of the Web has led to the development of prototypes and languages that enable three-dimensional representations – **virtual reality modelling language (VRML)**. This language allows graphical representations and models generated by computers to be broken into smaller components and transmitted across the Internet. One example is Pathfinder.[8] The development of such a complex structure and the loading process results from the small packages being transmitted independently in some structured order. VRML is the most commonly adopted protocol used across the Web to enable three-dimensional graphical representation and transmission. To enter the domains of VRML, it is essential to have a VRML browser – that is, a three-dimensional web browser.

In addition, software enables the delivery of on-demand audio and video across the Web. The process of audio and/or video streaming allows clients to order and be delivered pictures, video and audio associated with objects compressed to hold the digitised audio and video. Products such as StreamWorks, VDOLive and CU-SeeMe are all software packages that enable transmission and electronic commerce on the Web. CU-SeeMe allows real time video-video transmission that is suitable for face-to-face communications and negotiations.[9] One of the most popular forms of web-based audio streaming is the use of MP3 to listen to music or radio. MP3 is a form of compression for audio that is supplied through access to the Web. It allows a high level of compression with little loss in quality. However, MP3s are only *near* CD quality. The most common software programs available include: RealPlayer G2, Quicktime 4, WinAmp and MusicMatch. The experience of Napster (www.napster.com)[10] with regard to copyright issues demonstrates that although the technology is available, business and commercial principles can amend its use. The fall of Napster encouraged the establishment of a new web architecture, peer-to-peer (P2P) networking (Gnutella).

E-business interest in P2P models

In peer-to-peer networking, individuals allow access to specific files, such as music, so that other individuals can search and download them to their own

PCs. In this architecture each PC is both a client and a server and hence they are called servants.

If a user, called Adam, wishes to obtain a particular file (owned by Don), he connects via Gnutella to Barbara who is connected to Chris and Don. Within seconds Adam has searched all the drives, found the file and downloaded it. The search works instantly from 4 (the default number of connections that can be changed) to 16, to 256 to 1024. Thus, the method of finding the files makes it extremely difficult to track the origin of the initial query. Because of the decentralised nature of GnutellaNet, its software authors claim it can withstand a direct nuclear attack and even more destructive damage from lawyers.[11]

Corporations are investigating using P2P as a way for

- employees to share files without the expense involved in maintaining a centralised server
- businesses to exchange information with each other directly.[12]

One P2P e-business model that uses a distributed computing technology is called the **publish-subscribe system** (commonly referred to as pub-sub[13]). Pub-sub enables information producers (publishers) to disseminate relevant, high-value information to consumers (subscribers) via a P2P network. This is a communication infrastructure that enables data access and sharing over disparate systems and among inconsistent data models.[14] It is being used for distributing stock quotes and news updates.

Transmitting voice traffic

The Internet is also increasingly being used to carry voice traffic. This is particularly cost-effective for voice traffic between one country and another. A voice conversation is converted into digital data and this data is sent over the Internet as an IP packet, just as any other data would be sent. If two PC users have the voice-over IP (VOIP) software and a way of speaking and listening such as sound cards, speakers and microphones, they can talk to each other without paying telephone charges, apart from the Internet connection costs.

This has not taken over from 'normal' voice telephony because people have to pre-arrange a conversation time. However, it can be made more attractive by the use of a gateway. A VOIP service provider may have a gateway, say, in Singapore and a user in Adelaide connects to this gateway over the Internet. The gateway then connects to a local telephone in Singapore. The user in Adelaide pays the cost of the local call in Singapore plus something for the VOIP packets.

The use of two gateways allows a telephony provider to provide cheap long-distance calls. The user dials up using an access code, which routes the call through the gateway over the Internet to the gateway nearest to their destination, where it is converted back to go over the local telephone lines. In this case, the user is not aware that the call is being carried by VOIP.

SUMMARY

Electronic commerce offers businesses the opportunity to improve their access to markets, to increase their inter-organisational and intra-organisational efficiency and to complete business tasks more effectively. How these outcomes are achieved depends on which technologies that provide Internet access are available to businesses. The technologies are designed to support the structure of the Internet and the way this physical structure enables ease of access. The Internet works using the various telecommunications networks established throughout the world, including public telephone systems, private cable networks, public and private microwave networks, satellite networks and wireless links.

The technologies that make electronic commerce work include design elements that have enabled the development of intranets and extranets for businesses. The development of the Web has enabled better and more creative use of the Internet, increasing potential for improved and more effective marketing, sales, advertising, data exchange and communications. New and emerging architectures and technologies will continue to improve the effectiveness of the Internet for commerce. These developments will encourage the more frequent use of electronic commerce and the Internet in the global and local business environments.

Key terms

active server pages (p. 60)
common gateway interface (CGI) (p. 62)
electronic data interchange (EDI) (p. 57)
ethernet (p. 56)
extensible markup language (XML) (p. 60)
extranets (p. 52)
fat client system (p. 72)
file transfer protocol (FTP) (p. 60)
hotlink (p. 59)
Internet protocol (IP) (p. 57)
intranets (p. 52)
Java (p. 72)

JavaBeans (p. 72)
JavaScript (p. 61)
local area network (LAN) (p. 56)
middleware (p. 71)
multipurpose Internet mail extensions (MIME) (p. 60)
point-to-point protocol (PPP) (p. 57)
portals (p. 68)
post office protocol (POP) (p. 57)
protocols (p. 52)
publish–subscribe system (p. 74)
search engines (p. 65)
simple mail transfer protocol (SMTP) (p. 60)

standard generalised markup language (SGML) (p. 59)
structured query language (SQL) (p. 71)
thin client system (p. 72)
transmission control protocol/Internet protocol (TCP/IP) (p. 54)
very-high-speed backbone network service (VBNS) (p. 63)
virtual reality modelling language (VRML) (p. 73)

Case study

BARUNGA MUSIC ONLINE

By Amanda Toshack and Katina Michael, University of Wollongong © 2002

Barunga Music is a fictitious company, used for the sole purpose of creating this case study.

Barunga Music is an organisation that records, markets and sells Aboriginal compositions. Barunga is a small business that operates a physical store based in Melbourne. The organisation was established in 1994 by Stephen Clark and business partner Daniel Stone. The company employs 10 staff members, including a part-time IT professional.

SWOT ANALYSIS

After comparing historical sales revenue quarter by quarter, Clark decided to conduct a high-level SWOT analysis. He had not reached his sales target estimates in the last financial year and considered what opportunities there might be to reverse this trend. His findings are shown in figure C3.1.

It became apparent to Clark that investing in an electronic commerce strategy was a plausible solution, although lately he had read about the failures of the dot.coms and was not entirely convinced. Stone, on the other hand, was a savvy businessman who was not afraid to take calculated risks. After all, it was he who had brought to Clark's attention that Skinny Fish Music,[15] a major competitor, had gone online in 2000.

Strengths	Weaknesses
• Market niche focused on Aboriginal music • Barunga is a trusted label and brand that has been in operation for eight years	• Physical store located in Melbourne only • Customer base is relatively small • Budget for advertising is small

Opportunities	Threats
• Create an Internet presence • Market and sell music online • Extend customer base to a global market • Locate new talent abroad to record indigenous music of any background	• Main competitor has already invested in electronic commerce technology • The cost of compact discs is being driven down by market forces

FIGURE C3.1: SWOT analysis findings

PRELIMINARY CONSIDERATIONS

Before any decisions were made to adopt an e-commerce strategy for Barunga, Clark and Stone conducted further research. They examined the current market conditions and explored Barunga's main competitors. They estimated the potential online market in terms of size and location, and reviewed current competitor pricing, online promotional strategies and the identification of underdeveloped market niches.

After an analysis of Barunga's main competitor Internet sites, Clark realised that establishing an Internet presence would not automatically guarantee an increase in sales. Some of the competitor sites were riddled with defects and did not reflect the quality of product that was being promoted online. These defects included the inability to quickly locate particular information about products and/or use key-word searches on the site, the content was not updated regularly, little or no company information was displayed and, in most cases, a secure electronic payment system was absent. Barunga decided that it would differentiate itself using the online medium.

Clark and Stone considered several options, all of which sounded feasible until they invited their part-time IT professional to discuss them further. She quickly made her employers aware that adopting an e-commerce strategy would be costly and required careful planning, and that the implementation would most likely happen in stages. She also dispelled Clark's suggestion that she would take on the additional responsibility of building the site on top of her normal workload. She did, however, agree to conduct a requirements analysis based on information gathered from their meeting.

INTERNET SITE REQUIREMENTS

Company background and contact information

It is very important for an organisation, especially one that offers online shopping, to provide background information about the business to its customers. This builds customer confidence in conducting online transactions with the organisation. Barunga should also advertise its existing physical location, which will provide additional legitimacy to the online business. Further, a contact email address should be provided for customers who require additional information or support in addition to the information provided on the FAQ (frequently asked questions) page.

Products

Compact discs are a low-risk purchase, since customers are not usually concerned about colour, size or compatibility issues. Therefore, the factors that Barunga must focus on are inventory stock levels, price and value-added features. Value-added features include providing services such as the opportunity to purchase the music in digital format for the customer to download, for instance in mpeg3. A discount option for this type of sale can be granted, offset by the reduction in administrative costs.

Member facilities

A members' section within Barunga's web site will provide the capability to build a customer database of existing and potential clientele. While subscription to this service will be free, it will require the customer to complete a simple online form. Information collected through this form will not be so detailed that it potentially deters individuals who are conscious about parting with too much personal information. The following services will be offered to members: access to sample music and video clips; access to the public message board; and the ability to subscribe to a mailing list detailing upcoming events such as concerts and new releases. It is inherently implied that an online shopper must be a member to be able to make a purchase.

Search facility

Barunga's site will enhance the online customer experience by granting them the ability to find information quickly and easily through an online search facility capability. Customers will not only be able to search for key words within the site but also for words within a song, hence returning search results by title, theme, singer, songwriter, place and date. In addition, an easy-to-follow site map will aid customers.

Online purchasing facility

Barunga will use an Australian online electronic payment system (EPS) designed and provided by ANZ BizSite.[16] Unlike its main competitor, Skinny Fish Music (SFM), Barunga wants to encourage its customers to purchase online. SFM has found itself in a predicament as it has outsourced its EPS to an American-based company that does not hold itself liable for fraudulent activities resulting from Australian sales. In this manner, SFM has inadvertently discouraged its Australian customers from using the convenience of an online shopping cart, preferring instead to take their orders offline. Barunga, on the other hand, will not be responsible for securing customer data, as this too will be handled by BizSite. ANZ will also host the entire site, which will allow all information to be kept and managed in a centralised area.

Offline orders

Barunga has recognised that not all online customers will feel confident about providing their credit card payment details over the Internet. These customers will be accommodated offline through mail, facsimile or telephone. However, strong incentives will be offered to entice customers to shop online. Incentives will also be made to engage and retain customers. This will be implemented using a loyalty points system. For each dollar a customer spends, five points will be awarded. The higher the amount of money spent, the more points the customer will accumulate. The points can then be spent on selected products in the Barunga storefront.

Affiliate programs

Affiliations will be made with other sites such as www.aboriginal.com and www.aboriginalconnection.com. This will entail these organisations to direct customers to Barunga's web site through links and banner advertisements.

TECHNOLOGY OPTIONS: IN-HOUSE VERSUS OUTSOURCED SOLUTIONS

Upon reviewing the Internet site requirements Clark and Stone had to make a decision between an in-house solution and an outsourced solution. Knowing that the existing IT staff member would not take up a full-time position at Barunga (due to family commitments), they considered hiring an additional IT employee to work part-time on the implementation of the web site. After some initial investigations, however, they ruled out an in-house solution due to the amount of uncertainty that was associated with it. They were, after all, a company that sold Aboriginal music; they were not e-commerce specialists.

An in-house solution would have meant additional costs, such as the purchase of several pieces of software — for example, a web-publishing package such as Macromedia Dreamweaver, Microsoft's SQL2000 database and a shopping cart application. Barunga also would have had to purchase a new computer, find a reliable broadband Internet service provider and potentially host its own web site. The thought of not having a reliable 24×7 site for online customers, catering for shoppers in different time zones, was enough to convince them to go for an outsourced solution. Using ANZ's BizSite service meant that no additional costs would be required for the purchase of new software or hardware.[17] The process of building the customer database would also be handled by BizSite[18] and the site would be hosted on ANZ's web partner, MultiEmedia.com Ltd.

COST-BENEFIT ANALYSIS

After weeks of research, Stone had become convinced that an online business model was the right way forward for Barunga. Clark, on the other hand, still wished to build a cost-benefit model to ensure that his original motive to increase sales would be achieved by the introduction of the online storefront. Table C3.1 outlines Clark's cost-benefit assumptions.

Clark gave the go-ahead for the project only after calculating that benefits would indeed outweigh costs within the first year of the web site being established. The most significant cost was the web development and the ANZ application fee, which was a one-off start-up cost of $5000. Ongoing operational expenses totalled $2239 in the first year and $2099 in the second, as domain name hosting need only be renewed every two years with Melbourne IT.[19] It was also forecasted that a cost saving of $1580 would be achieved by showing promotional material on the web site, rather than through traditional methods such as the postal system.

CONCLUSION

Clark and Stone considered that Barunga's future web site would need to perform where their competitors had failed. Maintaining a parallel, almost seamless, strategy between the physical and virtual storefronts would be challenging but necessary.

To succeed, Barunga Music's web site must continually strive to meet the changing needs of customers. Internal intelligence gathered from site logs, such as the number of hits per page and consumer buying habits, as well as other demographics, will aid the development of personalised marketing campaigns that should inevitably help boost sales.

Clark believes that in the long term it may even be possible to go completely virtual, and dedicate the physical location as a place where musicians solely record music. But for now, the entrepreneur just wishes for the stage-by-stage development of a robust web site that has enough functionality to make him more money.

TABLE C3.1 COST–BENEFIT ASSUMPTIONS		
	2002 FORECAST ($)	**2003 FORECAST ($)**
Revenue from e-commerce (net of transactions costs)	25 000	35 300
Less: Cost of goods sold	(11 300)	(17 990)
Gross profit from e-commerce	13 700	17 310
Add: E-commerce cost savings		
Promotional material (four hours/month at $25/hour)	1 200	1 200
Reprinting costs for photos for promotional material	380	380
Total e-commerce cost savings	1 580	1 580
Gross benefit from e-commerce	15 280	18 890
Less: Ongoing e-commerce costs		
ANZ web hosting	(1 799)	(1 799)
ISP	(300)	(300)
Domain name registration	(140)	
Total ongoing e-commerce costs	(2 239)	(2 099)
Operating benefit from e-commerce	14 675	16 791
Less: E-commerce establishment costs		
Web development and ANZ application fee	(5 000)	
Research and development	(1 400)	
Total e-commerce establishment costs	(6 400)	
Net benefit from e-commerce	8 275	16 791

QUESTIONS

1. How will Barunga Music's B2C processes be impacted by the introduction of an online virtual storefront?
2. Visit ANZ's BizSite page at www.bizsite.com.au. What type of services does ANZ provide to its prospective online business customers?
3. Have Clark and Stone made the right decision in outsourcing the development of Barunga Music's web site? Why or why not? Compare the pros and cons of outsourcing the development with the pros and cons of in-house development.
4. Are there any costs that Clark has accidentally omitted from his cost-benefit analysis? Are Barunga's revenues, one-off and ongoing costs, accurate?
5. Visit Barunga Music's major competitor at www.skinnyfishmusic.com.au. Are there any recommendations you can make to this small business so that it can improve its web presence?

1. Log onto www.time.com/ and trace all of the site's paths by clicking the hyperlinks. Develop a tree diagram of all the hyperlinks allowed from the site. Each of these is developed in HTML language. How do you know this?

2. The URL for one of the world's best examples of Internet commerce is www.public.iastate.edu/~PremCourses/dutchauc.html. Find the site and undertake the following exercises to gain some practical understanding of Internet commerce.
   (a) Read about the Dutch Flower Auction and how it works.
   (b) Why was the auction site developed?
   (c) How does the flower trading operate?
   (d) What are the advantages and disadvantages of the Dutch Flower Auction?
   (e) When was the IT form of the flower auction developed?
   (f) How does the IT site work?
   (g) Complete the case questions on the site.
   (h) Write an evaluation of the assessment of the Dutch Flower Auction site.

3. Choice Mall (www.choicemall.com) is a shopping centre in cyberspace.
   (a) How many merchants are there on this site?
   (b) How effective is the site as a network provider of goods and services?
   (c) Which sector of the suppliers' market is the site aimed at?
   (d) What are the establishment costs involved in using this site?
   (e) Visit www.isworld.org/isworld/ecourse and navigate through to the knowledge section using the top navigation area. This section of the site contains a wealth of research material on web technology.

Suggested | reading

Baker, R. H. 1997, *Extranets: The Complete Sourcebook*, McGraw-Hill, New York.

Benett, G. 1996, *Introducing Intranets*, Que Corp, United States.

Department of Foreign Affairs and Trade 1999, *Creating a Clearway on the New Silk Road*, Commonwealth of Australia, Canberra.

Department of Foreign Affairs and Trade 1999, *Driving Forces on the New Silk Road*, Commonwealth of Australia, Canberra.

Kalakota, R. and Whinston, A. 1996, *Frontiers of Electronic Commerce*, Addison-Wesley, United States.

Kalakota, R. and Whinston, A. 1997, *Electronic Commerce: A Manager's Guide*, Addison-Wesley, United States.

Kosiur, D. 1997, *Understanding Electronic Commerce*, Microsoft Press, United States.

Liu, C., Peek, J., Jones, K., Buus, R. B. and Nye, A. 1996, *Managing Internet Information Systems*, O'Reilly and Associates, United States.

Maddox, K. 1998, *Web Commerce: Building a Digital Business*, John Wiley & Sons, New York.

May, P. 2001, *Mobile Commerce*, Cambridge University Press, United Kingdom.

McKeon, P. and Watson, R. 1996, *Metamorphosis: A Guide to the World Wide Web and Electronic Commerce*, John Wiley & Sons, New York.

End | notes

1. The following web site will provide additional information on PPP: www.cisco.com/univercd/data/doc/cintrnet/ito/55168.htm.
2. Further details on POP and post office software can be found at www.groupweb.com/email/es_soft.htm.
3. The history of the development of the Web and these protocols is available at www.w3.org/hypertext/www/History/1989/proposal.html.
4. You can view such a file by opening www.mastercard.com/press/970718a.html.
5. The SET protocol agreement process and details are available at www.set.org.
6. Software packages that use object-oriented programming techniques to develop programs and objects for display on the Internet or on PCs.
7. SQL is a language that enables object-oriented programming. Further details can be found at www.jcc.com/sql_stnd.html.
8. It would be worthwhile at this point to go to the Time site (discussed in question 1) and examine the way the home page for Time actually loads onto a computer (www.time.com/).
9. The development of CU-SeeMe can be found at goliath.wpine.com.au/cu-seeme.html.
10. More detailed information can be found by starting a search at www.mp3.com/help/.
11. FirstTake 2000, 'Gnutella – file sharing', *Australian Personal Computer*, June 2000, p. 35.
12. searchnetworking.techtarget.com/sDefinition/0,,sid7_gci212769,00.html\.
13. Wang, C. et al. 2002, *Security Issues and Requirements for Internet Scale Publish-Subscribe Systems*, Proceedings of the 35th Hawaiian International Conference on System Sciences.
14. Ibid.
15. Skinny Fish Music, www.skinnyfishmusic.com.au.
16. www.bizsite.com.au/RegisterAndSubscribe/bizSitePackages.asp.
17. www.bizsite.com.au/RegisterAndSubscribe/bizSiteFAQ.asp#1question0.
18. www.bizsite.com.au/RegisterAndSubscribe/bizSiteFAQ.asp#1question5.
19. www.melbourneit.com.au/help.php3?keyword=newpricing.

CHAPTER 4

World Wide Web commerce

LEARNING outcomes

You will have mastered the material in this chapter when you can:

- understand how to apply marketing strategies to Internet commerce
- know the new five P's of marketing and their application to Internet commerce
- know how to plan, organise, control and monitor an Internet commerce site
- appreciate the use and potential of intelligent shopping agents
- understand the importance of developing a community for products in Internet commerce.

'Yet EAI and related software, too, has its drawbacks. It is expensive, and so far it connects only a limited set of applications. But its biggest disadvantage, according to Don Ferguson, an IBM research fellow, is that it does not provide the flexibility of changing business processes in real time.'

'Timely technology', *The Economist*, 31 January 2002, www.economist.com.

INTRODUCTION

Smart technology is now assisting businesses to integrate their applications and offer better services to their clients. In this chapter we look at how companies need to rethink their marketing strategies and how best to approach setting up an e-commerce web site. It is important to look at web-hosting models, techniques for building a commercial web site, programming languages and electronic commerce software.

How to be seen on the Internet is a challenge. A business may decide to advertise through normal marketing channels, because most people are accustomed to seeing URLs on advertisements on buses and trains. Radio and television advertisements often give the web addresses of businesses, so people are becoming used to 'double ewe, double ewe, double ewe, dot cyber business, dot com, dot a ewe' either in spoken or written form. If the business name is the same as the web address name (e.g. the web address for David Jones is www.davidjones.com.au), this is a subtle form of advertising in itself. Failure to be as innovative as the competition and to use technology for strategic advantage means that a company may lose promotion opportunities. Failure to match competitors' unit costs is another strategic challenge. The Web allows businesses to promote online using advertisements such as banner ads, online catalogues, product information, competitions and electronic feedback.

The cyber business must not forget that people are a vital part of any business — including the people who run the business and the people who interact with the business. (Customer relations is dealt with fully in chapter 8.)

THE NEW FIVE P'S

Tom Patty, formerly a worldwide Nissan account director, believes that the old five P's of marketing (namely product, price, place, promotion and people, and packaging) were based on a world dominated by stability, a fast-growing economy and a much less competitive environment. He has proposed a replacement set of P's for the new world, where chaos has replaced stability, economies have slowed and global competition has increased.[1] These new P's are paradox, perspective, paradigm, persuasion and passion.

Paradox

The *Macquarie Dictionary* defines **paradox** as: 'A statement or proposition seemingly self-contradictory or absurd, and yet explicable as expressing a truth.'[2] Patty gives an example from his own field to explain the meaning of the word: 'All cars are the same; all cars are different.' He then shows how to master this paradox by:

- exploiting the differentiation — for example, Altima is the 'first affordable luxury car'

- creating a unique identity, such as a well-known brand name that suggests that this particular brand name is somehow better than the others, although essentially 'all cars are the same'
- becoming the 'first of something' in order to highlight a product that is essentially the same as its competitors.

In the cyber business it is very easy to exploit paradox. For example, Advance Bank (now St George Bank) was able to market itself as the first Australian Internet bank. Another example of paradox is Amazon.com, which has created a unique identity as a bookshop with over two and a half million titles on offer that does not have a physical shop.

The Australian Broadcasting Commission (ABC) is primarily viewed as a radio and television broadcaster. However, in 1996 the ABC established ABC Online as a new network in its own right (see figure 4.1). The ABC creates and packages content for an online audience rather than just value adding for radio and television audiences. The ABC sees the online audience as a unique entity, which it aims to attract. Online Coaching Colleges are providing virtual teachers to help students to prepare for their final examinations.

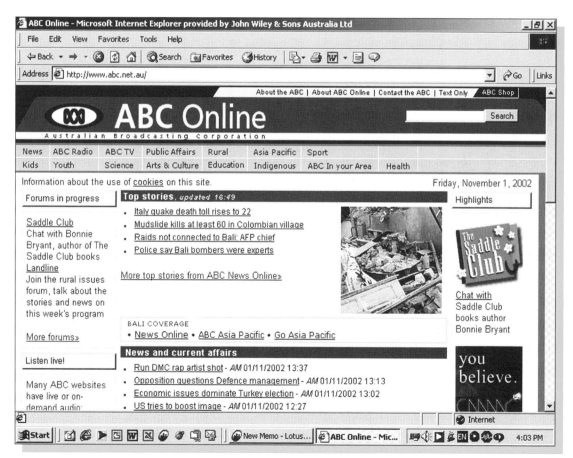

FIGURE 4.1: Home page of ABC Online (www.abc.net.au)

Perspective

Patty believes that it is vital to view the products from the consumer's **perspective**. The cyber business must determine:

- the consumer requirements that the product or service satisfies
- how its product satisfies those requirements differently and better than its competitors.

Banks such as St George Bank have targeted executives and women in their advertisements. They appeal to these busy people by stating that they understand how difficult it is to do domestic business during a frantic lunch hour: how much more convenient would it be to do your banking at home via computer, where there is no more queuing, no more rushing? The web shop www.greengrocer.com.au offers a wider range of products than most physical fruit and vegetable shops. It also provides added value, as follows:

- Products are rated according to the season.
- Value-for-money items are marked.
- Items are delivered to the door.
- There is a money-back guarantee if not satisfied.
- Customers save time by not going to the shops.[3]

Online trading has satisfied a need for investors to do their own trading from home. Software such as Business in a Box has helped entrepreneurs to set up their own web shops quickly (e.g. www.vetshoponline.com).

Paradigm

The third new P according to Patty is **paradigm**: a pattern example, a model way of doing things. In this new world, paradigms shift and we have to start anew. In chapter 1 the example was given of how retrenched executives have had to reinvent themselves from company people to individual consultants. Encyclopaedia Britannica had to change its mode of presentation from paper to CD-ROM. It is vital to identify the proper paradigm, and position the business accordingly.

Doing business on the Internet represents a paradigm shift in methods of doing business. Computer software sellers realised that selling over the Internet represents a major paradigm shift in the way they distribute their software. They can now download software directly to the customer's hard disk. In Netscape's Californian headquarters orders for its software used to come in at a rate of 1000 a day.

Web sites may hold audio and video files that can be listened to or watched by web users. Streaming technologies, such as audio streaming, allow users to play the multimedia files as they are being downloaded.

The ABC uses time shifting, an offshoot of audio streaming, to allow people to listen to ABC programs over the Internet, now that audio over the Internet is comparable to AM quality.[4]

Persuasion

All businesses try to persuade people to buy their product or service. As Internet commerce is a new medium, companies are attempting different ways to persuade people to visit their site and get them to buy. Patty states that in order to master **persuasion** it is essential to concentrate on:

- credibility
- content
- involvement of the listener.

Obviously, well-established physical businesses will have no trouble with the credibility angle in the virtual world. Start-up businesses, however, will need to establish credibility quickly. Content needs to be addressed in an online environment, because too much content bores the online reader. Speed of loading is vital to keep the potential client interested. In a web business there are many ways to involve the audience — after all, it is an interactive medium. Some of the methodologies include:

- allowing the consumer to see a demonstration of your products and services
- allowing visitors to email your staff directly or order online
- letting people see how many others visit your site
- running contests
- providing value-added services — for example, the Sofcom site allows the visitor to link to other interesting sites such as movie, gambling and online shopping sites.

A site that has been built to ensure a high level of interactivity is Libragirl (www.libragirl.com.au). The interactivity means that visitors spend more time there as they have opportunities to win prizes and ask for free samples of company products.

Passion

Patty states that he is passionate about his business objective — to develop exciting communication that persuades a consumer to visit a Nissan dealership. This **passion** could also be extended to the Internet commerce site. Remember that the Internet is an exciting communication channel, a brave new frontier in commerce, and the business needs to persuade the consumer to visit the web site. The web site CyberHorse (www.cyberhorse.com.au) caters for hundreds of followers of horse racing. Subscribers pay a monthly fee to access its Virtual FormGuide, which allows punters to obtain comprehensive racing form guides for all Australian TAB meetings.

Because Australians are passionate about sport it makes sense to have a sporting web site. Greg Norman markets his golf and casual apparel line from the Greg Norman Collection via the Web at the Shop@Shark.com Store (www.shark.com). Tips, articles and the marketing of his golf-course design company are also found on the site (see figure 4.2). Centrebet uses the

Internet to host sites in Australia, Denmark, Norway and Finland; conduct bets with clients; illustrate dates, times and locations of events for betting; and to conduct offshore banking.

FIGURE 4.2: Home page of Shark.com (www.shark.com)

CREATING A COMMERCIAL WEB SITE

Planning

Any type of work involves planning, organising, controlling and monitoring activities.[5] Creating a commercial presence on the Web involves all of these, but with important variations. The traditional paradigm of 'gather data, evaluate alternatives and select plan' does not work with the Web, and companies need to adopt an evolutionary and flexible approach for setting up a web site.[6] Because many companies have 1950s work philosophies, they react to the Web by setting up large committees to discuss policies, content and implementation strategies. They often lose strategic advantage by taking too long to get a web site online. It is better to get some web experience and to put projects online quickly and constantly improve them, rather than spending months arguing over policies and content. Instead of setting up large committees, companies should participate in strategic planning workshops, which should be conducted by professional web consultants and should assist interested participants, including senior management, to become aware of the potential of the medium. It is vital to have a senior person on side if the web site is to get approval quickly. The first step in achieving quality excellence is the decision to make quality leadership a basic strategic goal. One half-day could be spent training the participants in the Web and the next day working out strategies for how the company could create its commercial presence on the Web. It is essential to build quality into the web site at this early design stage to conform to the principles of total quality management.

An Internet commerce strategist begins by considering all aspects of the current business, its processes, people and customer base. The transition to e-business may involve many staff from within the organisation and potentially many from outside the organisation. Members of the information technology department must be involved in the successful execution of the strategy.[7] Some important aspects must be considered:

- new ways of doing business through technology
- evaluation of the organisation's response to customer needs
- ways to decrease costs and increase competitive advantage
- assessment of the customer base and its capacity to trade online
- assessment of products and services and how these may be marketed to the customer
- outsourcing requirements
- estimations of timing into the digital market, schedules for development
- assessment of the potential effects of disintermediation and reintermediation
- creation of a detailed partnering strategy
- financial requirements of the Internet business
- objectives for the first six months
- keeping up to date.

Organising

The commercial web site should be thought of as a continually growing and informative picture of the company. As such it is essential that it is updated and constantly improved as part of total quality management. There must be some hook to get people to return to the site, otherwise it will not be revisited. This can be done by running contests, offering incentives, and so on. Some companies are now adding in small advertisements for their own products and for the products of other companies.

It is also vital to organise training sessions for all members of the organisation who are interested in the Web. The more people involved and enthused by the Web the better, as they will be able to provide new ideas for running the online business. Harris Technology is a good example of this approach. Every staff member is involved with the web site design and implementation, and the online business is seen as just another way of serving the clients. Training covering all aspects of server operations and web presentations should be provided because such good training will contribute significantly to standardisation and 'corporate image'. This idea is in line with company-wide commitment and company-wide introduction of total quality management principles.

Controlling

In many large organisations control of the web site can become a power tool for a division or department. Office or organisational politics may cause serious conflicts over who has ultimate control. In some companies, divisions that have been downsized may see control of the web site as a way to get back into favour in the organisation. Other divisions, such as computing services, may see the web design and maintenance as just another chore that they have to do on top of their already busy schedule. A SPIDER (Strategic Planning for Internet Dissemination, Evaluation and Retrieval) team can assist in such ventures.[8] If different departments of an organisation want to become involved in the commercialisation of the organisation's web site, they need support in doing this, but not complete control of every page that is added. **Templates** and guidelines can be circulated. Templates are useful as they assist the different departments to quickly add a page and it helps if they feel that they are not starting from scratch. The guidelines need to set out who has formal authority to approve pages. Change control documentation is important when considering a large project.

Monitoring results

Once an organisation has a commercial web site it is a simple matter to gather statistics on the site. The online orders will provide the statistics but some companies favour visitor books or interactive forms. There is a danger of overkill on statistics. Web users tire of filling in large forms unless there is some incentive for doing so. It is possible to allow a daemon, a background process that runs on a Unix machine, to measure the number of hits. Each week, the service provider for Cyber.Consult emails the number of visits, or hits, to the Cyber.Consult home page. These figures are broken down into the countries of origin of the hits and the domain names. Obviously, if a company needs more information, interactive forms and visitor books will be necessary. These forms do help a business to build up a profile of its customers and after all not all visitors to the site will buy. It is handy if the cyber business knows why the potential client has not followed through with an order. In attempting to adhere to the principles of total quality management, the gathering of information from the customers who visit the organisation's page can be used as a tool to ensure that the customer requirements are incorporated into the design and continual development of the site.

Creating and sustaining an Internet commerce site means being prudent with external companies, Internet service providers (ISPs), network integrators and Internet specialists.

Creating a commercial web site quickly

One of the quickest ways to set up a business online is to go to a company that makes it easy for you. Yahoo has its facility to set up an online store, namely Yahoo!Store, which allows potential clients to set up an online business using a series of online wizards to help design the commercial site. If you want to set up your online business from scratch, you may have to spend between $7000 and $12000, with some businesses spending as much as $100000. Companies and individuals can buy templates for online catalogues and databases. Inter-World produces a software product called Commerce Exchange, which allows users to build up corporate catalogues and online malls, and manage accounts with multiple billing options, purchase ordering and invoice processing.

Internet commerce technology review

This section provides an overview of the technology needed for a commercial web site. (Refer to chapter 3 for more details.) The method of connecting to the Internet is the first decision to be made when establishing a web site. A commercial web site must be available to customers 24 hours a day, seven days a week. This is the major advantage that web buying has over physical shopping. The cyber business must have a dedicated connection to the Internet. In Australia there are many ISPs that will assist in setting up your communication link. They will also assist in making sure you have a domain name, which should reflect the company name. Melbourne IT is one company that registers commercial domain names for Australia. NetRegistry is another company that registers commercial domains, but it is important to be aware that it is possible to register in other countries as well.

Some of the items that need to be considered when choosing an ISP are:
- cost
- performance
- terms of service contract.[9]

The ISP might charge a flat rate fee, a set-up fee and a charge for hosting the electronic web site. Make sure that the ISP is able to support its customer base and that you have a disaster recovery plan in place if your ISP does not survive. Set-up costs for a virtual web server can vary from nothing to $450 (which includes domain name registration). Ongoing costs for a virtual server vary from $20 per month to several hundred dollars per month. Some ISPs also create web sites and prices vary from $70 to over $100 per hour. Alternatively, you might decide to buy package deals, such as a fully scalable solution as offered by InterWorld or e-business packages from IBM.

The cyber business must also decide on whether to connect to the Internet via fast modem or via ISDN (integrated services digital network). A 28.8-Kbps fast modem will support up to 20000 hits per day, whereas an ISDN line can support up to 80000 hits per day. The business will also need a network device to connect the computer to the TCP/IP-based Internet − either a modem for a dedicated voice line or a terminal adapter for an ISDN connection. Some ISPs have their own overseas backbone link and avoid the congestion that may occur on Telstra's backbone. The cost of setting up a permanent modem connection varies from $150 to over $650 with ongoing fees of between $120 and $650 per month. The permanent ISDN connections are much more expensive and may cost from $150 to $2000 to set up and ongoing costs for such a fast connection may run from $120 to $1050 per month.

Make sure you study the terms of the service contract to ensure you know what you are signing and what rights you have. In Australia disputes with ISPs should be referred to the Telecommunications Industry Ombudsman. The cost of setting up permanent web server hardware that has a lot of memory should also be remembered. Table 4.1 sets out some typical hardware considerations for large- and medium-sized enterprises.

TABLE 4.1	HARDWARE CONSIDERATIONS IN LARGE- AND MEDIUM–SIZED ENTERPRISES			
WORKSTATIONS CONNECTED	**SERVER OPERATING SYSTEMS**	**SERVER HARD DISKS**	**SERVER MEMORY**	**PROCESSORS**
3000 workstations: XP Professional, Windows 2000, Linux and SUN workstations, Macintoshes	Windows 2000, XP Professional, SUN OS Solaris, Linux	80 GB 120 GB	512 MB	Pentium and Alpha Processors, SUN, IBM, HP, Silicon Graphics, Unix, Linux

SOURCE: E. Lawrence 1998, 'Setting up a shopfront', *Hands-on Solutions: E-Commerce*, CCH, Sydney, p. 35.

The software that is required to operate web servers includes the following:
- directory indexing software to open uniform resource locators (URLs)
- audit log files to track every request for a file from your server, host name, date, time and type of request
- access control software that allows user access to be restricted by requiring a user name and password
- common gateway interface (CGI), which allows different types of networking software to interact with one another.

Table 4.2 shows the results of a survey of web server software usage on Internet-connected computers as well as active servers.

TABLE 4.2	MOST POPULAR WEB SERVER SOFTWARE				
	WEB SITES USING SOFTWARE, MAY 2002		**WEB SITES USING SOFTWARE, JUNE 2002**		**PER CENT CHANGE**
DEVELOPER	**NUMBER**	**PER CENT**	**NUMBER**	**PER CENT**	
Apache	10 411 000	65.11	10 964 734	64.42	–0.69
Microsoft*	4 121 697	25.78	4 243 719	24.93	–0.85
iPlanet**	247 051	1.55	281 681	1.66	0.11
Zeus	214 498	1.34	227 857	1.34	0.00

* Microsoft is the sum of sites running Microsoft-Internet-Information-Server, Microsoft-IIS, Microsoft-IIS-W, Microsoft-PWS-95 and Microsoft-PWS.
** iPlanet is the sum of sites running iPlanet-Enterprise, Netscape-Enterprise, Netscape-FastTrack, Netscape-Commerce, Netscape-Communications, Netsite-Commerce and Netsite-Communications.

SOURCE: Netcraft Web Server Survey, June 2002, www.netcraft.com/survey, accessed July 2002.

Web application hosting

As discussed above, Internet hosting was traditionally done as web site hosting in-house or with an ISP. Web application hosting is now common and can be done in-house or via an **application service provider (ASP)**. In this model 'application services' such as B2C e-commerce functionality or customer relationship management software are rented from a provider. As with any rental agreement the advantage is that there is no initial application purchase cost, so such a model may appeal to small- and medium-sized e-commerce enterprises. These companies do not have to employ high cost technical support staff or increase their bandwidth spending. However, as is common with rental agreements, there are some risks. What would happen if the ASP went out of business? What would happen if you wanted to change ASP? Can you trust the ASP with your data?

DIFFERENT METHODOLOGIES FOR DEVELOPING AN E-COMMERCE WEB SITE

There are various systems development methodologies that are used for developing e-commerce sites. Each methodology must deliver the ability to develop top-quality e-commerce sites at *Internet speed*; for this reason, **rapid application development (RAD)** and prototyping are important. A **prototype** is a working model of the proposed system that allows end users to interact with the system before it is completed to make sure it meets their needs. The use of **joint application development (JAD)** is also important in light of the multidisciplinary nature of e-commerce. Extensible markup language (XML) is rapidly becoming the *lingua franca* of interorganisational communications on the Internet and many systems developers and software engineers are using **unified modelling language (UML)** as a standard object-oriented design language. Almost every maker of software development products endorses UML, including IBM and Microsoft (for its Visual Basic environment).

Going online

The following list of issues should be considered when taking your business online:[10]

- Develop an online strategy document.
- Ensure that there are enough funds to go online and stay online – many dot.com companies have suffered from fast cash burn and have closed, for example dstore.com.au and thespot.com.au.
- Investigate current and future infrastructure needs.
- Study best-practice web-site design and hosting – it is often useful to visit web sites that set out best-practice guidelines, such as the one at www.treasury.gov.au.
- Factor in testing and maintenance of the web site.
- Ensure trust and security issues are taken seriously and that policies are posted online.

- Make sure customer relationship management is carried out online.
- Realise that marketing and branding have to be carried out both online and offline.
- Take into account legal matters such as copyright and contracts – get legal advice before putting up your web site.
- Maintain competitive advantage by value adding online.

The following steps should be used to build an Internet commerce site:

1. Gather the requirements.
2. Design the site.
3. Build the site.
4. Arrange hosting.
5. Monitor and maintain the site.

1. Gather the requirements

As with any information technology system it is important to know what the users want. The users may be the buyers, the clients, business partners and employees, and you need to know whether they want to perform transactions, browse documents, listen to music or download movies. It is also necessary to understand why the organisation is introducing a web-based e-business site. The organisation might hope to increase sales, cut costs or make life easier for its employees. The organisation must have obtained a meaningful web domain name. Understand the technical requirements for such a system in terms of operating systems, volume of use, bandwidth requirements and ease of use. Find out what type of content management software will be needed to ensure that the site is easy to maintain.

2. Design the site

It is imperative to look at the design of the content and how it is to be structured. The type of content must also be decided. A catalogue display should not allow graphics to hamper the speed of loading of the pages. The navigational aids should be easy to use and should provide a good impression of the corporation. The shopping cart capabilities should be documented, as well as how to handle the transactions. Decide on what amount and type of programming is required – even if you buy off-the-shelf software, some programming might be needed.

3. Build the site

The multidisciplinary nature of e-commerce generally means that a multidisciplinary team will be required to build the site. Such a team could consist of web developers, graphic artists, accountants, programmers and usability experts to handle the usability testing. Refer back to the SPIDER team mentioned above.

4. Arrange hosting

This has been discussed above – will the site be hosted in-house or by an ISP or ASP? If you opt to rent space on a provider's hosting service, the cost will be lower and your business will not have to invest in expensive equipment and highly paid technical staff. Some ISPs provide dedicated hosting whereby your business is provided with its own server that is managed by the ISP. This option is more expensive than shared hosting but has the advantage of giving you more control over the look and feel of your online site. The most expensive option is for the online business to have its own server and to totally control the site and its connections to the outside world. A useful site for comparing all these options in-depth is www.hostcompare.com/.

5. Monitor and maintain the site

The functions of building and installing a web site represent only a fraction of the time and effort that will be required over the life of the commercial web site. It is vital that the web site be regularly maintained and updated for 'freshness' and accuracy of content. As the web site grows, maintenance staff may find it necessary to modify or redesign the information architecture of the site to accommodate new site sections, navigation functionality and brand requirements.

E-COMMERCE SOFTWARE OVERVIEW

There are off-the-shelf e-commerce software packages available ranging from partial to total software solutions. Shopping cart software may be integrated into your web shop – one solution is provided by Cart32 Shopping Cart (www.cart32.com). The shopping cart software should allow users to click on the item to place it in their virtual shopping cart and should allow users to delete the item if they change their mind. Users should be able to proceed to the checkout and commit the transaction. Some online shops allow users two chances to make a commitment to the transaction. Large integrated total solutions are provided by such companies as InterWorld (www.interworld.com) and IBM e-business solutions.

Other software developments include e-commerce merchant systems connecting to telecommunications. NETcall Telecom and iCat Corporation are incorporating NETcall's Hyperphone links (the telephone equivalent of hypertext links) into e-commerce web shops. This will enable web shoppers to browse, shop, click a button and be automatically connected to the desired merchant, enabling them to complete the transaction by phone.

Email-filtering software is able to analyse queries sent by email and quickly generate a reply from a database of responses.

For small- and medium-sized enterprises it is useful to look at such cheap alternatives as Yahoo! Store Builder or Freemerchant.com. For as little as US$15 per month and a yearly fee of US$150 your online business can be up and running in a few hours. These sites offer the novice a set of effective page-building wizard tools to help design the web site, as well as statistics to help the store owner to check on the items sold, the number of visitors to the site, revenue and the number of orders. These data-mining tools are especially helpful to online businesses in showing up customer buying trends and relationships among data. It is a useful exercise to try your hand at building a sample store to see how effective these tools are.

If your business is classified as a medium-to-large-sized enterprise, it might be useful to look at IBM's WebSphere, an Internet infrastructure software known as middleware. It enables companies to develop, deploy and integrate next-generation e-business applications, such as those for B2B e-commerce, and supports business applications from simple web publishing through to enterprise-scale transaction processing. WebSphere transforms the way businesses manage customer, partner and employee relationships. For example, you can use it to create a compelling Web experience that improves the quality and quantity of site traffic, extend applications to incorporate mobile devices so the salesforce can service clients faster, or build an electronic e-marketplace to lower sourcing costs.[11] For further information on WebSphere visit www.ibm.com and enter the search term WebSphere.

Electronic shopping agents

Electronic shopping **agents** are software tools that assist users to search the Internet for product items. Users interact with a shopping agent by submitting agent requests. The agent then searches relevant online shops for items matching the search criteria. The agent returns to the user with:
- a detailed description of the items found
- the price of the items
- a direct link to the virtual store where the user can purchase the items.

The agent formats the information, perhaps by price or use, to help the shopper to compare products. Several agent-based systems have been developed for electronic commerce systems (e.g. PersonaLogic, Firefly, Bargain-Finder, Jango, Kasbah, AuctionBot). For more information on these agents visit bots.internet.com/search/s-shop.htm.

BUILDING AN INTERNET COMMERCE COMMUNITY

As illustrated in figure 4.2, building an Internet commerce community is helpful in ensuring the success of the cyber business. Some of the areas that could be classified as Internet commerce hotspots in Australia are discussed below.

Internet banking

In December 1995 Advance Bank (now St George Bank) began offering banking on the Internet and immediately took on the leader position as the first Internet bank in Australia. By June 1996 it was in second place in the *Money Page*'s Cyberspace Top Ten Banks, immediately behind Security First Network Bank of the United States.

Australians have rapidly adopted Internet banking — 23 per cent of people now use online services, compared with 12 per cent in the United Kingdom and 15 per cent in the United States.[12] However, 45 per cent of Australians are scared off Internet banking because of system outages and security scandals. Ibanks in the United States and the United Kingdom have addressed the problems of scalability (that is, handling the huge increase in online customers) and availability on a 24 × 7 basis, but the major banks in Australia have been slow to deal with these issues. It is thought that they will not be prepared for the massively quick uptake of online banking.[13]

Service–selling sites

Originally it seemed that cyber shopping malls would be the most effective way to get noted on the Web. Large department stores have not joined malls – they have set up their own sites. Retail shops that have succeeded have thrived by turning their customers into a community. The bookshop Amazon.com encourages community feeling by getting people to write reviews of books they have read, by encouraging buyers to interact with authors via email and by getting customers to register with Eyes, a service that notifies customers of new books that are likely to interest them.

> A general rule of thumb is that online consumers are interested in making better informed purchases more quickly, rather than getting the lowest price. The more tiresome a purchase is in the physical world, the more likely consumers are to try an online alternative. Because shopping for a mortgage is difficult and tedious, a site offering straightforward and easy-to-understand comparisons could be a hit. Because buying a CD is easy, (online music stores) must offer far more than a physical music store to draw in the shoppers.[14]

In the service area Qantas builds community identity on its web site by allowing members of its Frequent Flyer club to buy tickets and to check their points online. If customers have sent packages via Qantas, they can trace the progress of consignments using the web site.

Online publishing

This is an exciting area of Internet commerce. The major Australian newspapers are now online, and so far their offerings are free. They are making money from advertising. The *Sydney Morning Herald* accepts classified advertisements over the Internet. Publishers are extending their field of interest and joining with others in joint ventures.

The real power of the Internet lies in the user's ability to download finished products such as music, video and books digitally. For songs there are sound files that use a compression technology called MP3, which can shrink a 60-Mb sound file to less than 5 Mb by eliminating all the information the human ear cannot detect.

In October 1999, Yahoo! introduced an Internet broadcast service to position itself as a global distribution network for music, video and books online.[15] Yahoo! has identified four ways of making money from broadcasting over the Internet:

1. charging music labels to turn songs into streaming media and to distribute them to the Yahoo! user base
2. seeking a percentage of the transaction fee when consumers pay for music online
3. building a series of super-sized music databases
4. aggregating content and posting advertisements.

Digital books such as *SofBook* by Virtual Press, *RocketBook* by NuvoMedia and Everybook by Everybook, Inc., have also made their appearance.[16]

B2B transactions

B2B e-commerce refers to any transaction between two parties who are commercial in concept such as proprietary companies or partnerships. Also, if a seller enters into the transaction to make a profit and the buyer enters into the transaction as part of the means by which they will ultimately profit, then the transaction is business. Finally, the nature of the transactions often defines 'business' – for example, by looking at the following:

- the frequency of the transaction
- the dollar value of the transaction
- the quantity of items purchased in the transaction
- the role of the transaction in the supply chain.[17]

Coca-Cola Amatil Australia (CCAA) now uses eProcure, an Australian software product that connects requesters to approvers and buyers to suppliers, automating the functions from order making, sending and receiving the product. The self-service web interface ordering model has a level of access to the catalogue and is used for ordering IT equipment, stationery, travel, entertainment, contract and project-based services. GartnerGroup research has shown that online procurement can save companies up to 20 per cent in costs (or an average of 7 per cent to 10 per cent).[18] Examine the case study at the end of this chapter for an example of business-to-business e-commerce.

SUMMARY

This chapter has outlined the techniques and methods that are useful for making Internet commerce a reality in the business environment. The new five P's of marketing have been used to illustrate the ways in which Internet commerce can become a profitable business proposition. It is vital to take into account the five P's of marketing as set out by Tom Patty. These are paradox, perspective, paradigm, persuasion and passion. In this chapter we have looked at examples of Internet commerce sites that have shown attention to these new five P's of marketing. We have reiterated the need to plan, organise, control and monitor the web business. We have looked at planning for e-business and at some e-commerce software, as well as the need to use rapid application methodologies to set up e-business sites. Examples of successful sites that have concentrated on building a community have been given. Business-to-business e-commerce has been examined and an overview of setting up an e-commerce web site has been given.

Key terms

agents (p. 96)	paradigm (p. 86)	rapid application
application service	paradox (p. 84)	development (RAD)
provider (ASP)	passion (p. 87)	(p. 93)
(p. 93)	perspective (p. 86)	templates (p. 90)
joint application	persuasion (p. 87)	unified modelling
development (JAD)	prototype (p. 93)	language (UML)
(p. 93)		(p. 93)

Case study

THE ADOPTION OF E-COMMERCE BY MICROBUSINESSES

By Katina Michael, University of Wollongong © 2002

In Australia, about 89 per cent of businesses have less than five employees. This equates to 1 035 000 microbusinesses. What is important to note is that 637 300 of these are non-employing businesses (i.e. sole proprietors) according to the Australian Bureau of Statistics (ABS).[19] By studying these figures it becomes increasingly apparent what a challenging task the majority of business operators have in adopting and successfully integrating electronic commerce into their business. They only have their own resources and experiences to draw on and face a multitude of constraints such as time, money, lack of expertise and access to limited amounts of information. Many microbusiness owners are more concerned about making ends meet and how they will satisfy upcoming customer engagements than how they will venture online. Even though microbusiness computer penetration is very high,[20] at about 79 per cent, electronic commerce adoption is substantially lower. According to the ABS, only 64 per cent of microbusinesses have Internet connectivity and some 14 per cent have a web presence.[21]

MICROBUSINESS RESOURCE LIMITATIONS

For most Australian microbusinesses the first steps towards the adoption of electronic commerce can be very daunting. Companies with less than five employees can seldom afford a dedicated information technology (IT) professional on their payroll. More often than not, the IT role is bestowed upon the most naturally gifted computer-adept employee as an additional part-time job function. This individual is usually a self-motivated beginner who is provided with little training and usually learns 'on-the-job' by trial and error. Seemingly simple tasks such as purchasing a computer, finding a suitable ISP, registering a domain name and establishing a web presence can become unassumingly overbearing. Small business owners and key decision makers are usually too preoccupied with the day-to-day operation of the business to worry about formulating a proper electronic commerce infrastructure plan. Many businesses aimlessly seek to go online giving little thought to answering fundamental questions such as why they are doing so, how they will go about it, and within what time frame and budget. Requirements are usually satisfied on an ad-hoc basis and with little prior investigation into how going online may impact current business practices.

THE ROAD TO ELECTRONIC COMMERCE[22]

The road to electronic commerce can be segmented into four main stages: buying a computer, getting connected to the Internet, building an Internet presence and introducing electronic commerce functionality. These stages are discussed below.

Buying a computer[23]

The first hurdle for a new start-up may well be where to buy a computer. There are equipment vendors on the Internet such as Dell, retail department stores such as Harvey Norman and local stores that may sell no-name brands and second-hand computers. Deciding where to go to purchase can be a dilemma. The second hurdle may be related to getting a valid quotation that includes all the components that you have specified. Trying to compare several quotations can also be difficult, so they are best compared against minimum specification requirements. Consider what type of configuration is suitable for your needs. Should the computer be a desktop or a laptop? How much storage space is required on the hard drive? How much random access memory (RAM) and what type of processing speed? Will the office computers and other peripherals be networked via hub? In addition, what type of software does the business require to go online? Which Internet browser will be used and which email program? Finally, the decision to purchase or lease the equipment is also important as it has considerable tax implications.

Getting connected to the Internet[24]

Once the computer equipped with a modem has been purchased, getting connected to the Internet with the right ISP is a very important step on the road to electronic commerce success. Choosing the wrong ISP can be disastrous. Poor Internet connectivity, low modem-to-user ratios (leading to congestion during peak periods), inadequate customer support and expensive fees are enough to turn off any microbusiness owner from staying connected for long.

The *Australian ISP List*[25] is a good place to start looking for information on prospective ISPs.[26] Businesses that are located outside the Sydney metropolitan area may find it a particularly useful resource because it lists ISPs by their regional presence. The *Australian ISP List* also identifies additional services offered by ISPs such as web hosting and Internet training, and lists all the points-of-presence (POP) locations, network details, supported protocols and pricing. Depending on the type of microbusiness and the role the Internet will play in the business, it may also be useful to consider whether broadband connectivity is appropriate, either cable or ADSL. If narrowband is preferred because broadband is either too expensive or not offered in the serving area, ISDN could also be considered. Settling for a 56 Kbps dial-up connection may also be sufficient, but one or more additional dedicated telephone lines may be leased for the purposes of receiving email or browsing the Internet without interrupting the flow of incoming telephone calls.

Building an Internet presence[27]

Once you have found an ISP that offers reliable connectivity,[28] the next step is to establish an Internet presence. The same ISP that offers your business Internet access should also possess web hosting capabilities for an additional monthly or annual fee.

In most cases the ISP can also help you to register a domain name for your business[29] and offer some advice about professional web development services. Web-page design expertise can vary considerably in price and quality, so it is advisable to obtain several quotes and to inspect a portfolio of current web sites designed by the prospective vendors.

Setting up a company web site takes a lot of planning – participating in electronic commerce is more than just building a haphazard home page just for the sake of getting something onto the Web. For example, will you require macromedia flash, database integration and/or web site promotion on selected search engines and directories?[30] In some instances, business owners may decide to create their own web sites, but what should be contemplated is the steep learning curve associated with attaining professional web design skills. The time and effort exerted in a 'do-it-yourself' web site may not be reflected in the final result. An unprofessional site can do more damage than good, not to mention losing hours that could have been spent elsewhere in general business operations. This is not to say that outsourcing web development is a panacea – ongoing maintenance costs are not cheap to a microbusiness that is struggling to survive. Depending on the complexity of the web site, outsource fees are anywhere between $1200 and $5000 for a basic web site. For a microbusiness owner generating not more than $100 000 per annum this is a sizeable investment.

Introducing electronic commerce functionality[31]

After establishing a basic company web presence the microbusiness owner may want to get paid over the Internet as well. Credit card payments can be processed in either a manual or automatic fashion. The manual way is for credit card details to be emailed to the business owner and for these to be processed offline. In order to process payments automatically business owners establish a merchant services agreement with a chosen bank and authorisation is conducted in real time. It may also be convenient to set up Internet banking capabilities at the same time. Additional electronic commerce functionality could be applied to the web site by introducing an online product catalogue or even a shopping cart system that allows consumers to shop over the Internet.[32] When getting paid over the Internet, the business owner should enquire about secure payments. This can be implemented using 128-bit Secure Socket Layer (SSL) encryption or digital certificates.[33]

Finally, after the B2C transactions are in operation, conducting B2B electronic data interchange should also be considered, depending on the nature of the microbusiness. More and more large retailers and government organisations are insisting that smaller players use EDI to streamline processes and reduce overheads.[34]

THE ONLINE REALITY

The four main stages to electronic commerce may seem straightforward; however, it is one thing to read about these stages, but it is another thing to plan to do them, and yet another to implement them successfully.

High failure rates are synonymous with new start-up businesses,[35] and it should be noted that electronic commerce does not miraculously make all other conventional business problems go away. In fact, a recent national survey conducted by Dun & Bradstreet (D&B) in Australia has revealed some very interesting trends. In short, Australian businesses are either 'loving or leaving the Internet'.[36] They either think it is having a positive impact on their business, or they think it is not contributing at all and subsequently they are dropping out of the electronic commerce game altogether. According to Dun & Bradstreet '[b]usiness experimentation with e-commerce in the last 12 months has revealed that while a small proportion are doing more online, a larger proportion are doing less'.

How should these results be interpreted? Should this report deter microbusinesses from going online? Not at all. But it should at least act to raise the awareness that adopting electronic commerce requires some serious thinking. Inadequate research by a microbusiness can lead to the misalignment of tens of thousands of dollars with very little to show in terms of a functional company web site at the conclusion. Perhaps a suggestion would be to follow the path to electronic commerce as outlined above. At the completion of each stage, the business should reassess its business goals and what it hopes to gain from the Internet before committing to the next phase of implementation. The business may require only a basic company web site initially, but as the company grows in stature additional functionality can be added.

QUESTIONS

1. What are the main steps involved on the road to electronic commerce?
2. What are some of the hurdles that microbusinesses face in deciding to go online?
3. What types of benefits can electronic commerce offer to microbusinesses?
4. Visit the National Office of Information Economy (NOIE) web site at www.noie.gov.au. What kind of resources does NOIE make available?
5. Visit the *Australian ISP List* at www.cynosure.com.au and study three ISPs. How do they differentiate themselves from each other?

1. Prepare a discussion paper to outline the benefits of Internet commerce for a particular business of your choice.
2. Prepare a marketing plan for getting a business ready for an Internet presence.

Suggested | reading

Bayles, D. 1998, *Extranets: Building the Business-to-Business* Web, Prentice Hall, New Jersey.

Hill, T. 1993, *The Essence of Operations Management*, Prentice Hall, United Kingdom.

Kalakota, R. and Robinson, M. 1999, *E-Business: Roadmap for Success*, Addison-Wesley Longman, United States.

Kalakota, R. and Whinston, A. 1997, *Electronic Commerce: A Manager's Guide*, Addison-Wesley, United States.

Lawrence, E. et al. 2002, *Technology of Internet Business*, John Wiley & Sons, Brisbane.

net.Genesis Corporation 1996, *Build a World Wide Web Commerce Center*, John Wiley & Sons, New York.

Pfaffenberger, B. 1998, *Building a Strategic Extranet*, IDG Books, United States.

End | notes

1. Patty. T. 1997, *Mastering the New Five P's of Marketing*, www.chiatday.com/raw_materials/insights/5ps/5p_mkt.html.
2. *Macquarie Dictionary*, 3rd edn, 1997, Macquarie Library, Macquarie University, NSW, p. 1559.
3. Lawrence, E. 1998, 'Setting up a shopfront', *Hands-on Solutions: E-commerce*, CCH, Sydney, p. 25.
4. Creedy, S. 1997, 'Aunty casts Net to catch up with PC generation', *Australian*, 12 August, p. 33.
5. Hill, T. 1993, *The Essence of Operations Management*, Prentice Hall, United Kingdom.
6. Newton, S. 1999, Electronic Business: Factors For Success, MA thesis for School of Computing Sciences, University of Technology, Sydney.
7. Lanfear, K. 1995, private email on strategies for implementation of World Wide Web, Networks Information Products Coordinator of United States Geographic Services.
8. Ibid.
9. Lawrence, op. cit.
10. Williams, G. and Behrendorff, G. 2000, 'To web or not to web?', *Australian CPA*, August 2000, p. 51.
11. 'WebSphere for newcomers', www7b.boulder.ibm.com/wsdd/zones/newcomers/.
12. Dearne, K. 2002, 'Security fears hurt e-banking', *Australian*, 5 March, p. 31.
13. Ibid.
14. Anderson, C. 1997, 'In search of the perfect market', *Economist*, 10 May, p. 9.
15. Needham, K. 1999, 'Yahoo broadcast tunes in Web's absolute power', *Biz.Com, Sydney Morning Herald*, 28 September, p. 32.
16. Silberman, S. 1998, 'Ex Libris: The joys of curling up with a good digital reading device', *Wired*, July, pp. 98–104.
17. Macpherson, A. 1998, 'Business-to-business transactions', *Hands-on Solutions: E-commerce*, CCH, Sydney, p. 7.
18. *E-Commerce Today* 1999, 'Coca-Cola Amatil embraces online procurement', issue 61, 23 September, www.ecommercetoday.com.au.
19. ABS, 2002, 'Characteristics of small business', Cat. No. 8127.0, www.abs.gov.au.
20. ABS, 2002, 'Business use of information technology', Cat. No. 8129.0, www.abs.gov.au.
21. A strong relationship between business size and the adoption of electronic commerce is apparent when comparisons are made with medium and large business types, which have close to 100 per cent IT penetration.
22. See also AUSe.NET's eight general stages that a small organisation will go through in adopting electronic commerce, www.ause.net/.
23. AUSe.NET 2000, 'How to buy a computer', www.ause.net/, v3.6.
24. AUSe.NET 2000, 'How to buy a computer', www.ause.net/, v2.3a.

25. Davies, K. 2002, *The Australian ISP List*, www.cynosure.com.au.

26. As well as looking at well-known ISPs such as Telstra BigPond or OptusNet, it is also worth looking at what some of the other ISPs have to offer.

27. AUSe.NET 2000, 'How to set up a web site', www.ause.net/, v2.3a.

28. Some ISPs are well known for focusing on offering business connectivity, such as connect.com.

29. A domain name in the form of .com, .org, .net or .info can be obtained with or without the .au extension for Australia.

30. See the services offered by Metro Software Developments, www.webdevelopmentaustralia.com/.

31. NOIE and ABA, 1999, 'Getting paid on the Internet', www.ause.net/.

32. iNETstore Corp, www.inetstore.com.au.

33. SecureNet certificates, www.securenetca.com.au/.

34. To learn more about EDI visit www.reims.net/Resource_Zones/EDI/edi_resources/edi_standards.html.

35. Hindle, K. G. and Rushworth, S. M. 2000, *Yellow Pages Global Entrepreneurship Monitor*, Swinburne University of Technology, Melbourne.

36. CyberAtlas 2002, 'Australian biz loving or leaving Internet', CyberAtlas, cyberatlas.internet.com/big_picture/geographics/print/0,,5911_979161,00.html.

CHAPTER 5

Electronic payment systems

LEARNING outcomes

You will have mastered the material in this chapter when you can:

- explain the various types of electronic payment systems
- define electronic purchasing
- explain the benefits and list the forms of transactions that can be used to transact electronic purchasing
- identify the security needs of offline and online electronic purchasing systems
- describe and explain the value of various e-cash systems and smart cards
- define EDI and demonstrate how invoicing and payments can be made
- explain the advantages and disadvantages of EDI relative to other forms of electronic payment systems.

'The future of wireless lies in creating lifestyle-altering solutions that will lead to a bigger market than can be imagined. For example, some predict that everyday items, such as passports and wallets, will be augmented or even replaced by mobile devices that carry proof of identification, bank balances, and reservation information, and deliver this information to merchants through a low-cost, wireless network.'

G. Raczkowski 2002, *Mobile Ecommerce: Focusing on the Future*, WorldCom white paper, © 2002 dash30 Inc, www1.worldcom.com/global/resources/whitepapers/, pdf/WorldCom_White_Paper_On_MobileEcommerce.pdf, accessed July 2002.

INTRODUCTION

Since the publication of the second edition of this textbook, many changes have taken place in the area of electronic payment systems. There has been an explosion in new forms of ways to pay for items over the Internet. Some, such as Floox and Beenz, never survived the great dot.com crash of 2000, while others, such as E-Gold and PayPal, are still operating, and no doubt new e-payment systems will continue to be developed. This chapter begins by examining some background issues to e-payment systems, and then looks at electronic payment systems in B2C and B2B environments. It also studies emerging forms of payments suitable for mobile e-commerce.

ELECTRONIC PAYMENT SYSTEMS

Purchasing is the process of exchanging currency or value in the form of **money** for goods, services or information. **Electronic payment systems (EPS)** involve that same exchange process but use an electronic intermediary to facilitate the exchange. Instead of paying for groceries with cash, for example, customers commonly use an electronic transfer of funds system using the same cards they utilise for their personal banking. The electronic system validates the value of the exchange, debits the customer and credits the supplier, all electronically. These systems eliminate cash and eliminate the need for frequent banking just to obtain cash. It is worth thinking about all the forms of transactions that can occur using EPS. They range from the small-scale, such as individuals buying groceries and household items, to the large-scale exchange of products and components, valued in millions of dollars, using **electronic data interchange (EDI)** processes.

   In the global trade in services (including software, entertainment and information products and professional services), which now accounts for well over $40 billion of US exports alone, electronic purchasing has the potential to revolutionise trade by lowering transaction costs. It will also assist in increasing the potential implementation of **just-in-time (JIT)** manufacturing processes, improving delivery time of component parts and facilitating new types of commercial transaction. Real-time ordering of and payment for supplies, components, services or information must facilitate greater efficiency and induce the potential for expanded trade at regional, national and international levels.

From traditional payment methods to EPS

Throughout recorded history we have engaged in the exchange of value in many ways. In earlier times goods and services were exchanged by barter or by tokens of various sorts. Some two or three millennia ago, the first forms of symbolic tokens with specific values emerged. These primitive coins and tokens formed the basis of the modern forms of exchange, which derived their value from societies' recognition of the value of precious metals such as gold. In the twenty-first century, the value of coinage and paper money is found in the comparison of one currency against another. Coinage and paper notes (plastic in Australia and Thailand) now have their own intrinsic value and an acceptance in society that generates and maintains that value. If a currency is overvalued because of government policy or because of economic conditions, governments can now devalue the currency relative to the currencies of other countries, as been the case in Thailand and Argentina.

No matter what form money takes, it performs four functions.
- Money is a medium of exchange.
- Money is a means of account (stating how much is owed and by whom to whom).
- Money provides a standard of deferred payment.
- Money is a defined store of value.

Any asset that performs all four of these functions can be defined as money. The question we are confronted with in discussing electronic forms of money or exchange is: Do the various types of electronic purchasing perform all four functions? This question needs to be considered as this chapter is read and discussed.

Today, we also have the added impact of exchange processes that allow us to exchange the value of goods and services in ways other than by using coin or paper money. For many decades bills of exchange, gems and precious metals have been used as alternative forms of exchange. In the 1990s, the emergence of EPS further revolutionised the way we buy and sell goods and services. Traditionally, we exchanged value in a process that engaged us in a multi-step process (see figure 5.1). Today, that multi-step process has been significantly changed to reflect the electronic exchange of value (see figure 5.2).

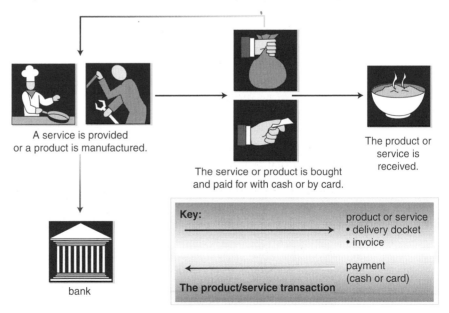

A service is provided or a product is manufactured.

The service or product is bought and paid for with cash or by card.

The product or service is received.

bank

Key:
→ product or service
• delivery docket
• invoice

← payment (cash or card)

The product/service transaction

FIGURE 5.1: Paying for goods and services in the traditional way

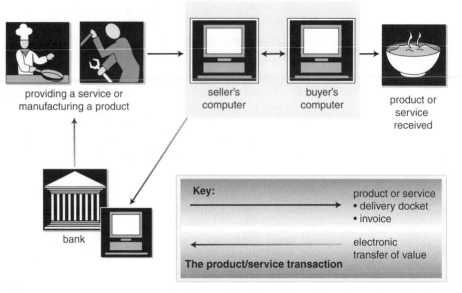

providing a service or manufacturing a product

seller's computer

buyer's computer

product or service received

bank

Key:

→ product or service
• delivery docket
• invoice

← electronic transfer of value

The product/service transaction

FIGURE 5.2: Paying for goods and services using electronic technology

In Australia, a number of policies have been put in place to facilitate a process where payments can be facilitated for an efficient exchange process. Australian businesses are not only affected by the decisions of governments and the Reserve Bank on exchange processes, but they are also required to report to the Australian Securities and Investments Commission about the nature, extent and impact of their payment systems and business activities.[1] To facilitate efficient clearing of payments lodged electronically, systems have been developed to improve the speed at which transfer payments can be verified to' support better cash flows in business.[2]

Electronic payment systems operate in various ways. The ways that exchange can occur electronically include:

• electronic financial payment systems (where value is exchanged using a system where a card is debited with some value or where a card allows value to be transferred from one account to another)

• Internet payment systems (where systems are in place that allow value to be exchanged using specified protocols on the Internet)

• **smart card** payment systems (where a silicon chip is used to transfer stored value from a card to a business system in exchange for goods and/ or services).

B2C ELECTRONIC PAYMENT SYSTEMS

There are many ways to pay for goods electronically, such as credit cards, e-cash, e-cheques (e-checks) and stored value cards. The most popular form of payment over the Internet is via the use of credit cards. Banks all over the world have invested in magnetic strip card technology to ensure that the processing of credit cards and cheques is done efficiently, securely and quickly.

Credit cards on the Internet

A credit card transaction is an instruction by a customer for funds to be transferred into a business's account and charged against the customer's account. The customer gives the instruction to the seller directly, by handing over the card or by telephoning, emailing or faxing details such as the card number, the name on the card, the expiry date and the type of card (e.g. VISA or MasterCard). Normally, once a month customers are expected to make a payment to their bank to either settle all recent transactions or pay some minimum amount. In addition, it is now possible for an Australian to visit a web site such as www.expedia.co.uk, purchase an airline ticket, pay with an Australian credit card and have the tickets delivered to a friend or relation in London. The primary steps involved are shown in figure 5.3.

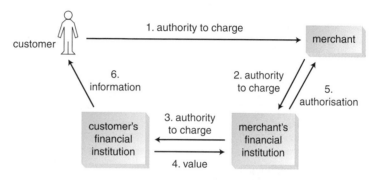

FIGURE 5.3: Steps in a credit card transaction

SOURCE: Australian Information Industry Association Ltd 1999, 'Getting paid on the Internet: what you need to know to receive credit-card payments', www.xamax.com.au/AIIA/CrCards.html.

Credit card numbers can be sent over the Internet encrypted or unencrypted. Encryption is the process of enabling information/data/knowledge to be coded in such a way that it cannot be read without a decoding system or key. All Internet browsers provide some level of data security. A 40-bit Secure Socket Layer (SSL) is typical for most browsers available worldwide and is adequate for most common data transfer situations. A 128-bit SSL is used by financial institutions and Internet-capable software suppliers. Roughly speaking, 128-bit encryption (the number refers to the size of the encryption key) is 309 485 009 821 345 068 724 781 056 times stronger than 40-bit encryption![3]

Web sites should inform buyers that their credit card is protected by encryption. Unencrypted dealings with credit cards are analogous to giving your credit card number over the phone. Customers can check if their browser supports session encryption by looking for a small closed lock in Internet Explorer or small unbroken key in the Netscape browser family.

Prodigy Internet® and MasterCard® have been specially developed for online and offline purchases. The Prodigy card guarantees online fraud protection and offers a points-based reward program that allows credit card holders to redeem points for free Prodigy Internet Access.[4]

How credit cards work on the Internet

Table 5.1 sets out the way in which credit card payments are processed.

As mentioned in table 5.1, Trintech is a specialist software company offering online credit card transactions for both e-business and mobile e-business (see figure 5.4).

TABLE 5.1	CREDIT CARD OPTIONS
TYPES OF MERCHANTS	**HOW THEY DEAL**
Offline merchants	Open a merchant account with a bank
	Accept only point-of-sale transactions or those that occur when you present credit card at the store.
Special Internet merchant account	Processed by banks or third-party services — e.g. www.cybercash.com, www.icat.com or www.camtech.com.au
Specialised software	Trintech offers online credit card transaction capabilities (for e-business and mobile e-business) — see www.trintech.com

SOURCE: H. M. Deitel, P. J. Deitel and P. R. Nieto 2000, *E-business and E-commerce: How to Program*, Prentice Hall, New Jersey, pp. 136–7.

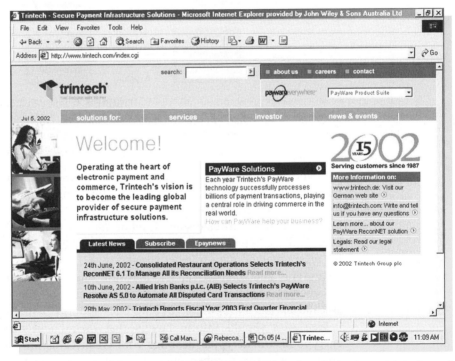

FIGURE 5.4: The Trintech web site (www.trintech.com)

ANSI Standard X4.13-1983 is the system used by most US national credit card systems. This is what some of your credit card numbers mean:[5]

- The first digit in your credit card number signifies the system − 3 = travel/entertainment cards (such as American Express and Diners Club), 4 = VISA, 5 = MasterCard and 6 = Discover Card.

- The structure of the card number varies by system. For example, American Express card numbers start with 37, and Carte Blanche and Diners Club with 38.
- For American Express, digits 3 and 4 are type and currency, digits 5–11 are the account number, digits 12–14 are the card number within the account and digit 15 is a check digit.
- For VISA, digits 2–6 are the bank number, digits 7–12 or 7–15 are the account number and digit 13 or 16 is a check digit.
- For MasterCard, digits 2–3, 2–4, 2–5 or 2–6 are the bank number (depending on whether digit 2 is a 1, 2, 3 or other). The digits after the bank number up to digit 15 are the account number, and digit 16 is a check digit.

There is a wealth of information on how credit cards work at www.howstuffworks.com, and more on the workings of credit cards on the Internet can be found in Alex Toussaint's 'Processing credit cards for online payment' at msdn.microsoft.com/workshop/server/commerce/creditcard.asp.

Virtual credit cards

Virtual credit operates by being able to generate a single use card number. In an Internet commerce environment a unique credit card number is used to purchase goods at a single web site so that a card member's actual account number never travels to the online store. Members of American Express Private Payments[SM] are assigned random, unique numbers to use in place of their actual card account numbers, so that their actual account numbers are never transmitted over the Internet. The numbers are valid for one month and can be used once only to make a purchase online.[6] Obviously, such a system has its drawbacks, because, for instance, these cards cannot be used for orders designated to be shipped as the items become available. Normal credit cards would have to be used in such instances.

Because each single use card number becomes exclusive to the online store where purchases are made, recurring charges such as Internet service provider fees or back-ordered items can be billed to that same number. One example is the Discover Deskshop® 2.0 virtual credit card, which is shown in figure 5.5.

EFTPOS

Electronic funds transfer at point of sale (EFTPOS) refers to when the purchaser is physically at the point of sale, such as the checkout in a supermarket or in a petrol station. EFTPOS operates either on credit or debit cards, immediately debiting the value of the exchange against an existing bank account. On credit cards, EFTPOS systems check the validity of the card status and then credit the value of the exchange against the credit card account for future payment by the cardholder (see figure 5.6). This method of payment has proved popular with virtual shoppers too, as several online shops (e.g. www.woolworths.com.au) use mobile EFTPOS machines when they deliver goods to clients.

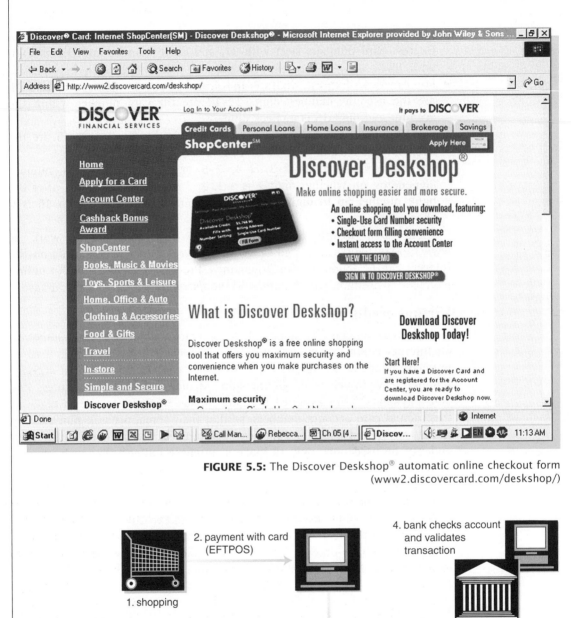

FIGURE 5.5: The Discover Deskshop® automatic online checkout form (www2.discovercard.com/deskshop/)

2. payment with card (EFTPOS)

1. shopping

3. store information system dials bank

4. bank checks account and validates transaction

5. EFT from customer's bank to store's bank

FIGURE 5.6: EFTPOS, payments and shopping

Electronic cheques

Electronic cheques (spelt *checks* in the United States) operate as though you were being issued a set of numbers from the bank: each number represents a cheque. This is a virtual chequebook without the physical cheques. You use each set of numbers only once – like a cheque. An example of an eCheck™ can be found at www.echeck.com.

With eCheck™, the payer
- writes the cheque on a computer
- signs it
- emails it over the Internet.

The payee
- receives the cheque
- verifies the signature
- endorses the cheque
- writes a deposit slip and signs it.

The endorsed cheque is then sent by email to the payee's bank for deposit. Bank personnel
- verify signatures
- credit the deposit
- clear and settle the endorsed eCheck™ by sending it on to the payer's bank, where signatures are once again verified and the amount of the eCheck™ is debited from the payer's account.[7]

For more information on eChecks™ visit www.echeck.org/, where you will find tutorials on how these e-cheques work, such as www.echeck.org/demos/meeting92299/EcheckTutorialMMA.pdf.

Electronic wallets

Electronic wallets have been designed to make it easier to shop online. If customers sign up for e-wallet, later when they shop online they need to enter their billing and shipping information only once. The e-wallet software will then instantly fill out online order forms with a click of a mouse. To make gift-giving easier, the wallet can also store the shipping addresses of friends and family. Electronic commerce modelling language (ECML), a universal format for online checkout form data fields, was launched in June 1999. ECML provides a simple set of guidelines for web merchants that enables digital wallets from multiple vendors to automate the exchange of information between consumers and merchants. ECML works with any web-security software and enables electronic wallets to feed customer information automatically into the payment forms of participating merchants.[8] For further details see the web site www.ecml.org.

Web services

Some companies are trying to solve electronic payment problems by using what are known as web services. Web services range from such major services as storage management and customer relationship management (CRM) to much more limited services such as the furnishing of a stock quote and the checking of bids for an auction item. The accelerating creation and availability of these services is a major Web trend.[9] For example, the Commonwealth Bank's Netbank connects its site with the BPAY online bill payments site by using web services. The web services wrap the BPAY accounts and present them to Netbank using such web technology as XML and HTTP. They use Sun Servers and Java to accomplish this.[10]

Digital cash

At a more experimental level, the increasing use of the Internet and the Web for commerce is creating a need for another type of EPS – digital cash. In the world of digital cash there are numerous brand names that have become common forms of description for digital money in general. One experiment that has been trialled since 1994 using the digital cash concept is the **DigiCash** Corporation based in the Netherlands. This **eCash**™ system uses electronic tokens to exchange goods and services in an online environment. Banks are used to verify the value of the token. It is important to note that eCash™ is a trademarked commercial application of digital money implemented in banks in the United States, Finland and Germany since 1995. **CyberCash** is a company that offers a secure means to conduct credit card transactions on the Internet. It is designed specifically for use by CyberCash's operators. However, digital cash has had a difficult time: its issuers either went bankrupt (DigiCash), dropped the product (CyberCash) or moved into another business.

Digital cash consists of a small string of encrypted digits, or electronic tokens, that can be used as a substitute for money to purchase various goods and services in an electronic environment, usually the Internet. For example, token or exchange value certificates can be used on the Internet or on private networks such as SITA (Société Internationale Transportation Aéronautiques), which provides a private network that supports the booking processes and traffic planning of most of the world's airlines. Digital cash replaces money in the transaction but depends on an institution, such as a bank, to provide the monetary value for the digital transaction.

Yahoo! offers PayDirect at its web site at www.paydirect.yahoo.com. This system allows consumers to:
• send money to anyone in the United States with an email address
• pay for an auction item they have won
• create custom links on their web page to expedite direct payment by creditors
• send a group bill to collect money for a party.

Another area that looks promising is prepaid cards. Research is being undertaken by CommerceNet – see the CommerceNet Security and Internet Payments Research Group at www.commerce.net. Prepaid cards that are used for online payments are typically distributed as simple scratch-off, embossed plastic or magnetic strip cards. The cards are available in different denominations and can be purchased from a retailer with any payment mechanism, but most typically using anonymous cash. When distributed to retailers the cards are inactive and they must be activated prior to use as a payment instrument.[11] Prepaid cards offer an attractive alternative to credit cards, especially for young people who are not eligible for a credit card.

The prepaid cards are easy to source, brand and distribute. The required Internet technologies can be readily assembled using commodity building blocks such as the generic browser, SSL, any SQL database, any server technology and the appropriate scripting language, given the technical ability to set it up. The only real area of technical differentiation is in passing purchase authorisation back to online merchants. Research is continuing, but already some well-known credit card companies have been moving into the area. American Express has signed a distribution agreement with 7-Eleven to create and distribute the 7-Eleven® Internet Shopping Card. VISA has recently started to offer prepaid cards, called VISA Buxx, through some of its member banks.

One of the problems with using digital-cash systems is the need to ensure the security of the payment being made. Three major protocols have been developed to try to ensure that all electronic payments over the Internet are secure. These protocols are:

- *STT*: Developed by Microsoft and VISA, STT uses a two-keyed authentication and encryption system that enables purchases to be completed using credit cards in a method similar to offline credit card usage. Each user is authenticated by an electronic certificate or credential that is unique to them. Any transaction must be verified by this credential.

- *SEPP*: This protocol was developed by IBM, MasterCard, Netscape, Verisign, RSA, Terisa Systems, SAIC, GTE and CyberCash using existing credit card procedures. However, SEPP differs from STT in that SEPP uses other forms of communication and other existing and private networks, as well as the Internet, to process the exchange of value involved in the transaction. In effect, it uses existing EFT infrastructure to operate.

- *SET*: This protocol was developed by both of the major credit card providers, VISA and MasterCard, to establish a uniform, secure communication standard for Internet commerce and is designed to become the standard for Internet commerce. SET trials began in 1997. SET uses the Internet rather than existing EFT infrastructure. On 4 June 1998 SET Co. awarded the right to use the SET trademark to the first four vendors of SET-compliant software: GlobeSet Inc., Spyrus/Terisa Systems, Trintech and Verifone. These companies' wallet applications were determined to be compliant with the SET 1.0 protocol. Check www.setco.org for SET protocols.

The following points illustrate the advantages of SET.[12] Primarily a secure communications standard, SET:

- enables bankcard payment on the Web
- provides special security needs
- ensures privacy of financial data

- features strong authentication policies for participants
- offers special purpose certificates
- provides message integrity
- offers non-repudiation for dispute resolution
- hides bankcard number from most merchants
- sustains existing relationships − cardholders with their banks, merchants with their banks
- provides interoperability
- supports end user choice of payment card
- provides links to existing systems.

IBM's superSet project is to extend SET to other payment instruments such as micropayments and cheques. However, the uptake of SET has been slow, and it appears that SSL has become the de facto standard.

One global organisation that has an interest in EPS is CommerceNet (www.commerce.net). CommerceNet has put in place portfolios that deal with five initial areas:

- infrastructure (EDI, robustness, network management and related infrastructure services)
- financial service (payments, Rosetta Net, eCheck™)
- trust and security (public key infrastructure (PKI), security showcase and encryption)
- information access (catalogues, directories, agencies and search interoperability)
- architecture and markets (eCo framework, iMarkets, vertical markets).

CommerceNet issues an email newsletter on electronic commerce matters. To receive it, send an email to buzz-request@lists.commerce.net. In both the subject line and the body of the message, type the word 'subscribe'.

Other digital currency products

New digital cash products are entering the market. These products are being marketed for a variety of reasons.

- People like the anonymity of digital cash as opposed to credit cards.
- Many people do not have access to credit cards: young people do not qualify for a credit card, and some cultures do not feel comfortable with credit cards.
- Auctions and C2C e-commerce have also created a need for online payment systems between individuals other than via a credit card.
- Merchants might find digital cash more convenient since credit card costs cut into merchants' revenue. Therefore, sites selling small items, such as a single song, need to be able to accept micropayments ranging from a tenth of a cent to $10. Millicent is an account-based micropayment scheme originally developed at DEC's System Research Center in 1995 (see www.millicent.digital.com). Development has now ceased on this project so it remains to be seen if the product will continue.

Some of the new digital cash techniques are listed below.

- Consumers can now store value in an online account and deduct from it the price of small purchases. This technique was pioneered by iClick-Charge. IBM and Compaq use a similar technique, as does Fairfax for its archived articles.
- Qpass makes no initial charge but accumulates payments and deducts the final amount from a credit card.
- Trivnet uses ISPs to track customers' online spending and add it to their bill.
- PayPal has been developed by Confinity to enable people to open an account at the web site and then email dollars to other people (money can be transferred via Palm Pilots). By 2002, over 15 million people worldwide were using the system. It is particularly useful for dealing with transactions over the auction site eBay. For up-to-date information check the web site at www.paypal.com.
- E-Gold allows clients to fund their accounts by purchasing gold or other metals and then transferring units of those metals (measured by weight) by entering a recipient's account and a password. The usage of such a currency scheme is spreading and is also accepted by other players such as eBay. For further information visit the web site at www.egold.com.
- Various online bartering schemes exist such as BarterTrust and BigVine.
- A British firm called Oakington has developed software that allows for the automatic payment of taxed and 'time escrow' so that a transaction does not clear until the goods arrive.

Another digital cash product is the wallet, a small software program that is used for online purchase transactions. It allows for several methods of payment to be defined within the wallet. It may take several different kinds of credit card. Microsoft offers its Passport wallet to store credit card details and shipping addresses. This information is sent over a secure connection to online merchants.

Research on digital cash has concentrated on trying to resolve the difficulties that exist technically and socially. As a result, a number of new alternatives are being developed. For example, in 1995 at the University of Newcastle, the Monetary Systems Engineering Group developed an account-based transaction protocol for low-value transactions that allows a vendor to verify a transaction without contacting a central authority and without expensive encryption.

A more detailed discussion of digital cash systems is to be found in Furche and Wrightson (1996).[13] Developments in the design and use of digital cash in Australia can be viewed at www.cs.newcastle.edu.au/Research/pabloins/mseg.html.

Mobile e-payments

With the advent of the third-generation (3G) Internet, mobile commerce (m-commerce) will become increasingly important. For this reason Ericsson considers the wireless Internet to be 'the biggest growth opportunity we will see in the communications industry'.[14]

The Texas company Kedemon, Inc. announced in May 2002 its Mobile Companion solution for shopping over the Web, making a payment at the convenience store, ordering food at a drive-in or getting help from a local server. The Mobile Companion includes a Bluetooth transceiver that features a wireless invitation token interface. This patent-pending technology should solve the problems that exist when establishing transient associations between a personal mobile device and a radio-enabled point of service.[15] Information about the Mobile Companion and the wireless invitation token technology can be found on the Kedemon web site at www.kedemon.com.

M-commerce transactions still present many potential problems, namely:
- speed of transactions
- anti-fraud potential
- cost
- security.[16]

Popular SMS-based systems were advocated as a potential universal remedy. However, because transactions can be slowed by a busy SMS system, some rethinking is being done. M-commerce is being tested 'in pockets' in the United States and other world regions.[17] In Alon in the United States, a wireless marketplace is available in petrol stations. In DoCoMo in Japan, specialised vending machines that dispense products and electronic goods such as ring tones and screensavers are being tested. In Singapore, CityCab started a pilot trial in May 2002 to allow customers to pay their taxi fares via mobile phone.[18] Users first register for free with www.telecab.com.sg or www.telemoney.com to obtain a personal identification number. The system works in the following manner:

1. The passenger dials a TeleCab hotline, follows the prompts and keys in a personal identification number, the taxi driver's identification and the amount of the fare.
2. The request is sent to the TeleMoney server, which triggers a call to the driver's mobile phone to accept the amount.

Smart cards (stored value cards)

Smart cards are a form of EPS that uses a plastic card with a microchip that stores information, usually about value. Value is stored on the card and acts as a substitute for cash. Smart cards, or more correctly **stored value cards (SVCs)** where it is the value of money that is stored, can store more information and perform more functions than the magnetic strip cards that are more commonly in use throughout the world (see figures 5.7 and 5.8). It is estimated that there are over 600 million smart cards in operation throughout the world, either as magnetic strip cards or as SVCs with microchips. They are used to store information about people's health, they are used as identity cards and security cards, and they form the electronic signature in digital mobile phones. Australian and European trials of smart cards as substitutes for cash by companies such as VISA and Mondex suggest that smart cards will eventually replace the common magnetic strip cards now used in EFTPOS and banking transactions using ATMs.

Smart cards are really microcomputers that rely on another medium or reader to supply the power source to make them work. Smart cards have a small chip embedded, usually in a plastic card. This chip acts like a microcomputer with a typical input/output device, a microprocessor, and ROM and RAM memory (see figure 5.9).

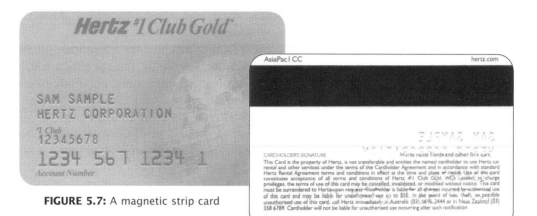

FIGURE 5.7: A magnetic strip card

FIGURE 5.8: A stored value card (SVC) — the front and back of one of Telstra's phonecards

FIGURE 5.9: Components of a smart card and internal communication flow

SOURCE: A. Furche and G. Wrightson 1996, *Computer Money: A Systematic Overview of Electronic Payment Systems*, dpunkt.verlag, Heidelberg, p. 65.

Smart cards or SVCs can store everything found in a wallet or purse. They operate mostly by transfer of data/value from the card to a business system, usually without verification, which makes them different from online payment systems. The protocols used in this process are:

- the programming of cards, assigning serial numbers and loading keys to increase and decrease the value of cards – this is called personalisation[19]
- the allocation of transaction reload capability, which enables the stored value on the card to be added to when desired
- a debit transaction process facility that enables a business system to download value and debit the loading system for the value of a transaction.

Smart cards can also store university transcripts, personal records, medical information, hospital files, social security information, employment records – in fact, any personal or organisational information that needs to be stored and be portable. It is not beyond the realms of thinking that in Australia an SVC could be developed that would be our driver licence, Medicare card, bank card and bank debit card and contain our medical records and personal CV (see figure 5.10). The limitations to this development have to do with privacy and other legal, social and political issues, which are discussed in chapter 6 and which can be more fully explored in Tyree (1997).[20]

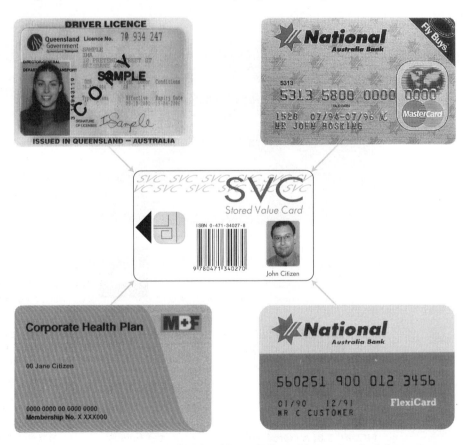

FIGURE 5.10: An SVC could contain all of these elements

In Thailand, Lenso has developed an SVC for international telephone calls that operates at Lenso telephone points. In this case, the consumer buys a card for either 250 baht or 500 baht (A$10 or A$20) and then uses the value stored on the card to make international phone calls. The value stored on the card is downloaded at the conclusion of the telephone call. This is a closed system. The cards are manufactured by Lenso, which receives payment when they are purchased. The business system, the international telephone point, downloads the value, capturing the payment just as coin-operated telephones capture coins. This SVC is non-reusable and discarded after the value is used up. A similar smart card system is used in the Melbourne Central car park. On entering the car park, the customer is given a smart card that can then be used to store/record the value of purchases made throughout this very large shopping complex. The system is designed to give the exiting customer a 50 per cent discount on car-parking charges for every $10 spent in the shopping complex. The system also recognises each additional $10 unit of purchases as a credit for further discount at future use of the car park.

The Microbus public transport system throughout Bangkok has recently introduced an SVC that is purchased from the bus driver and then given value by the consumer passing bank notes into a machine either on the bus or at a number of offices throughout metropolitan Bangkok. Each trip is then debited against the card when it is put into the card reader in the bus. In this case, the SVC is reusable and can be 'topped up' at any time.

In China reusable SVCs are being used to activate electricity meters and in Singapore a tourist card (SVC) is being developed to eliminate the need for moneychangers. Already there are banks in Asia that have electronic reader machines that change currency from one to another by reading the currency electronically, eliminating the human interface in the transaction. These are true EPS because each eliminates the intermediary process of human handling. Stored value is transferred from a card to another organisation's account. This is then adjusted through an electronic banking system.

Types of SVC

Closed-system stored value cards are smart cards where the intrinsic value of the card is fixed. Such cards include fixed-price, prepaid telephone cards or prepaid transport tickets. In this case, the owner of the card and the provider of the service are the same. Open-system stored value cards are smart cards where the intrinsic value of the card can be changed. These cards can be recharged in value. They can be described as an electronic wallet where the value on the card can be increased each day or at any regular interval. Most commonly, the owners/issuers of such open-system stored value cards are not the service providers. For example, a bank can issue an open-system SVC (e.g. Thai Danu Bank's SMART Cash card) and this card can then be used in any store or for any purchase or transaction where there is a card reader.

With both closed- and open-system stored value cards there will be an impact on the transaction process and the accounting of money throughout the economic systems they engage. In effect, they complicate the value exchange process (see figure 5.11).

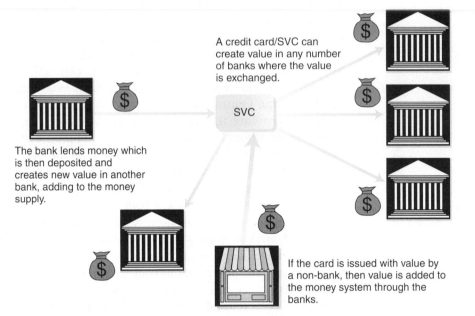

A credit card/SVC can create value in any number of banks where the value is exchanged.

The bank lends money which is then deposited and creates new value in another bank, adding to the money supply.

If the card is issued with value by a non-bank, then value is added to the money system through the banks.

FIGURE 5.11: Stored value cards in the exchange process

Advantages and risks of SVCs in business

In a very detailed evaluation of smart cards in Australia, the Centre for Electronic Commerce at Monash University has concluded that:

- Smart cards will have a significant impact on the banking system and the way it operates.
- Smart cards will affect the way money is exchanged.
- Smart cards may erode the traditional role of banks in the payment systems used in society, although the Australian banks and others, such as in Thailand, are acting at the forefront of the development and issue of stored value cards and other smart cards to maintain their traditional roles.
- Smart cards have the potential to allow institutions other than banks to issue value and thus create money that has been the traditional role of banks. For example, a company could issue smart cards for transactions in its own stores or enterprises which could be developed and issued on credit and thus create money. This could impact on the supply of money and the level of inflation in an economy.
- Smart cards and stored value cards are expensive to establish and the potential profitability of the new value and service created by the stored value cards will be lessened at least in the short run.

- Stored value cards should improve the efficiency of electronically transferring funds for low-value, high-volume transactions.
- Stored value cards should offer consumers a great range of choice in payment methods and improve convenience.
- Stored value cards and smart cards will probably increase the cost to consumers by the need of suppliers to cover costs.
- Stored value cards may not be affordable by all consumers, thus raising equity issues in society.
- The protections that are in place to protect consumers when using existing payment systems/cards do not always apply with stored value cards.
- Smart cards are more secure than magnetic strip cards.
- Stored value cards could be more secure than cash, depending on the card design and the method of recording stored value.
- The trials on stored value cards that are currently in operation in Australia (VISA, Transcard, MasterCard, Quicklink and Mondex) are technically incompatible!

B2B ELECTRONIC PAYMENT SYSTEMS

The notion of electronic commerce was coined in the 1960s by financial institutions that began investigating ways to automate their back-end banking systems. Initially, these systems were capable of basic electronic processing of cheques; however, soon they managed to process credit card and wire-transfer transactions electronically.

Electronic funds transfer and EFTPOS

The 1970s saw the introduction of **electronic funds transfer (EFT)** between banks and financial institutions and the gradual emergence of the customer-focused automatic teller machine (ATM), which has since proven to be immensely popular with the general public.

EFT and EFTPOS are electronic tools currently in use to effectively transfer the value of exchange process for goods or services or information. EFT is any transfer of funds initiated through an electronic terminal, telephone, modem, computer or magnetic tape so as to order, instruct or authorise a financial institution to debit or credit an account.[21] EFT utilises computer and telecommunication components both to supply and transfer money or financial assets.

Electronic data interchange

During the late 1970s and early 1980s, another component of electronic commerce emerged as a result of businesses striving to reduce the 'paper trail' and improve efficiency. Electronic messaging technologies and in particular EDI lead the automation of business process and, intrinsically, business process re-engineering. EDI is the automated exchange of structured business documents (such as purchase orders and invoices) between an organisation and its customers, suppliers or other trading partners.

Traditional (non-Internet) EDI is actually a set of specifications for formatting documents designed specifically to automate business flow within a business – and between businesses – by replacing paper documents with electronic ones.

Using EDI, a business document (such as a purchase order) may be transmitted by a communications application across the trading network and automatically processed by a receiving application residing with the trading partner. Subsequently, the trading partner's communications application can generate and send back to the original party a reply EDI document (such as an invoice), which can be automatically interpreted at the receiver end. This entire process becomes paperless, is highly efficient and requires little or no human intervention.

The strength of EDI lies in its ability to enable organisations with different business and computer systems to link those systems cost-effectively. By structuring the transfer process and standardising the format of these electronic documents, EDI enables purchasers and suppliers to communicate and transact in a faster, more efficient manner. Thus EDI represents an effective technology for reducing the overheads associated with paper processing, product verification, handling and storage.

EDI processes must have the following characteristics:

- The exchange of information must be in a structured format so that the data is placed and found in predetermined places in the electronic message.
- The format or structure of the information must be agreed upon by both the receiver and the sender.
- The data must be machine readable. EDI does not involve the sending of data by fax from one organisation and then the re-keying of that data in the new place of operation.

Traditional EDI

Traditional EDI systems require communication between two or more trading partners. Hence, the network infrastructure must contain two major components – a communications channel that delivers the EDI documents across the trading network, and conformance to EDI standards. See figure 5.12 for an overview of the EDI process.

Communications channels

The communications channel of a trading network is dictated by the complexity of the trading network and the type of communication link. There are three major communications channels available to EDI users.

Direct link EDI

Direct link networks (ISDN leased lines and high-speed modem dial-up) represent the simplest EDI communications method. Direct link EDI allows a business to communicate with trading partners by 'dialling up' the trading partner's network and transmitting EDI documents as required.

Typically, trading partners install and maintain their own direct link lines. Issues with speed, protocols and reliability across the trading partner network make direct link EDI prohibitive to smaller businesses. Hence, direct link EDI is suited primarily to large organisations transmitting large volumes of data on a regular basis.

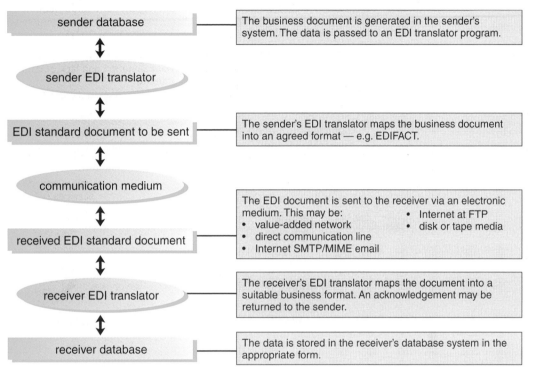

FIGURE 5.12: The EDI process

SOURCE: PIEC and TradeGate, www.tradegate.org.au/ec-projects/ec-for-industry/pharmaceutical/directions2.pdf.

Private networks

A private (proprietary) network is a closed network available to a selected group of trading partners. Typically, a 'hub' company manages document-handling overheads and protocol conversion facilities for 'spoke' trading partners. These 'spoke' companies can dial up the private network using a standard modem and perform their EDI transfers for the cost of a phone call.

Value-added networks

A **value-added network (VAN)** is a third-party network or intermediary capable of providing reliable, secure transmission of documents between trading partners. Typically, VANs are analogous to a post office or clearing house, providing not only transmission services, but also EDI support services such as protocol conversion, speed conversion, mailbox services and value-added services such as technical support, consulting, training and EDI-to-fax services (see table 5.2 and figure 5.13).

TABLE 5.2	ADVANTAGES AND DISADVANTAGES OF VANS	
ADVANTAGES	**DISADVANTAGES**	
▪ 24 × 7 operation, accessible globally	▪ Interruption of VAN services	
▪ Typically toll-free or local phone number	▪ VAN processing delays	
▪ Multi-speed, multi-protocol support across trading partners.	▪ Data alteration and lack of data integrity.	

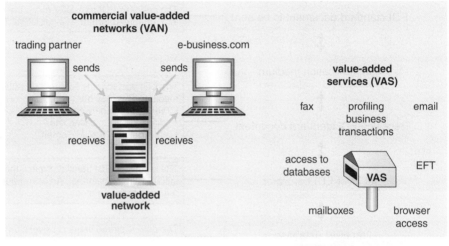

FIGURE 5.13: VAN architecture

Initially, VANs provided mailbox services to trading partners on the network. Incoming EDI documents from trading partners were stored in electronic 'mailboxes' from which they could be retrieved at a later time by the intended recipient. VANs now also support administrative facilities such as document auditing, message tracking, usage reporting and billing services.

VANs can also convert EDI documents between formats for trading partners. Using in-house EDI translation software, a VAN offers translation services that convert documents between standards such as X12 and EDIFACT, between standard and proprietary formats, and to other media types such as email and fax.

VANs store and send on information and data in forms that are acceptable to the businesses receiving the data. VANs act as intermediaries for large numbers of businesses, acting as a focal point in the multi-transactional, multi-nodal nature of most businesses. VANs act as a router of data, and act as a consultancy point for new business. The most important VANs in Australia include Tradelink and T-Net, which are run by Telstra, and EXIT, which is run by OTC, Australia. The network processes used in an EDI transaction are shown in figure 5.14.

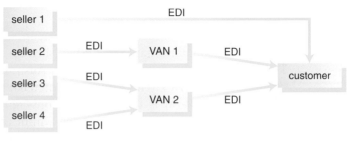

FIGURE 5.14: How EDI works

EDI standards

The EDI communication process illustrated in figure 5.14 depends on the existence and acceptance of specific EDI standards and protocols that have to be adopted by each user in both simple and complex EDI relationships. Linking a customer with a supplier in an EDI relationship involves a hierarchy of communication levels, each of which has different accepted standards and protocols.

Most standards and protocols used in EDI communications are derived from the International Consultative Committee for Telephony. EDI standards for messages usually involve the data being broken down into smaller packages for transmission and sent to a receiver where they are reassembled into a coherent message (see figure 5.15).

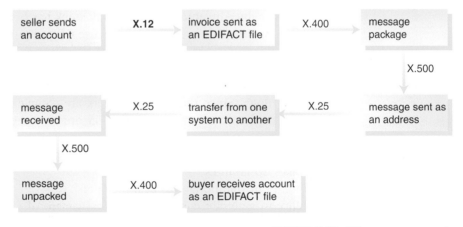

FIGURE 5.15: EDI process protocols

The exchange protocols used in the EDI process above perform different functions. The X.25 standard allows electronic messages to be broken up into specific packages of information (packets), which are sent to the receiving PC and enable reassembling of the original information sent. The **X.25 protocol** controls the EDI process at the communications level. At another level, the

X.400 protocol and the **X.500 protocol** enable the message to be handled by the sending and receiving PCs. They are not concerned with content but, in the case of the X.400, with how the data can be broken up and packaged and, in the case of the X.500, with addresses and directories used in the EDI process.

As a result of the need for specific standards for successful EDI processes, a number of standards have been established throughout the world including **TRADACOMS** in the United Kingdom. In Australia, **EDIFACT** is the standard used in EDI. EDIFACT (electronic data interchange for administration, commerce and transport) is the United Nations-agreed standard for EDI transmission. This protocol is recommended within the framework of the United Nations. The rules of EDIFACT are approved and published by UN/ECE in the United Nations Trade Data Interchange Directory (UNTDID) and are maintained under agreed procedures. The details of EDIFACT syntax, message structures and specific protocols can be found at www.unece.org/trade/untdid/texts/d422_d.htm.

Benefits of traditional EDI

Firms worldwide have benefited from productivity gains through using traditional EDI by this leveraging of computer-to-computer transaction exchange. Traditionally, only large firms have employed EDI technology because it is an expensive, proprietary technology. Nonetheless, EDI is found to be a standard part of nearly all large and medium-sized firms because it can typically save 5 to 10 per cent of procurement costs. Two notable examples[22] are set out below.

- General Electric (GE) in the United States uses EDI with its trading partner network to reduce inventory levels. Safety stock has been reduced from 35 to 10 days worth. This has occurred because GE can purchase material and have it delivered more often and more efficiently using EDI. The average cost of purchase orders has fallen from US$52 to US$12.
- Astra Pharmaceuticals in Australia receives orders from customers using EDI technology. Since the types of orders are complex (often 90 lines in length), the chance of error and incorrect ordering are high in a manual system. With EDI and the use of standard electronic documents, order errors are dramatically reduced. Order fulfilment once took 24 hours – it now takes 20 minutes.

Advantages of traditional EDI also include:
- an ability to maintain control over the movement of materials
- a reduction in labour costs
- a reduction in routine tasks that can often cause errors
- a reduction in stockholding and accounts receivable
- an increase in cash flow due to the effective management of trade creditors
- an increase in customer service
- a move to one-time entry and elimination of superfluous administration.

Shortcomings of traditional EDI

Although EDI has provided such firms with many benefits in terms of cost reduction and general efficiency improvement, EDI is an expensive means of doing business. Small and medium-sized firms tended not to be EDI-capable because of the inherent costs in proprietary software purchase, hardware installation and ongoing maintenance.

Typical costs of implementing translation software may range from $5000 (for a PC-based system) through to $250 000 (for a mainframe application). Transaction and subscription fees may also apply. In general, typical monthly fees are $50 and transaction fees of $0.50–$0.70 per transaction apply.[23]

Internet EDI

The traditional e-commerce landscape has seen EDI as an effective means for the transmission of business documents between organisations. However, economies of scale have proven to favour the large organisations that perform a large volume of transactions. Although EDI has been standardised through ANSI and EDIFACT, high operational costs, extensive customisation requirements and the need for value-added network providers have hindered widespread adoption.

The ubiquitous and open nature of the Internet brings a new dimension to EDI – Internet EDI. The Internet's inherent low-cost transport mechanism and standardised protocols offer organisations the opportunity to participate in B2B e-commerce at low cost. Moreover, the Internet offers a deeper interaction for trading partners.

Internet EDI offers the trading partner community not only basic transactional capability, but also online catalogues, pricing information, scheduling and delivery information, and even new ways of actioning procurement such as online auctions.

Internet EDI also offers broad connectivity through worldwide connections, allowing buyers and sellers to transact on a global scale. It offers a simple, platform-independent vehicle for information exchange through the TCP/IP protocol and the emerging common standard **open buying on the Internet (OBI)**.

OBI provides trading partners with a simple standards-based solution through a flexible platform-independent architecture. The OBI standard focuses on the Internet transaction and the components of which this is comprised – namely EDI, digital certification and supporting back-end database systems.

The Bank Internet Payment Systems (BIPS) project developed by the Financial Services Technology Consortium (FSTC) will enable better B2B e-commerce. BIPS is a project to develop an open specification for bank customers to securely negotiate and communicate payment instructions to bank systems over the Internet. This project, which began in 1996, is supported by a number of large banks, including Citibank, and is closely linked with existing EFTPOS payment systems like SWIFT, which is used across Australia.

SUMMARY

Electronic payment systems are becoming an increasingly important part of B2B and B2C payment transactions and the exchange of value. The Internet has enabled consumers to access many products and services that can be selected, ordered and paid for electronically. Electronic catalogues are being developed that will allow businesses and consumers to order anything from car components to pizzas and wine. EPS using smart cards, online EFTPOS-type systems and digital-money systems enable businesses and consumers to pay electronically.

EPS can vary from simple transactions using magnetic strip cards, in which customers' details are exchanged for goods or services and an account is sent, to more complex systems where an online purchasing system can debit existing bank accounts of the purchaser and credit bank accounts of the seller. This new form of purchasing has reduced the importance of cash or money as the only form of transaction or exchange of value. Traditional forms of exchange such as money are being replaced by these new methods of exchange, which are effectively diversifying the nature and complexity of B2B dealing and consumer-to-seller transactions in terms of both cost and convenience. In a more complex way, B2B transactions of data and exchange of value have been used increasingly in many industries, especially in the retailing and car industries. EDI transactions enable more efficient allocation of resources for production and servicing.

Electronic purchasing enables more cost-effective and time-effective transactions to occur. However, in the process there are security demands that have to be recognised and addressed by both business and consumers. EPS have had a difficult time since the dot.com crash of 2000. It is clear that the majority of Internet commerce purchasers still use their credit cards for purchasing items over the Internet. The fear about adequate security still deters many people from shopping on the Internet. The idea of having a special credit card with a low credit threshold is thought to be one way to make potential consumers feel safer. One-use credit cards are thought to be another way to ensure that people feel comfortable sending their credit card details over the Internet. The nature of these security issues as they affect e-commerce and EPS is discussed in detail in chapter 6.

Key terms

CyberCash (p. 114)
DigiCash (p. 114)
eCash™ (p. 114)
EDIFACT (p. 128)
electronic data
    interchange (EDI)
    (p. 106)
electronic funds transfer
    (EFT) (p. 123)
electronic funds transfer
    at point of sale
    (EFTPOS) (p. 111)

electronic payment
    system (EPS) (p. 106)
electronic purchasing
    (p. 106)
just-in-time (JIT) (p. 106)
money (p. 106)
open buying on the
    Internet (OBI) (p. 129)
smart card (p. 108)
stored value cards (SVCs)
    (p. 118)
TRADACOMS (p. 128)

value-added network
    (VAN) (p. 125)
X.25 protocol (p. 127)
X.400 protocol (p. 128)
X.500 protocol (p. 128)

Case study

By Katina Michael, University of Wollongong © 2002

FROM THE ENIAC TO CHIP IMPLANTS

The top-secret ENIAC project, at the Moore School of Engineering at the University of Pennsylvania, was first made known to the public in February 1946. Reporters used 'anthropomorphic' and 'awesome characterisations' to describe the computer. In an article entitled 'The myth of the awesome thinking machine', Martin stated that the ENIAC was referred to in headlines as 'a child, a Frankenstein, a whiz kid, a predictor and controller of weather, and a wizard'.[24]

Photographs of the ENIAC used in publications usually depicted the computer completely filling a small room, from wall-to-wall and floor-to-ceiling (see figure C5.1). In fact, the ENIAC 'weighed 30 tonnes, covered 1500 square feet of floor space, used over 17 000 vacuum tubes ... 70 000 resistors, 10 000 capacitors, 1500 relays, and 6000 manual switches, consumed 174 000 W of power, and cost about $500 000'.[25] People were usually shown interacting with the machine, feeding it instructions, waiting for results and monitoring its behaviour. One could almost imagine that the people in the photographs were 'inside the body' of the ENIAC.

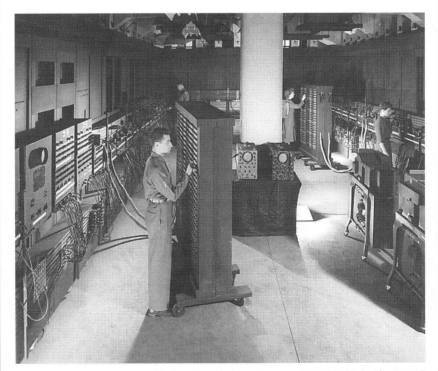

FIGURE C5.1: The ENIAC
(www.library.upenn.edu/special/gallery/mauchly/jwmintro.html)

In August 1998, BBC News published an online article entitled, 'Technology gets under the skin'.[26] Professor Kevin Warwick of the University of Reading was depicted with a tiny chip being inserted into his left arm (see figure C5.2). This chip allowed Warwick to be 'wired up to the computers in his building at the university'.[27] There is much in this potent image that even a lengthy volume could only just touch the surface of its philosophical meaning. How could humans ever have imagined back in 1946 that the large machine filling the size of a room would one day be smaller in size than a grain of rice, and be capable of being inserted into the arm of a human? Professor Warwick was to single-handedly turn the image of the 'awesome' ENIAC upside-down. A secular prophecy fulfilled perhaps, the *electronic brain* united with the *anthropos*.

FROM ANIMAL TO HUMAN IMPLANTS

For years now animals have been implanted with microchips for tracking and monitoring purposes. Some cities have made it compulsory through legislation for pets to be identified in this fashion. Companies like AVID[28] market their microchip ID systems to cater for the needs of domestic pets and also livestock. The latter is a growing industry,[29] especially in these times of global concern over diseases such as 'foot-and-mouth'. So if it works for animals, it might also work for humans. In just a few years consumers have become comfortable with the implanting of microchips in animals; there is little to suggest that this idea will not be just as successfully transferred to human applications.

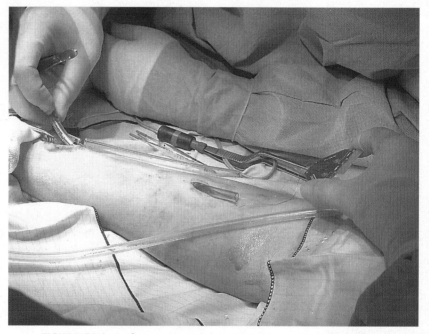

FIGURE C5.2: Professor Warwick having a chip implanted into his left arm (news.bbc.co.uk/hi/english/sci/tech/newsid_158000/158007.stm)

In fact, the number of microchip implant patents has increased rapidly since the late 1990s. Applied Digital Solutions is just one company that is pioneering efforts that are focused on providing human chip implant services. The company markets its VeriChip[30] solution to people who would like to use it for medical identification and emergency situations. The idea seems harmless enough: an implant the size of the nib on a ballpoint pen is inserted into the subdermal layer of the skin and is used only for identification purposes. A remote database that stores more specific information about the individual is then queried once identification has been determined. The invention has the potential to be a life-saving device and could be used as a complementary component in any location-based system.

Perhaps the big commotion that followed Warwick's implant was a little over the top. After all, pacemakers have been used for decades, and cochlear implants are becoming so common that even the youngest of toddlers can undergo the operation.[31] Major breakthroughs are also occurring in the area of retinal implants, helping the blind to see.[32] And many believe that researchers are not that far off from providing concrete evidence that suggests that paralysis, Parkinson's and neurodegenerative disorders could be treated using brain implants.[33] However, biochips for drug delivery,[34] for instance implantable insulin pumps,[35] are set to make the biggest impact on consumers in the short term. The chips can release chemicals into the body either in a pre-programmed mode or by being triggered remotely.

FROM MEDICAL APPLICATIONS TO COMMERCE APPLICATIONS

Most consumers would accept implants for life-saving and life-enriching procedures related to increasing life expectancy. However, it is too early to tell whether or not consumers would adopt implants for such everyday applications as electronic payments, citizen identification, driver's licences, social security, ticketing or even retail loyalty schemes. While the adoption of other automatic identification technologies in the past has indicated that consumers are willing to adapt the manner in which they live and conduct business due to technological change, the process takes time. The difference between chip implants and other previous auto-ID devices is that the latter are non-invasive by nature. Bar codes are located on the exterior of goods, magnetic strip cards and smart cards are carried by cardholders and, more recently, biometric systems have required contact with only some external human characteristics such as the fingerprint or palm print for identification.

Perhaps what Warwick was demonstrating by using the chip implant for commercial applications was that life could be somewhat simplified if consumers did not have to carry ten different cards in their wallet for a multiplicity of applications.

One implant would suffice for any number of applications, as long as the identification number used to identify the individual was unique. And there would never be a chance of losing the implant because it would be inside the body, unlike traditional card devices that can be stolen and misused. Biometrics also have the shortfall that they exclude some members of society who are incapable of using the technology either due to some form of disability or because of age.

THE FUTURE

Warwick believes that the ultimate goal of the transponder technology is to connect humans more closely with computers and perhaps have a direct connection from the brain to the computer. While this is perhaps a little too futuristic for now, Warwick is correct in pointing out that chip implants could be used to track employees while they are at work, prevent mass murders by keeping track of gun owners and tag paedophiles to keep them away from schools or childcare centres. Coupled with the power of the Internet and global positioning systems (GPS), microchip implants could become increasingly important. Warwick is not the first to propose 'thought-to-thought' communication, making the telephone redundant.[36] British Telecom researcher Peter Cochrane is well noted for his interest in naturally progressing towards a superhuman species.[37]

It is very difficult to forecast what the future will bring but we can use past and present developments to make educated guesses. What is apparent today is that technological convergence is gathering stimulus and humans are considering becoming an intrinsic part of this process. Microchip implants for commercial purposes such as electronic payment systems was once a far-fetched idea that people would not pay much attention to. This may have been the case in the early days of the ENIAC, when it would have been hard to imagine that this giant calculating machine would one day be under our skin.

QUESTIONS

1. What types of electronic applications could chip implants be used for?
2. Could chip implants replace the need for magnetic strip or smart cards to make electronic payment transactions? Why or why not?
3. How would chip implants potentially change the way business is conducted on the Internet?
4. What are biometric systems? Visit the site www.biometrics.org/html/examples.html. What different biometric characteristics can be used to verify an individual at an ATM?
5. Consider the automatic identification selection environment. What types of trends are currently taking place as techniques have evolved since the widespread introduction of bar codes in the late 1960s in the retail industry?
6. What are the social implications of introducing chip implants for humans? Consider this in the context of government services.

Quest ions

1. Find out as much as you can about the following EDI standards and protocols: WINS, IDI, CCITTX.25, CCITX.400, CCITX.500, ANSI X.a2, EDIFACT, TRADACOMS, EANCOM, Financial EDI and Hybrid EDI.
2. Prepare a report on smart cards examining:
    (a) privacy issues
    (b) anonymity and smart cards
    (c) technology that protects and/or enhances privacy for smart card users.

Suggested | reading

Centre for Electronic Commerce 1996, *Smart Cards and the Future of Your Money*, Report for the Commission for the Future, Monash University.

Churchman, P. 1987, *Electronic Payment Systems*, Basil Blackwell, Oxford.

Emmelmainz, M. 1990, *Electronic Data Interchange: A Total Management Guide*, Van Nostrand, New York.

Furche, A. and Wrightson, G. 1996, *Computer Money: A Systematic Overview of Electronic Payment Systems*, dpunkt.verlag, Heidelberg.

Gattorna, J. and Walters, D. 1996, *Managing the Supply Chain: A Strategic Perspective*, Macmillan, London.

Hammond, R. 1996, *Digital Business: Surviving and Thriving in an On-line World*, Hodder & Stoughton, London.

Kalakota, R. and Whinston, A. 1996, *Frontiers of Electronic Commerce*, Addison-Wesley, United States.

McKeown, P. and Watson, R. 1996, *Metamorphosis: A Guide to the World Wide Web and Electronic Commerce*, John Wiley & Sons, New York.

O'Mahony, D., Peirce, M. and Tewari, H. 2001, *Electronic Payment Systems for E-Commerce*, 2nd edn, Artech House.

Timmers, P. 2000, *Electronic Commerce: Strategies and Models for Business-to-Business Trading*, John Wiley & Sons, Chichester, United Kingdom.

Tran, V. G. 1995, 'EDI: good for what ails the healthcare world', *EDI World*, September, pp. 28–30.

Tyree, A. 1997, *Digital Money*, Butterworths, Sydney.

End | notes

1. The Australian Securities and Investments Commission web site is www.asic.gov.au/.
2. See the Australian Payments Clearing Association's web site, where the schemes in operation in Australia are set out: www.apca.com.au/Paymentsystems.htm#Financial.
3. help.netscape.com/kb/consumer/19971208-6.html.
4. Deitel, H. M., Deitel P. J. and Nieto, T. R. 2000, *E-business and E-commerce: How to Program*, Prentice Hall, New Jersey.
5. 'How credit cards work', www.howstuffworks.com/credit-card.htm?printable=1.
6. 'Using American Express private payments', www.amazon.com/exec/obidos/tg/browse/ -/519796/104-6699126-3237519.
7. 'What is an eCheck?', http://whatis.techtarget.com/WhatIs_Definition_Page/ 0,4152,283970,00.html.
8. www.ecml.org/.
9. Definition from www.whatis.com.
10. Maher, W. 2002, '.Net or not yet', *APC Magazine*, June, p. 114.

11. Jones, R. 2001, 'Prepaid cards: an emerging Internet payment mechanism', www.commerce.net/research/ebusiness-strategies.

12. Aaron, M. 1997, 'Internet payments: opportunities and status', *IBM Computer Money Day*, April, Sydney.

13. Furche, A. and Wrightson, G. 1996, *Computer Money: A Systematic Overview of Electronic Payment Systems*, dpunkt.verlag, Heidelberg.

14. Statistics for Mobile Commerce, http://www.epaynews.com/statistics/mcommstats.html#.

15. Kedemon web site at www.kedemon.com.

16. 'Deloitte: phones "will be key payment tool"', *Wireless Newsfactor*, 26 April 2002, www.epaynews.com.

17. Ibid.

18. 'Asia: pay your taxi fare by mobile phone', *Australian*, 7 May 2002, p. 2.

19. Furche, A. and Wrightson, G. 1996, *Computer Money: A Systematic Overview of Electronic Payment Systems*, dpunkt, verlag für Technologie GmbH, Heidelberg, p. 68.

20. Tyree, A. 1997, *Digital Money*, Butterworths, Sydney.

21. Kalakota, R. and Whinston, A. 1996, *Frontiers of Electronic Commerce*, Addison-Wesley, United States, p. 298.

22. Hyndes, M. et al. 1999, *Creating a Clearway on the New Silk Road: Annex 1 — Impact of the Internet on Business Efficiency*, Department of Foreign Affairs and Trade, Canberra.

23. Fu, S., Chung, J-Y., Dietrich, W., Gottemukkala, V., Cohen, M. and Chen, S. 2002, 'A practical approach to web-based Internet EDI', *Proceedings of the 19th International Conference on Distributed Computing*, IBM IAC, T. J. Watson Research Center, NewYork, www.research.ibm.com/iac/papers/icdcsws99/index.html.

24. Martin, C. D. 1993, 'The myth of the awesome thinking machine', *Communications of the ACM*, vol. 36, no. 4, p. 126.

25. Martin, C. D. 1995, 'ENIAC: press conference that shook the world', *IEEE Technology and Society Magazine*, Winter, pp. 3f.

26. 'Technology gets under the skin', *BBC News*, news.bbc.co.uk/hi/english/sci/tech/newsid_158000/158007.stm, 25 August.

27. Sanchez-Klein, J. 1998, 'Cyberfuturist plants chip in arm to test human-computer interaction, *CNN*, 28 August, www.cnn.com/TECH/computing/9808/28/armchip.idg/.

28. www.avidmicrochip.com/.

29. Geers, R. et al. 1997, *Electronic Identification, Monitoring and Tracking of Animals*, Cab International, Oxford.

30. www.adsx.com/prodservpart/verichip.html.

31. Canham, L. and Aston, R. 2001. 'Will a chip every day keep the doctor away?', *Physicsweb*, July, physicsweb.org/article/world/14/7/11.

32. Ahlstrom, D. 2000, 'Microchip implant could offer new kind of vision', *The Irish Times on the Web*, 9 November, www.ireland.com/newspaper/science/2000/1109/sci1.htm.

33. 'Brain pacemakers', *Technology Review*, September 2001, www.technologyreview.com/articles/hall0901.asp.

34. The pharmacy-on-a-chip notion can be found in the following article: 'MIT bioengineering and beyond', October 2001, p. 1, alumweb.mit.edu/opendoor/200110/.

35. 'Implantable insulin pumps', *Biology*, 6 October 1999, biology.about.com/library/weekly/aa061099.htm.

36. Warwick, K. 2000, 'Cyborg 1.0', *Wired*, February, pp. 145–51.

37. Cochrane, P. 1998, *Tips for Time Travellers*, McGraw-Hill, London.

Security and Internet commerce

LEARNING outcomes

You will have mastered the material in this chapter when you can:

- list the major security issues that underpin networks and their application to electronic commerce
- explain the major risks to businesses and other organisations from security failure when using the Internet for transactions of any sort
- explain how viruses affect the security and integrity of online and electronic communication and electronic commerce
- describe how confidentiality, integrity, availability and authenticity issues can be addressed in Internet commerce
- define and explain how firewalls and proxies are used in securing networks running electronic commerce applications.

'All parties in the e-commerce chain realised that the real problem with online transactions was not security; rather, the problem was authenticating that the person entering the credit card details was indeed the real cardholder.'

G. Knapp 2001, 'Standards rise to combat e-commerce fraud', *Image and Data Manager*, November/ December, p. 6.

INTRODUCTION

E-commerce is concerned with doing business using electronic technologies. It can involve the transmission of data, transactions and payments, or marketing and value adding to existing products or databases. That data can be as simple as an invoice or an order form in an EDI exchange. E-commerce can also involve the exchange of tokens that represent value or the exchange of credit card numbers that represent purchases by a consumer from a retailer. In all of these cases there is an acceptance that the integrity and safety of the exchange has been secure from capture or interference from **hackers** or others wishing to gain information illegally. Data transferred across networks needs to be protected and it needs to be confidential. In this chapter, we review those issues relating to the **security** of business done in an online context or business that uses other electronic methods.

The first issue that we must be concerned with is identifying and dealing with the risks associated with Internet commerce; the first part of this chapter deals with those elements. Once they are understood, businesses and other organisations must be able to develop management strategies and then manage security issues and implement practices that will be effective and efficient and meet organisational goals.

INTERNET COMMERCE SECURITY CONCERNS

Security of networks and systems operating in business organisations is of paramount importance to all businesses engaged in electronic commerce and online commerce. This security needs to be well organised and systematic. Systems can function very effectively and improve the efficiency of businesses to a significant degree. However, if the **confidentiality** of the data transacted, the communications sent or the files stored cannot be assured, then the system is of less value to the organisation. Business done electronically relies on the integrity of the data being sent. If data is corrupted by poor systems, poor system management, inadequate or incompatible software and hardware, or by viruses, then the business transacted is of no value whatsoever.

Business organisations need to be able to protect the goodwill and value of their business. They need to be assured that their data and files cannot be stolen or made accessible to those who have no right of access. Network systems must be made secure from prying computers and the eyes and intelligence gathering of hackers. Business systems must ensure that the identity of both senders and receivers of information, data or communications is correct and appropriate for the information or transaction desired. It is only with the development and implementation of proper IT policies and the establishment of an **IT audit** for security that businesses will gain proper and thorough security in the operation of their networks.

From the time a business installs a web server or hires space on a commercial web server from an ISP, there is the potential for the business systems in the organisation to be exposed to breaches of security and confidentiality across the entire Internet. Any link to the Internet exposes businesses to tampering (Internet graffiti), where data can be altered or covered with meaningless scribble, pictures or electronic junk in the same way that a graffiti artist scrawls on walls. Links to the Internet also expose the business to the theft of data. Databases can be captured whole and transferred for other uses such as industrial espionage very easily. Almost as big a problem is the deliberate alteration of data that might influence decision making or change the ways business decisions are made. The TCP/IP protocol developed to run the Internet was not designed with security in mind. This protocol, the basic system running Internet communication, is vulnerable to interception. Any movement of data from browser to a server or back is vulnerable to eavesdropping.

Web site security is about keeping strangers out but at the same time allowing controlled access to a network. Sometimes, achieving both of these elements can be very difficult. However, this raises the question of whether there is any real difference between security in a paper-based business organisation and an electronic-based business organisation. The security of data and information is just as important in both cases. What is different is that the electronic-based business is exposed to very fast capture of large volumes of data. In the paper-based organisation, it would take considerable time to capture and transcribe large volumes of data. Even the process of theft of files is not really a quick process. Special security measures have to be taken in an electronic environment to prevent access to confidential data.

There is one more question that needs to be raised. Are the security issues of networks any different from other security issues? There is a great deal of debate about security on the Internet. However, there can be as much concern about security of transmission using other electronic forms. When a fax is sent from one machine to another, what certainty is there that the fax has reached its original destination or that the fax has not gone to another location, been altered and then sent on again? There is concern by consumers about sending their credit card details over the Internet. They fear that their transaction information will be intercepted and used by someone else. On the other hand, people now readily telephone their credit card details when paying accounts. Is there any more security on a telephone network than on the Internet? Probably not! However, all security issues revolve around resolution of business risk. Business risks can be associated with products that may or may not sell and with services that people may or may not want, and can also be generated by inadequate legal provisions as in most parts of the world where the law does not adequately address the needs of Internet commerce. This includes a lack of recognition of digital signatures and a lack of application of consumer protection laws for goods purchased outside the country. However, where attention to the details of the protection of data and the protection for trading has been considered, as has occurred in Singapore,[1] there is always a greater chance that risk will be reduced and business made more secure. In addition, risk can result from poor reliability of trading partners, from staff behaviour within organisations and as a result of problems with ISP security.

For businesses to be established and run effectively it is imperative that as much attention as possible is paid to information and security risks as is given to financial risks. Risk analysis 'entails identifying ways in which the confidentiality of data, the integrity of data and systems, and the accessibility to data and systems can be compromised, as well as identifying other loss-related outcomes and their probable impact'.[2] Such a risk analysis needs to take into account:

- the financial significance of data
- the impact on the competitive advantage of the firm
- the exposure to fraud
- confidentiality
- privacy.

Risks in electronic commerce systems management must be assessed in all e-business systems. For example:

1. Businesses need to know what they have to make secure.
2. Copyright protection techniques need to be understood.
3. Businesses need to understand and assess the principles of competitor monitoring.
4. Businesses need to establish competitor intelligence and understand its role in new-product development.
5. Businesses need to evaluate the use of security monitoring services.
6. Firewalls and other hardware and software considerations need to be integral in a business.
7. Businesses need to plan for dealing with viruses and electronic sabotage and have a plan for dealing with attacks.

Security of data and transmission of information in an electronic form, whether online or not, is a fundamental issue for businesses and individuals engaged in electronic commerce. All businesses must ensure that the security and integrity of their data and transmission of sensitive information is protected from bugs and misconforming system interference, from graffiti and data alteration, from browser-side interference and corruption of data, and from interruption from telecommunication infrastructure problems.

SECURITY ISSUES IN NETWORKS RUNNING ELECTRONIC COMMERCE APPLICATIONS

Security issues in online and electronic forms of business can be classified in various ways. The issues to be addressed by businesses have been classified by Kalakota and Whinston,[3] who suggest that the concerns are of two broad types: client-server security, and data and transaction security. The World Wide Web Consortium (W3C) (www-genome.wi.mit.edu/WWW/faqs/wwwsfl.html) propose that there are basically three overlapping types of risk:

1. bugs or misconfiguration problems in the web server that allow unauthorised remote users to:
   - steal confidential documents not intended for their eyes
   - execute commands on the server host machine, allowing them to modify the system

- gain information about the web server's host machine that will allow them to break into the system
- launch denial-of-service attacks, rendering the machine temporarily unusable.

2. browser-side risks, including:
   - active content that crashes the browser, damages the user's system, breaches the user's privacy or merely creates an annoyance
   - the misuse of personal information knowingly or unknowingly provided by the end user.

3. interception of network data sent from browser to server or vice versa via network eavesdropping. Eavesdroppers can operate from any point on the pathway between browser and server including:
   - the network on the browser's side of the connection
   - the network on the server's side of the connection (including intranets)
   - the end user's ISP
   - the server's ISP
   - either ISP's regional access provider.

It is important to realise that 'secure' browsers and servers are only designed to protect confidential information against network eavesdropping. Without system security on both browser and server sides, confidential documents are vulnerable to interception.

The following discussion highlights the major risks involved with network security and suggests how these issues might be addressed. In this chapter, security issues are treated individually as many of the issues can apply to all types of security issue classifications like those referred to above.

Confidentiality of data

Confidentiality of data in e-commerce is concerned with the notion of protection from intrusion, that no one can access the contents of data or information being sent and that no one can identify who is sending or receiving a message. This is especially important where highly sensitive documents such as strategic plans, business plans and marketing strategies are exchanged electronically. Such confidentiality is also important in the transmission of data where credit card users and the operators of business can be identified or where their own security card or electronic payment system is involved.

Confidentiality is very closely linked with the issue of privacy for individuals and businesses using the Internet or using any form of electronic business communication. One of the problems with maintaining privacy lies with the protocols actually used in electronic commerce. Almost all servers log every access and record the IP address and/or host name, the time of the download, the name of the user (if obtained by user authentication or by protocol), the URL requested, the status of the request and the size of the data file(s) transmitted. Immediately this occurs there is a chance the privacy of the user can be affected. In addition to the capture of this information, browsers can also provide the URL that the client came from and the user's email address. Browsers maintain a record of all users of sites and of any browsing patterns. In terms of privacy, a network manager or 'the web police' may investigate the use of the Web inside any organisation. This collection of data can be used to build a user profile that might contain information that may affect the individual's position within any organisation.

Integrity of data

Integrity of data requires that data transmitted electronically cannot be altered, defaced or lost during transmission. Integrity relies as much on ensuring that data is not lost accidentally as it does on ensuring it is not lost intentionally. Ensuring **data integrity** involves the operators of business systems understanding that data is protected at all levels in the operation, from the operator (the human element) to the systems being used (browsers, systems, networks, servers and communications infrastructure).

The process of ensuring data integrity must include an auditing process. Some would argue that with no auditing there is no security. The data trail of transactions and transmissions must be secure to ensure data integrity. In traditional practice it is common for responsible managers to check data for accuracy.

In addition, business managers will check for the reliability of the source, for the accuracy of any figures and charts, for the standing of creditors and suppliers, and for an assessment of credit limits where those form part of that business transaction. This process is slow and often requires a number of people to manually check every element of the transaction/data that is supplied in paper format. This process is shown in figure 6.1.

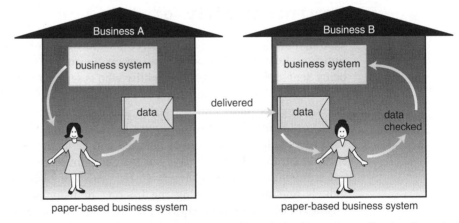

FIGURE 6.1: Traditional checking process for data integrity

With a change to electronic business practices, the data is often transmitted from machine to machine. Therefore, new controls must be developed and implemented to check the validity of the data and to check for errors — processes that were previously done manually. Electronic checks need to be built into the system. Key data needs to be electronically matched. This could, for example, be a simple process of electronically matching data from invoices with delivery dockets and purchase orders. This electronic checking system needs to be under constant review and subject to continuous scrutiny to maintain appropriate levels of data integrity (see figure 6.2).

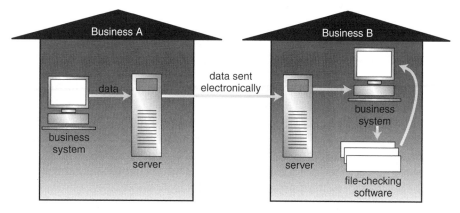

FIGURE 6.2: Checking data integrity in an electronic environment

The interaction/transactions must be authorised and authenticated by the business. In addition, there must be constant vigilance in searching networks for **viruses**, because viruses are probably one of the major causes of destruction of data integrity.

Viruses

The fear that viruses can affect business operations, business systems and transactions and communications between businesses and between business and customer can cause as much, or more, damage than the actual virus. The management problem for businesses is to develop and enforce controls to trap and eliminate computer viruses, and to disseminate information about appropriate software so that a distinction between normal control structures and viruses is available to users of business systems. Internet commerce is very susceptible to virus damage because of the complexity of the Internet connections network and the **availability** of sites for hackers and virus creators to hide and load their software. The oldest forms of interference are called **worms**. Worms propagate and exist independently. They do not have to attach to another program or part of the operating system, distinguishing them from viruses.

A computer virus is defined by its ability to replicate itself. A computer virus cannot replicate itself independently. It requires some form of carrier or 'host'. A computer virus creates damage to the computer system 'infected', either accidentally or deliberately. Computer viruses can occur everywhere in a personal computer's software, as boot blocks, in file allocation tables, in .EXE and .COM files, and in ordinary files masquerading as functional files. Computer viruses come in all shapes and sizes. These programs seek out unused resources and use them to resolve master program problems or tasks. Cracks are programs that have been copy protected, and have been illegally broken.

Computer viruses are classified by their mode of infection, the path used to replicate the virus and the type of system infected. Boot viruses infect the boot block on a floppy or hard disk. These computer viruses usually replace the boot block with all or part of a virus program. The virus files hide in memory and the virus moves the boot block on the disk to another location. File viruses infect ordinary .EXE or .COM files. Usually they just attach the virus code to the file. Multipartite viruses infect both boot blocks and executable files. Being opportunistic, they find available files at random. A systemic virus attacks the system files necessary to run DOS. These files control the allocation of system resources such as directories. Polymorphic viruses attack the integrity of the operating system used in business system computers and servers. While trying to conceal their existence, stealth viruses can modify file structures to conceal additional codes added to files. The newer viruses, meta viruses, use meta languages embedded in powerful modern programs like Microsoft Word to create damage to existing files and potential files as they are created.

Virus infection is not always very obvious in business organisations. Computer viruses behave in an exponential way. They initially spread and multiply quickly until saturation is reached and then they slow down. Any infection can go undetected for months. In most cases damage caused by the virus will be widespread before the problem is recognised. In business organisations it is therefore essential that infection is detected as early as possible. The earlier it is detected, the easier it is to stop.

Another problem for businesses engaged in electronic commerce is that the origin of the infection can source multiple infections all with different paths of infection. The importance of virus detection becomes increasingly important in organisations as they rely more and more on computer systems for their management and operations and for trading. The more reliant a business is on computer systems, the more vulnerable it becomes to damage caused by computer viruses. A strong company policy against any illegal software is the simplest step in preventing virus infection.

Useful resources from the Internet are the *Users Security Handbook* (info.internet.isi.edu:80/in-notes/rfc/files/rfc2504.txt) and its companion site, *The Security Handbook* (SSH) (info.interact.isi.edu:80/innotes/rsc/files/rfc2196.txt). Tips on how to protect systems from viruses are found in these publications.

It is impossible for a computer virus to be created accidentally. They are invariably introduced into business systems by contact with virus-infected disks, from downloaded information from web sites or from Internet commerce transactions. Software bugs that cause virus-like damage can be created accidentally but such bugs are not viruses as they are not created specifically to do malicious damage; they do not propagate and they can be easily tracked and rectified.

Virus infections must be dealt with quickly and with expert knowledge. A lack of understanding about the location of the virus or the nature of the virus can be catastrophic for a business. Properly designed computer virus repair software must be used as it is often the case that attempts to clean up viruses that may, or perhaps may not, exist can create far more damage than could be caused by the viruses themselves if inadequate repair software is used. Therefore, businesses engaged in electronic commerce must ensure that their networks are secure from external or internal accidental or deliberate damage caused by computer viruses.

Having understood the risks, it is essential that businesses clearly understand how to manage these risks and ensure safety.

SECURITY MANAGEMENT FOR INTERNET COMMERCE

Availability issues

Availability requires that the communications infrastructure and the network systems in place can receive and send information and data and enable electronic transactions in business. There is a requirement that the actual electronic business process gets through. Systems and networks have to be secure enough to ensure that there is no blocking. For the business this must mean that the computer systems, the network, the servers and the software are reliable. It is also essential that the engineering supporting the systems and networks is both sound and reliable and therefore that no technical hitches occur that affect the quality or speed of any transactions or transmissions. Common gateway interface (CGI) scripts are essential software programs. CGI scripts link servers and software and servers and other resources such as databases. These scripts are themselves small servers and this can create problems in making information too available. The problem with CGI scripts is that each one creates opportunities for exploitable bugs. CGI scripts may leak information about the host system that will help hackers to break in. These leaks may be either intentional or unintentional. CGI scripts that process remote-user input, such as the contents of a form, may be vulnerable to attacks in which the remote user tricks them into executing commands. Therefore, it is essential that business organisations ensure the security of not only servers but also the CGI scripts that link their servers to other resources used in the business. Each business must establish a well-written, precise and coherent policy to ensure that all possible traps and leaks are covered.

To ensure availability, it is essential that business organisations, ISPs, network managers and telecommunication infrastructure companies have a well-formed and implemented security policy. Such a policy has to not only affect action plans in cases of emergency and the requirements of quality delivery and service, but also ensure that the sending or receiving system is set up to do what is intended. In some cases the system could be set up to block everything except some specific tasks. In a purchasing/ordering system, transactions using VISA or MasterCard can be allowed through and all other transactions blocked. Such policy is essential not only to make the system do what it is intended to do but also to ensure that any fraud can be detected. Security policy of all forms requires that the developers of the systems understand the nature of the organisation they are working for. Organisational knowledge is essential to ensure that systems do not do too much or handle tasks that are extraneous to the core function of the business. It is generally accepted in networks that 'knowledge is power' — the more a hacker can establish about a system, the more chance there is for the hacker to find loopholes and break into the system. Denial of service attacks on major e-commerce sites such as Yahoo!, eBay and Buy.com illustrate the fragility of the Internet.

Authentication issues

Authentication of data and information transmission in online and electronic form requires that the message sent must reach the intended recipient and only that recipient. The receiver also needs to be sure that the identified sender is really the one sending the message and that there has been no intermediary sender involved in the process. The simplest means of authenticating data and information transmission is with a name and a password. This is one way of establishing a trust relationship in B2B or C2B electronic links. The most common way business organisations can establish authentication is with an Access Control List. The platforms on which network systems are most usually operating (Unix, Banyan, Windows NT, Novell) all have established protocols built in that enable read, write, print and execute functions.

One final way of managing security and authentication is via the use of a digital signature, which is a piece of data that identifies the originator of a document. It is established by encrypting the contents of the document using the originator's cryptographic key. Wilson argues that this makes the signature unique to both the file and the owner of the key.[4] More sophisticated access barriers for authentication use **encryption** or coded messages that operate on a dual system of codes or 'keys' (see figure 6.3).

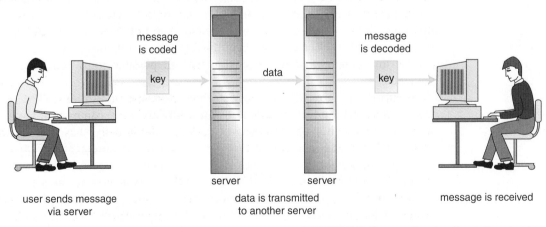

FIGURE 6.3: Keys and codes for authentication

Security writing and encryption

Encryption is the process of enabling information/data/knowledge to be coded in such a way that it cannot be read without a decoding system or key. In an authentication system everyone owns a unique set of codes (keys). In one type of authentication both the receiver and the sender own the same encryption key to transmit and read transmissions. This is often called symmetric encryption. In another form of encryption one of the keys is a public key that is widely distributed and owned by all the people using the system. The second key is a private key that is kept secret. With this system a message is sent with the public encryption key but it can be read only by the recipient with the private key. This is an asymmetric or public form of encryption. In this process the person sending the message 'owns' a certificate, digital signature or identification file, which ensures that the person sending the message using the public key is who they say they are. The most commonly used public key encryption system at the moment is RSA.[5]

Using this form of authentication is very important in web-based communications as the TCP/IP protocol is very easily tapped into. There are devices called packet sniffers that can listen to TCP/IP traffic on any network and pull down any files, codes, documents or data that is passing across the network. It is therefore vital that any measure that avoids this form of detection must be implemented in a business organisation committed to doing business electronically.

Restricting access to servers and therefore to files, documents, data, plans or business operations in an electronic commerce environment means restricting access in three ways: specifying access, specifying user names and passwords, and using codes and encryptions to restrict access.

Specifying access

Access can be restricted to specific IP addresses, sub-nets or domains that are defined by the business organisation at its server. This process will prevent 'noise' – that random hacker or nosey investigator who is seeking easy access. However, such a process will not prevent the determined, well-organised and structured hacker. With the proper equipment and readily available software, hackers can make it seem as if they are connecting from a location different from their real one. This act of an intermediary hacking into the message process is called 'spoofing'.

There is no guarantee that a person contacting a server from an authorised host is in fact the person the receiver or the web manager thinks they are. The remote host may have been broken into, tampered with and used as a hidden access route. To ensure proper authentication, IP address restriction must be combined with something that checks the identity of the user, such as a check for user name and password.

Specifying user names and passwords

A password is only good if that password is chosen carefully. Many people choose their names, their middle names, their birth dates, their office phone numbers, their children's names or even QWERTY![6] Each of these types or forms of names can be randomly found by clever hackers who send random search messages over the Internet hoping to break into sites where simple passwords of this form have been used. A patient hacker can work for hours trying to get into a server, because some servers do not impose a limit on the number of attempts at access. The hacker can try over and over to get in. This is very different from access to bank accounts using an ATM. In this case, the ATM has been programmed to take only three attempts. After the third error the ATM captures the card and disables any more attempts until the card is retrieved from within the bank itself.

Passwords have to be clever and randomly developed. If the business sells a certain type of car, such as a BMW, it would be very sensible not to include these three letters in the password. Numbers rather than letters are also not a good idea as there are many software packages that can generate large volumes of random number series that can be applied to access attempts at Internet sites. Some combination of letters and numbers that make sense only to the person creating them or make no sense at all are safer. However, it must be noted that any use of letters and numbers is never really safe. The longer the password, the better for safety, and perhaps the use of other characters from the keyboard, such as '$', '&' and '^', can help.

Using codes and encryption to restrict access

In encryption protection both the request and the document being sent are coded in such a way that the text cannot be read by anyone but the intended recipient. At this stage there are no universal solutions to the problems of security and encryption. However, there are some newer developments with software becoming available to ensure that electronic commerce can be done in a more secure way.

Recent developments in security

The newer schemes for Internet security include SSL (Secure Socket Layer) proposed by Netscape Communications. This is a low-level encryption scheme used to encrypt electronic commerce communications and transactions in higher-level protocols such as HTTP, NNTP[7] and FTP. The SSL protocol can authenticate servers (verifying the server's identity), encrypting data in transit and verifying client identity. SSL is available on several different browsers, including Netscape Navigator, Secure Mosaic and Microsoft Internet Explorer.

This software is also available on a number of servers including those from Netscape, Microsoft, IBM and Quarterdeck. SSL uses public key encryption to exchange a session key between the server and the client accessing the server. This session key is used to encrypt the HTTP transaction. A different session key is used for each transaction. Therefore, if a hacker manages to decrypt a message or a transaction, it does not mean that the key protecting all the data has been discovered. Decrypting another transaction will require the same amount of effort involved in decrypting the first message or transaction.

Another security protocol has been developed that operates with HTTP, the highest-level protocol most commonly used on the Web. SHTTP (secure HTTP) works only with the HTTP protocol. However, with more advanced encryption techniques becoming available, there is a demand for governments to take a more regulatory role in the further development of electronic commerce.

One new exciting development in security protocols is Cryptolope. **Cryptolope** is IBM's trademark for its *crypto*graphic enve*lope* technology. Cryptolope objects are used for secure, protected delivery of digital content. They are similar to secure servers. Both use encryption to prevent eavesdroppers from stealing or interfering with content. Both use digital signatures to offer the end user a guarantee that the content is genuine. However, IBM argues, cryptographic envelopes go further:

- A single envelope can incorporate many different, but interrelated, types of content – for example, text, images and audio – and keeps the package intact.
- A Cryptolope object is a self-contained and self-protecting object, and can be delivered any way that is convenient. For example, Cryptolope objects can be placed on CD-ROMs, mirrored to different FTP sites or even passed casually from user to user, all without breaking the underlying security.
- A Cryptolope object ties usage conditions of the content to the content itself; for example, the price or specifications that viewing the content can only be done with a special viewer or specifications that data can be delivered only to a system that is capable of applying a digital watermark. Because the Cryptolope object is digitally signed, usage conditions cannot be tampered with without invalidating the cryptographic envelope.

The Cryptolope components are all written in Java and the 'envelope' is nothing more than a JAR (Java archive) file. The opener is simply a program that causes the Cryptolope object to begin execution. This allows the maximum flexibility in applying Cryptolopes to an application.

Non-repudiation issues

Non-repudiation requires that senders and recipients of messages can validate their role in the transmission of data. The sender and the recipient must not deny their role in the transmission of a message of an electronic transaction using credit cards or digital cash.

ADDRESSING SECURITY ISSUES IN ELECTRONIC COMMERCE

IT audits

In operating a business in an electronic environment it is essential that companies ensure that a proper audit of all the factors leading to the issues referred to in the previous sections of this chapter are addressed. The process of an IT audit will ensure that those factors creating an insecure environment are addressed. Figure 6.4 illustrates a framework that encompasses all of the processes necessary to implement an effective IT audit to ensure secure and effective electronic commerce.

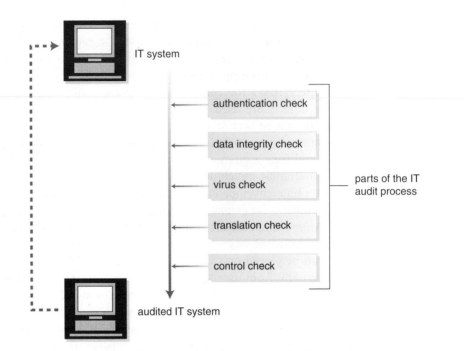

IT system

authentication check

data integrity check

virus check

parts of the IT
audit process

translation check

control check

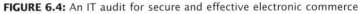

audited IT system

FIGURE 6.4: An IT audit for secure and effective electronic commerce

This audit trail requires a five-step process:[8]

1. *Authentication check*

   Systems checks need to be made to ensure that:
   - secure passwords are allocated within the organisation
   - documented and delegated levels of authority are established and are reflected in the password structure
   - all unused passwords are deleted
   - login attempts are monitored, controlled and limited
   - the number of login accounts available on the machine is limited
   - control systems are established to ensure that the sender of any message can be verified
   - customer and trading partner agreements are in place
   - established and agreed protocols for communication are in place
   - control systems are established that will automatically generate verified receipts for all electronic communications
   - agreements and legal documents exist that will assure acceptance and non-repudiation of electronic communications with or without electronic signatures.

2. *Data integrity check*

   The implementation of electronic and online trading necessitates the development of new controls to detect invalid data and to check that data sent matches data requests and is aligned with data already processed in similar transactions. To implement data integrity in an online system, it is important that:
   - systems and software are in place to enable data matching electronically
   - exception reports are checked and verified according to previously sent data

- systems check the accuracy of data in data communications involving requests
- systems are in place to check previous documents exchanged and follow up on requests at regular intervals
- policy exists and systems are developed and implemented to review edit checks and ensure continued data integrity.

3. *Virus check*

Viruses are the most common form of data corruption in online and electronic commerce environments. Internet viruses are becoming more common and the ease of download of secreted viruses necessitates that checks are both immediate and continuous on all servers and on all machines linked to servers. It is therefore imperative that businesses establish:
- virus check systems and install virus detection and repair software on servers and all linked PCs
- a process of daily checks of all systems for delayed virus impact
- an immediate reaction policy to the detection of viruses in engaging in online or electronic commerce.

4. *Translation check*

In many instances of Internet commerce and online commerce there is a need to enable the translation of data from one form to another that allows access to existing databases and files within a business organisation. This is especially important in old and newer versions of EDI where data files are translated out of the sender's server and into the receiver's server. Therefore, it is important that:
- any translation process implemented is tested
- quality control procedures are in place to ensure that the quality of data received is compatible with the needs of existing business databases and processes
- shells and interpreters not absolutely essential have been removed
- a policy and appropriate software is in place to direct and alert operators when translation failures occur
- there is a system check that ensures that only information designed to be processed has been sent
- systems are in place that report data that is incompatible or not processed.

5. *Control check*

In Internet commerce it is essential that the data is correct and whole when sent and received by the intended parties. To achieve this goal it is important that all businesses operating in an electronic environment have established control systems where:
- all data is received by using sequence checks that check data trails, check for errors and constantly monitor the audit process
- communications between clients and the host business are immediate and reliable to ensure there are no delays in transmission
- data sent on each occasion is filed within correct data files and overwriting of previous data does not occur

- appropriate archiving of all data sent and received is achieved to enable checking where there are disputes
- all unused servers are turned off.

In response to typical business practice, many organisations outsource their IT, electronic commerce and sometimes security processes. **CERT (Computer Emergency Response Team)**[9] and **AusCERT (Australian Computer Emergency Response Team)**[10] provide a comprehensive process to support security in organisations. AusCERT provides a single, trusted point of contact in Australia for the Internet community to deal with computer security incidents and their prevention. AusCERT aims to reduce the probability of successful attack, reduce the direct costs of security to organisations and lower the risk of consequential damage. Secure communications are facilitated on request. AusCERT is a member of the international Forum of Incident Response and Security Teams (FIRST) and has close ties with the CERT Coordination Centre, with other international incident response teams (IRTs) and with the Australian Federal Police. AusCERT also:

- provides a centre of expertise on network and computer security matters
- centralises the reporting of security incidents and facilitates communication to resolve security incidents
- provides for the collation and dissemination of security information including system vulnerabilities, defence strategies and mechanisms, and early warning of likely attacks
- acts as a repository of security-related information, tools and techniques.

Hutchinson and Warren have researched the attributes of Australian information systems managers with regard to policies and audits.[11] They conclude that while a majority approve of doing something, only a minority are prepared for an external attack. The need to shield a business from information compromise is argued by Helms et al. to be best done by being pro-active and thus setting a long-term strategy in place.[12] There is one other method that will facilitate higher levels of security in organisations undertaking electronic commerce using the Web or other networks. This is the implementation of **firewalls** and proxies within the system servers.

Server security, firewalls and proxies

Most commercial servers are constructed as an intermediation process between the Internet and database and other servers behind the network they support. These network servers tend to store various software packages that enable mail, FTP, newsgroups, network operating systems, the Web, CGI scripts and telnet. With such an array of software, the server is vulnerable to attack. Security policy and the technology practices an organisation adopts must address these vulnerabilities.

Server security can be flawed because of intrusion from either in front or behind the server. It is imperative that security checks are made on networks servers and regular tests are made on a server's operation and on the security of each of the component software packages it operates. This involves not only implementation of a security policy and security audit; it also requires the use of additional features to ensure screening and repetitive testing.

Firewalls are pieces of software or hardware that allow only those users from outside a system with specified characteristics to access that system. Firewalls can protect a system or a network or a section of the Internet from unauthorised use both from outside and from within. Levels of access to various parts of a system can also be protected when an internalised firewall system is implemented. Firewalls are devices that can enable secure access and communications between intranets that have been secured and where levels of trust are ensured, and between the Internet and external networks where the level of security and trust is not well established.

Firewalls are part of the audit strategy that has already been discussed. All of the checks and controls referred to in that audit process can be made more effective with a policy that stipulates implementation of a firewall. To enable the types of protection the audit process requires, firewalls are located at an access point into or out of a system or network (see figure 6.5).

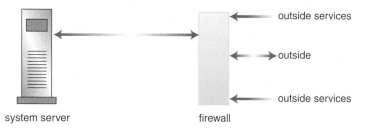

system server   firewall

FIGURE 6.5: Firewall and security from the outside world

If a firewall is placed inside an existing network server, an internal site is created that is insulated from the outside and is accessible only from within the local area network (LAN). Such a firewall might be one that is suitable for the development and implementation of an intranet in a business organisation. These types of firewalls can enable businesses to control access to various levels of information within the organisation and ensure that there is internal security of the operations of that organisation (see figure 6.6).

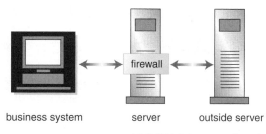

business system   server   outside server

FIGURE 6.6: Firewall and internal protection

If the business organisation wants its business server to have access to an external network or wants its server to be accessed by the outside world and other users of the Internet, there is a need to place the business network's server outside of the firewall (see figure 6.7).

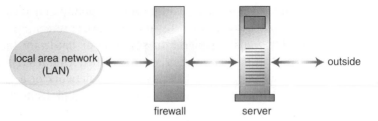

FIGURE 6.7: Firewall allowing external access

Firewalls can provide three levels of security depending on the level of security desired by a business organisation. Firewalls can:

- simply log traffic into and out of a server
- screen or filter information passing through the firewall by using various protocols that can establish which IP addresses (in and out), domains, names or passwords are acceptable – this operation can effectively block undesired or unrecognised incoming traffic and limit the extent and routing of outgoing traffic
- control all traffic with strict protocols and include levels of access, which include information hiding, or maintain regular audits of all data trails and/or communications (e.g. email) – this level of firewall security is the most developed and when rigorously enforced can maintain a strict level of control of and knowledge about the use of a business's server.

However, there is a danger in the overdevelopment of firewalls. As with all servers and the software loaded on them, the more things that run on the server and the firewall, the more things that can be cracked open by a hacker and, thus, the more difficult it is to maintain and ensure security.

One of the more common forms of firewall is the use of a **proxy**. A proxy is a small program that is able to read messages on both sides of a firewall. Requests from outside users for information, files, transactions or communications from the web server are intercepted by the proxy, checked and then forwarded to the server machine. The response is eventually forwarded back to the requester (see figure 6.8).

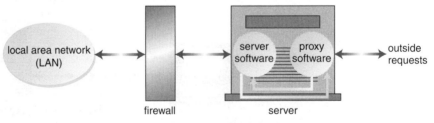

FIGURE 6.8: Role of the proxy in firewall security

Proxies increase network security because they can strictly control authentication processes and check all logins to the server. Proxies can support high-level protocols that can enable and deny access to the server and thus to the business organisation's business systems. Proxies also enable better network management because they provide an intermediary in the transaction process, which increases the potential for checking and adds another level to the transaction process that will also enable a higher level of security. However, one disadvantage of using proxies is that by having an additional level of activity in the business systems interacting with the Internet there is a greater chance for viruses to infiltrate the system and escape detection until some damage has been done.

SUMMARY

Bernstein et al. suggest that there are three critical paths to maintaining and managing a security audit trail to ensure business security in Internet commerce.[13] These paths are shown in figure 6.9.

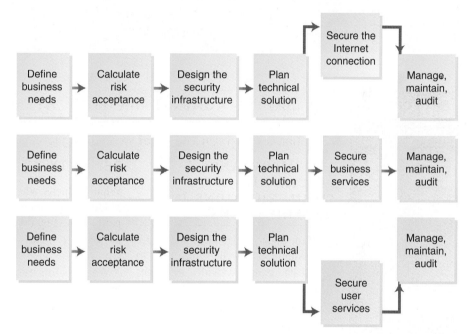

FIGURE 6.9: Three critical paths to manage and maintain a security audit

SOURCE: Y. Bernstein, A. Bhimani, E. Schultz and C. Siegel 1996, *Internet Security for Business*, John Wiley & Sons, New York, p. 80.

Systems can function very effectively and improve the efficiency of businesses significantly. However, if the confidentiality of the data transacted, communications sent or the files cannot be assured then the system is of less value to the organisation. Business done electronically relies on the integrity of the data being sent. If data is corrupted by poor systems, poor system management, inadequate or incompatible software and hardware, or by viruses, then the business transacted is of no value whatsoever. Business organisations need to be able to protect the goodwill and value of their business. They need to be assured that their data and files are not stolen or made accessible to those who have no right of access. Network systems must be made secure from prying computers and the eyes and intelligence gathering of hackers. Business systems must ensure that the identity of both senders and receivers of information, data or communications is correct and appropriate for the information or transaction desired. It is only with the development and implementation of proper IT policy and the establishment of an IT audit for security that businesses will gain proper and thorough security in the operation of their networks.

Key terms

AusCERT (Australian Computer Emergency Response Team) (p. 152)	confidentiality (p. 138)	proxy (p. 154)
	Cryptolope (p. 149)	security (p. 138)
	data integrity (p. 142)	server security (p. 153)
authentication (p. 146)	encryption (p. 146)	viruses (p. 143)
availability (p. 143)	firewalls (p. 152)	worms (p. 143)
CERT (Computer Emergency Response Team) (p. 152)	hackers (p. 138)	
	IT audit (p. 138)	
	non-repudiation (p. 149)	

Case study

THE BATTLE AGAINST SECURITY ATTACKS

By Katina Michael, University of Wollongong © 2002

THE IMPORTANCE OF ELECTRONIC COMMUNICATIONS IN ORGANISATIONS

Medium-to-large-sized companies are increasingly using their intranets to broadcast company-wide messages and store valuable information. Employees can choose to view multimedia-based messages from company executives, link to the latest product success stories, download the most recent technical specifications or refer to the most up-to-date pricing figures. Whatever the requirement, organisations have become very reliant upon electronic intra- and intercommunication methods. Whether it is sending an email with an attachment to a client, downloading information from the knowledge management system (KMS) or placing files in one another's public folders, employees now expect the technological capabilities to be available all the time.

SECURITY THREATS

What happens when the availability of electronic communication methods is threatened by external factors such as security breaches like viruses or worms?

An organisation's productivity level can be crippled in an instant if the right security measures have not been taken. Employees stop receiving emails (while clean-up filters detect and delete the offending emails), might not be able to download important files from the KMS and, even worse, may realise that every file in their public folder has been deleted without warning. In the case of employees who are about to submit a response to a multimillion-dollar tender, this is perhaps the 'point of no return'. But, of course, it all depends on the severity of the problem and the number of hours or days the 'forced' outage lasts.

Learning from your mistakes

I cannot help but recall the day back in 1999 when my senior manager came out of his office waving his arms in disbelief. 'I've lost everything', he said. Our small department ceased work, got up and huddled around him. 'What do you mean?', we asked. He kept shaking his head. 'I made my D drive public read/write so that the account team in Sydney could download or upload whatever they needed to my computer whenever they needed ... and now nothing is there!' The problem was magnified when we realised that our manager's laptop had never been set up for automatic back-ups. He had indeed lost 'everything' and we too slumped in the knowledge of what this meant for our team of eight – a few late nights in desperate recovery of the files we had permanently lost in time to meet an upcoming deadline, although some of us had older versions of files floating about on our machines. We decided from that point onwards to seek a process of centralising our files on a common computer that had plenty of storage space and was backed up daily.

Loss in worker productivity

By late 2000, our company had invested in a corporate-wide KMS. Initially, we considered that this would protect us from viruses and worms – until Code Red hit in 2001. By that time the team had successfully migrated to using the KMS and whole projects were successfully being run on it. Code Red infected the servers and it took two days for our operations to get back to normal. In the meantime, employees were limited in what they could do until the servers were restored. I recall people making lots of cups of coffee and talking about going home because they could not do much without being able to access the Internet or download files they needed to complete work. Some people used the telephone instead to communicate with peers and reassessed their strategies while the problem was being sorted out, whereas others just took the opportunity to sort through their desks and desktops and carry on with minor administrative tasks or reading.

The impact on small business

Small businesses are often severely devastated by breaches in security, not in terms of scope but in terms of the havoc that can eventuate from files that have been corrupted or lost permanently. Small business employees are usually the easiest targets since many are not aware that some worms can act to completely destroy their systems.

While many are becoming more educated about how to protect their business, there are still some who are coming to terms with their past mistakes. I know of one small business owner who lost five years worth of customer contacts because multiple viruses brought his computer to a complete halt. He had no back-ups and was in complete shock when informed by several computer technicians that there was no way to retrieve the information from his hard drive. He spent six months trying to rebuild the database, before coming to the realisation that some of his contacts had been lost forever.

THE INCREASING MALICIOUSNESS OF VIRUSES AND WORMS

What has become apparent is that, since 1996, security breaches have increased in their level of attack and maliciousness.[14] In the past, the IT department had to combat simple macro viruses that would attach themselves to Microsoft files and become menacing pests. Then attackers realised that email could be used to infect many more people. Not only could employees unknowingly initiate a virus by opening an executable file, but the email would be subsequently sent to every person in the address book as well.[15] And it is no longer the humble desktop that is under fire; more and more hackers are targeting servers, machines that are responsible for maintaining network stability. Thus, infection has moved from a file-to-file problem, to a computer-to-computer problem, to a server-to-server problem. Whole 'systems' are now under fire and information services security teams are being tested like never before.

It has begun to dawn on me that corporations are not the only potential victims – the risk of widespread damage to government organisations is also high. Once upon a time we were alerted to the notion of Defcon 4 in movies like *War Games* (1983) that related to thermonuclear war battles. Today, we talk about Risk 4 and the possibility of cyber-terrorism battles. What about the possibility of a worm that could permanently destroy computer systems? Of course, the infected machine could be completely stripped of all its software, including the operating system, and everything could be reinstalled (as happened to machines infected by Code Red). But what if something worse was possible – for instance, the ability to bring down the major data centres that control international network traffic flows? This could have the potential to send normal day-to-day processes into chaos. One cannot help but ask whether or not society has become over-reliant on technology. It has become an intrinsic part of life, not just something we rely on to automate certain routines.

THE REQUIREMENT FOR A SECURITY POLICY

Security policies usually only work well when there is compliance by all individuals within the corporation. It is no good 90 per cent of the employee base complying with suggested security measures against viruses, for instance, if the other 10 per cent ignore the procedures. The latter have the ability to start a virus that will rapidly spread throughout the organisation.

The security policy should also be holistic in nature. You cannot claim to have any single security issue under control if you leave the others unchecked for a time. That is like accidentally locking your keys in your car and leaving them dangling from the ignition. There is a chance that no one may see them, but there is also a chance that someone will be tempted to break in and drive off with a minimal amount of effort.

Some information services teams are now becoming very strict with their requirements. Machines that are detected as being unprotected from standard anti-virus software, for instance, may be removed from the network without consultation, and individual access privileges may be reinstated only when the appropriate measures have been taken and subsequent clearance has been given by information services. In addition, organisations can use email filters to detect and delete viruses before they are executed. Personal desktop firewall programs can also be applied to minimise attacks. Even relatively simple measures like password-protecting public folders and turning off services that are not required (e.g. FTP or telnet) can increase a company's defences. Furthermore, all employees should be warned not to open any suspicious email attachments, no matter how big the temptation is to read something like LoveLetter.[16] And, of course, organisations should always download the latest virus definitions.

The aftermath

Inevitably, computer viruses and worms will hit corporations. The question of what to do after they hit is critical. Even the most up-to-date virus protection software will not curb new or mutated strains that are continually surfacing all over the world. When some worms are breeding on the network, information services may seek a 'bandaid solution' to the problem by applying patch after patch without completely getting rid of the problem. In fact, there is something in this: we are learning to live with viruses, virus strains and their consequences, just as we have developed vaccines to prevent deadly diseases. But there is a chance that our bodies will get weaker and will be unable to resist the diseases if mutated strains eventuate.

QUESTIONS

1. What is the difference between a virus and a worm?

2. Visit the Symantec virus encyclopaedia at www.symantex.com/avcenter/ vinfodb.html and offer three recommendations for dealing with breaches in security.

3. What effects can viruses and worms have on the productivity of an organisation?

4. Visit www.cert.org/. What kinds of measures can information services implement to curb security breaches?

5. Research the Code Red worm. What was the official infection target of this worm? Fundamentally, how did the worm work?

6. Investigate iHug's iSpy online protection services at www.ihug.com.au/ ispy. Should this service be adopted by all of iHug's residential Internet customers? Should consumers have to pay extra for this service or should it be provided as part of the ISP's basic Internet service?

Questions

1. What are the major security issues affecting network security?
2. How can the authenticity of messages be verified on the Internet? How does authentication affect Internet business?
3. Why is government policy for security so important?
4. Should all governments attempt to develop an international agreement on information law? Why or why not?
5. How and why are firewalls and proxies so important?
6. How do viruses affect the security and integrity of online and electronic communication and electronic commerce? What can businesses do to protect themselves from security breaches by viruses?
7. Prepare reports on:
   (a) site spoofing
   (b) denial of service attacks.

Suggested | reading

Ahuja, V. 1997, *Secure Commerce on the Internet*, Academic Press, London.

Badamas, M. A. 2001, 'Mobile computer systems − security considerations', *Information Management & Computer Security*, vol. 9, no. 3, pp. 134–6.

Bernstein, Y., Bhimani, A., Schultz, E. and Siegel, C. 1996, *Internet Security for Business*, John Wiley & Sons, New York.

Centre for Electronic Commerce 1996, *Smart Cards and the Future of Your Money*, Report for the Commission for the Future, Monash University.

Chapman, D. B. and Zwicky, E. D. 1997, *Building Internet Firewalls*, O'Reilly & Associates, United States.

Churchman, P. 1987, *Electronic Payment Systems*, Basil Blackwell, Oxford.

Dhillon, G. 1999, 'Managing and controlling computer misuse', *Information Management & Computer Security*, vol. 7, no. 4, pp. 171–5.

Emmelmainz, M. 1990, *Electronic Data Interchange: A Total Management Guide*, Van Nostrand, New York.

Ford, W. and Baum, M. 1997, *Secure Electronic Commerce*, Prentice Hall, New Jersey.

Furche, A. and Wrightson, G. 1996, *Computer Money: A Systematic Overview of Electronic Payment Systems*, dpunkt.verlag, Heidelberg.

Furnell, S. M., Chiliarchaki, P. and Dowland, P. S. 2001, 'Security analysers: administrator assistants or hacker helpers?', *Information Management & Computer Security*, vol. 9, no. 2, pp. 93–101.

Garfinkle, S. and Spafford, G. 1997, *Web Security and Commerce*, O'Reilly & Associates, United States.

Gattorna, J. and Walters, D. 1996, *Managing the Supply Chain: A Strategic Perspective*, Macmillan, London.

Ghosh, A. K. 1998, *E-Commerce Security*, John Wiley & Sons, New York.

Gritzalis, S. and Gritzalis, D. 2001, 'A digital seal solution for deploying trust on commercial transactions', *Information Management & Computer Security*, vol. 9, no. 2, pp. 71–9.

Hammond, R. 1996, *Digital Business: Surviving and Thriving in an On-line World*, Hodder & Stoughton, London.

Hawkins, S., Yen, D. C. and Chou, D. C. 2000, 'Awareness and challenges of Internet security', *Information Management & Computer Security*, vol. 8, no. 3, pp. 131–43.

Higgins, H. N. 1999, 'Corporate system security: towards an integrated management approach', *Information Management & Computer Security*, vol. 7, no. 5, pp. 217–22.

Kalakota, R. and Whinston, A. 1996, *Frontiers of Electronic Commerce*, Addison-Wesley, United States.

Kalakota, R. and Whinston, A. 1997, *Electronic Commerce: A Manager's Guide*, Addison-Wesley, United States.

Kokolakis, S. A., Demopoulos, A. J. and Kiountouzis, E. A. 2000, 'The use of business process modelling in information systems security analysis and design', *Information Management & Computer Security*, vol. 8, no. 3, pp. 107–16.

Labuschagne, L. and Eloff, J. H. P. 2000, 'Electronic commerce: the information-security challenge', *Information Management & Computer Security*, vol. 8, no. 3, pp. 154–7.

Liu, C., Peek, J., Jones, K., Buus, R. B. and Nye, A. 1996, *Managing Internet Information Systems*, O'Reilly & Associates, United States.

McKeown, P. and Watson, R. 1996, *Metamorphosis: A Guide to the World Wide Web and Electronic Commerce*, John Wiley & Sons, New York.

Pfleeger, C. 1997, *Security in Computing*, 2nd edn, Prentice Hall, New Jersey.

Phukan, S. and Dhillon, G. 2000, 'Ethics and information technology use: a survey of US based SMEs', *Information Management & Computer Security*, vol. 8, no. 5, pp. 239–43.

Rubin, A., Geer, D. and Ranum, M. 1997, *Web Security Sourcebook*, John Wiley & Sons, New York.

Tran, V. G. 1995, 'EDI: good for what ails the healthcare world', *EDI World*, September, pp. 28–30.

Tryfonas, T., Kiountouzis, E. and Poulymenakou, A. 2001, 'Embedding security practices in contemporary information systems development approaches', *Information Management & Computer Security*, vol. 9, no. 4, pp. 183–97.

Tyree, A. 1997, *Digital Money*, Butterworths, Sydney.

Udo, G. J. 2001, 'Privacy and security concerns as major barriers for e-commerce: a survey study', *Information Management & Computer Security*, vol. 9, no. 4, pp. 165–74.

End | notes

1. See www.ec.gov.sg/policy.html for further information.
2. Bernstein, Y., Bhimani, A., Schultz, E. and Siegel, C. 1996, *Internet Security for Business*, John Wiley & Sons, New York, p. 59.
3. Kalakota, R. and Whinston, A. 1996, *Frontiers of Electronic Commerce*, Addison-Wesley, United States.
4. Wilson, S. 1999, 'Digital signatures and the future of documentation', *Information Management & Computer Security*, vol. 7, no. 2, pp. 83–7.
5. A detailed discussion of RSA can be found in Furche, A. and Wrightson, G. 1996, *Computer Money: A Systematic Overview of Electronic Payment Systems*, dpunkt.verlag, Heidelberg.
6. QWERTY are the first letters on a keyboard from the top left working across. These letters have been commonly used as a password.
7. NNTP is the network news transfer protocol designed to enable newsgroups to run supporting Windows 95 and Windows NT.
8. The thin IT audit process was developed from work carried out by G. Behrendorff from the Centre of Electronic Commerce, Monash University.
9. See www.cert.org for more information.
10. See www.auscert.org.au/Information/Auscert_info/whatis.html for more information.
11. Hutchinson, W. and Warren, M. 2001, 'Attitudes of Australian information system managers against online attackers', *Information Management & Computer Security*, vol. 9, no. 3, pp. 106–11.

12. Helms, M., Lawrence, P. E. and Morris, D. J. 2000, 'Shielding your company against information compromise', *Information Management & Computer Security*, vol. 8, no. 3, pp. 117–30.

13. Bernstein, Y., Bhimani, A., Schultz, E. and Siegel, C. 1996, *Internet Security for Business*, John Wiley & Sons, New York.

14. Symantec rates security threats using a risk factor of between one and four, which is based on the potential harm the threat could cause. Some of the current Risk-4 threats include W32.Klez.H@mm, W32.Badtrans.B@mm, W32.Nimda.A@mm, W32.Sircam.Worm@mm and W95.Hybris.Gen.

15. The Melissa virus that spread in 1999 is an example of a Microsoft Word 97 and Word 2000 macro virus that was propagated via email attachments.

16. LoveLetter is the name of a worm that was spread through email attachments in May 2000.

The Internet customer

C H A P T E R

LEARNING outcomes

You will have mastered the material in this chapter when you can:

- define the Internet customer
- understand how to reach the Internet customer
- provide examples of different approaches to Internet marketing
- understand the common online activities of the Internet customer
- understand ways of marketing to the Internet customer
- understand database marketing
- know the difference between direct and database marketing
- appreciate the importance of cyber security.

'The interest driven nature of the Internet means that by the time the customer comes to our website, we already owe them something in return for the time they have spent seeking us out — meeting this debt will increase the perceived value of the Internet for the end user.'

S. Dann and S. Dann 2001, *Strategic Internet Marketing*, John Wiley & Sons, Brisbane, p. 100.

INTRODUCTION

The Internet and Web create some distinct challenges for those who wish to find, develop and interact with **customers**. The Internet consumer could be thought of as a different breed to the traditional consumer. The Internet has enabled them to access information on products and services from a variety of competitors, from across the globe. Customer acquisition is the name of the game on the Internet and companies have to adapt by paying attention to them and providing better levels of service. Research has shown that Internet customers:

- are brand loyal (but within limits)
- take to new concepts easily
- accept risks
- are averse to rules (Why can't I do that?)
- are willing to pay (but demand value)
- want to customise their own solutions quickly and easily.[1]

DEFINING THE INTERNET CUSTOMER

At first, defining who is and who is not an Internet customer seems easy: an Internet customer is anybody who makes purchases via the Internet. From this perspective the Internet customer is anybody who engages in a transaction with a vendor. Such a definition focuses on those people who browse the Internet and make a purchase (perhaps using a credit card) from a vendor of some product. This definition, however, is unnecessarily narrow. Perhaps a better definition of 'customer' might be to borrow from the Quality movement and view the customer as any consumer of goods and services, regardless of the type of financial transaction. This definition can be modified to include any consumer of content on the Internet, where content can include tangible goods, as well as services and information.

With this shift in mind the focus has moved from purchasers of things to the wider community of those who use the Web. This large and nebulous group becomes a somewhat unruly mass to understand and an even more difficult one to interact with. Included in this broad category of Internet customer are:

- readers of company web pages
- recipients of company emails
- online subscribers to newsletters
- direct purchasers of goods (e.g. software and graphic art)
- indirect purchasers of goods (e.g. books and CDs).

With this view in mind, there are many Internet customers, only some of whom are involved in traditional transactions with a vendor.

Other subtleties exist when thinking about who is the customer. Some have suggested that not only are there external customers, but internal customers too. Intranets serve as content providers for employees of a given organisation. Silicon Graphics provides an excellent intranet for its employees, or internal customers.

Just who is the Internet customer?

Are you having trouble finding Internet customers? Look in the office next door and you will find one. A survey by IDC found that over a third of Australian consumers had made an online purchase in 2001/2002, with predictions that this figure will rise to just over 50 per cent of consumers engaging in Internet shopping. Included in this was the fact that buying locally was more popular than international sales with Australian sites accounting for 42 per cent of the transactions, compared to 35 per cent for US sites.[2] According to IBM's E-Commerce Assistant page,[3] the success or otherwise of a product on the Internet depends on six overall factors:

1. The target market should preferably be one that consists of:
   * computer users
   * technology early adopters
   * people with above-average levels of income
   * people with above-average levels of education
   * a mix of men and women now that the balance is getting to be 50/50.
2. Preferably, the product should:
   * be computer-related
   * not need to be touched or tried on before purchase
   * be simple and easy to understand
   * be easy to ship to a customer
   * be standardised
   * be innovative
   * have global appeal
   * occupy a niche market.
3. The product needs a known brand so that customers will be more trusting.
4. To be an attractive product on the Internet, the product:
   * should be easy to distribute globally
   * should not have local, non-Internet distributors competing.
5. An attractive Internet product will:
   * not be too expensive or too inexpensive
   * have a price that can be changed frequently
   * be able to leverage off existing publicity and advertising
   * have a lower cost structure on the Internet
   * not have too much competition to drive prices down.
6. The market environment should:
   * allow anonymity for purchase
   * be in growth rather than depression
   * be in a developed region or country.

There are several sites you can access to check out the types of people who use the Web. The Brigham Young University study identified a series of types of online buyers and non-buyers in a survey conducted in 2001.[4] The study into usability uncovered significant factors for non-purchasing as being fearful browsers (10.7 per cent) who use the Internet for window shopping online, shopping avoiders (10.7 per cent) who have concerns regarding transaction security, technology muddlers (19.6 per cent) who don't spend much time online and feel under-confident with their computer skills, and the final category of fun seekers (12.1 per cent) who mainly go online for leisure rather than shopping.[5] As with most studies into non-shopping behaviours, fear of credit card fraud dominated the security reasons for not buying online.

According to a survey of 3000 US consumers with Internet access, Greenfield Online found that Generation X is doing the most buying online. Consumer purchasing increased by 11 per cent over 12 months, nearly 75 per cent of the participants buy online and 82 per cent buy more than one item per session.

Clearly, the Web is an important place in which to find out about products and services, and it is a slowly growing forum for more traditional transactions.

The issue of culture cannot be ignored.[6] As the non-English speaking and reading world moves online, it is expected that an English-only web site will not be understood by approximately 35 per cent of the Internet audience.[7] While translation software exists in the form of machine translators such as Babelfish (babelfish.altavista.com) these cannot replicate the subtle nuances of a human translation. In traditional face-to-face, or even traditional distance-based, customer interactions, the cultural identity of the customer could be rather easily known. On the Web, culture is expressed through a keyboard. This creates new difficulties and challenges. Subtleties of language may become easily lost on the Web, potentially creating communication barriers. It is important to be aware of cultural difference when operating within the Web.

REACHING INTERNET CUSTOMERS

Getting to customers is a central problem in Internet commerce. In more traditional times business proprietors could rely upon such simple activities as physical proximity to ensure that customers were reached. Putting up a billboard sign over the highway assured that local shoppers knew about products. Now, however, the Web has exploded physical proximity as a variable in the customer relationship. Steering the customer to a given product is a much more difficult and complex process. In fact, it has been suggested that rather than see the customer passively awaiting the marketer, the customer and marketer should work together in developing the Web marketplace.[8]

Very early attempts at facilitating the meeting between customer and provider were found in hotlists. Lists of providers, organised around themes or products, were available on such services as Yahoo! A natural progression from the hotlist was the **Internet shopping mall**, which is a more highly structured and organised form of hotlist. For example, The Internet Mall solicits businesses, without charging an access fee. The mall makes money through corporate sponsorship and **advertising**. The Internet Mall differs from the CyberMall in New Zealand where a small monthly charge is levied.

Such malls, however, are targeted towards small and often new businesses. Sofcom, an Australian Internet publisher operating the Sofcom mall, bills at a rate of $40 per month.

Advertising to reach customers

More sophisticated methods of reaching customers are evolving, such as advertising. **Banner advertisements** are passive advertisements that are encountered by simply visiting a web page. These banner advertisements have not proved as popular as advertisers had hoped as many web surfers do not click through. One solution to this is the live banner, which lets a user get more information about the product without leaving the current site. The problem with live banners is they work slowly (especially with slower modems) and are expensive to develop. **Target advertisements** are active. These advertisements are those on which a user must click in order to visit; they invite the user to act. Target advertisements are appearing more often on the Web, encouraging would-be customers to visit pages.

Sponsorship of search engines is a way of gaining high visibility and contact with customers. For example, IBM e-commerce carries a banner advertisement on the search engine Web Wombat. Clicking on the advertisement directs the customer to the IBM e-commerce site. There, customers can read about new products, register products or discover more about the company. By positioning an advertisement on a search engine, US Robotics–Australia ensures that its message is seen by a wide number of web users. Search engines are a favoured place for advertisements, because they offer the marketer an important advantage.

As searchers enter their searches, the key words are used to determine what type of advertisement will come up on the screen. For example, if you were to search using the key word 'car', the page that appears listing the web sites containing that key word would also feature advertising from businesses such as car dealerships. For example, a search using the key word 'telephone' will result in an advertisement by Optus.

DoubleClick is a major international online advertising company that both sells and manages web advertising (see figure 7.1). It provides a service called DART to send online advertisements to specific web pages. DoubleClick came under attack from privacy groups in 1999 and 2000 over its advertisement serving and data collection practices and has decided to hire a chief privacy officer and retained PriceWaterhouse Coopers to do regular privacy audits.

Commercial vendors of other products may also carry advertising. For example, Telstra sponsors advertisements on the National Rugby League (NRL) web page. Fans of the NRL can click on the sponsor's logo, or the Telstra advertising, to be taken to the Telstra site.

Advertising is sold using three different methods.[9] First is **flat-fee advertising**, which simply charges a set fee for the advertisement over a time period. In this arrangement no assurances are made concerning who sees the advertisement, or its effectiveness. In many ways the flat-fee model harks back to the days of a simple billboard sitting by the roadside.

Slightly more sophisticated than this model is the **CPM** (cost per thousand presentations model) **advertisement**, which calculates the number of times the advertisement is viewed. Thus, the higher the bill for the advertisement, the greater its visibility. The average cost of the CPM advertisement is about US$40, with advertisements appearing on soap operas, mysteries and dramas peaking at an average of US$50.[10]

A third model of advertising billing is **'click-through' advertising**. This model bills on the basis of the number of times the advertisement is clicked on, taking the viewer to the advertising page. Thus, billing is on the number of times somebody actually undertakes an action.

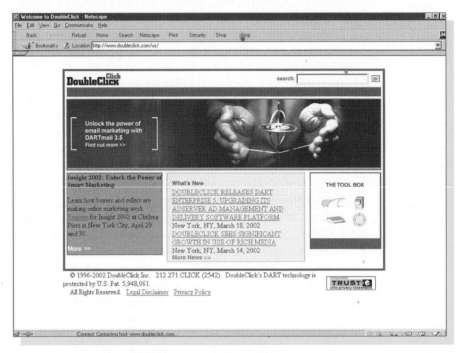

FIGURE 7.1: Advertising on the Web: home page of DoubleClick (www.doubleclick.com/US)

Satisfying customer needs

Thus far, these approaches to guiding customers to the desired site have been replications of very traditional advertising plans. Technically, they are increasingly sophisticated, but they rely upon some very tried and true methods.

Use of the Web, however, has led many to interact with customers in much richer ways. For example, the NRMA provides membership services via the Web. Customers can access the NRMA's survey of new car prices, a technical hotline and other motoring news using their membership number and membership expiry date.

In providing these services, the NRMA attracts customers to its site. It has now released its first online sales facility allowing customers to purchase travel insurance over the Web. Users can obtain a quote online and before departure secure the transaction using a credit card. Obligation-free quotes are available and to attract new users NRMA is offering a discount of 25 per cent for any travel insurance purchased over the Internet.

Consumer activities online

Online consumer behaviour consists of two things – the behaviours that drive people onto the Internet, and influence what they do when they get there, and the behaviours that can only be done while online. There are nine specific motivators for using the Internet, and these are:

1. *Anonymity*: The individual consumer uses their time online to engage in sites and places without being actively recognised by other people. For example, people can search out medical information regarding conditions that they don't want other people to know they have (e.g. athlete's foot) without the web sites identifying who they are.
2. *Communications*: People use the Internet to email or chat with people or companies. The success of the Internet as a communications medium is most clearly felt in the areas of B2C communication, as customers can email instant feedback to organisations as they peruse the Web.
3. *Convenience*: The consumer uses the Internet to make their life easier, and goes to sites that offer the advantage of being able to save time (and/or money). These sites will offer online shopping with easy to use ordering and well supported delivery mechanisms that allow for fast and accurate delivery.
4. *Information seeking*: The consumer comes online in pursuit of knowledge in a specific area, and uses search engines or news sites to research their goal. Sites accessed in this type of activity tend to be text orientated, or facilitation sites – such as search engines – which the consumer uses to find the information.
5. *Global access*: The consumer uses the Internet to access the world. During this sort of surfing activity, the consumer is most likely to seek overseas sites for their international perspective.
6. *Community*: The consumer is online to be part of a social gathering, or a gathering of online friends, rather than to perform any specific task.
7. *Utility*: The consumer goes online simply because they have no alternative but to use the Internet service. This is increasingly common for bank services and bill payment transactions which are limiting the availability of offline transactions in order to emphasise online delivery.
8. *Recreation, leisure and pleasure*: The consumer uses the Internet for fun and relaxation, and may incorporate other motivations such as community or communications. This tends to be the motivation that draws people to entertainment and gaming web sites.
9. *Inherent merit*: The consumer uses the Internet because it's the Internet, and it's there. This last form of Internet usage is usually of limited interest to marketers as the user is focused on using new and different parts of the Internet for the sake of exploration.

The three major Internet-specific behaviours are:

- *Self representation*: This is where the consumer can use the Internet to develop an avatar personality for their online behaviour. Avatars can either be used for direct interaction in chat groups or online gaming, or as the basis around which a web site or web journal is based.
- **Cybercommunity**: The development of community structures in online environments such as mailing lists, IRC channels and similar interactive environments.
- **Flow state**: This is where the consumer awareness of the passage of time during their Internet activity is reduced and they find themselves spending longer online than they planned, or expected. Flow is often reported in association with recreation-based surfing, and usually is associated with an expression of surprise at the current time (e.g. It's midnight already?) as the consumer feels that they have been online for only a short period of time.[11]

These Internet-specific activities represent the combination of the benefits of a computer-mediated environment with specific consumer motivations. Easy access to virtual space assisted the development of the self-representation behaviours, particularly with the widespread access to web-based journals or hosted web sites. In turn, shared infrastructure such as web diaries can often lead to the creation of communities of shared experiences between the consumer publishing their work and their readers. Spending time engaged in the writings of the open diaries and involvement in the community structure can also engage flow-state behaviour more easily than can occur with online bill paying.

CUSTOMER RELATIONS

Customer relations is a vital subject in the evolution of Internet commerce. Developing that affinity between providers and customers is crucial for successful online commerce. In Australia there are roughly 100 000 businesses online. The unfortunate reality is that most of these businesses fail to maximise their use of the Web. Ideally, relating to and interacting with customers is more than simply putting up a web page. Elaine Rubin, Senior Vice-President of Interactive Marketing of iVillage and one-time head of the highly successful interactive services group 1-800-Flowers, has advice on customer relations:

> The power of online marketing, she says, comes from one-to-one communications between retailers and manufacturers and their customers. Used right, the technology can actually build affinity and relationships. Unfortunately, many corporate web sites are nothing more than repurposed advertising and use the Internet simply as a way of lowering costs.[12]

Perhaps the most basic way of relating to customers is through email, which is an efficient and simple way of interacting with customers. Assisting customers in interacting through email serves the interests of everybody. For example, Amazon communicates extensively with its customers via email.

Each book order that is placed with Amazon receives an acknowledging email containing the specifics of the order and the order number. The signature of the email contains a hypertext link back to the Amazon web page. Further facilitating the ease of communication are simple directions for sending a return email, which is routed to the appropriate department automatically.

To follow email best practice, consider the following:

- Offer email facilities only if you are prepared to support them at a high level.
- Every email deserves a response.
- Answer the questions posed by the email sender.
- Match the medium's expectations (i.e. people who send email expect a rapid response).
- Implement a staffing model that matches your customer's needs.
- Treat every email as a sales opportunity (but with care).[13]

Providing a web-based form for communication may enhance email use. This makes communication easier for the customer, who does not need to create a structured reply but rather supply only specific answers to questions. It also allows the content provider to classify responses by field. So, for example, customers may be asked to give demographic details such as age. The customer might click only on an age category, rather than give an exact age. The content provider can simply classify responses to categories, which are then automatically logged into a database (e.g. FileMaker Pro). No data entry need be done in order to compile a database.

Of course, some may wish to combine both fields with specific questions and open comment fields. Qantas, for example, allows visitors to its site to combine both specific feedback as well as open-ended commentary (see figure 7.2 on the following page).

Establishing relationships beyond the simple buyer–seller relationship can be accomplished by providing information of interest to customers. For example, TMP Worldwide has compiled a comprehensive web page providing visitors to the page with a wealth of information about employment. While the TMP Worldwide mission is to trade in employment services, its site may be used by anyone interested in employment issues. Not only does the company provide information, but it also solicits participation in various surveys and questionnaires. TMP Worldwide surveys often are reported on in the news, thus enhancing the sense of participation.

The TMP Worldwide experience, however, is a not a common one. Most web pages are designed with little or no consultation with customers. In fact, according to a recent GartnerGroup report, 90 per cent of the companies surveyed had created their web sites without ever asking what their customers wanted on those sites![14] This, once again, supports the conclusion that most businesses on the Web fail to work with customers in an effort to meet their needs. Developing methods of consulting with customers is vital to web site success. Ideally, customers are consulted not just once, but repeatedly, in order to better ascertain their needs over time.

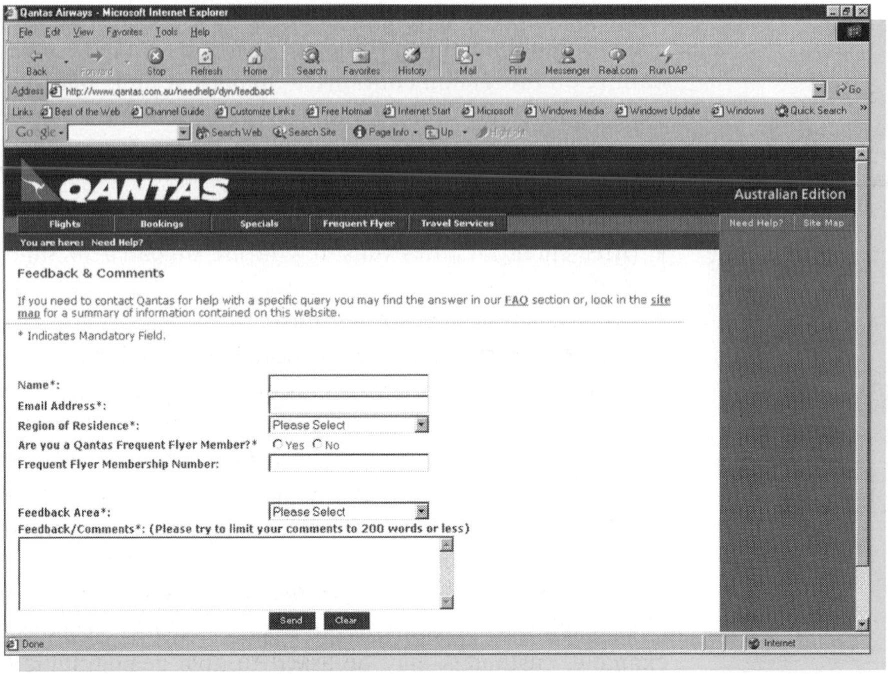

FIGURE 7.2: Provision for feedback on Qantas's web site (www.qantas.com.au/needhelp/dyn/feedback)

Generating repeat business from customers is essential for successful online and offline trading. It hinges on developing a positive relationship between client and seller called customer relationship management. The goals of such a framework are set out in table 7.1 below.

TABLE 7.1	CUSTOMER RELATIONSHIP MANAGEMENT		
TACTIC	**METHODOLOGY**	**EXAMPLE**	**WEB EXAMPLE**
Use existing relationships to grow revenue	Identify, attract and retain the best customers	Maximise relationship via up-selling and cross-selling	www.barnesandnoble.com
Use integrated information for excellent service	Use customer information to save customers' time and ease their frustration	Don't make them repeat information	www.aol.com
Introduce repeatable processes and procedures	Improve consistency in account management and selling	Make sure the different employees know the customer	www.CDNow.com
Create new value and instill loyalty	Make this your point of difference	Offer discounts for buying online	www.nrma.com.au
Implement a more pro-active solution strategy	Use a customer-focused business solution across whole enterprise	Eliminate issues before they reach crisis point	www.amazon.com

SOURCE: Based on R. Kalakota and M. Robinson 1999, E-business: Roadmap for Success, Addison-Wesley Longman, United States, pp. 111–12 © Adapted with permission of Pearson Education, Inc., Upper Saddle River, New Jersey.

Sometimes, however, customer relations break down. Responding to customer complaints in a quick and speedy fashion is vital. Standards Australia has outlined the essential steps to handling **complaint resolution** in developing the Australian standard **AS 4269**. The essential elements are:

- possess a commitment to efficient and fair resolution of complaints
- commit the resources necessary to handle complaints
- have a visible process for handling complaints
- ensure the complaints-handling process is accessible
- provide assistance for the lodgement of complaints
- be responsive to complaints
- ensure that remedies for complaints are available
- ensure that data is systematically collected
- account for complaints and classify them to allow their later analysis
- review complaints handling annually.

Ideally, a web-based form should be available so that complaints can be lodged. If not a web-based form, then at least a hypertext email address inviting customers to comment and provide feedback should be used. Following these guidelines ensures that customer interactions, when and if things go wrong, result in building relationships and not breaking them down.

DATABASE MARKETING STRATEGIES

Database marketing is the storage and retrieval of customer and client data — such as name, address and purchase history — for the purpose of better understanding customer and client needs and delivering goods and services that satisfy these needs in a manner that achieves organisational objectives.[15] This is particularly important on the Web where it is vital to encourage existing customers to buy more and to buy more frequently.

Direct marketing differs from database marketing in that direct marketing focuses only on promotion because it relies on advertising to generate a measurable response and/or transaction. Database marketing focuses on four elements, namely targeting, tailoring, tying and tapping.

Table 7.2 outlines some of the strategies that are vital in database marketing.

Some issues that need to be addressed in developing a database marketing system include:

- What will it be used for (e.g. list management, identifying segments) and will its use be legal and ethical?
- Who will be using the database (e.g. marketing or other departments)?
- How will the database be used (e.g. are clear and precise applications noted)?
- What further data is required from external sources (e.g. census data or Internet-behaviour data)?
- Who will be responsible for implementing and maintaining the database (e.g. on-site or outsourced)?[16]

TABLE 7.2	THE FOUR T'S OF DATABASE MARKETING	
THE T'S	**EXAMPLE**	
Targeting	Micromarketing and finetuning of customer segments to find out who should be targeted in promotions, which customers should be retained, etc.	
Tailoring	Adapting the offer to suit the customer's needs — communicating the right message to the right person	
Tying	Building permanent customer relationships by developing trust and satisfaction, e.g. using frequent-buyer programs	
Tapping	Tapping into increased profits by using satisfied customers as sources of references for prospective buyers, e.g. giving away gift certificates to customers encourages them to recommend the site to their friends	

SOURCE: C. Perry and H. Master 1999, *Module 3, Strategies for Database Marketing, E-business Strategy Study Book,* University of Southern Queensland, pp. 3.6–3.7, adapted from K. Rohner 1998, *Marketing in the Cyber Age: The Why, The What and The How,* John Wiley & Sons, New York.

CUSTOMER SECURITY

Customer security remains the most problematic issue for commercial transactions. Surveys consistently cite security as the main reason for not engaging in online transactions. Yet, most customers poorly understand threats to security. Security threats fall into two groups – those threats against individual accounts and those that threaten whole databases. Industry is more concerned, obviously, with the latter, whereas individuals more so with the former. More often than not, however, newspaper headlines fail to make these distinctions. There have been cases of databases being broken into and credit card details stolen. These are security issues of great relevance, but have little or nothing to do with the individual customer. The holder of credit card data on the database is responsible for ensuring that the data is protected. In this case, there is no way to personally guarantee the user that his or her credit card is protected from unwanted use.

Instead, most customers worry about the actual transaction in which they are involved. Most believe that their credit card details are being stolen or can be stolen during a transaction. Few, if any, cases exist where this has occurred. Even more troublesome for individuals involved in commercial transactions is the misunderstanding concerning liability. Credit card holders are liable for only the first $50 of stolen credit card transactions; the banks carry the majority of risk. Yet, it seems that most credit card holders fail to make this observation. Some Internet customers keep an Internet-only credit card (with a low credit limit) for online purchases.

In an effort to overcome security concerns and allay customers' worries, credit card companies in conjunction with banks are working to develop encrypted transactions, thus protecting the entire transaction. In August 1997 the ANZ Banking Group became the first of the major Australian banks to employ a secure mode for Internet banking. Credit card holders with the ANZ Bank used **virtual wallet software**, which was loaded on their PCs. These virtual wallets used **Secure Electronic Transaction (SET)** encryption to protect transactions. However, it appears as if secure socket layer (SSL) has become the de facto security standard, particularly with Australian banks.

Of course, commercial transactions are not the only sorts of transactions to occur on the Web. Other data can be accessed via the Web, such as personal records. This data must also be protected from unwanted examination. Recent experience in the United States suggests that security concerns stop at financial matters. US citizens wishing to access their social security records could do so briefly via the Web. Reality outweighed expectations when thousands of people accessed their social security information. The experiment was closed in less than a week, when demands outweighed expectation and after concerns were raised that insufficient security safeguards might allow unwanted access to private files.

SUMMARY

The customer relationship on the Web is fraught with possibilities and challenges alike. It is not a traditional customer relationship as might have existed in other commercial contexts. Rather, it is one that demands a high degree of participation from all parties. It is important that content providers respond to customer needs and ask what those needs are on an ongoing basis. It is also important to guide the customers to information you wish them to have. Establishing this ongoing two-way relationship will greatly enhance the business-to-customer relationship.

Key terms

advertising (p. 166)
AS 4269 (p. 173)
banner advertisements (p. 167)
'click-through' advertising (p. 168)
complaint resolution (p. 173)
CPM advertising (p. 168)

customers (p. 164)
customer relations (p. 170)
customer security (p. 174)
cybercommunity (p. 170)
flat-fee advertising (p. 167)
flow state (p. 170)

Internet shopping mall (p. 166)
secure electronic transaction (SET) (p. 175)
target advertisements (p. 167)
virtual wallet software (p. 175)

Case study

INTEGRATING ISLANDS OF INFORMATION THROUGH CRM

By Katina Michael, University of Wollongong © 2002

SERVE YOURSELF

It was not so long ago that one would pull up into a service station and be greeted by an attendant who would customarily ask whether or not to fill up the car with petrol. Of course, today things have changed. Petrol station attendants have been replaced by something called 'self-service'. The customer is empowered and has the responsibility to fill up their own car with as much petrol as they want. A little extra effort perhaps but no one seems to mind, apart from the countless number of people who lost their jobs as attendants. What is noticeable, however, is the human contact between the attendant and the driver which has been forgone. The local service station is no longer where people will get a chance to talk to *Jack*, but merely fill up their car with petrol to make sure they can reach their destination. To this end, driver loyalty has diminished; people will fill up their car with petrol at any service station convenient to them. The traditional customer care that has disappeared along with the role of the petrol station attendant has had to be replaced by a new relationship based on loyalty card schemes and the like. The key message here is how to engage existing and potential customers and how to retain them, given that the new relationship is managed on new terms of interaction. One can almost hear customers saying *'if you want me to fill up my car here every week, you must give me something in return that I value or a good enough reason not to look elsewhere.'*

MEETING THE BUYER IN CYBERSPACE

More than any other technology, the Internet has changed the rules of engagement between the buyer and the seller. In a physical store it is the salesperson that will approach the customer; in a virtual store it is the customer who will approach the seller. In a physical store the seller usually has minutes to convince the customer to shop further; in a virtual store the seller has seconds. Why? Because like using the telephone, the Internet allows the customer to shop around without exerting too much additional effort. A customer can make a decision based on quality, price, availability, aesthetic attributes and after-sales support, by comparing the different product or service offerings over the Web, in the privacy of their own home and at a time that suits them. Some traditional 'bricks and mortar' companies have been left dumbfounded by the changes the Internet has borne, opting to stay offline; others are barely coping with some form of Internet presence. However, there are a growing number of companies that have successfully implemented a parallel online business model to their existing operations.

ISLANDS OF INFORMATION

The term customer relationship management (CRM) is not new though its importance is only now being realised more completely. Before the Internet, CRM systems existed, albeit in a primitive form.

The most common implementations of CRM included using direct mail, the telephone or face-to-face communications to develop and maintain relationships, building a lead customer database, knowing the buying behaviours of existing customers, and getting customers to fill out product satisfaction surveys.

The problem with these traditional forms of CRM was that separate stand-alone software systems were used. For instance, buying behaviours were not linked to product satisfaction surveys and aggregate results from surveys were not fed back to product engineers who were responsible for creating the products. And even if they were linked, they provided little insight into strategies of how to best serve the customer and how to encourage a uniform approach to retaining them.

This led to untimely and misguided marketing campaigns that were sometimes more confusing for the customer than beneficial – a problem that very large organisations are still struggling to overcome, despite the technological advances that have taken place in the last decade. The larger the organisation it seems, the more difficult it becomes to know your customer and offer a personalised service where they feel valued. This is especially true for global companies that offer products through different channels in different countries. The same product or service is not transferable from market to market with exactly the same success, and customers in different geographies with different socio-cultural influences will react differently to one another. For instance, what may be a perfectly valid approach to customer relationship management in the United States may be considered offensive in China.

THE FACE OF CRM TODAY

Enter the need for an integrated and intelligent approach to online and offline customer relationship management. Whether a customer physically visits a store to shop, fills out a paper-based customer request form, rings a call centre seeking post-sales support, faxes through an order, emails a sales representative related to a product feature, visits the company web portal searching for a technical specification or makes an electronic payment, every single touch point should be recorded. The CRM system may be distributed in nature, but the information must be accessible by the people who need it, when they need it.

Take the example of a customer who has purchased a product over the Internet and is waiting for its arrival via post. At the time of purchase, the online catalogue indicated that the product was in stock, and the customer checkout screen provided a date of arrival. The product does not arrive when the customer expects. The disgruntled customer (who needed the product immediately) sends the company an email asking why the delay has occurred.

An automated response is sent to the customer indicating that a sales representative will attend to the matter and subsequently respond accordingly. Twenty-four hours lapse, the customer sends another email and receives yet another automated response with the same message.

By this stage the customer is so frustrated that they decide to pick up the phone to call a representative. After being put on hold for some twenty minutes, they finally talk to a representative who knows nothing about their situation: *'I'm sorry, we don't handle the email system, only incoming calls.'* The customer realises that they must repeat themselves again, and is left with a negative impression of customer service even though their inquiry was eventually sorted out.

Perhaps the moral of the story is that the customer should be given the choice to engage the seller or be engaged through any medium they wish. If they prefer to send emails with queries rather than to speak with a sales representative, then they should have this option. The problems begin when a response to that specific email query is automated with either information that is too generic or wrong information; or even worse, when a reply to that email is never sent. The kind of impression projected forward to the customer in this instance is *'that company obviously does not want my business – I'll go somewhere else next time.'*

THE CRM PHILOSOPHY

CRM has been touted the new philosophy that will empower not only the seller but the buyer as well. CRM is not just about customer care, it is a corporate philosophy; a strategy that encompasses the process of customer engagement, browsing and purchase. But it does not stop there. CRM is also concerned with post-sales follow-up support, evaluating the customer and placing them into an appropriate market segment, and introducing ways to retain the customer so that they continue to make purchases. At best, CRM is about making the customer feel so valued that they will not only make repeat purchases but also tell all their friends about how good your customer service was and subsequently how happy they are with the products they have purchased. Companies like Dell[17] have been used time and time again as examples of good CRM (see figure C7.1). Dell gives customers who want to purchase computers the option of configuring computer hardware online in parallel to talking to a local sales representative, and also offers customers the capability to track their order from the point of manufacture to arrival. CRM vendors like Siebel Systems[18] are offering businesses the capability of implementing such processes through their integrated call centre and web-centric solutions.

In the not too distant future, CRM will also be linked to granting sales and field service teams timely information, and offering resellers and channel partners access to up-to-date records. Salespeople, the automated back office, and account and/or product managers will be responsible for producing this integrated knowledge that will filter through to different parts of the business.

The necessity to see or speak to the seller is something that varies product by product and service offering by service offering. What may be feasible for one business may not work in another. With this in mind, companies must define the needs of their customers to help serve them better.

Today, there are several factors that are constraining CRM from being all that it can be. These factors are related to Internet penetration, limited broadband access, the infancy of credible IP-based applications, and security and privacy concerns. The future of CRM is being able to grant customers the ability to use the Web to shop while having the simultaneous option to click on either a voice button or multimedia conference button and hear or see the actual sales representative they are interacting with. Perhaps it is not so much about seeking to recreate what the physical world offers, but giving the customer the choice to shop and buy in an environment that they feel comfortable in.

FIGURE C7.1: Dell system configuration page
(austore1.dell.com.au/au/bsd/cart/configuratornw.asp)

QUESTIONS

1. What is customer relationship management (CRM)?
2. How has the Internet impacted traditional CRM methods?
3. What are the main technologies that are used to implement CRM processes? Give examples from solutions featured on the Siebel Systems web site (www.siebel.com).
4. How has CRM changed the customer shopping experience?
5. What are the major constraints associated with the implementation of CRM systems today?
6. Visit the Dell web site (www.dell.com) and indicate the various CRM features that have been implemented by the company.

Questions

1. Assume that your manager has asked you to recommend whether your company should or should not start marketing its products or services on the Internet. What factors about Internet marketing would you include in your report?
2. Investigate whether or not there is a difference between direct marketing or database marketing. Access an e-commerce site, decide which model the site uses and explain your decision.
3. What sort of customer-based issues might you need to consider when designing a presence on the Web?
4. What are the strengths and weaknesses of the various methods of advertising on the Web?
5. How can commercial vendors address customer concerns over transaction security?
6. How can companies on the Web enhance their relationships with customers?
7. What are some methods you can use to identify and attract customers to a web site?

Suggested | reading

Dann S. and Dann S. 2001, *Strategic Internet Marketing*, John Wiley & Sons, Brisbane.

Department of Foreign Affairs and Trade 1999, *Driving Forces on the New Silk Road: The Use of Electronic Commerce by Australian Businesses*, Commonwealth of Australia, Canberra.

eMarketer, *eMarketer Weekly Newsletter*, www.eMarketer.com.

Hanson, W. 2000, *Principles of Internet Marketing*, South Western College Publishing, Thomson Learning, United States.

Kalakota, R. and Robinson, M. 1999, *e-Business: Roadmap for Success*, Addison-Wesley Longman, Boston, United States.

Maddox, K. 1998, *Web Commerce: Building a Digital Business*, John Wiley & Sons, Toronto, Canada.

Nesheim, J. 2000, *High Tech Start Up*, The Free Press, New York.

NUA, *NUA Internet Surveys*, www.nua.ie.

Rohner, K. 1998, *Marketing in the Cyber Age: The Why, The What and The How*, John Wiley & Sons, New York.

End | notes

1. Maurice, D. 1999, *Trading in Cyberspace: Satisfying the Internet Customer*, E-commerce and the Internet, KPMG seminar, 31 August 1999.
2. NUA Surveys 2002, 'Over a third of Aussies buy on-line', 26 Mar., www.nua.ie/surveys/?f=VS&art_id=905357694&rel=true.
3. Perry, C. and Sweeney, A. 1999, *Module 2, Internet Marketing, Unit 75707, E-business Strategy Study Book*, University of Southern Queensland, pp. 2.13–2.15, based on E-Commerce Assistant program on IBM site at advisor.internet.ibm.com/inet.nsf.
4. NUA Surveys 2001, 'Brigham Young University: Would-be shoppers still worry on security', 13 July, www.nua.ie/surveys/?f=VS&art_id=905356976&rel=true.
5. Smith, S. and Swinyard, B. 2001, 'The Internet useability study', July. www.byu.edu/news/releases/archive01/Jul/internet.htm.

6. 'The Global Internet', *The Internet Economy Indicators*, www.internetindicators.com/globalinternet.html.

7. Hoffman, D. and Novak, T. 1996, 'A new marketing paradigm for electronic commerce', *The Information Society*, www2000.ogsm.vanderbilt.edu/novak/new.marketing.paradigm.html.

8. Capron, H. L. 2000, *Computer Tools for an Information Age*, Prentice Hall, New Jersey, p. 250.

9. Novak, T. and Hoffman, D. 1996, 'New metrics for new media: toward the development of web measurement standards', *Project2000*, www2000.ogsm.vanderbilt.edu/novak/web.standards/webstand.html.

10. Focalink Communications 1997, 'Focalink reports web serial sites charge an average CPM of US$250', www.focalink.com/home/fc/fc26ad.html.

11. Dann, S. and Dann, S. 2001, *Strategic Internet Marketing*, John Wiley & Sons, Brisbane.

12. 'Content is still king, says the queen of online marketing' 1996, OtR, www.hotwired.com/market/96/15/index1a.html.

13. Maurice, D. op. cit.

14. Kline, D. 1996, 'Memo to the boss: your web site is useless', *Hotwired*, hotwired.lycos.com/market/96/15/index1a.html.

15. Schoenbachler, D., Gordon, G., Foley, D. and Spellman, L. 1997, 'Understanding consumer database marketing', *Journal of Consumer Marketing*, CD-ROM, vol. 14, no. 1, pp. 5–44, www.mcb.co.uk/jcm.htm.

16. Perry, C. and Master, H. 1999, *Module 3, Strategies for Database Marketing, E-business Strategy Study Book*, University of Southern Queensland, p. 3.9.

17. www.dell.com.

18. www.siebel.com.

CHAPTER 8

Organisational communication

LEARNING outcomes

You will have mastered the material in this chapter when you can:
- define organisational communication
- understand the effect the Web has on organisational communication
- provide examples of different approaches to organisational communication
- understand the various methods of interacting within and between organisations
- understand organisations' use of ERP systems and CRM for effective and efficient communication with customers and trading partners.

'The Internet is a communication medium that allows, for the first time, the communication of many to many, in chosen time, on a global scale. As the diffusion of the printing press in the West created what MacLuhan named the "Glutenberg Galaxy", we have now entered a new world of communication: the Internet Galaxy. The use of the Internet as a communication system and an organising form exploded in the closing years of the second millennium.'

M. Castells 2001, *The Internet Galaxy: Reflections on the Internet, Business and Society*, Oxford University Press, Oxford, pp. 2–3.

INTRODUCTION

The Internet is changing the way that organisations conduct their business and communicate with their customers and trading partners. The Internet allows organisations to distribute information faster (by email and intranets) than traditional modes of communication (fax and post). This new way of distributing and disseminating information is only possible with the use of electronic data storage and transmission. In the near future, the dream of the paperless workplace may become a reality, a place where documents, forms and information will be stored digitally for reference and use by organisations. This phenomenon of the future office requires a new way of thinking about organising and managing communication within and between organisations, using the Internet effectively as a medium for information transmission and communication.

By having a well-managed communication process with customers and trading partners, organisations are now in a strong position to provide better customer service in a real-time manner, so that email messages and online enquiries can be attended to in a matter of minutes. Organisations can see that the next wave of customer-centric innovation requires business integration of processes, applications and systems on a new and grander scale. Sue Bostrom of Cisco Internet Business Group suggests that businesses should 'develop an e-culture mind-set by looking at the Internet across the entire system of their business.'[1] Looking at the potential of the Internet as a new tool for communication and dissemination of information will assist organisations to reach potential customers and build relationships and loyalty with existing customers. With a better-managed communication system, organisations can also streamline their processes with trading partners, minimising costs and improving relationships.

This chapter looks at the impact that the Internet is having on organisational communication. It focuses on both intra-organisational and extra-organisational communication via the Internet. The chapter also introduces the concept of enterprise resource planning systems for supply chain management and communication with trading partners. Before focusing on these topics, however, we examine some broader themes of the Internet and organisational communication.

HOW THE INTERNET IS CHANGING ORGANISATIONAL COMMUNICATION

The Internet is changing the dynamics of organisations in many ways. Three primary points of focus are the new publishing paradigm, the Internet and work, and just-in-time information.

The new publishing paradigm

The problem of creating, printing, using and storing information has long plagued organisations. Consider the daunting task of creating, printing, using and storing information that the Commonwealth government faces.

Whole legions of public servants spend hours collating, distributing and searching for information. It is a monumental task. The number of hours it takes to generate publications or look for old ones is huge. Under the old publishing paradigm labour was intensively used to create, print, use and store information. Research officers collected data, analysts created information, public affairs specialists distributed it and librarians collected it. Under the new publishing paradigm, however, creating, printing, using and storing information is no longer as labour intensive. Equally important is the fact that organisations no longer have to plan for long lead times in order to get information out to their stakeholders. Instead of creating a newsletter in a fortnight, Internet publishers can create and distribute newsletters in as little as a few hours. Consider the changes wrought by the new publishing paradigm in table 8.1.

TABLE 8.1	CHANGES WROUGHT BY THE NEW PUBLISHING PARADIGM	
OLD PUBLISHING PARADIGM	**NEW PUBLISHING PARADIGM**	
Publishing control centralised	Publishing control decentralised	
Long lead time to publication	Very short lead time to publication	
Labour intensive	Not labour intensive	
Once published, almost impossible to change	Easily changed and altered	
Static medium with little interaction	Dynamic medium with a high level of interaction	

The new publishing paradigm provides many new changes and challenges for organisational communication. It has the potential to create a far more fluid, and perhaps even chaotic, publishing environment. This will create new challenges for managers in the years to come. Two professors from the Harvard Business School formulated what is known as the Law of Digital Assets.[2] Unlike physical assets, digital assets are used but not consumed, which means that digital assets can be used over and over again. The organisation can create more value by continually recycling its digital assets through a large, nearly infinite, number of transactions. However, it is still vital to revise, enhance, improve and repackage these digital assets. Many newspaper firms, such as the *New York Times* and the *Sydney Morning Herald*, allow web surfers to read articles online for free but charge for archived material.

Bertelsmann Online (BOL), a German bookseller, plans to launch downloadable books that can be read by the Rocket eBook, which can display 36 000 pages from its battery powered memory. The German book wholesaler Libri has launched a service digitally printing single copies of hard-to-find books.[3]

The Internet and work

Donald Tapscott, in his book *The Digital Economy*, argues that networked organisations are changing not only how they do things, but their very structure as well. He writes that a '. . . radical rethinking of the nature and functioning of the organization and the relationships between organizations' is occurring.[4] Large organisations have long had the advantage of being able to draw on economies of scale and resources. The smaller companies who can adapt to change more rapidly, however, are quickly overcoming the advantage held by the larger organisations. Small companies can use the Internet to tap into pools of information previously unavailable, partly because the Internet overcomes the tyranny of distance. Previously, organisations were constrained by distance and time in use of resources. Now with the Web, such problems of distance and time are largely overcome.

Global software teams provide a good illustration of how the Internet is changing traditional organisational structures and communication. A global software team is a team that actively collaborates on a common software/systems project but is separated by national boundaries.[5] The reasons why global software teams are formed include:

- the availability of experts in various countries who are not willing to relocate to a new country
- cost reductions, whereby staff can be employed at a lower rate
- organisational expansion, whereby an organisation acquires another organisation or expands to a new country
- organisational strategic location, when it is important for an organisation to have a presence in the global economy.

BAAN has its headquarters in the Netherlands but has remote sites in the United States, Canada, Germany, India, Japan, Israel and Brazil. Whenever a new project is initiated, a global team is formed. The team members come from a variety of countries depending on their expertise and experience. The team is not required to be in a specific location and the team members can remain in their own locations. Many tools can be employed for communication between team members. Videoconferencing can be used to conduct virtual meetings. Email and intranets are used to inform members and distribute information. The intranet can also be used to store electronic documents, which team members can then access. Team members interact virtually by using email or the intranet. All documents and code can be exchanged via a team intranet for comments and action. Global software teams can achieve efficient outcomes for projects by effectively utilising the Internet for communicating and exchanging information. The characteristics of global teams are different to traditional team structures. Table 8.2 compares traditional team structures with virtual team structures.

Teleworking, the new mode of work adopted at the end of the last millennium by numerous organisations, also represents the change from traditional team structures to new team structures. Teleworking enables teams to function across national boundaries through the use of electronic media, such as the Internet, mobile phone and other wireless networks, and private computer networks. Using such communication networks, global teams can design and develop software, manage computer operations in remote places as application service providers (ASPs), and facilitate intra- and inter-organisational communication.

TABLE 8.2	CHARACTERISTICS OF VIRTUAL TEAMS VERSUS TRADITIONAL TEAMS	
TRADITIONAL TEAMS	**VIRTUAL TEAMS**	
Co-located members	Distributed members	
Face-to-face interaction	Electronic communication	
Members from same organization	Members from different organizations	
Hierarchical	Networked	
Mostly informal communication	Continuous structured communication	
Position authority	Process and knowledge authority	
Information distribution (push)	Information access (pull)	
Information on paper	Information electronic	
Sharing completed work	Continuous sharing of incomplete work	
Knowledge hoarding	Knowledge sharing	
Transparent process	Computer-visible process	
Culture learned through osmosis	Culture learned through electronic-based communications and artifacts	

SOURCE: E. Carmel 1999, *Global Software Teams: Collaborating Across Borders and Time Zones*, Prentice Hall PTR, New Jersey, p. 15 © Reprinted with permission of Pearson Education, Inc., Upper Saddle River, New Jersey.

Just-in-time information

Just-in-time (JIT) information was an important change in inventory control. Just-in-time business processes, whereby organisations introduce the use of electronic communications and enterprise resource planning systems, have been an important change in inventory control. Many organisations, such as wholesalers and manufacturers, are often stuck with large inventory of unused parts and products on their warehouse shelves. Overordering of inventory means increased costs and valuable space is lost on warehouse shelves as parts and products are stored. Many organisations want to order and receive parts or products when their stocks are just about to run out. This means that parts that will be used today are delivered today. However, orders must be completed well before the parts actually run out, so organisations are trying to streamline their processes by incorporating their suppliers into their supply chain management processes. Intel established an extranet or private Internet to communicate real-time inventory levels and demand to suppliers and customers.[6]

An extranet is a specialised and customised online information service provided by a company to its valued clients (individuals or organisations). Its platform is Internet connectivity and web technology. A business needs to look at its suppliers and customers as strategic allies. The business is part of a group providing high-quality products and best possible services and needs to design its extranet with that in mind.[7]

JIT inventory control meant that the size of an inventory was controlled to match current production as closely as possible. The same principle now applies to information because of the Internet. No longer are organisations slaves to traditional methods of information collection and dissemination. Instead, JIT information now provides organisations with the capacity to create, acquire and disseminate information in a much more efficient fashion. Corporate newsletters, intranets and email now make JIT information a real possibility.

Consider a simple example of a sales meeting. A meeting scheduled for 2.00 p.m. is cancelled. Before network solutions were available someone had to first call around to those who were supposed to attend the meeting and let them know it had been cancelled. In addition, considerable effort was spent in trying to set up a new meeting time convenient to all involved. By linking offices together via an intranet, a meeting can be cancelled with ease. Broadcast emails further facilitate schedule changes, as do online calendars. The amount of time wasted in inefficient communication is significantly reduced if the networked solution is used effectively.

JIT information allows organisations to more quickly focus their energies on things that matter. Thus, as organisations become more efficient in their use of information, they gain important competitive advantages.

ORGANISATIONAL ISSUES

Organisational issues that affect business communication by employing electronic communication technology include:

- *Building infrastructure for sharing information*: organisations require a well-formed strategic plan when using technology enabling electronic communication and information dissemination within the organisation and with trading partners. This strategic plan relies on a stable and well-integrated IT infrastructure, which is well maintained, regularly audited and consistently monitored.
- *Managing knowledge*: in making full use of infrastructure and technology such as an intranet, organisations should carefully plan the storage of organisational knowledge, which employees use as a source of reference and to assist in their decision making. Managing the purposeful use of IT resources is a key part of ensuring this.
- *Maintaining flexibility*: organisations should think about the compatibility of their infrastructure and technology with that of their customers and suppliers. Organisations also need to select infrastructure and technology for future upgrades.

- *Flattening organisational communication processes*: electronic communication reduces the hierarchical nature of communication structures in organisations because messages can be sent directly to intended receivers.
- *Organisational culture*: electronic communication technologies need to be implemented carefully without disrupting organisational culture. Thus, if face-to-face communication is the culture within an organisation, email can be used to support and organise face-to-face meetings, for example through the distribution of documents, and electronic calendars can be used to establish the availability of participants. Organisational culture can impose limits on the use of electronic communication. In some organisations restrictions are imposed. However, creative organisations implement strategies to bring about the required changes in organisational culture.
- *Organisational commitment*: organisations that commit to using electronic communication need to educate and train their employees to gain the full benefits from the new infrastructure and technology.

A comprehensive communications capability should be a fundamental part of an organisation's infrastructure, for example providing email facilities or setting up a Lotus Notes database to share information among employees. Organisations should not have one system for internal communication and a different system for customer service (e.g. different email packages for communication within the organisation and for communication with customers) – they should be converted into a common data platform.

INTRA-ORGANISATIONAL COMMUNICATION

The Web has affected **intra-organisational communication** in a variety of ways. It also has the potential to completely revolutionise intra-organisational communication, but that potential is yet to be realised. The three primary vehicles of change have been the use of email, the development of the intranet concept and the use of graphical browsers as the front-end for other applications.

Email

Email has dramatically affected intra-organisational communication. Billions of messages are sent around the world each day and email has become a key driver behind the explosion of electronic commerce. In the 12 months ending June 2001, 50 per cent of Australians had used the Internet. In 2001, over half of Australia's 1.2 million small businesses used the Internet in dealing with customers and finding information.[8]

It is used to transfer company data orders, invoices, word-processed documents, spreadsheets and CAD files between business partners saving time and the expense of sending paper communications.[9]

Michael Dertouzos, Director of the Massachusetts Institute of Technology's Laboratory for Computer Science, underscores the importance of email, writing,

'Email is a basic function on all information infrastructures.'[10] Email provides a number of benefits to intra-organisational communication, including:

- efficiency
- speed
- accountability (the receipt of an email can be electronically monitored)
- automation
- embedded HTML (allowing text, graphics, images, sound and video in an email)
- visibility (email makes it easier to find people, especially if they are overseas because they will be listed in an email directory somewhere on the Internet).

The disadvantages of email for intra-organisational communication include:

- people stop talking to one another
- people spend too much time emailing each other
- communication is inappropriately targeted
- email readers become bogged down in a sea of email
- mind dumping (where people send emails on subjects that they might not otherwise have written a letter about).

A survey conducted by PricewaterhouseCoopers in 1998 found that 13 per cent of Australia's top 100 companies regularly monitor email and about 6 per cent read messages. About 15 per cent of companies that monitor do not tell their employees. In the United States about 27 per cent of companies monitor workers' email.[11] According to a recent study released by the Denver-based Privacy Foundation, 14 million employees, or just over one-third of the online workforce in the United States, have their Internet or email use monitored by their employers.

> Worldwide, the number of employees under such surveillance is about 27 million, the study reports. The availability of inexpensive technology is driving the growth of employee monitoring, according to Andrew Schulman, the Privacy Foundation's chief researcher. Within the past few years, employee monitoring, as measured by the sales of surveillance software, has increased at least twice as fast as the number of US employees with Internet access, according to the study. Worldwide sales of employee-monitoring software are estimated at $140 million a year, or about $5.25 per monitored employee per year, the foundation said.12

According to Rosen (2000),[13] legally companies need only warn their employees in writing that their emails may be monitored. Rosen suggests that this will lower employees' expectations of their privacy being considered. Other research suggests that large numbers of organisations in the United States, for example, are using a similar policy.

Email is becoming an essential element in virtually any information infrastructure. Sending emails to multiple recipients will distribute the message to an almost infinitely large number of people. This is an effective way of broadcasting important information to a wide spectrum of employees. Of course, email can be targeted to specific individuals as well.

Attachments may be added to email, allowing the inclusion of documents created in a number of word-processing, database and spreadsheet packages. A sales presentation can be prepared in one part of an organisation, reviewed by another, and modified by yet another, before being presented. All of this may take place in a large geographical area, and may occur easily within hours. The **interactive mail access protocol (IMAP)** allows for better control over the way messages are delivered. Instead of having all the new email messages delivered from the email server onto the user's computer in one go, IMAP gives the user greater flexibility in interacting with the inbox. The user may choose to download only the subjects of the new email messages, then select and download only relevant messages. It also allows the user to see what files are attached to an email and then decide which ones to download. Obviously, this is ideal for users receiving email over slow connections such as a laptop computer connected to the Internet via a mobile telephone.[14]

Companies should ensure that they have an electronic communications policy that expressly categorises certain conduct as prohibited and outside the scope of employment contracts. Further details on email are found in chapter 10, pages 255–7.

Intranets

Another change in intra-organisational communication has come from the development of the intranet. An intranet is simply a smaller, local version of the Internet. Whereas the Internet is accessible and accesses information from around the globe, an intranet is accessible and accesses information locally. Douglas Cruickshank explains:

> Intranets employ the same information-organizing principles as the World Wide Web, a graphically-oriented, highly flexible approach that can be tailored to the existing structure of virtually any organization or project. Yet unlike the Internet, an intranet can only be accessed by individuals within an organization, and by outsiders who've been given passwords to allow them in. A special network security device known as a 'firewall' keeps out all others.[15]

Intranets give organisations the capacity to provide JIT information to any part of an organisation. In addition, intranets act as a resource to employees; for example, John Wiley & Sons Australia has a useful intranet for staff (see figure 8.1 opposite). Staff can download all forms used in general business, check the schedules for projects, read updated information about the company and company social events, and find links to useful web sites.

Intranets have been adopted quickly by a wide range of organisations throughout the world. Some of the features of an intranet include:
- the ability to transmit timely, important information rapidly throughout the organisation
- web browser software capable of browsing the Internet as well as the intranet (e.g. Netscape Communicator)

- high bandwidth, assuring speedy communication
- security
- front-end access to other internal software applications (e.g. databases).

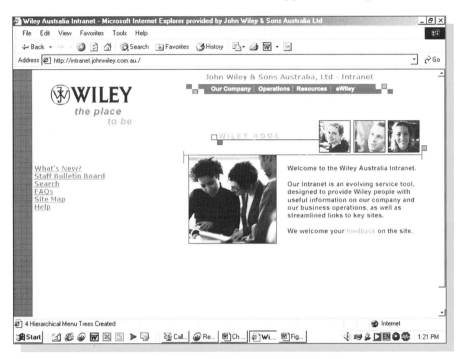

FIGURE 8.1: The intranet home page of John Wiley & Sons Australia
(intranet.johnwiley.com.au)

Useful downloadable software applications can also be linked to intranet pages so that employees need only download and configure software to their local machine. For example, human resource managers may wish to electronically support the assessment of employee performance. Software is available that supports the performance appraisal process by keeping track of employees and their key performance indicators. The **Performance and Assessment Results 4 (PAR4)** software can be linked through an intranet. Managers can then download and configure PAR4 to their local machines as needed. Human resource managers can use the intranet to provide managers with software that makes their job of assessing employee performance more manageable.

Intranets ensure that information can be disseminated quickly throughout the organisation, that everybody has the same information, and that those important tools and resources are universally available.

Software from companies such as Macromedia makes it easier for companies to build web applications to handle e-commerce, business process automation and dynamic information publishing on intranets, extranets and the Internet. Macromedia has a series of software applications that assist in the production of sites that deliver high-impact, low-bandwidth web sites to browsers. These include Flash, Fireworks, Shockwave and Dreamweaver. Visit www.macromedia.com to see sites using some of these applications.

Organisational knowledge management

Knowledge management is the process of managing organisational knowledge to create business value, sustain competitive advantage through knowledge sharing, generate new ideas, solve problems and apply the knowledge gained from customer interactions to maximise business growth and value.[16] Organisational knowledge comes in different shapes and forms, including memos, letters, forms, models, figures, personal knowledge, team knowledge, individual skills and images. Some of the knowledge can be captured electronically and stored in an organisational database for sharing and dissemination. Tiwana defines the word 'knowledge' as:

> a fluid mix of framed, contextual experience, values, situated information, expertise, and grounded intuition that provides the framework for evaluating, understanding, and incorporating new experiences and information. Such knowledge becomes not only embedded in documents or repositories but also in organisational routines, processes, practices, and norms.[17]

Thus, organisational knowledge needs to be managed carefully so that knowledge can be shared among the organisation's employees to assist with daily operations and strategic operations. An intranet is a good tool for managing and sharing knowledge within an organisation. Knowledge can be easily communicated and disseminated to employees. The intranet can be used to disseminate organisational knowledge such as rules and procedures, expert knowledge and past experiences in solving certain type of problems. Employees can then access this knowledge and use it for the benefit of the organisation.

Using graphical browsers as front-end interfaces

Another change in intra-organisational communication is in the use of graphical browsers as front-ends, or access points, for other software applications. Within organisations financial information and customer databases may be accessed remotely using a graphical browser interface. For example, the Macquarie Graduate School of Management has trialled handling queries through online forms. Prospective students fill out the form and send it. The data is used to update a FileMakerPro database and a copy is emailed to the university marketing group. The customer helps both build the database and initiate the process of sending out marketing information. While this application starts with an external user initiating communication, it results in a change in how the organisation communicates internally. No longer is data entry required. Equally important, updated figures can be generated about online marketing.

At the University of Hong Kong, prospective students of the Master of Science degree in Electronic Commerce and Internet Computing can apply for the program online (see www.ecom-icom.hku.hk/admission.htm). The online application system for admissions is a web-based system developed by the MSC ECom-IComp Programme Office, and can be used by the public to apply for admission to the degree program. The system aims at speeding up the whole admission process. As soon as an online application is confirmed, the Programme Office processes the application. In addition to the online application form, the system tracks application status. To prevent data being captured by a third party when being transmitted over the Internet, a Secure Socket Layer connection is used for data encryption. A certificate is issued by the Hong Kong Post CA (Certification Authority), which is the public certificate authority in Hong Kong, to ensure authenticity.

Remote tracking of mailed packages is fast becoming an important web application. The application was originally pioneered by Federal Express. Other companies now using a web interface to track packages include Qantas, DHL Australia and TNT.

The final change brought about by graphical browsers is the use of videoconferencing and Internet telephone calls. Videoconferencing and Internet telephones have been available, in varying quality, for a short period on the Internet. Telephone calls within an organisation but outside of the existing telephone network can also be made via the intranet. Videoconferencing is also available, linking a number of intra-organisational sites together by way of a video camera and web-based software. As web technology improves, it is becoming increasingly possible to engage in a live videoconference through a corporate intranet, linking people within a single company who are geographically dispersed.

Equally appealing for intra-organisational communication are groupware applications, such as Lotus Notes, which allow users to interact remotely with one another in a structured environment. Such groupware is ideal for group meetings, brainstorming sessions or other such applications. Groupware brings to group meetings the immediacy of videoconferencing, with the logical structures found in many software applications.

EXTRA-ORGANISATIONAL COMMUNICATION

Extra-organisational communication is also changing. Extra-organisational communication is that which occurs between the organisation and some group or individual outside the organisation.

Many of the same tools that are changing intra-organisational communication are also changing extra-organisational communication. Two primary examples of how extra-organisational communication is changing are found in modifications to the supply chain and the recruitment of employees.

The supply chain

One example of the electronic **supply chain** is found at Woolworths. The Woolworths web page provides instructions on how to establish an electronic supply chain (see figure 8.2). Woolworths makes no software prescriptions. Rather, the company helps would-be suppliers to understand the electronic supply chain.

At Ford Direct's web site, Ford Motor Company allows users to link with their local Ford dealers to search for a new or used car (see figure 8.3).

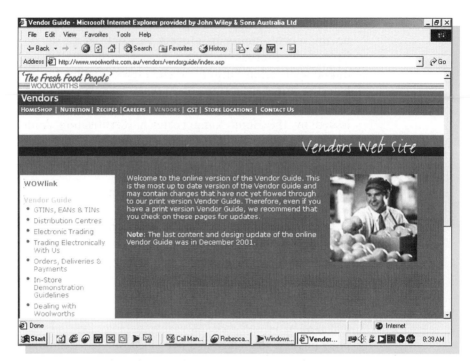

FIGURE 8.2: Easy to follow instructions from Woolworths on the electronic supply chain (www.woolworths.com.au/vendors/vendorguide/index.asp)

FIGURE 8.3: Ford Direct's web site, where customers can build a customised order, search the inventory of local Ford dealers, obtain a quote from local dealers and search for a used car (www3.forddirect.fordvehicles.com/Dispatch.jsp)

General Motors has set up the e-Gm online service division to tighten its supply chain and retail sales processes. General Motors, Ford and Daimler Chrysler are driving forces behind the Automotive Network Exchange (ANX) – an initiative to force car-industry suppliers to communicate via the Internet. The e-GM system will provide the car maker with a worldwide web configuration and ordering platform in the first quarter of 2000. Since November 1999, Ford has accepted customised web orders on a limited range of vehicles.[18]

Recruiting employees

The recruitment of employees is also changing dramatically via the Web. Traditionally, recruitment has been limited to a few methods – newspaper classifieds, bulletin boards or recruitment agencies. Time and control limit all of these methods. Newspapers come only at a given time of day, space is limited and they cannot be updated. To add something to a newspaper one must wait for the next edition. Bulletin boards and recruitment agents both take control away from the prospective employer and place it in the hands of another.

Monster Board Australia, an offspring of Monster Board in the United States, provides employers and prospective employees with greater functionality than a simple classified advertisement. Monster Board solicits and touts jobs, but also provides assistance to job seekers through the use of an online résumé engine. In addition, it also contains a 'virtual interview' as well as feature articles, user polls and a résumé posting service. Also available are employer profiles that can be surveyed by job seekers at any time and job seekers are able to register their job preferences on some sites and have job listings emailed to them daily.

Companies, of course, need not depend upon the services of an intermediary at all. Job postings are a common occurrence in organisations. Often, no one knows about the job posting except those who happen to read it in the coffee room or wherever it may be posted. The Web takes the in-house posting and makes it globally available. For example, InterWorld, an electronic commerce consulting firm, advertises directly on its web page rather than publishing its job announcements through some third party.

The web site www.employment.com.au offers jobseekers a user-friendly site (see figure 8.4). Another web site that offers jobseekers a similar, but equally user-friendly, interface is www.monster.com.

There can be little doubt that the Web affects extra-organisational communication. We have seen two ways in which that impact is realised. The supply of goods, services and people is greatly affected by the Web. What other impact will the Web have on organisational communication? One of the new impacts comes about from the complex, integrated software packages that have played a significant role in organisations. These are enterprise resource planning systems.

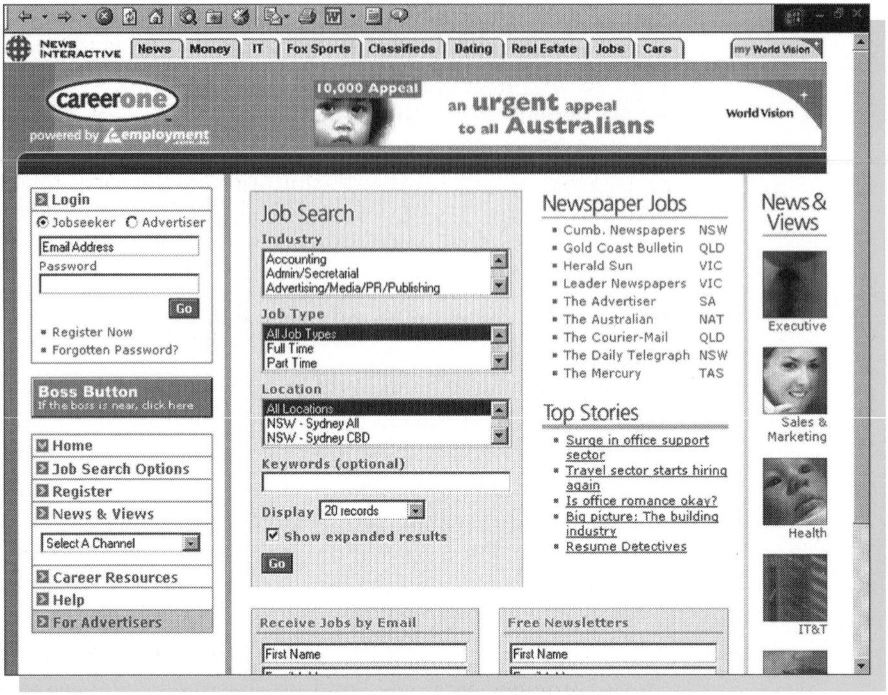

FIGURE 8.4: Australia's longest running employment site (www.employment.com.au)

ENTERPRISE RESOURCE PLANNING SYSTEMS

Enterprise resource planning (ERP) systems, as mentioned earlier, enable organisations to streamline their processes with their suppliers as well as enabling easier and more efficient communications within and between organisations. ERP systems focus on managing an organisation's internal systems and information through data interchange and streamlining organisational processes as a whole. By successfully installing an ERP system, an organisation will be able to manage its internal information more effectively and efficiently to meet organisational goals and objectives. The system will also assist the organisation to manage its knowledge.

ERP systems enable organisations to communicate, exchange and process information with their suppliers in one integrated information system. With an ERP system, only one software package is required for the whole organisation. ERP systems normally come in modules, for example manufacturing, finances, human resources, and sales and marketing. Organisations are not required to purchase and install all the modules in an ERP package. They can install only one module or more modules, depending on their requirements. The major ERP vendors are SAP (www.sap.com), People Soft (www.peoplesoft.com), JD Edwards (www.jdedwards.com) and BAAN (www.baan.com).

The successful installation of an ERP system will enable effective communication throughout an organisation. For example, when a part is running low, an ERP system can automatically generate and send an email with a purchase order to a preferred supplier (see figure 8.5). However, the organisation needs to set the stock levels that trigger the ERP system to communicate with suppliers and generate purchase orders. After emailing a purchase order to the supplier, the ERP system sends a copy of the email to both the person in charge of ordering and to the accounting department. The organisation's accounting module is then updated automatically and an email message is sent to the accountant to advise them of the changes made by the ERP system.

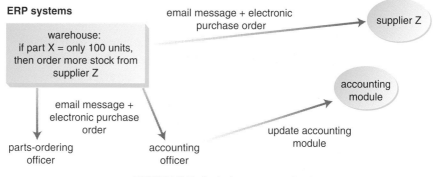

FIGURE 8.5: Ordering communication process in ERP systems

ERP systems enable organisations to move to a new level of communication where information can be exchanged and processed in a streamlined manner. In traditional supply chain management, even with computerised information systems, many organisational legacy systems cannot communicate and exchange information with other legacy systems. Therefore, time and money have to be spent setting up protocols for data transmission and for formatting data from one organisation to another. Some organisations also have problems with the compatibility of information within their own information systems, because assorted systems have been implemented by different units within the organisation. An ERP system allows the organisation to focus its energies on things that matter. Thus, as organisations become more efficient in their use of information, they gain an important competitive advantage. This impacts on those inside the organisation and informs the human factor in relating to web technologies and organisational communication. At the forefront of this is communication between organisations and their customers.

Customer relationship management

Communication and information exchanges between organisations and their customers are important for building good relationships and loyalty. Numerous customer relationship management (CRM) software packages are available, for example from Siebel Systems (www.siebel.com), Onyx Software (www.onyx.com), FrontRange Solutions (www.frontrange.com), Oracle Corporation (www.oracle.com) and Interact Commerce (www.interactcommerce.com). These applications allow organisations to capture knowledge about customer purchasing behaviour.

Such useful information about customers may include:

- frequency of purchases
- types of products or services purchased
- amount of money spent for each purchase
- customer's general interests.

This information is important because organisations can use it to generate personal letters or newsletters to customers and treat each customer as an individual rather than as part of a group (e.g. a monthly newsletter can be generated to include only topics of interest for a particular customer). Personalised service makes customers feel better and promotes trust. Promotional material and advertising can then be directed to customers strategically, so that promotional materials such as letters or email messages are sent only to customers who have expressed an interest in the products. While some companies can better target their promotional material, email has made it cheaper to send advertising material, and some organisations send copious amounts of advertising material to as many people as they can, including those who do not want it (and who therefore treat it as junk mail). With personalised service, however, customers who have not expressed an interest about a product do not receive the promotional material.

Thus, CRM enables organisations to communicate effectively with their customers and treat each customer as an individual. By providing customers with only the information they require and thus by providing better customer service, organisations can improve their relationships with their customers. Again, this reinforces the need to understand the human factor.

THE HUMAN FACTOR

There can be no doubt that the Web is affecting organisational communication. In so many ways organisations can win huge efficiencies by its intelligent use. There are, however, some human factors that need to be acknowledged. For example, consider the human issues that are present in teleworking. Some of the positive benefits from teleworking are:

- increased worker autonomy
- enhanced worker control over their own schedules
- reduction in family/workplace conflicts
- increased morale and enhanced trust
- higher productivity
- fewer occurrences of workplace bullying and confrontations between employees and their bosses.

Yet, Lamond, Standen and Daniels also observe problematic areas in teleworking, including:

- decreased opportunities for development and promotion
- increased conflict between home and work
- less time in face-to-face contact with fellow employees
- reduced job security
- social isolation
- increased hours of work.[19]

While teleworking provides ample benefits to both the organisation and the worker, one should not forget the downside. Considering how human problems will be addressed and handled remains a vital challenge for any organisation, no matter what technological advances are made. Ongoing training is certainly one answer to developing and maintaining mastery over the Internet. Other areas to consider when reflecting upon the management of the human factor include:

- recruiting and selecting employees with appropriate Internet experience
- assessing Internet skills and abilities during performance appraisals
- maintaining a fair and equitable Internet environment
- ensuring occupational health and safety (e.g. repetitive strain injury)
- planning future Internet uses and needs
- developing organisational policies on use and misuse of the Internet.

Even with the best planning in place, however, the technology that drives the Internet will continue to change. At what pace this change will occur is anybody's guess. Just think about the impact that information technology has already had on organisations. In 1997 Reuters commissioned the report *Dying for Information*, which outlined the various ways in which information technology like the Internet is impacting on organisations. The report found that roughly two-thirds of surveyed managers found that information over-load resulted in stress and lowered job satisfaction.[20] One spokesman from Reuters commented, 'Information has truly become a bit of a liability.'[21]

We are caught in a dilemma. On the one hand, we need more and better information to stay competitive. Yet on the other hand, too much information leads to stress and even organisational dysfunction. The challenge is to try and manage this dilemma. Dertouzos reflects on the human factor, writing:

> Human emotions and foibles have a huge effect on all professional exchanges within an organization. Solid bonds or rifts among employees, the boss's mood, motivation or lack thereof to achieve goals, passion, greed, jealousy, and altruism are all at play in any human organization. The Information Marketplace will have greater impact on organizations if it can effectively handle these subtle links among humans along with the more straightforward exchanges of information.[22]

The Web creates a myriad of new interactions between people. Managers must account for the many ways in which people will react to these new interactions. One cannot forget the human factor.

GLOBAL COMMUNICATION ISSUES

As the use of electronic communication and the Internet becomes more common as part of inter- and intra-organisational communication, there are some issues that organisations need to consider:

- *Attitudes towards communication technology*: Different countries have different attitudes towards communication technology. Some countries prefer face-to-face communication rather than virtual communication. For example, the Nepalese prefer oral communication rather than written communication. Their meetings are called in an informal manner, and minutes of the previous meeting and agendas are not distributed beforehand.[23] Therefore, the use of email or other written forms of communication may not be suitable in countries such as Nepal.

- *Language*: The most common language used on the Internet is English, and most software applications are written in English. However, there are many people who do not have English as their first language and who might find it difficult to communicate and use an English-based application. This could reduce the effectiveness of communication between organisations and customers.
- *Existing technology and infrastructure*: Countries such as the United States, Australia, Canada, New Zealand, Singapore and Malaysia have invested in improvements to their technology and communication infrastructure, which enables them to have faster speed data transmission. However, some countries still have inadequate telecommunications infrastructure, and this prevents them from using and transmitting data effectively on the Internet. The so-called 'digital divide' is the gap between those who can effectively use new information technology such as the Internet and those who cannot and who do not have access to it.[24]
- *Legislation*: Data transmission between countries sometimes needs to take into consideration legal issues and local legislation, for example encryption of data, which is not permitted in France, and some strong encryption algorithms, which may not be used in the United States.

Intra-organisational communication, particularly between countries, is becoming more common with the use of email and other technologies such as videoconferencing and web cam. However, local values and attitudes towards communication technology need to be understood. Organisations need to select communication technologies that will be accepted in other parts of the world. For example, if customers prefer face-to-face communication, then videoconferencing would be a more suitable form of communication than email or voice messages. Organisations need to understand that different countries have their own unique ways of communicating among their employees and citizens. For instance, in Thailand email has been embraced as a communication tool between friends and relatives who study or work overseas. Email and SMS messaging are used extensively by the younger generation. However, email is rarely used as a formal communication tool within organisations — written memos and documents are preferred. Thais prefer face-to-face communication, because this allows them to show politeness and respect during meetings and can be used to strengthen relationships between trading partners, friends and colleagues. Therefore, in such circumstances communication technologies would be more appropriate as support tools.

Some global companies might want to use an intranet to share information among branches in different countries. If the organisational culture is fairly similar across the world, then this is not a problem. However, this is rarely the case. Different cultures operating in different branches of a global company will more than likely impact on the adoption of specific forms of communication. Some degree of inaccuracy and misinterpretation may result from the different attitudes to different forms of communication.

SUMMARY

In this chapter we have examined the ways in which the Web impacts upon organisational communication. Generally, the Web is creating a new set of dynamics in which organisations are operating. Two of the key changes highlighted were the adoption of online collaboration, for example global software teams, and the use of ERP systems for organisations to achieve just-in-time information. Online collaboration has changed the nature of work. Specific locations and work times are being replaced by hot-desking (more than one person sharing an office or a computer in a business), the home office and mobile workplaces. Traditional hours of work are being replaced by flexible hours. For example, in global software development teams, team members can be situated in different parts of the country or in different parts of the world. Global software teams use email and intranets to communicate and disseminate information among team members.

This chapter also focused on both intra-organisational and extra-organisational communication. In intra-organisational communication it was seen that email, intranets and the use of the graphical browser as a front-end for software are the key influences. In extra-organisational communication it was observed that the Web is changing the ways in which supply chains operate as well as where future employees are located. ERP systems enable organisations to improve their communication, and thus their relationships, with their suppliers. CRM is also now becoming an important issue for organisations for creating loyalty with their customers.

The human factor was also emphasised. No technological change or solution stands apart from human issues. The key to benefiting from the Web will ultimately be found in matching human requirements with technological solutions. Finally, global communication issues were investigated by looking at cultural differences between countries, which can limit the use of some communication technology. Organisations need to select communication technologies that are compatible with their customers' communication values. This issue will arise wherever cross-cultural communication is conducted.

Key terms

attachments (p. 190)	global software teams (p. 185)	just-in-time (JIT) information (p. 186)
enterprise resource planning (ERP) systems (p. 196)	interactive mail access protocol (IMAP) (p. 190)	Performance and Assessment Results 4 (PAR4) (p. 191)
extra-organisational communication (p. 193)	intra-organisational communication (p. 188)	supply chain (p. 193) teleworking (p. 185)

ORGANISATIONAL COMMUNICATION: WILL IT BE IMPROVED BY ADOPTING INFORMATION TECHNOLOGY?

By Theerasak Thanasankit, Monash University

Smith Textiles Pty Ltd is a textiles company located in Bangkok. The company has been established for more than 35 years and has gained its reputation by producing high-quality cloth and clothing products, and because of trust among its loyal customers.

The company's organisational structure is rather flat, comprising a CEO, who is the owner of the company, and three managers (see figure C8.1). Two of the managers are the CEO's sons and the other is his daughter-in-law. The organisation has three locations, all in Bangkok. The headquarters is a cotton-knitting enterprise; the second factory produces sports and designer T-shirts, with most of its customers in the United States and other Asian countries; and the third factory, which is located approximately five kilometres from the headquarters, also produces knitted cotton materials for export. Each branch has its own organisational registration. The headquarters is Smith Textiles Factory Co. Ltd, where the CEO and his third son are located. The second branch is called Ni-Ke-Matsu Factory Co. Ltd and is run by another son. The third branch, which is run by the CEO's daughter-in-law, is called Nutty Textile Factory Co. Ltd.

The manager of Ni-Ke-Matsu has a strong vision for his factory to move forward in the new millennium by introducing information technology for organisational processes and communication. The knitting machines are the most up to date for high-quality manufacturing for high-profile multinational clients.

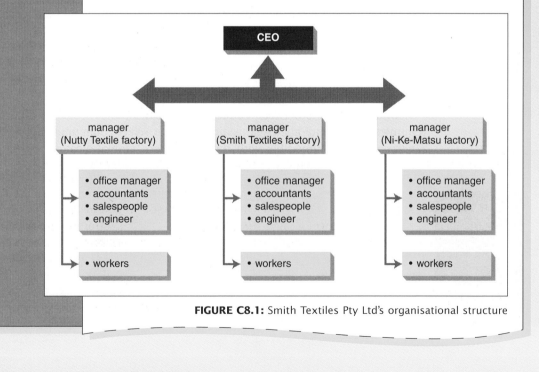

FIGURE C8.1: Smith Textiles Pty Ltd's organisational structure

This organisation is being wired and linked together by the introduction of computer networking. The network system has allowed the office employees, who are doing clerical work and maintaining contacts with clients, to use email for communication with overseas and local clients. The manager has also introduced a centralised information system for the organisational database management system. The information that is kept in the database management system includes customer information, purchase orders, accounts, inventory and manufacturing. The organisation's information system is accredited with ISO 9002. The manager has stated that it is important for his company to present itself as a high-technology organisation by employing the use of network computing and the Internet for communicating and exchanging information with clients and suppliers.

Figure C8.1 shows that the organisational structure of each of the organisations is flat. This is a result of the ownership and management being one and the same. Essentially, the company follows the very representative family business structure common throughout Chinese family businesses in Asia. The managers oversee every aspect of the organisation's activities. The immediate family members of the CEO (his sons and daughter-in-law) are the managers of each of the different organisations. However, the CEO, as patriarch of the family, is still the person who makes the final decisions and who oversees the whole management of the three companies.

At Smith Textiles, the CEO is still doing business in the same way that he has for the past 30 years. Many documents, such as purchase orders, invoices and payroll, are recorded manually. There are four PCs in the office, which are used for spreadsheets (accounting) and word-processing.

The business processes in the Smith and Nutty factories start after salespeople receive orders from their clients. Obtaining orders from clients is still conducted in an old-fashioned way. Salespeople use their personal contacts to acquire new clients and visit existing clients to make presentations showing materials and styles of fabrics. It is also common for these salespeople to drop in to visit clients for informal chats. This is one way that they strengthen their connections with clients and improve trust. Many businesses in Thailand operate in this manner, as this strengthens the relationships between them and their clients. Many business relationships turn into friendships, and this becomes an important part of business practice in Thailand. Therefore, salespeople become an integral part of the business for keeping good relationships with their clients. It is not surprising to see gifts being prepared for clients during Western New Year celebrations. The gifts vary from big cakes to expensive jewellery and white goods.

Every morning the salespeople and the CEO get together, keeping each other up to date with order details. The meeting is very informal as the CEO also receives information about the wellbeing of his clients, such as their general health, the state of business, and so on. This is the only time that the salespeople get together each day.

The salespeople work closely with the CEO and the three managers. Communication between the sales staff, the CEO and the three managers is fundamental for business planning, production planning, inventory ordering of raw materials and order delivery.

The orders are given to the managers. They then investigate the availability of the machines for knitting each customer's order. Machine availability and delivery times are estimated by consulting with the engineers who look after the factory machinery and its scheduling. After machine availability is established the job is placed in the production queue. The raw materials (cotton) required to meet the order are estimated. The inventory staff investigate the availability of colours and types of cotton required for the order. If there is not enough cotton, the inventory officer orders the cotton from suppliers. Communications with suppliers are mainly via telephone calls or fax. It is very difficult to predict when the inventory will arrive — it depends on the suppliers and availability. The world market for cotton also impacts on availability.

Up to this stage, some of the problems emerging for processing customer orders include estimating manufacturing and delivery time and estimating inventory delivery. Most of the time estimation comes from staff experienced in dealing with suppliers and clients. The estimates change when staff encounter difficulties or delay from suppliers. Staff then communicate with clients and rearrange a new delivery time.

One of the major problems is machine breakdowns. The knitting machines are imported from Japan, Germany and Taiwan. The suppliers of the knitting machines are located in Bangkok. However, many of their specialised technicians are located at their company headquarters in Tokyo, Frankfurt and Taipei. The companies need to contact their respective agencies for assistance when the knitting machines break down. The agencies then need to contact their headquarters and ascertain the availability of technicians. Then the technician has to fly to Bangkok for consultations and to fix the knitting machine. If any parts need to be ordered, this delays the delivery time to fulfil customer orders. The whole schedule for every knitting machine then needs to be rearranged.

Within the organisation, communication between the sales staff and CEO/manager (to look at the planning process), the engineer (to estimate production time), the inventory manager (to order supplies of raw materials) and the engineer again (for maintenance), is a complex process. The son in charge of Ni-Ke-Matsu factory is trying to put these processes into an IT framework but is having difficulties with the old-fashioned practices of the CEO, who is comfortable with the 'old ways'.

Delivery of products is also difficult to estimate and thus creates problems when trying to advise clients exactly when the products will arrive. As mentioned earlier, the delivery date is estimated based on staff experience and intuition. However, there is no way to estimate the exact date of delivery until production is finished.

After each roll of cotton fabric is produced, it is quality checked for damage, oil stains, punctures and consistency of colour. This process may take up to four days, depending on the amount of checking that needs to be done. After the quality checking process is completed, the invoice is generated manually. Each roll of fabric has to be weighed and noted on the invoice for verification at the customer's site.

Generating invoices is sometimes tricky. Most of the time, invoices include the total shipment. However, many customers, especially those who are 'preferred customers' and who have a very close relationship with the CEO, are issued with an invoice without the total price, as this is negotiated later or prior to delivery. The customers then fill in the total amount of the invoice. This process is very much based on trust and for the past 30 years the CEO has never experienced any dishonesty from his 'preferred customers'. Trust and honesty are highly valued in Thailand when conducting business. Communication and connections form the basis and stability of this trust.

It is clear that there are many problems with the company's existing systems. The three organisations want to be able to exchange information between them and also to improve inter- and intra-organisational communication between staff and customers. The CEO recognises that the current processes at Nutty Factory and Smith Textile are cumbersome and need improvement via the use of new applications and information technology.

QUESTIONS

1. How could an ERP system improve inter-organisational communication and data exchange between the three companies?
2. How could a CRM system be used to improve communications with the company's clients?
3. Could a CRM system achieve the same level of trust and good relationships that the three companies currently have with their clients?
4. Would the remote worker environment be suitable for the sales staff?
5. Do you think a tightly integrated system like an ERP system will allow the companies to process invoices the way they prefer?

Questions

1. Visit SAP's web site on customer relationship management (www.sap.com/solutions/crm/) and investigate how SAP's software can be used to achieve CRM in organisations.
2. What are the strengths and weaknesses of using the Web for organisational communication?
3. How can an organisation use an intranet to achieve knowledge sharing among its employees?
4. How can an intranet be used to prevent information overload in an organisation?
5. How can an ERP system be used to achieve e-business with supply chain management?

Suggested | reading

Bayles, D. 1998, *Extranets: Building the Business-to-Business Web*, Prentice Hall, New Jersey.

Department of Foreign Affairs and Trade 1999, *Driving Forces on the New Silk Road: The Use of Electronic Commerce by Australian Businesses*, Commonwealth of Australia, Canberra.

Kalakota, R. and Robinson, M. 1999, *E-Business: Roadmap for Success*, Addison-Wesley Longman, United States.

Kosiur, D. 1997, *Understanding Electronic Commerce: How Online Transactions Can Grow Your Business*, Microsoft Press, United States.

Lamond, D., Daniels, K. and Standen, P. 1997, 'Virtual working or working virtually? An overview of contextual and behavioural issues in teleworking', *Proceedings of the Fourth International Meeting of the Decision Sciences Institute, Decision Sciences Institute*, Sydney.

Lamond, D., Standen, P. and Daniels, K. 1997, 'Contexts, cultures and forms of tele-working', *Proceedings of the ANZAM conference*, Melbourne.

Norris, G., Hurley, J. R., Hartley, K. M., Dunleavy, J. R. and Balls, J. D. 2000, *E-Business and ERP: Transforming the Enterprise*, John Wiley & Sons, New York.

O'Leary, D. E. 2000, *Enterprise Resource Planning Systems: Systems, Life Cycle, Electronic Commerce, and Risk*, Cambridge University Press, Cambridge, MA.

Pfaffenberger, B. 1998, *Building a Strategic Extranet*, IDG Books, United States.

Phillips, M. 1997, *Behind Australia's Most Successful Websites*, Bookman, Melbourne.

End | notes

1. Newton, S. 1999, 'Electronic Business: Critical Success Factors for Implementation – A Case Study of ACME Connectors', Collecter99 Conference, Wellington, New Zealand, 29 November.
2. Kosiur, D. 1997, *Understanding Electronic Commerce: How Online Transactions Can Grow Your Business*, Microsoft Press, United States, p. 229.
3. Grimming, R. 1999, 'Booksellers buy the digital title', Computers/Cutting Edge, *Australian*, 26 October, www.news.com.au.
4. Tapscott, D. 1996, *The Digital Economy*, McGraw-Hill, New York, p. 54.
5. Carmel, E. 1999, *Global Software Teams: Collaborating Across Borders and Time Zones*, Prentice Hall PTR, New Jersey.
6. Kalakota, R. and Robinson, M. 1999, *E-Business: Roadmap for Success*, Addison-Wesley Longman, United States, p. 225.
7. Pfaffenberger, B. 1998, *Building a Strategic Extranet*, IDG Books, United States, p. 70.
8. www.newsbyte.com.
9. Braue, D. 1999, 'E-mail features that make every post a winner', Jargon, *Sydney Morning Herald*, 28 September, p. 32.
10. Dertouzos, M. 1997, *What Will Be*, Harper Edge, New York, p. 89.
11. Lowe, S. 1999, 'This mail may knock twice', *Sydney Morning Herald*, 23 September, p. 11.
12. Rosencrance, L. 2001, 'Monitoring employee e-mail, Web use escalates', *Computerworld*, 9 July, www.nwfusion.com/news/2001/0709email.html, accessed July 2002.
13. Rosen, J. 2002, *The Unwanted Gaze: The Destruction of Privacy in America*, Random House, New York.
14. Braue, D. op. cit., p. 32.
15. Cruickshank, D. 1996, *The Intranet Reinvents Business*, www.sigraf.co.yu/sigraf/oblasti/sgi/www/intmain.html.

16. Tiwana, A. 2001, *The Essential Guide to Knowledge Management: E-business and CRM Applications*, Prentice Hall, New Jersey.
17. Ibid., p. 35.
18. Tebbutt, D. 1999, 'E-commerce to save General Motors $18 bn', *Australian*, Computers/Net News, 12 October, p. 49, www.news.com.au.
19. Lamond, D., Standen, P. and Daniels, K. 1997, 'Contexts, cultures and forms of teleworking', *Proceedings of the ANZAM conference*, Melbourne.
20. Lowe, S. 1997, 'Information technology – overload control', *Sydney Morning Herald*, 30 September, p. 6.
21. Ibid., p. 6.
22. Dertouzos, G. 1997, *What Will Be*, Harper Edge, United States, p. 204.
23. Malling, P. 2000, 'Information systems and human activity in Nepal', in C. Avgerou and G. Walsham, *Information Technology in Context: Studies from the Perspective of Developing Countries*, Aldershot, Ashgate, UK.
24. The Digital Divide Network 2002, 'Digitial Divide basics', www.digitaldividenetwork.org, accessed June 2002.

CHAPTER 9

Taxation of Internet commerce

You will have mastered the material in this chapter when you can:

- appreciate the impact of Internet commerce on the administration of the Australian taxation system and the implications for Australia's tax base
- assess the extent to which the government's potential responses to the growth in Internet commerce are affected by international agreements or conventions
- research the policy approaches being taken by other countries and the scope for international cooperation.

'If you are a state and you want more money, Internet access is a very juicy target.'

Grover Norquist, president of the anti-tax group Americans for Tax Reform, in T. Wolverton 2001, 'Beware the Internet tax man', *ZDNet News*, 29 October, zdnet.com.au.

'Taxation relies on order and certainty. It is built on concepts such as residence, source and tangible goods. Cyberspace, however, has no place for such quaint notions.'

L. Schmidt 1997, 'The tax man's nightmare', *Business Review Weekly*, 24 February, p. 1.

INTRODUCTION

Geographical boundaries have been used for centuries to define the limits of power that governments have over people. It is taken as self-evident that laws made in Australia will affect the people of Australia and have little or no impact on the citizens of other countries. The relationship between a geographical boundary and a legal boundary falls into four areas: power, effects, legitimacy and notice.[1]

Power is the ability to enforce laws, and the level of power asserted by a single government is limited to actions that are acceptable to the peoples within its geographical boundaries. Civil strife and war can result where governments try to exert unacceptable power on their citizens or try to operate outside their geographical boundaries.

The actions of a person or a business in traditional commerce have a greater *effect* on people and things that are physically closer to them. Hence, a restaurant in Sydney can be called 'Chinese Garden' and will not be in conflict with a restaurant of the same name in France. But if another 'Chinese Garden' restaurant opened in the same Sydney street, this could be a problem.

The *legitimacy* of a government's power resides with the people who live in the geographical area controlled by the government.

Geographical boundaries are a convenient means of signalling to people that they are moving from one jurisdiction to another. Legal systems contain the idea of *constructive notice*, that in crossing a geographical boundary people become subject to the laws of the country or state even without being specifically told.

In many countries it has been accepted that geographical boundaries result in two tiers of control, one at the local level, say, at state level, as in Australia and the United States, and one at the federal level. In recent decades there has been another layer of legislative agreement and enforcement above the federal level where countries have cooperated within larger frameworks. For example, the United Nations is accepted by its member countries as having the power to override national jurisdictions in extreme circumstances. The European Union has added a layer of legislation above that of its member countries. However, in all the centuries of jurisdiction geography has been used to determine the limits of that jurisdiction. But in this new millennium the traditional rules are being exploded by the Internet and its lack of geographical boundaries.[2]

The Internet poses a threat to traditional governing structures in terms of information that is accessible to people and to the taxation systems that provide governments with their sources of revenue. The jurisdictional issues that arise from the Internet and e-commerce are complex. In particular, the problem of taxation across e-commerce is complex:

> E-commerce represents a new business model. As such, it creates some challenges to tax systems that were designed with a different model in mind. Two key reasons help explain why e-commerce raises tax issues:
> 1. Location — Existing tax systems tend to determine tax consequences based on where the taxpayer is physically located. The e-commerce model enables businesses to operate with very few physical locations.

2. Nature of products — E-commerce allows for some types of products, such as newspapers and music CDs, to be delivered in digitized (intangible) form, rather than in tangible form. Digitized products may not be subject to sales tax in some states. Also the ability to deliver digitized products, as well as services over the Internet also reduces the need for physical locations, thus creating fewer taxing points.[3]

The failure of so many dot.coms may have reduced the urgency to resolve the taxation problems of e-commerce during this respite in the volume of e-commerce trade, but the underlying problems remain and need to be resolved before e-commerce becomes a dominant trading platform.

BACKGROUND HISTORY

In 1997, the Australian Taxation Office (ATO) published the *Discussion Report on Tax and the Internet.* The ATO's concern has been mirrored around the world and electronic commerce issues have been raised at many international forums. The Organisation for Economic Cooperation and Development (OECD) has conducted three major international conferences to address Internet issues, including tax issues.

In January 1999 a technical advisory group (TAG) was set up by the OECD 'to examine the characterisation of various types of electronic commerce payments under tax conventions'.[4] The TAG identified 26 categories of transactions and has begun the task of identifying issues relevant to the OECD Model Tax Convention.

In 1999 the ATO produced *Tax and the Internet: Second Report of the Australian Taxation Office,*[5] which delivers the results of discussions with business representatives, academics and government agencies. The resulting action plan outlines some immediate action that can and should be taken to enable the ATO to meet the challenges and take advantage of the opportunities afforded by the emerging digital economy.

In July 1999, the Australian government passed tax reform legislation that set in motion the issuing of an Australian Business Number (ABN) to each Australian business as part of the Goods and Services Tax (GST) registration process. A digital certificate is issued as part of the registration process and enables all businesses to positively identify themselves to agencies such as the ATO. Government departments are monitoring the ABNs to ensure they are up to date.[6] The new Australian GST package began operation in July 2000 and mirrors the operation of similar taxes such as VAT (Value Added Tax) in the United Kingdom, which has been in operation for some years.

The Australian Society of Certified Practising Accountants is supportive of **tax neutrality**, which rejects the imposition of new or additional taxes on electronic transactions. Neutrality requires that the tax system treat similar income equally, regardless of whether it is earned through electronic or existing means.

However, Australia's fragile tax base is under a lot of pressure and massive changes are being made to our taxation system. Many countries are grappling with what to do about taxing Internet businesses. There exists the possibility of individuals being able to set up accounts with cyberbanks in tax havens to circumvent the international banking system. In such a scenario, the transfer of currency could be completed directly between the cyberbanks and account holders through personal computers, leaving no traceable information trail for revenue officials. Tax evasion on a wide scale will be easier and more difficult to catch when carried out over the Internet.[7]

The Australian government wants to be seen to be encouraging innovation and improvement of our business infrastructure. However, certain businesses will see the Internet as a way of operating without bureaucratic red tape. Companies will be tempted to choose countries that offer them legal advantages such as bank secrecy and low or no tax. Australian and international taxation laws are being examined as they relate to corporate and individual residency, **tax avoidance** and **tax evasion**, **money laundering** and technology transfer.

Some of the questions that governments in countries such as Australia are trying to answer include:
- If cyberbanks are set up, how will they be regulated so that the Australian government does not lose potential taxation revenue?
- How will the jurisdictional issues be determined for the levying of taxes, with regard to electronic payments over the Internet?
- What will be the likely impact of offshore electronic credit facilities on government taxation revenues?

AUSTRALIAN BUSINESS INTERNET USAGE

The number of Australian businesses using computers, accessing the Internet and using web sites or home pages continues to grow. Computer use has shown steady growth, rising from 49 per cent of Australian businesses in 1993–1994 to 84 per cent of businesses at the end of June 2001. The proportion of businesses with a web presence has grown rapidly, rising from 6 per cent in 1997–1998, to 16 per cent in 1999–2000, to 22 per cent in 2000–2001. The proportion of businesses with Internet access has also risen rapidly, from 29 per cent in 1997–1998, to 56 per cent in 1999–2000, to 69 per cent in 2000–2001.[8]

This level of information technology usage is supported by Australia's expenditure on information technology and telecommunications (IT&T). The Australian Bureau of Statistics special article, 'Information technology and telecommunications in Australia (1999–2000)',[9] demonstrates that Australia's IT&T expenditure in 1998–1999 was around $62 billion (or US$39 billion). This level of expenditure represents over 10 per cent of Australia's GDP and moves Australia ahead of Columbia, Sweden, the United Kingdom and New Zealand.

However, this spending is not even across all businesses and IT&T usage within different industry sectors varies considerably (see table 9.1). The proportion of Australian businesses using computers or with access to the Internet was lowest in the accommodation, café and restaurant sector (71 per cent and 53 per cent, respectively) and was highest in the electricity, gas and water sector (95 per cent and 89 per cent, respectively).

TABLE 9.1	IT&T USAGE ACROSS VARIOUS INDUSTRY SECTORS			
INDUSTRY	NUMBER OF BUSINESSES ('000)	BUSINESSES USING COMPUTERS (%)	BUSINESSES WITH INTERNET ACCESS (%)	BUSINESSES WITH WEB PRESENCE (%)
Electricity, gas and water supply	—	95	89	44
Property and business services	164	93	85	25
Finance and insurance	26	90	81	22
Wholesale trade	48	89	77	33
Retail trade	119	78	57	22

SOURCE: Australian Bureau of Statistics 2002, *Business Use of Information Technology, Australia*, Cat. No. 8129.0.

AUSTRALIAN HOUSEHOLD INTERNET USAGE

In April 2002, the National Office for the Information Economy released statistics regarding home Internet usage (see figures 9.1 and 9.2). According to this report, an estimated 52 per cent of Australians are online, placing Australia equal seventh with Norway.[10]

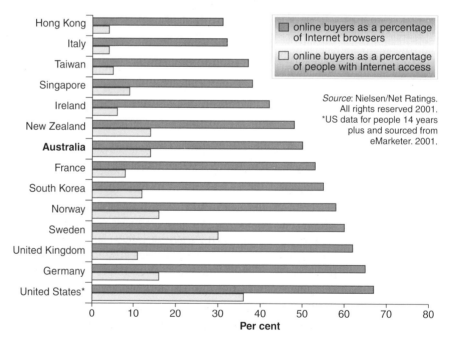

FIGURE 9.1: Percentage of people 16 years and over purchasing online in the six months to September 2001

SOURCE: National Office for the Information Economy 2002, *The Current State of Play: Australia's Scorecard*, April, p. 31.

The number of registered users of online banking in Australia almost doubled from 2001 to 2002, reaching 5.23 million at the end of March 2002, up from 2.77 million in 2001.[11] Overall, Australia is ranked eighth in terms of the take-up of online shopping (see figure 9.1). Countries ahead of Australia in terms of online purchasing penetration levels are the United States, Germany, the United Kingdom, Sweden, Norway, South Korea and France (taken from the combined scores in figure 9.1).[12]

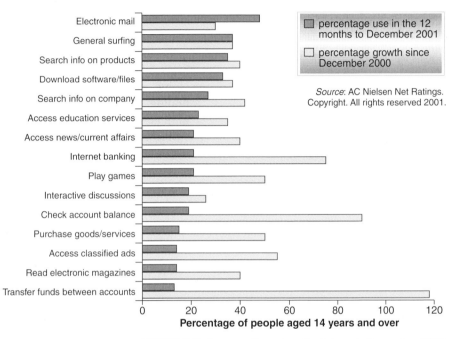

FIGURE 9.2: Reasons for using the Internet, December 2001

SOURCE: National Office for the Information Economy 2002, *The Current State of Play: Australia's Scorecard*, April, p. 32.

INTERNATIONAL PROGRESS IN INTERNET COMMERCE

The development of technology and, in particular, online services, has resulted in the breakdown of geographical restrictions allowing consumers easy access to services provided abroad. Within this region, Australia's main competition is with Singapore, Hong Kong and the United States. Other economies such as Malaysia and Taiwan are also developing similar strategies to develop online financial service facilities.[13]

During the 1990s the Singaporean government implemented a strategy to attract financial services, other business service enterprises and the regional headquarters of overseas multinationals by offering incentives such as low taxation, infrastructure, co-investment opportunities, transparent regulation and an educated, disciplined workforce. The Singaporean government intends to take Singapore's stake further to become Asia's prime financial hub. Singapore is building a digital infrastructure that will provide *disciplined broadband Internet access*. This initiative, referred to as 'Singapore One', aims to establish Singapore as an e-commerce hub for Asia, connecting the three million residents of the island to the Internet.

Hong Kong established its Innovation and Technology Fund in order to solicit innovative research and development proposals. It is hoped that the proposals will help Hong Kong to better utilise the Internet for electronic commerce and develop a high level of security on wireless Internet communications.[14]

Malaysia has created the Multimedia Super Corridor, in which two 'smart cities' are being developed: Putrajaya and Cyberjaya. The Multimedia Super Corridor is 50 kilometres long, stretching south from Kuala Lumpur, and aims to attract leading technology-led companies to Malaysia. Putrajaya will be the new government and administrative capital of Malaysia and it is where the concept of 'electronic government' will be introduced. ('Electronic government', or 'e-government', refers to making the Internet the main means of enabling access to government information, services and processes.) Cyberjaya will be the centre for multimedia industries, a multimedia university, research and development centres, and operational headquarters for multinational companies that want to run their global manufacturing and trading activities using multimedia technology.[15]

Australia also has undertaken a number of initiatives, including the establishment of the Australian Centre for Global Finance (AXISS Australia), the creation of the National Office for the Information Economy (www.noie.gov.au), whole-of-government approaches to online delivery, and initiatives such as the Building on IT Strengths program. AXISS aims to make Australia a leading financial service centre in the Asia–Pacific time zone.[16]

BARRIERS TO E-COMMERCE

One of the main reasons cited by consumers for not using the Internet to make purchases is their perception of the lack of security and the possibility that their credit card details will be used fraudulently.

Businesses have to overcome the barrier of being able to accept payments in different currencies and ensure that payments will be authorised by the credit card company or banking institution. In October 2001, an Australian company, Pure Commerce, won the award for Innovation in E-Commerce.[17] Pure Commerce enables Internet merchants to accept payments securely in all major currencies and using international credit cards. It provides services to protect against Internet fraud and foreign exchange risk and also supports e-commerce over mobile devices.

Through innovative technology consumers and businesses are gaining more confidence in global e-commerce transactions, encouraging a dramatic rise in commercial transactions that are not restricted by geographical boundaries. Other innovations are increasing the variety of payment methods, money transfer and settlement methods, and transaction protocols. The web site ntrg.cs.tcd.ie/mepeirce/Project/oninternet.html summarises some of these methods, which are shown in table 9.2.

These are just some examples of the enormous variety of technologies supporting global payments, settlements and money transfers. Within this complex financial environment taxation authorities need to consider if and how they will align e-commerce with traditional revenue collection.

TABLE 9.2	EXAMPLES OF PAYMENT SYSTEMS ON THE INTERNET
PAYMENT SYSTEM	**FEATURES**
ACH Datasoft	Allows online payment from a US bank account using the automated clearing house (ACH) bank network
Bank Internet Payment System (BIPS)	A non-proprietary protocol for enabling payment through banks over the Internet
CashBox	Payment management system that supports Internet loading and spending of a variety of Internet payment types, including Mondex
CheckSpace	A user-to-user account-based scheme, linked to a US bank account, with a cheque-like Web interface. Targeted at small businesses, it allows email payment requests/invoices
Clickshare	A publishing system to track movements and settle charges for digital transactions
Cybersource	Offers real-time credit card processing
Ecash	A fully anonymous electronic cash system, using Chaum's blind signatures
eCharge Phone	Allows purchases to be charged to a local telephone bill
E-coin	A token-based micropayment system, which uses a client wallet plugin
Electronic Funds Clearinghouse	Provides payment transmission and intake conduits over the Internet.
GlobalConnect	A payment provider based in the Netherlands, provides cross-border collection of consumer payments made using local payment cards, bank transfers and cheque payment options
Jalda	An account-based system for making both micropayments and macropayments from any IP device
Mondex	Smart-card based payment system
PayCash	A fully anonymous electronic cash system from Russia
Proton	A stored value smart card system (e-purse) originally issued in Belgium as an alternative to physical cash; it is now being adapted for Internet payments
WebMoney	An account-based system with some anonymity, allowing transfer between temporary accounts using wallet software

SOURCE: Network and Telecommunications Research Group 2001, 'Payment mechanisms designed for the Internet', ntrg.cs.tcd.ie/mepeirce/Project/oninternet.html, accessed July 2002.

AUSTRALIA AND TAXATION

Even before the electronic revolution, it had been apparent in Australia for many years that our tax system needed reform. Unfortunately, experts have not been able to agree on how to achieve such reform. Australia has a reputation for having high marginal income tax rates because our top rate of 48.5 per cent, including the Medicare levy, applies to incomes of $50 000 and above. By comparison, in the United States the top rate is 39.6 per cent and it applies from incomes of $US260 000 or A$410 000 and above.

Many Australian politicians have found the issue of tax reform to be a 'poisoned chalice'. Joh Bjelke-Petersen, ex-Premier of Queensland, advocated a flat tax in the 1980s and was spectacularly unsuccessful in his attempt to get into Federal Parliament. The then leader of the Federal Opposition, Dr John Hewson, advocated a GST in the 1993 election and was soundly beaten. In 1998, the Prime Minister, John Howard, won his second term of government after advocating a GST of 10 per cent, but was returned with a significantly reduced majority. GST was introduced in July 2000 and is now part of the Australian taxation system.

However, reports are surfacing that Australia's tax system has become so complex and the paperwork so overwhelming that even tax agents are pulling out of doing tax returns. Tax agents are still struggling with the system two years after the GST was introduced.[18]

Australia's Board of Taxation is expected to present its review of international taxation arrangements by the end of 2002. The director of tax services at Hall Chadwick, Keith Burchill, says the government needs to renegotiate the double tax agreements it has with other countries, including Russia and the United States. He says withholding tax rates on foreign investors also need to be reduced to attract more foreign investment to Australia.[19]

TAX IMPLICATIONS OF INTERNET COMMERCE

In order to consider the impact of Internet commerce on the tax system, it is necessary to examine the nature of the liability imposed by a particular tax, whether it be income tax, sales tax or fringe benefits tax.

- **Income tax**: Income tax is an aggregate tax, whereby the liability is arrived at after adding up all items of assessable income and subtracting all allowable deductions. Income tax imposes a personal liability on the person who derives the income. Thus, personal identity is extremely important. In cases of taxpayer defaults in the payment of income tax, the identity, whereabouts and financial position of the taxpayer are all relevant.
- **Sales tax**: Sales tax is an example of transaction tax, whereby liability results from an imposed tax on particular types of transaction. A consumer buying a car, for example, is subject to a sales tax on that car and the advantage for the government is that the car dealer collects the tax for the government.

- **Goods and services tax (GST)**: In Australia, the GST is set at 10 per cent and is added to fees and the sale of business assets. Businesses collect the GST on behalf of the Australian Taxation Office and businesses must pay GST on expenditure such as overheads and capital expenditure. The net amount of GST collected (that is, collection minus GST on business expenditure) is paid over to the ATO.[20]
- **Fringe benefits tax**: Some taxpayers seek to minimise their taxation burden by using flexible salary packages. In such a case, a person might have his or her children's school fees paid directly to a school or parking fees paid directly to the parking station. This money therefore does not appear as salary and lowers the person's tax burden. Obviously, the ATO is interested in ways in which the Internet could be used to help minimise taxable income.

TAXES ON INTERNET PURCHASES AND INCOME GENERATED BY INTERNET PURCHASES

Businesses

Applying sales taxes to Internet purchases is a very complex area. It depends on where the trader is located, where the customer is located and where intermediaries are located. This area of taxation is being grappled with across the world and is a very difficult taxation area to control. For example, in New Zealand traders with international customers are advised:

> For GST purposes if you want to zero-rate sales made to customers overseas you'll need to obtain sufficient evidence that the customer is outside New Zealand and therefore that the transaction can be zero rated. The email address by itself does not constitute sufficient evidence that the customer is outside New Zealand.[21]

Similarly, an online business has to be aware of income taxes in other countries:

> It is unlikely that simply selling goods electronically through a web site located in New Zealand to customers in another country will make you liable to tax in that country.
> But if you carry on any other activities in that other country you may have a taxable presence there. For example, if you own and operate a server in that country you may be liable for tax there.[22]

Most countries seek to tax residents on all income regardless of its source, while non-residents are taxed only on income derived in the taxing authority's country of jurisdiction. Otherwise, such a situation could lead to inequities where residents are taxed on the same income twice. International treaties exist to cover these types of problems but the rules will have to be modified to take the Internet into account. International cooperation on allocation of taxing rights and **compliance** measures to secure those rights will be crucial.[23]

The ATO maintains its interest in commercial transactions over the Internet, but it has recognised the following difficulties inherent in the commercial usage of the Internet:

- A web site can be moved quickly from one location to another, even to another country. Cheap hardware can be discarded or disposed of quickly.
- 'Stock on hand' can be merely a set of data files, which can be updated periodically and automatically from afar.
- Customer orders and payments can be handled by a back-end database system, with payments (electronic cash or credit card details) being channelled somewhere entirely unconnected with other parts of the site.
- A third party can deliver physical goods such as books or CDs on an agency basis.

Professor Tyree believes that international cooperation will be vital, but points out that it is a certainty that some small countries will establish 'computer money havens', just as they have established tax havens and bank havens.[24]

It is clear that taxation authorities recognise the difficulties inherent in the commercial usage of the Internet.[25] The use of a web site allows for the material value of items such as software, data and goodwill in a business to be both indefinite and mobile. The ATO may find it difficult to use its full powers under ss. 263 or 264 of the *Income Tax Act* to assess the income of a commercial web site because:

- components of the web site do not have to be physically co-located
- logically integrated business operations can be spread over a number of places.

Consumers

From the consumer's point of view, there is no tax advantage or penalty in Australia simply because they make purchases over the Internet. GST will be charged on goods and services bought over the Internet just as if they had been bought by mail order (see table 9.3). For example, Standards Australia sells all Australian, ISO and IEC standards through its web shop (www.standards.com.au/catalogue/). Clients can choose an instant PDF download or order a hard copy that is delivered by mail. There is a 10 per cent discount on PDF downloads, no mailing costs and the Standard publication arrives within seconds. Standards Australia accepts all major credit cards and GST is added whether the client downloads or collects via snail mail. However, this premise is only valid if the trader and the consumer are within Australia, and for many Internet purchases the consumer is dealing with an organisation outside of Australia.

The information in figure 9.3 is taken from the Australian Customs Service web site (www.customs.gov.au) and is valid as at July 2002.

In addition to the duties imported goods may be subject to one or more indirect taxes. These indirect taxes comprise the GST, the wine equalisation tax and the luxury car tax. Taking the GST as an example, GST is applied at

10 per cent of the value of the taxable importation. The value of the taxable importation is the sum of:

- the customs value of the imported goods
- any customs duty payable
- the amount paid or payable to transport and insure the goods.

It is clear that for physical goods purchased over the Internet the point of import is a fairly straightforward taxation and control point for countries to focus on.

TABLE 9.3	EXAMPLES OF DIFFERING RATES OF DUTY AND SALES TAX FOR GOODS BOUGHT OVER THE INTERNET			
GOODS CATEGORY	**DUTY RATE (%)**	**SALES TAX (%)**	**COMBINED RATE (%)**	**GOODS VALUE AT WHICH $50 MINIMUM COMBINED DUTY AND SALES IS EXCEEDED***
Clothing	34	0	34.00	$147.06
Car parts	15	22	45.36	$110.23
Jewellery	5	32	45.32	$110.33
Photographic materials	5	22	32.72	$152.81

* Goods that are below certain set value limits and have a combined sales tax and duty less than $50 are exempt from sales tax and duty.

SOURCE: Department of Communication, Information Technology and the Arts 2002, *Shopping on the Internet: Facts For Consumers #4*, last updated 28 April, www.dcita.gov.au, accessed July 2002.

Taxable importations

Are Internet downloads taxable importations?

No, because there has not been an importation of goods. [Section 13-5]

The downloading of something is a taxable supply if the supply is connected with Australia, there is consideration, the enterprise test is met and the supplier is registered or required to be registered. It is connected with Australia if the supplier makes the supply through an enterprise that they carry on in Australia. [Section 9-25(5)(b)]

The downloading of something where the supply is not connected with Australia may still be a taxable supply in some circumstances. The circumstances are:

- the recipient of the supply acquires the thing supplied solely or partly for the purpose of an enterprise that the recipient carries on in Australia; and
- the recipient is registered or required to be registered; and
- the supply is for consideration; and
- the thing is going to be used solely or partly for making input taxed supplies or for a private or domestic purpose.

In these circumstances, the GST is payable by the recipient. This is known as 'reverse charging' [Division 84].

FIGURE 9.3: Australian Customs Service information on Internet downloads

SOURCE: Australian Customs Service 2002, *Customs Tax Reform Issues Log*, www.customs.gov.au/taxref/issues.htm#TaxImp, accessed July 2002.

Digitised goods

As more goods become digitised, for example books, newspaper articles, music, films and software, they can be directly purchased over the Internet and become vulnerable to GST avoidance. In this environment tax administrators face three main problems:

- ascertaining when a transaction occurs
- determining where the place of supply is
- attaching a value to the transaction.

The April 2000 report of the US Advisory Commission on Electronic Commerce recommended the following:

- a five-year moratorium extension of the 1998 three-year moratorium on new Internet-based taxes
- elimination of the 3 per cent federal tax on Internet service providers
- special tax exempt status for goods sold in digital form.[26]

It is clear that Internet e-commerce presents tax and customs authorities with a series of problems:

- no central control, as the Internet pays little or no regard to national boundaries
- weaknesses in the domain name system, which mean that taxation and customs authorities have trouble determining the location of the business behind the web site and the identity of the person controlling it
- the absence of an audit trail, as the untraceable use of an Internet site is relatively easy to arrange
- paperless electronic invoicing and receipting, which will be a feature of e-commerce
- increase in the number of digitised goods – in Europe, digitised goods are classified as services and are subject to VAT (sales tax)
- reconfigurable goods, such as the integration of downloaded software into a physical product
- the increased number of imports such as books in small packages, leading to an increased workload for customs officials
- distortion of competition, where duty free goods are cheaper than locally sold goods (as is happening in Australia with books, CDs and fishing tackle)
- prohibition, restrictions and surveillance – the World Trade Organisation has declared goods supplied over the Internet to be services and, as such, they are not within the purview of customs; however, the Internet may be used to acquire pornographic material that would contravene customs laws if imported in physical form.

Internet gambling

Australians are known to enjoy gambling. Indeed, every November, the nation almost comes to a standstill to watch the Melbourne Cup. Around the world countries have been trying to formulate legislation to govern

Internet gambling. In October 1999, the special committee set up by the Australian federal government to review gambling across Australia stated in its conclusion:

2.127 Australia has established itself as a market leader in the emerging online gambling industry. Locally based operators are experiencing rapid growth mainly due to increasing gambling activity from overseas based gamblers. Currently Australian gamblers comprise a small proportion of the online gambling market.

2.128 The types of gambling activities that the Internet will allow are potentially unlimited. However, currently, most gambling is based on traditional activities such as casino type games and sports betting.

2.129 There is evidence that more operators will enter into the online gambling industry, as Australian governments continue to issue appropriate licences. Further, technologies are being developed and implemented to expand the types of gambling activities that will become available. Consequently it is likely that the industry will undergo significant change in the short to medium term.[27]

The report listed the current online gambling operators in Australia, shown in table 9.4.

TABLE 9.4	ONLINE GAMING AND BETTING IN AUSTRALIA		
OPERATOR	**LICENCE**	**TYPE OF GAMBLING**	**DATE STARTED/LICENSED**
Canbet	ACT	Racing and sports wagering	November 1998
Capital Sports	ACT	Racing and sports wagering	1996
Centrebet	NT	Sports wagering	1992, Internet approval 1996
City Index	ACT	Racing and sports wagering	1996
Davidson Sports Betting	NSW	Racing and sports wagering	1 June 1999
GOCORP Limited	QLD	Casino gaming	June 1999
International All Sports	NT	Racing and sports wagering	1997, Internet approved 1998
Lasseters Casino	NT	Casino gaming	12 April 1999
Megasports (ACT)	ACT	Racing and sports wagering	February 1999
Network Gaming	TAS	Casino gaming	1999
OzBet (WA TAB)	WA	Racing and sports wagering	July 1997
NetTAB (NSW TAB)	NSW	Racing and sports wagering	1998
TAB Qld	QLD	Racing wagering	1999

SOURCE: Senate Information Technologies Committee 2000, *Netbets: A Review of Online Gambling in Australia*, Commonwealth of Australia, March, www.aph.gov.au/senate/committee/it_ctte/gambling/ChapTwo.doc.

For many operators the tax regime influences where they will base their operations. In reporting to the Senate committee Centrebet confirmed that it would continue to operate out of Alice Springs because 'the advantages of operating in the Northern Territory, which include a competitive wagering tax rate for sports betting and business orientated regulators... are required to offset the disadvantages of remaining in Alice Springs [e.g. recruiting skilled staff]'.[28]

In other countries, online gambling is meeting with a mixed response.

- In India, the Maharashtra government has granted permission for the Royal Western India Turf Club to introduce online gambling on horse racing.[29]
- In Denmark, the Danish taxation minister established a working group to investigate updating and unifying Denmark's existing gaming legislation to cater for Internet gambling. The working group was also asked to investigate the possibilities of keeping the Danish online gambling industry out of foreign hands.[30] Details about the working group's report may be found at www.skm.dk/pub1/internetspil/english/kap7eng.htm.
- In North Korea, an Internet lottery site went live in April 2002. South Korea was planning to block the site due to its links with the North. (It is illegal for South Koreans to make contact with North Koreans and the two countries are in a technical state of war.)[31]
- In the United Kingdom from late 2002, lottery players will be able to buy tickets over the Internet. In March 2002, the UK government released a report that proposes the regulation of the online gambling and gaming sector.[32]

As reported by Rose in *The Law of Internet Gambling*,[33] online gambling can be fraught with problems for the consumer and the trader. For example, smaller countries, often island nations in the Caribbean and South Pacific, have issued licences, usually to foreigners. Government background checks of these gaming operations are often sporadic or non-existent. For example, Grenada sold an exclusive licence to one operator, Sports International, and allowed that operator to sell sub-licences without having to check the applicant's background. Players have little guarantee that these gaming operations are run honestly or that they will be paid if they win, or even if they will get their front money returned.

INTERNATIONAL RESPONSE TO INTERNET COMMERCE: A REVIEW

Australia is not alone in trying to set up guidelines to cope with the impact of Internet commerce. In 1996, Australia, Canada and the United States jointly produced a paper for the Organisation for Economic Cooperation and Development called *Implications of the Communications Revolution for Tax Policy and Administration*, ref. CFA (96) 46. In the Framework Document, issued by former President Clinton in July 1997, the United States backed a tariff-free approach to the sale of electronic goods and services over the Internet. It does not apply to tangible products ordered and paid for over the Internet but delivered via conventional means.

Germany toyed with the idea of taxing business sites by way of a licence, much like the television licensing system as used in the United Kingdom. However, they rejected this taxation model in August 1997. In Europe, Internet retailers are supposed to collect VAT, which is similar to GST. The idea of a transmission tax has been put forward as preferable to taxing the 'value' of the almost intangible information. Belgium's Ministry put forward a Bit Tax proposal, whereby they would attempt to tax data travelling over their communication links. The Minister of Telecommunications in Belgium stated that the number of bits crossing Belgium's border would yield $10 billion in annual tax revenue (about 4 per cent of Belgium's GDP).[34]

US response

According to Nicolas Negroponte, Director of the Massachusetts Institute of Technology's Media Lab, tax regulation is the biggest issue facing the Internet for years.[35] In the United States, the *Framework for Electronic Commerce (Framework Document)*, which was issued by the authority of former President Clinton on 2 July 1997, looked at financial, legal and market access issues.[36] The United States supports a tariff-free approach to transactions involving electronic goods and services over the Internet, with the exception of tangible products ordered and paid for over the Internet but delivered via conventional means.

The United States proposes that Internet trading be placed under a universally agreed global framework, while many developing countries want the United Nations to control the Internet.[37] Ira Magaziner, President Clinton's top adviser on the electronic economy, outlined the US position at the Internet Industry Association of Australia (INTIAA) (now called the Internet Industry Association) annual conference in December 1997, namely:

- a tariff-free electronic commerce trading environment without new taxes
- minimally regulated secure electronic payment systems
- a common commercial code that accepts electronic signatures and other authentication procedures and that has a dispute resolution mechanism, liability exposure rules and access to registries of Internet users.

Magaziner put forward two possible ways to tax electronic transactions:

- introduce a corporate profits tax similar to the US taxation regime
- develop a smart card to automatically deduct sales taxes or value-added taxes at the time of a trade (this would require taxes to be internationally uniform) — the major advantage of this method would be that it ensures taxation authorities get 100 per cent of the sales tax revenue due compared with present sales tax revenue yields of about 60 per cent.[38]

The US position rules out any kind of new taxation of e-commerce transactions and no discriminatory taxation on the Internet; in other words, no new taxes on Internet access or Internet telephony. Again, developing countries are opposed to this as they often use state-owned telephone monopolies as a source of foreign currency. The Internet is therefore potentially valuable to such countries. The United States has the following Internet commerce strategy:

- create a predictable environment for industry by securing international agreement that there will be no censorship of the Web nor will there be discriminatory or overly bureaucratic ways of taxing the Internet
- create a predictable legal environment for the Internet on an international scale so that, for example, digital signatures in one country would be recognised in another.[39]

The above gives the impression that all is working well in the United States, but the reality is somewhat different. The US form of government, where government power is shared between the states and the national government, creates a legal environment in which businesses must deal not only with federal law but also with the law in each state in which they have customers. Standards for determining the constitutionality of state and local taxes have been set by the Supreme Court. To meet the constitutionality standard a state tax on interstate businesses must pass a four-part test (as seen in the *Complete Auto Transit, Inc v. Brady*, 430 US 274 (1977)). State taxation of interstate business must:

- tax only interstate activities with a sufficient connection to the taxing state
- be fairly apportioned to the taxpayer's activities in the taxing state
- not discriminate against interstate commerce
- be fairly related to the services provided by the state.[40]

Two well-known instances of imposing unconstitutional tax obligations are in the sales and use tax area. Twice the US Supreme Court has told states that tax collection obligations cannot be imposed on businesses that have no physical presence in their states. The states, led by the Multistate Tax Commission (an organisation of state tax administrators), engage in 'tax terrorism' according to Caldwell.[41] This consists of states claiming that existing legal precedents no longer apply, revising state standards and then forcing the companies to litigate the case all the way to the Supreme Court again. Thus, state laws, be they tax laws or other laws, that discriminate against interstate commerce will have a negative effect on the ability of electronic commerce businesses to access nationwide markets. Caldwell believes that the United States needs to create a single market environment in which companies can thrive.[42] The growth of electronic commerce necessitates a more nationwide and indeed global marketplace, which will force 'badly behaving' states to drop policies that discriminate against interstate commerce.

The US National Tax Associations Electronic Commerce Taxation Project

The original goal for the US National Tax Association's Electronic Commerce Taxation Project[43] was for industry and the states to develop a broadly available public report that identified and explored the issues in applying state and local taxes and fees to electronic commerce and that included recommendations to state and local officials regarding the application of such taxes and a model legislation designed to implement the recommendations of the project.[44] The government extended the moratorium on Internet tax up to November 2003.[45]

Caldwell believes that there are several remedies that Congress could implement to ensure that state and local governments do not impose unconstitutional forms of taxes on e-commerce companies. She recommends a remedy that works to prevent the collection of unconstitutional taxes such as denying attorney's fees in tax cases where the tax is found to be unconstitutional and ensuring the refund of taxes that have been declared unconstitutional.

Caldwell believes that in order for electronic commerce to develop to its fullest potential and provide consumers with the maximum benefit from the low-cost Internet marketplace, a national standard on state and local taxation of interstate businesses is required. Will state tax be 'roadkill on the information superhighway'?[46]

Canada's response

The Canadian government in its report, *The Canadian Electronic Commerce Strategy*, emphasised that the private sector has the lead role in the development and use of electronic commerce in Canada and it is the role of governments to support the private sector. It recommends three ways to provide this support:

1. Provide a supportive and responsive domestic policy environment for electronic commerce by ensuring consistent treatment of digital and paper-based commerce.
2. Work with other governments and international organisations to establish a truly global regime that provides consistent and predictable global rules.
3. Show leadership by acting as model users of new technologies to demonstrate the advantages of electronic commerce and build trust among businesses and consumers.[47]

In June 2001 Montreal hosted a conference attended by government officials from around the world. Its focus was 'Tax Administrations in an Electronic World'.[48]

History of Europe's response

Germany investigated the idea of taxing business sites by way of a licence, but rejected this taxation model in August 1997. Belgium's Ministry put forward a Bit Tax proposal, whereby they would attempt to tax data travelling over their communication links. This idea of a tax on each packet of data sent across the Internet where revenue is derived directly from Internet traffic on a volume basis was ruled out by the US government when President Clinton announced there would be no new taxes on the Internet.

The President of the European Union (EU) agreed in principle to the Internet becoming a duty-free environment. He expressed support for the development of an internationally uniform, simple system of taxation based on the principle of tax neutrality, which requires that the tax system treat similar income equally, regardless of whether it is earned through electronic means or through existing means.[49]

At the 'Internet, Web, What Next?' conference in Geneva in July 1998, the prospect of large web income flows encouraged many governments to think about cashing in on the Internet boom by introducing taxes and tariffs. Ronert Verrue, Director General of the European Union's DG XIII, demonstrated his case for Web legislation that would impose VAT on commercial transactions. The EU ruled that cross-border retailers should collect tax at the rate of the state in which their products are consumed.

In contrast to the tax perspective, international trade opinion favours minimal intervention in the growth of electronic commerce, despite such insights as that of OECD Secretary General, Donald Johnston:

> The emergence of electronic commerce – commercial transactions based on the electronic transmission of data over communications networks such as the Internet – heralds a major structural change in the economies of the OECD countries. Its impact may be as far-reaching as the invention of the printing press and the automobile. It will affect all aspects of the economic environment, the organisation of firms, consumer behaviour, the workings of government and most spheres of household activity.[50]

The EU's 1997 *A European Initiative on Electronic Commerce* established EU policy and objectives on key issues relating to the implementation of electronic commerce in Europe.[51] Details are at www.ispo.ce.be/ecommerce/, and include:

- the need for access to infrastructure, products and services necessary for e-commerce to be as widely available as possible
- establishment of a coherent regulatory structure throughout the union based on its single-market principles
- promotion of skills and awareness of e-commerce business opportunities
- coordination of EU regulatory principles with a compatible global regulatory framework.

The European Commission singled out taxation as an area of concern, asserting that no new taxes should be introduced in electronic commerce. In 1998 the European Commission formally rejected the idea of a Bit Tax on the basis of the following five points:

1. *The Bit Tax triggers double taxation*: Communication activities on the Internet are already taxed as communication services and equipment.
2. *The Bit Tax would not solve the particular taxation issues raised by electronic transactions*: As with the traditional supply of goods and services, with electronic transactions companies are required to levy sales tax where appropriate.

3. *A tax on 'physical' transactions is extremely difficult to implement*: Here the term 'physical' refers to bit throughput. Counting bits, they argue, will tend to cost more than the revenue raised and a Bit Tax creates incentives for tax avoidance by compressing data.

4. *A Bit Tax would create inefficient distortions*: The Internet offers new forms of goods and services. Internet suppliers will practise some type of price discrimination, for example between supplying a CD and supplying software online. Any taxation on the Internet will induce distortions, but a Bit Tax would introduce even larger ones.

5. *Internet development*: Europe is lagging behind the United States in terms of Internet development. For this reason, taxation is considered inappropriate.

The EU's position from 2003

Under current laws, European customers who buy goods over the Internet pay VAT when they are imported. But under the new rules, which come into force in July 2003, non-European suppliers who sell downloadable services into Europe will have to register with the tax department in one of the 15 EU member states and then levy that state's VAT on all their Internet sales into the EU.[52]

The OECD's response

The Organisation for Economic Cooperation and Development has taken a leading role among international institutions on electronic commerce policy and analysis.[53] Details are at www.oecd.org/dsti/sti/it/ec/index.htm. The governments of the OECD countries have realised they needed to develop a common approach on how to respond to the challenges that the Internet and global commerce will place on their taxation systems.

In 1997, at the Turku, Finland, conference on e-commerce entitled 'Dismantling the Barriers to Global Electronic Commerce', organised by the OECD, the following issues were addressed:
• access to and use of infrastructure
• building user and consumer trust
• minimising regulatory uncertainty
• easing logistical problems.

The Turku conference concluded that the Committee on Fiscal Affairs (CFA) of the OECD was the international body that would be most able to coordinate and further the taxation matters of electronic commerce. This was primarily due to the work that the CFA did in developing and maintaining the Model Tax Convention. The CFA was given the task of developing the taxation framework conditions that are applicable to electronic commerce.[54]

The OECD 1998 Ottawa Ministerial Conference, entitled 'A Borderless World: Realizing the Potential of Global Electronic Commerce', had the active participation of a large cross-section of the stakeholders in electronic commerce. The OECD recognised the need for all the stakeholders to work collectively in order to find solutions. The participants included international organisations, business, labour, consumer and public interest groups.[55] This conference adopted three formal Ministerial Declarations on the subjects of:

- protection of privacy on global networks
- consumer protection in the context of electronic commerce
- authentication for electronic commerce.

The ministers also endorsed the OECD report on *Taxation Framework Conditions for Electronic Commerce.* In the area of international tax arrangements and cooperation, the OECD has agreed to undertake the following actions:

- clarify how concepts used in the OECD Model Tax Convention apply to electronic commerce in particular
- determine taxing rights, including the concepts of 'permanent establishment' and the attribution of income
- classify income for the purpose of taxation; for example, intangible property, royalties, services and, in particular, digital information
- monitor the effect that electronic commerce has on the application of OECD Transfer Pricing Guidelines
- improve administrative assistance to taxation authorities by the use of existing bilateral and multilateral agreements
- investigate the effect of electronic commerce on harmful tax competition in the context of the recommendations on geographically mobile activities, which accompanied the OECD's report *Harmful Tax Competition.*[56]

The following recommendations were formulated at the OECD Ottawa Ministerial Conference in 1998:

- Small advisory groups from both the public sector and business should be developed rather than using large conferences.
- Clarification of how the concepts of the OECD Model Tax Convention apply to electronic commerce should be sought; namely, determining taxing rights and classifying income for taxation purposes.
- The effect that electronic commerce has on the application of OECD Transfer Pricing Guidelines should be monitored.
- Administrative assistance to taxation authorities should be improved using existing bilateral and multilateral agreements.
- The effect of electronic commerce on harmful tax competition in the context of the recommendations on geographically mobile activities should be investigated.[57]

Ireland's approach to tax and electronic commerce

The intensity of the international debate underlines the importance of the taxation issues surrounding e-commerce and the need for Ireland's Revenue Department to be able to articulate Irish national interests on the issues arising. The national reports of Australia, Canada, Japan, the United States, New Zealand and the United Kingdom and the reports of the international bodies such as the World Trade Organisation, the EU and the OECD stress the need for the implementation of an agreed international framework for the taxation of e-commerce.[58] International debate must move away from discussion of tax principles and focus on delivering practical arrangements for international e-commerce. Until practical tax arrangements are agreed and implemented, the free flow of global e-commerce will be impeded.

Ireland wants to be the centre of e-commerce in Europe. It has passed e-commerce laws and offers tax incentives to IT players. The paper, *Electronic Commerce and the Irish Tax System*, was released in July 1999 (see www.revenue.irlgov.ie). From a tax perspective, the Irish Revenue Department wants to ensure that tax rules do not stifle the development of e-commerce in Ireland. While it is vital that this policy goal remains central, the Revenue Department must ensure that the growth in business on the Internet is not at the expense of national revenues. The department wants to keep tax rules and tax compliance neutral between e-commerce and other forms of commerce. To work properly, tax rules may need to be tailored to cater for the technicalities of the Internet.

Japan's response

Japan believes in the creation of a global Internet taxation system on music, video and other entertainment software. Japan wants taxation of Internet transactions because it is worried about the inequalities between physical and Internet transactions. The Ministry of Finance in Japan has expressed the wish for software vendors to keep records of transactions and pay taxes to countries where consumers reside. Tax practitioners believe the method proposed by the Ministry of Finance is unrealistic and difficult to implement. Japan's position is not shared by the United States, which is against any cross-border Internet taxes.

International cooperation in dealing with taxing Internet commerce

> The cross border dimensions of many economic transactions over the Internet require not only that national regulations and practices be adapted to this new environment, but also that international co-operation is necessary if fiscal sanctuaries are to be minimised.[59]

Although there are 1500 international tax treaties in existence, the majority are between only two countries and concern income and capital taxation. Most of these treaties are based on the *OECD Model Tax Convention on Income and Capital*[60] and the rest are based on the *1997 OECD Model Tax Convention between Developed and Developing Countries.*

In 1991 Professor Richard Vann described how a specialist international institution could work:

> A more flexible approach to international tax problems may be possible in the context of an international tax institution structured like the Trade in Goods (GATT)... The advantage of this approach is the flexibility it offers... Nations could adopt from a menu of options a greater range of undertakings, such as tax ceilings (without reciprocity) and non discrimination in much the same way as tariff undertakings and side agreements operate in the GATT.[61]

There are many reasons why such an international body would not work in practice, namely:

- many countries have been aggressive in taxing income to get a greater share of the international tax take on multinational enterprises
- conflict of interest among countries
- traditional barriers to international cooperation, namely reciprocity
- time and difficulty involved moving from bilateral agreements to multi-national agreements
- some countries will remain outside the system.[62]

The role of cypherpunks

Cypherpunks or 'crypto-anarchists' are dedicated to building anonymous systems. In the *CypherPunks Manifesto*, Eric Hughes states: 'We are defending our privacy with cryptography, with anonymous mail forwarding systems, with digital signatures and with electronic money.' By combining encryption technology with digital signatures and remailers (which allow people to send anonymous emails) people will be able to move funds in the form of anonymous digital cash without a trace. Governments will not be able to tax what they cannot see and even if they try to break the encryption, the resources necessary to decipher potentially millions of transactions would be beyond those available to taxation authorities.

Anguilla, in the Caribbean, has been marketed by Vince Cate as a tax-effective jurisdiction in which to locate. His web server (www.offshore.com.ai) supplies businesses with their place of effective management and, hence, Anguillian residency. Cate believes that more than 50 per cent of pure Internet business will operate from tax havens within 10 years.[63]

What this means to taxation authorities is obvious. In *accounted* electronic payment systems, the issuer of the payments keeps a record of the flow of electronic money through the system; hence, accurate identification of the parties involved is possible. In *unaccounted* electronic payment systems, no records of the flow of electronic money are kept. With no audit trails, it is impossible to identify the parties involved.

Anonymous digital money will allow people to have instantaneous access to offshore banking facilities where there is no central body to control the issue and exchange of electronic cash. The growth of e-commerce will mean people will have the ability to avoid scrutiny of the taxation authorities.

ELECTRONIC TAX PACK

The Australian Taxation Office has used the Internet to assist it to gather tax. (More details are found in the case study at the end of this chapter.) Australian taxpayers were able to complete their first online tax returns in 1999 after the completion of a successful pilot in 1998 when 1200 personal income tax returns were filed over the Internet.[64] To participate, the taxpayer must use Windows and download the e-tax application from the ATO's web site. The taxpayer must also enter his or her tax file number and any requested details about his or her previous tax assessment. The taxpayer then receives a password, which is generated when personal details are verified. The software security company Baltimore developed the security technology. Digital certificate technology is used to sign the data on the return to ensure authenticity. The data is then encrypted before being sent over the Internet.

In the United States, electronic tax returns have raised concerns about security, with electronic tax returns being considered prime targets for hackers. More than 42 million Americans file their tax returns electronically and they have been warned that the Revenue Service will not be responsible for any breach of confidentiality. Tax returns contain valuable information such as social security numbers, names, addresses, bank details and employment details. A security audit of the Revenue Service in 2001 found that its firewalls did not restrict access to its networks, e-filed returns were stored unencrypted and intrusion detection was poor.[65]

ONLINE BANKING AND TAXATION ISSUES

A major growth market will be found in servicing and securing the global information flows of the mobile rich, who are taking their businesses offshore. It is estimated that 60 per cent of the world's private banking is held in trust in offshore, unsupervised tax havens.[66] Grand Cayman, a tiny tax haven in the Caribbean, has become the fifth largest banking centre in the world, with 500 banks and nearly 3000 registered companies.[67] The Internet is changing so fast that tax officials are becoming frustrated with the time it takes to change the existing inflexible tax rules. Bishop (2000) has quoted one vexed taxman as saying: 'They can move millions of dollars at the click of a mouse, and five years later, when we've changed the rules, they've come up with another scheme.'[68]

BUILDING TRUST WITH CUSTOMERS PURCHASING OVER THE INTERNET

Before consumers and businesses engage in debate over the appropriate taxation for e-commerce, there has to be an established trust that the basic commercial transactions of buying over the Internet fall within accepted commercial principles and that the business of e-commerce is part of everyday life.

At the end of 1999, and after 18 months of negotiation, the OECD completed and adopted guidelines for consumer protection in the context of electronic commerce. The guidelines set out the core characteristics of effective consumer protection for online B2C transactions. The guidelines are a first step in encouraging a global approach to consumer protection in the online marketplace, a sector that is by its nature borderless.

Eight simple concepts form the basis of the recommendations.[69] These are:

1. *Transparent and effective protection*: E-commerce consumers should be no less protected when shopping online than when they buy from their local store or order from a catalogue.

2. *Fair business, advertising and marketing practices*: Advertising should be clearly identifiable. Businesses should respect consumers' choices not to receive email they don't want. Businesses should take special care when targeting children, the elderly and others who may lack the capacity to understand the information as presented.

3. *Online disclosures about the business, the goods and services, and the transaction*: Disclosure should include complete and accurate information about the business, about the goods or services for sale and about how the transaction is made. What this means is that e-customers should know which business they are really dealing with. They should have a complete description of what they are buying. And they should have enough information about the transaction process to be able to make an informed decision.

4. *Confirmation process*: The confirmation process for a sale should give consumers a chance to see what they have agreed to buy and a chance to change their mind if they want to before the purchase is completed.

5. *Secure payment systems*: Payment systems need to be secure and easy to use.

6. *Redress*: In an international transaction, redress is one of the most difficult areas to address, and the OECD recommendations recognise that further work is needed. The guidelines articulate the principle that international e-commerce transactions are subject to an existing framework on applicable law and jurisdiction, but that it may be necessary to modify, or apply differently, this framework to make it effective to provide redress for e-commerce. The use of alternative dispute resolution is strongly recommended.

7. *Privacy*: The OECD has been at the forefront of international privacy work for decades. Over 20 years ago, the OECD developed *Guidelines Governing the Protection of Privacy and Transborder Flows of Personal Data* (1980). These guidelines were developed long before everyone started worrying about privacy in e-commerce (because there was no e-commerce). Today, the OECD privacy guidelines are considered to be a

'flagship' OECD document and still serve member countries as the basis for current international work on privacy in the online environment. The guidelines set out the following privacy principles:

- collection limitation principle
- data quality principle
- purpose specification principle
- security safeguards principle
- openness principle
- individual participation principle
- accountability principle.

The OECD consumer protection guidelines point directly to the 1980 privacy guidelines as the benchmark for providing privacy protection by recognising that 'business-to-consumer e-commerce should be conducted in accordance with the recognised principles set out in the 1980 OECD privacy guidelines'.

8. *Education*: The OECD guidelines encourage governments, businesses and consumers to work together to educate consumers about electronic commerce, to foster informed decision making by consumers participating in electronic commerce, and to increase business and consumer awareness of the consumer protection framework that applies to their online activities.[70]

The Australian Competition and Consumer Commission (ACCC) is also concerned that Internet businesses deliver high standards of security and customer service. The ACCC organises an annual 'Internet Sweep Day' to examine business sites over a 24-hour period. The sweep covers issues related to:

- disclosure of physical address
- telephone number or email contact details
- itemisation of costs
- information about the security of the online payment methods
- applicable currency for the purchase
- possibility of any restriction on the purchase (geographical, parental approval)
- refund and exchange policies
- information about how to lodge a complaint
- applicable law
- privacy policy.

The sweep day involves international agencies in countries such as Hong Kong, Taiwan, Germany, New Zealand, Portugal, Ireland, Poland, Austria, Canada, Norway, Finland, France, Denmark, Hungary and Jamaica.

The ACCC has also produced a series of Internet shopping fact sheets covering issues such as:

- What are the benefits and risks of shopping online?
- What type of information should I look for in a web site?
- How safe is it to use my credit card?
- Do I have to pay sales tax or duties on imported goods?

- What happens to my personal information?
- What if something goes wrong with my purchase?
- Banking on the Internet
- Seal of Assurance.

It is recognised that shopping on the Internet may have more problems than traditional retail or mail order and a number of organisations have produced information to support consumers, including:

- the Department of Communications, Information Technology and the Arts (www.dcita.gov.au/shoponline)
- VISA (www.visa.com)
- Australian Competition and Consumer Commission (www.accc.gov.au).

SUMMARY

Taxation of Internet commerce is a vexed issue. Governments throughout the world are examining their taxation laws as they relate to corporate and individual residency, tax avoidance and evasion, international taxation agreements, money laundering and technology transfer. Taxation reform for the entire system in Australia is an ongoing political debate and various special interest groups and politicians have proposed a radical overhaul of the system. The Australian Taxation Office has released two reports, one in 1997 and one in 1999. The ATO has also embraced the idea of using the Internet to carry out its business of processing taxation packs.

Gambling on the Internet is another area of special interest to the Australian government as it is a high revenue earner for state and federal governments. Some states and members of the gambling industry have been cooperating with the government to ensure that Australia becomes a major player in online gambling. Jean Baptiste Colbert, Louis XIV's treasurer, advised 'the art of taxation consists in so plucking the goose as to obtain the largest possible amount of feathers with the smallest possible amount of hissing'. It remains to be seen how the taxman will catch the virtual goose of Internet commerce.

Key terms

compliance (p. 217)	income tax (p. 216)	tax evasion (p. 211)
fringe benefits tax (p. 217)	money laundering (p. 211)	tax neutrality (p. 210)
Goods and Services Tax (GST) (p. 217)	sales tax (p. 216)	
	tax avoidance (p. 211)	

E-TAX FOR AUSTRALIAN INDIVIDUALS LODGING INCOME TAX RETURNS

By Jeff Chamberlain, Deakin University

The Australian Taxation Office is the federal government's prime revenue collector, responsible for the collection of around 96 per cent of its revenue (approx. $140.6 billion per year). The ATO Commissioner, Michael Carmody, acknowledged in his foreword to the ATO *Strategic Statement 2000–2003* that one of the five key issues that will shape the future of Australia's revenue administration is the impact of internationalisation and the growth of the Internet and electronic commerce.

The ATO advocates that for the majority of its clients, interactions will increasingly be performed online. The ATO has long been recognised as a government leader in the provision of services online. This is exemplified through programs it has delivered, including the Electronic Lodgement Service (a secure online tax return lodgement system for tax agents), Australian Business Number registrations online, Business Activity Statement lodgement online (via a secure tailored electronic commerce interface (ECI) software program, downloaded by businesses to their Internet-connected personal computers), and the individual's tax return preparation and online lodgement program, 'e-tax'. The e-tax product forms part of a major ATO online strategy to revolutionise the way it does business and its relationships and interaction with the community.

E-tax is a computer program that can be downloaded by individual taxpayers from the ATO's web site. It provides taxpayers (citizens) with extensive help, worksheets and calculation facilities to assist in the preparation of tax returns and then lodges those returns securely over the Internet. This is quite distinct from the facility used by tax agents to lodge individual and business returns. The tax agents' system is known as the Electronic Lodgement Service (ELS) and has been in operation for at least 10 years. It uses exclusive, secure, value-added network (VAN) architecture. There are around 10 million individual taxpayers in Australia.

E-tax helps users to determine whether they should lodge a tax return and, if so, asks a series of questions requiring user input to complete the actual return. A series of 'interview screens' guide users and intelligent rules built into the system ensure that only questions pertinent to respective users are asked. The program collates all of the typically required tax return data, including information on the taxpayer's income, deductions, losses, tax offsets and rebates, the health-care levy and adjustments. E-tax includes worksheets for computations and various information and help screens. It also provides an estimate of the taxpayer's assessment (i.e. the dollar amount owing or refundable). Validation and consistency tests check answers, figures and incomplete items, and users can print copies of completed returns for their records.

E-tax also offers the advantage that partly completed returns can be saved and several members of a household can use the software on the same computer after downloading their individual secure electronic keys and digital certificates. Taxpayers can also elect for EFT refunds (direct deposits into nominated bank accounts) before securely and electronically remitting the return to the ATO.

Public key encryption technology is used to attain security, privacy, authenticity and integrity. This has been adopted by the ATO to secure information transactions conducted with clients. The unique private keys enable the ATO to check the authenticity of transactions. By encrypting and signing documents using private and public keys, the ATO can detect whether an electronic document has been altered, thus ensuring the integrity of documents sent and received from clients. Use of public key encryption technology is enhanced through the use of Secure Socket Layer (SSL) technology for secure data transmission sessions.

Original business arguments presented in favour of the initial trial of the e-tax product included:

- the improvements brought to client assistance
- the ease of tax return preparation
- the speed of tax return preparation
- the reduction in compliance costs (e.g. lodgement over the Internet)
- higher data quality as a result of software error checking.

These arguments reflect the efficiency and effectiveness objectives and rationales of all governments when implementing such innovations. Efficiencies in this context related to such gains as perceived reductions in processing and compliance costs and increased effectiveness in terms of client service and data quality. All arguments reflect the ATO's wider strategic plans in place at that time.

Currently, the major ATO alternatives to e-tax include:

- *Lodgement of paper-based returns via a product called 'Tax Pack'*: This is a kit containing over 100 pages of information and forms that individuals work through. It is available at newsagencies and ATO branch offices. Completed returns are forwarded by post to an ATO branch office for processing, which can take up to two months because ATO officers are required to check and key the information manually. Thus, users are unlikely to receive prompt refunds.
- *Electronic lodgement via Australia Post with the 'Tax Pack Express' system*: This essentially involves a taxpayer handing a completed Tax Pack form to a postal clerk, who keys in information from the form for a fee and electronically submits that information to the ATO on behalf of the taxpayer. A prompt refund can then be expected.
- *Lodgement via an accountant or tax agent using a secure VAN-based Electronic Lodgement Service*: Taxpayers lodging via the ELS method have the advantage that they are not bound by the lodgement period (which falls between July and October every year) and also that a professional accountant prepares and lodges the tax return for them. However, this is the most expensive of all the lodgement methods.

E-tax lodgements have increased exponentially since implementation. Significantly, e-tax lodgements increased from around 26 000 in 1999 to around 274 000 in 2001. ELS lodgements increased by 1.8 per cent in 1999 compared with 1998, but then decreased by 2.8 per cent in 2000 against 1999 lodgement figures. Tax Pack lodgements consistently decreased during the same period. Tax Pack lodgements for 1999 were 8.9 per cent less than in 1998 and in 2000 were 2.1 per cent less than in 1999. Tax Pack Express lodgement enjoyed a surge in popularity in 1999 when lodgement figures increased by 17.2 per cent against 1998 figures, though in 2000 an almost equivalent reduction in lodgements occurred with a reduction of 15.8 per cent against 1999 figures. Generally, therefore, uptake rates for e-tax lodgements have surged ahead while returns lodged using the other methods have waned.

The ATO has identified various legal impediments to the provision of online services. The ATO must act in accordance with the statutory obligations placed upon it by the *Privacy Act* and the secrecy provisions of the *Income Tax Assessment Act*. In this sense, taxpayer information must remain confidential when transacted online and the security of that information, when obtained, must be maintained. The ATO is also required to ensure the authenticity of the individuals it transacts with and provide personal information only to individuals who are entitled to receive it. The ATO does this by following a rigid set of 'proof of identity' procedures. The ATO must also ensure the integrity and accuracy of documents that it receives from its online clients by ascertaining that the information contained in such documents has not been improperly altered.

The major issues emerging from e-tax can be summarised as follows:

- e-tax is a major ATO electronic service delivery strategy, which, in turn, is driven by the ATO's comprehensive strategic management system
- e-tax is relatively new; few countries in the world offer online facilities for individual tax administration
- the ATO is seen as a leader in electronic service delivery initiatives among the Australian federal government departments
- e-tax is available only over the Internet and is therefore not available to those without Internet access
- e-tax arguably accelerates the time it takes to prepare and lodge a tax return compared to manual preparation such as Tax Pack
- e-tax (in part) uses an expert systems paradigm that enables clients to detect some claims that would not necessarily be detected if completed manually
- e-tax users are required to download the program to their personal computer and the download is around four megabytes in size
- e-tax is free (similar online tax preparation initiatives emerging from the private sector entail completion and lodgement charges); individuals have yet another incentive to save on their accountant's expensive tax preparation fees

- the e-tax methodology has the potential, if successful, to extend to other types of tax return preparation (e.g. company returns) and even statutory return lodgements in other government departments (nationally and internationally)
- e-tax and other internal ATO electronic service delivery initiatives and proposed initiatives require coordination and congruence
- a wholly online solution is not yet available (i.e. e-tax still requires a software download), though some consider that a fully online solution would be more effective and efficient.

QUESTIONS

1. Debate whether the ATO should continue to develop the e-tax product given that it still serves only a minority of Australian taxpayers.
2. Should the ATO provide Internet access facilities, such as Internet kiosks, for those individuals who are unable to access the e-tax product because they lack private facilities to do so? Give reasons for your answer.
3. Why is it crucial that the ATO uses strong security for e-tax data transmission? How would a breach of this affect client trust, the ATO's brand and the future of the e-tax product?

Questions

1. Select three countries and research their approach to the taxation of electronic commerce. Compare and contrast their approaches with Australia's approach.
2. Visit the ATO's tax site (www.ato.gov.au) and find its e-tax area. Investigate how taxpayers obtain a 'digital signature'. What are the advantages and disadvantages of filing a tax return online?
3. Investigate the progress made by the taxation authorities in:
   (a) obtaining and putting into place a computer program that automatically deducts the appropriate tax from each online transaction
   (b) obtaining international cooperation to ensure that all computer programs match the tax needs of individual nations.
4. Investigate the idea that the ATO could use the Internet to monitor the number of transactions conducted over the Internet without invading anyone's privacy.
5. Debate the following statement: 'The e-tax system should allow the ATO to do its work with much fewer staff.'

Suggested | reading

Allen Consulting Group 2002, *Australia's Information Economy: The Big Picture*, a report for the National Office of the Information Economy, April, www.noie.gov.au/projects/information%5Feconomy/research%26analysis/ie%5Faust/start.htm, accessed July 2002; see also www.allenconsult.com.au.

Deutsch, R. L. et al. 1999, 'Residence and source', in *Australian Tax Handbook*, Australian Tax Practice, Sydney, pp. 25–38.

'A survey of globalisation and tax: the mystery of the vanishing taxpayer – special report', *Economist*, 29 January 2000, pp. 1–25 (special insert).

Ford, W. and Baum, M. 1997, *Secure Electronic Commerce*, Prentice Hall, New Jersey.

Furche, A. and Wrightson, G. 1996, *Computer Money: A Systematic Overview of Electronic Payment Systems*, dpunkt.verlag, Heidelberg.

Goolsbee, A. and Zittrain, J. 1999, 'Evaluating the costs and benefits of taxing Internet commerce', *National Tax Journal*, September, vol. 52, issue 3, pp. 413–28.

Lawrence, E. 1999, 'Virtual tax reform', *Hands-on Solutions: E-commerce*, CCH, Sydney.

McCouat, P. 1998, 'Taxation in cyberspace', *Hands-on Solutions: E-commerce*, CCH, Sydney.

National Office of the Information Economy 2002, *The Current State of Play: Australia's Scoreboard*, April, Commonwealth of Australia, www.noie.gov.au.

Pinto, D. 1999, Taxation Issues in a World of Electronic Commerce, unpublished paper, Curtin University of Technology, Perth, pp. 1–67.

Vann, R. 2000, *Tax Treaties – Spring 2000*, New York University School of Law, www.law.nyu.edu/vannr/spring00/, accessed July 2002.

End | notes

1. Schneider, G. P. and Perry, J. 2001, *Electronic Commerce*, 2nd edn, Course Technology, Thompson Learning, Cambridge, MA, pp. 397–400.
2. Ibid.
3. Joint Venture Tax Policy Group 2000, *Summary of Approaches for Applying Sales and Use Taxes to E-Commerce*, www.jointventure.org/initiatives/tax/I-Report.pdf, accessed July 2002.
4. OECD TAG, *Treaty Characterization Issues Arising from Electronic Commerce*, report to working party, number 1, www.tax-news.com/asp/res/tcofecom.pdf, accessed July 2002.
5. Electronic Commerce Project Team 1999, *Tax and the Internet: Second Report of the Australian Taxation Office*, December, Australian Government Publishing Service, Canberra, p. 4.
6. Davidson, J. 1999, 'Taking care of business on the net', *Australian Financial Review*, 23 July.
7. Muscovitch, Z. 1996, 'Taxation of Internet commerce', *ILSA-Ottawa*, Papers Archive #1, www.globalserve.net/~zak/index.html.
8. Australian Bureau of Statistics 2002, *Business Use of Information Technology, Australia*, Cat. No. 8129.0.
9. Australian Bureau of Statistics 1999–2000, 'Information technology and telecommunications in Australia (1999–2000)', special article in *Finance, Australia*, Cat. No. 5611.0.
10. National Office for the Information Economy 2002, *The Current State of Play: Australia's Scorecard*, April, p. 16.
11. Gal, O. 2002, 'Banking online grows', *Australian*, 10 July, www.theaustralian.news.com.au/common/story_page/0,5744,4677567%255E462,00.html.
12. National Office for the Information Economy, op. cit., p. 31.
13. Australian Bureau of Statistics 1999–2000, op. cit.
14. 'HK innovation and technology fund receives 103 applications', *People's Daily*, 12 January 2001, english.peopledaily.com.cn/200101/12/eng20010112_60264.html, accessed July 2002.
15. Multimedia Development Corporation, 'Creating the multimedia super corridor', Malaysian Government, www.mdc.com.my, accessed July 2002.
16. Australian Bureau of Statistics, 1999–2000, op. cit.

17. Pure Commerce 2001, 'Australian innovators shine at AIIA iAwards', 18 October, www.purecommerce.com.au/media-releases.asp#19, accessed July 2002.
18. Walker, F. 2002, 'Tax returns just too hard – even for the experts', *Sunday Herald*, 28 July, p. 19.
19. Stensholt, J. 2002, 'Tax review too hasty, firms fear', *Business Review Weekly*, 30 May, p. 76.
20. NSW Bar Association, on behalf of the Australian Bar Association, 2000, *A Practical GST and PAYG Overview for Members of the Australian Bar Association*, April, p. 5.
21. Inland Revenue, *Guide to Tax Consequences of Trading over the Internet*, New Zealand Government, p. 11, www.ird.govt.nz/library/ecommerce, accessed July 2002.
22. Ibid.
23. Ibid.
24. Tyree, A. 1997, 'Regulation of international electronic trading', *Proceedings of the Second Australian Computer Money Day*, University of Newcastle, Department of Computing Science and Software Engineering, Sydney.
25. Lawrence, E. 1999, 'Harmonizing global Internet tax: a collaborative extranet model', *South Africa Computer Journal*, no. 24, November, pp. 119–27.
26. Advisory Commission on Electronic Commerce 2000, *Report to Congress*, United States Government, April, www.ecommercecommission.org/acec_report.pdf, accessed July 2002.
27. Senate Information Technologies Committee 2000, *Netbets: A Review of Online Gambling in Australia*, Commonwealth of Australia, March, www.aph.gov.au/senate/committee/it_ctte/gambling/ChapTwo.doc, accessed July 2002.
28. Ibid, p. 17.
29. Gambling Licences.com 2002, 'Global news – India Maharashtra', www.gamblinglicenses.com/LicencesDatabaseDetail.cfm?Licenses_ID=110&Region=Asia%20Pacific, accessed July 2002.
30. Gambling Licences.com 2002, 'Global news – Denmark', www.gamblinglicenses.com/LicencesDatabaseDetail.cfm?Licenses_ID=87&Region=Europe, accessed July 2002.
31. Gambling Licences.com 2002, 'Global news – North Korea', www.gamblinglicenses.com/LicencesDatabaseDetail.cfm?Licenses_ID=107&Region=Asia%20Pacific, accessed July 2002.
32. Gambling Licences.com 2002, 'Global news – United Kingdom', www.gamblinglicenses.com/LicencesDatabaseDetail.cfm?Licenses_ID=77&Region=Europe, accessed July 2002.
33. Rose, I. N 1999, *The Law of Internet Gambling*, www.gamblingandthelaw.com/internet.html, accessed July 2002.
34. Soete, L. and Kamp, K. 1996, *The 'BIT TAX': The Case for Further Research*, www.ispo.cec.be/hleg/bittax.html.
35. Davidson, J. 1997, 'Holes in the tax net', *Australian Financial Review*, 18 October, www.afr.com.au.
36. United States Government 1997, *Framework for Electronic Commerce*, www.iitf.nist.gov/eleccomm/ecomm.html.
37. Lynch, A. 1998, 'Tax office stems net evasion', *Australian*, 26 November, p. 8.
38. Ibid.
39. Riley, J. 1997, 'US lobbies against Internet taxation', *Australian*, 16 December 1997, p. 42.
40. Caldwell, K. 1999, 'States behaving badly: the public policy report', *Electronic Commerce Core Series*, June, vol. 1, no. 6, p. 1.
41. Ibid.
42. Ibid., p. 2.
43. See the project's web site at www.nhdd.com/nta/ntaintro.htm.
44. Caldwell, K. 1999, 'Federalism: should Congress take a more active role in restraining the states from interfering in interstate commerce?', *Electronic Commerce Core Series*, vol. 1, no. 6, p. 12.

45. 'Bush to sign bill extending Internet tax ban', *USA Today*, 16 November 2001, www.usatoday.com/life/cyber/tech/2001/11/16/net-taxes.htm, accessed July 2002.

46. Bishop, M. 2000, 'The happy E-shopper: globalisation and tax survey', *Economist*, 29 February, p. 11.

47. Taskforce on Electronic Commerce, *The Canadian Electronic Commerce Strategy*, e-com.ic.gc.ca and www.connect.gc.ca.

48. 'Tax Administrations in an Electronic World', Montreal, 4–6 June 2001, www.oecd.org.

49. Riley, op. cit.

50. Johnston, D. J. 1997, 'Commerce goes electronic', *OECD Observer*, no. 208, p. 4.

51. Townsend, op. cit.

52. Taylor, L. 2002, 'Australia caught in middle of e-commerce tax battle', *Australian Financial Review*, 9 May, p. 49.

53. Townsend, op. cit.

54. Wilcox, C., MacKenzie, G., Grishenko, N., Fitzpatrick, P. and Hay, W. 1998, 'Case Study: Tax and Internet Commerce', project for Internet commerce and commerce on the Internet, University of Technology, Sydney, November, p. 41.

55. Wilcox et al., op. cit., p. 50.

56. Wilcox et al., op. cit., p. 52.

57. Lawrence, E. 1999, 'Virtual tax reform', *Hands-on Solutions: E-commerce*, CCH Publications, Sydney.

58. Revenue Department 1999, *Electronic Commerce and the Irish Tax System: A Revenue Discussion Document*, Irish State, p. 17, www.revenue.ie/e-commerce/e-commerce.htm.

59. Townsend D. 1999, *Briefing Report on Telecommunications Regulatory Issues for Electronic Commerce, ITU Regulatory Colloquium No. 8: The Changing Roles of Government in an Era of Telecommunications Deregulation*, ITU, Geneva, February, p. 39.

60. Wilcox et al., op. cit.

61. Vann, R., quoted in Pinto, D. 1999, Taxation Issues in a World of Electronic Commerce, unpublished paper, Curtin University of Technology, Perth, Australia.

62. Ibid.

63. www.offshore.com.ai, accessed October 2002.

64. Tebbutt, D. 1999, 'Net return to taxpayers', *Australian*, 6 July, p. 40.

65. 'E-tax targeted', *Australian*, 30 April 2002, p. 31.

66. Angell, I. 2000, *The New Barbarian Manifesto: How to Survive the Information Age*, Kogan Page, London, p. 88.

67. Ibid., p. 90.

68. Bishop, M. 2000 op cit, p. 11.

69. Asia Pacific Economic Cooperation Electronic Commerce Steering Committee Workshop on Consumer Protection: Consumer Protection in Ecommerce.

70. www.accc.gov.au/fs-search.htm.

CHAPTER 10

Legal and ethical issues

LEARNING outcomes

You will have mastered the material in this chapter when you can:

- appreciate how the Internet may be regulated by government concerns over such matters as censorship and consumer protection
- understand how copyright and defamation laws may be infringed by making information freely available over the Internet
- identify the problems associated with determining which legal jurisdiction applies to international transactions conducted via the Internet
- assess the differences between the establishment of a contract for goods or services in the traditional marketplace and a contract established via the Internet
- appreciate the potential for fraud and other criminal activities using the Internet
- understand how privacy of the individual and company records may be eroded by users of the Internet and what safeguards are required to preserve that privacy.

'Cybercrime won't stifle the expansion of e-commerce — it will accompany it. As technology becomes more sophisticated, entire markets will be created for cyberwarfare entities and then for counter entities. And the focus will be on defending the individual.'

Christine Canabou 2001, 'Life of Crime', *Fast Company*, 1 April, p. 60, www.fastcompany.com/online/45/futurist.

INTRODUCTION

Commercial transactions are subject to a comprehensive system of controls consisting of:

- the common **law**
- **legislation** at the state, federal and international levels
- industry codes of practice.

These controls have been established over time in an ad hoc fashion in response to the need to provide a high degree of certainty in contractual relationships and to give the consumer confidence that they will obtain 'a fair deal' in any spending decision. Both of these are necessary ingredients in the promotion of trade and commerce upon which modern economies depend. The controls have evolved and have been adapted to new technologies as they arise, although there is always a lag time before the controls 'catch up' with the latest technology.

We are still at an early stage in establishing controls over commercial transactions on the Internet despite the large volume of transactions taking place daily. Unique features of the Internet compared with earlier technological changes are:

- its rapid proliferation
- the multiplicity of communication channels
- the enormous volume of information and range of services available
- the ease and speed with which trans-border transactions can be conducted.

All of these pose a unique set of problems.

Although international agreements do exist for the regulation of international trade, they are not keeping pace with commercial realities. The principal problem is that existing agreements and even those proposed only deal with business or trade transactions. They do not deal with consumer purchases which are responsible for the huge growth in transactions over the Internet.

Major concerns include how security of commercial transactions over the Internet can be maintained and how the consumer's interests can be protected, including the individual's rights to **privacy**. Added to this are issues associated with protecting a society's values, exemplified by government's role in controlling content on the Internet, particularly in relation to **censorship**.

CONTROL OF INTERNET CONTENT

One of the first steps in trying to establish a legal framework for any new technology is to classify it in order to establish how existing legislation may be made to fit the new technology. Although the Internet service provider has become the major focus for attempts at legislative controls there is a wide variation between each country's approach.[1] Singapore, for example, has classified the Internet service providers as broadcasting media, requiring them to be registered. It thereby exercises control by allowing access only to authorised web sites. In the United States, the *Telecommunications Act 1996* considers the Internet service provider to be a telecommunications carrier. The US Supreme Court struck down the *Communications Decency Act 1996*, which would have restricted indecent material on the Internet, as unconstitutional and an attack on free speech.[2] In a recent development the US Supreme Court has also struck down the *Child Pornography Prevention Act 1996*. This Act prohibited the use of computer technology to knowingly produce child pornography, essentially treating computer-generated child pornography the same as pornography using real children. However, the Court found that the Act was an attack on free speech and that no real children were harmed in the creation of virtual pornography.[3]

An international working group, the Internet Content Rating Association (ICRA), supported by computer industry heavyweights such as Microsoft, has been formed to establish worldwide standards for content rating.[4]

In Australia, a Senate select committee report argued that Internet content should be treated in the same manner as a broadcast medium such as television. One of the outcomes of the report was to make the federal government's Telecommunications Industry Ombudsman available to hear complaints from users of the Internet.[5] The more significant outcome, however, was the enactment of the *Broadcasting Services Amendment (On-Line Content) Act 1999* (The On-Line Services Act). This regulates Internet content hosted both within Australia and offshore by restricting the use of the Internet for transmission of objectionable material including, most importantly, pornography, and to promoting measures to protect children from viewing such material.

The Act requires Internet service providers (ISPs) and Internet content hosts (ICHs) to comply with guidelines based on pre-existing film and video classifications and encourages the industry to adopt a code of practice or suffer the introduction of mandatory standards by the Australian Broadcasting Authority (ABA),[6] which is charged with responsibility for implementation of the Act. The ABA is able to initiate investigations into Internet content on its own initiative or as a result of a complaint from the public and issue notices requiring ISPs or ICHs to take down or deny access to prohibited content.

The Act was introduced in the face of prolonged opposition by industry groups[7] who consider that measures of control are impractical and costly, and represent an invasion of privacy of users.

The On-Line Services Act requires ISPs to supply software filters, but research has shown that less than 2 per cent of people are using them.[8] Software, such as Cybersitter (www.cybersitter.com), Surfwatch (www.surfwatch.com) and Net Nanny (www.netnanny.com),[9] allows parents to block incoming material using key words or phrases and other indicators. Blocking and filtering technologies allow users to decide what material can or cannot be accessed on their browsers, but they lack refinement. Typical examples of blocked words and letters include 'xxx', which blocks out Superbowl XXX sites; 'breast', which blocks web sites and discussion groups about breast cancer; and the consecutive letters 's', 'e' and 'x', which block sites containing the words 'sexton' and 'Mars exploration', among many others.[10] In the United States this software could potentially be considered a violation of First Amendment rights in that the user is never in control of what can and cannot be viewed. A recent report by the US National Academies, *Youth, Pornography and the Internet*,[11] contains a comprehensive review of these problems.

INTELLECTUAL PROPERTY

The law provides well-established protection for owners of **intellectual property** which covers many areas of human and corporate endeavour. The Internet provides increased opportunities for eroding that protection in regard to three types of intellectual property: copyright, patents and trademarks.

Copyright

Copyright protects a wide array of material including writings, artwork, music, films and computer programs and extends to broadcast material, quite separate to the copyright in the material which is transmitted. The copyright automatically belongs to the creator, or the owner, from the time of creation of the material. International treaties such as the Berne Convention provide for protection of Australian copyright owners overseas and vice versa although the rights vary from country to country according to different subject matter. The copyright notice '©' is not required for protection in Australia.

The copyright owner has the right to use the material in a variety of ways and the rights may be assigned or leased with or without limitations or conditions. Use of copyright material, usually by copying without the permission of the owner, will ordinarily be an infringement of copyright, except in certain circumstances — for example, copying by a student of a limited portion of a book (the 'reasonable portion' test).

In Australia, the *Copyright Amendment (Digital Agenda) Act 2000* came into force in March 2001 and updated copyright laws for the Internet and the digital age. The Act established the copyright owner's right of communication which applies to 'active communication', such as broadcast or cable transmission, and to 'passive communication', such as making material available on a web site, for example, to be viewed or downloaded. There are criminal penalties and civil remedies for making, importing or commercially dealing in devices and services — such as decryption software — that circumvent technological copyright protection measures. There are, however, 'permitted purpose' exceptions, such as for governments and decompilers of software. Liability of carriers and ISPs for infringing copyright is also dealt with. Factors to be taken into account when determining whether a person is liable for authorising or infringing copyright are based on existing law. The Australian Copyright Council provides comprehensive resources for review of copyright law.[12]

Copyright issues have had most publicity in connection with copying of music without possession of an original, using compression software to produce files which provide high-quality playback on computers or CD players. The music industry succeeded in shutting down dozens of web sites which stored and allowed access to pirate copies of music in MP3 format. Then, the popularity of MP3 soared in 1999, when Napster was launched. The free program could be downloaded from napster.com and enabled users to search for and download MP3 files from the shared directories of the users online at the time. At its peak, Napster had over 50 million users.

The heavy metal band Metallica commenced legal proceedings against Napster in November 1999, followed one month later by the Recording Industry Association of America (RIAA),[13] both alleging copyright infringement. In July 2000, Napster sought to dismiss the case against it by claiming that it was similar to an ISP (the *Digital Millennium Copyright Act 1999* (DCMA) in the United States provides that ISPs are not liable for copyright infringement if they are mere conduits for material passing through their networks). The motion was dismissed on the grounds that Napster did not have the necessary characteristics of an ISP, which, anyway, ought to have removed material once it became aware of copyright infringement.

While proceedings were in train, Bertelsmann AG, one of the five major music companies suing Napster, agreed to withdraw from the proceedings provided that Napster instituted a subscription-based service for new members. Bertelsmann later bought out Napster, hoping to capitalise on Napster's name to attract subscribers willing to pay for downloaded music.

With the demise of Napster, peer-to-peer technology 'filled the gap' with such software as Gnutella and Freenet, allowing users worldwide access to a huge variety of digital information but with a level of privacy and security not possible in the present client–server architecture of the web.[14] How copyright owners respond to these services remains to be seen.

Patents

A **patent** is a right granted for any device, substance, method or process which is new, inventive and useful. A patent must be applied for at the Patent Office and once granted is legally enforceable and gives the owner exclusive right to commercially exploit the invention for the life of the patent.[15] There is no such thing as a 'world patent'. Separate applications must be made for each country.

Applying for patents can take a long time and become expensive. www.PatentWizard.com gives an indication of the scope of the process, and provides assistance to businesses and inventors for drafting and filing patent applications with the United States Patent and Trademark Office (USPTO).

Patents covering software or programming related to web sites are the fastest growing sector at the US Patent Office.[16] US Internet companies have been lodging patent applications for online business models since a 1998 US court ruling in *State Street Bank & Trust Co. v. Signature Financial Group Inc.* that business methods, if novel and non-obvious, could be patented.[17] Some examples of such patents where companies are pursuing actions in the courts to protect their patents are given below.

Amazon was granted a US patent for '1-click' shopping, a system which records customers' shipping and payment details so that they do not have to re-enter their details during subsequent visits. Amazon commenced proceedings against Barnes & Noble for infringement of copyright, initially gained an injunction preventing Barnes & Noble using its 'Express Lane' system, but then lost the case on appeal. Priceline was able to obtain a US patent for its reverse auction system. This allowed consumers to nominate how much they would pay for goods and services, such as airline tickets and hotel rooms and then Priceline would seek vendors who were willing to accept the bid. Priceline is currently seeking an Australian patent over objections from local companies. DoubleClick patented the Internet technology known as 'adserving', which allows users to deliver, manage, measure and track online advertisements and provides feedback as to the effectiveness of their advertising campaigns.

Such patents have been criticised for stifling the growth of the Internet. The World Wide Web Consortium (W3C) is promoting its royalty-free patent policy as a means of overcoming some of these problems.[18]

Trademarks

A registered **trademark** gives the owner exclusive legal rights to use, license or sell the protected item for the goods and services for which it is registered under the provisions of the *Trademark Act*.[19] A trademark can cover not only words and pictures but also sound and smell. The law provides penalties for infringing a trademark either by using it or by showing something similar to the trademark.

From July 2001, Australia acceded to the Protocol to the Madrid Agreement in International Registration of Trademarks. The effect is that international registration of Australian trademarks will have to be done only once to gain registration in the 50 member countries (those members include European Union states and several Asian countries) with the United States moving towards joining.

Trademark infringement on the Internet has occurred through the use of **meta tagging**, whereby a word is incorporated into a site in order to increase the chances of a search engine returning the site. The first successful case of trademark protection against meta tagging was *Oppedahl & Larson v. Advanced Concepts, No 97CV1592 (D Co filed 24 July, 1997)*. The law firm brought the action against three companies and the corresponding ISPs when it found that a search on Oppedahl & Larson returned the defendants' web sites but the sites did not appear to contain either term. Only a review of the source page revealed the hidden text.

Two actions brought by Playboy Enterprises illustrate the importance of the degree of confusion in the mind of the Internet searcher as being a relevant consideration in actions for the protection of trademarks. In *Playboy Enterprises Inc. v. AsiaFocus International Inc. 1998 US Dist LEXIS 10359 (E D Va Feb 2, 1998)* the court found that the owner of two adult web sites, by using Playboy trademarks 'Playboy' and 'Playmate' within its sites was likely to lead consumers to believe that the defendant's sites were affiliated with Playboy and awarded damages to Playboy. However, in *Playboy Enterprises Inc. v. Terri Welles Inc., 78 F Supp 2d 1066 (S D Cal 1999)* the court found that Terri, being a Playmate of the Year, was entitled to describe herself as a 'Playmate' and dismissed the action.

Microsoft has recently commenced proceedings against 'Lindows', a new dot.com company promoting a Linux-based Windows compatible interface, for trademark infringement on the basis that Lindows was deceptively similar to Windows. Microsoft has been unsuccessful in lower US courts which found that the term 'Windows' had been in use well before Microsoft registered the term.

DOMAIN NAMES

Domain names are administered on a national basis around the world. Any name may be registered as a domain name provided that the name has not been previously registered by another company or individual.[20] Registration of a domain name is not backed up by legislation and in common with registration of a business or company name (which do, however, have a legislative basis), does not automatically give the registrant the right to use that name as a trademark. However, the registrant can also register their domain name as a trademark providing it meets the requirements of the *Trademarks Act*.

One aspect of domain names which has generated redress to the legal system is domain name squatting, whereby individuals have registered famous or significant names with the hope that the owner of the name would be prepared to pay considerable amounts of money to purchase the domain name. Court action by well-known companies to protect domain names has been successful where the domain name is in fact a trademark and some success has also been had in protecting well-known names where no trademark existed. Action has succeeded under the legal heading of 'passing off' where the name has been used to induce readers into believing that they are dealing with the real entity. Legal proceedings have also been successful against domain name owners who have registered mispellings of a popular name to catch browsers who mis-type the name for which they are searching. For example, Microsoft was able to evict the holder of the Internet address 'microsof.com'.

A '.com' can be registered for up to 10 years but '.com.au' domain names can be registered for only two years. It is important to renew the registration as there have been several examples of domain names having been snapped up by competitors or cybersquatters after the web site owner failed to renew. This has become more of a problem with the dot.com collapse. In a process known as 'porn napping' online pornographers are re-registering lapsed Internet domain names previously held by a legitimate company and then publishing sexually explicit content on the Internet at that address. Software is available to test externally linked web pages to identify such problems.[21]

The Internet Corporation for Assigned Names and Numbers (ICANN), which oversees the domain name system, has established an international system for mediating cybersquatting disputes. The arbitration process provides an alternative to the courts for a company which alleges that a holder of a domain name has no legitimate interest in the name. In Australia, au Domain Administration Ltd (auDA)[22] is the government-endorsed manager of the Australian domain name space. auDA licenses registrars who sell .au domain names and facilitates the .au dispute resolution policy. Problems have arisen in Australia whereby unsolicited domain name renewal notices have been sent out to domain name owners in attempts to 'poach' owners from their existing registrars, often at exorbitant rates.

JURISDICTION

Every country has established its own network of laws governing most aspects of private and commercial life in response to the country's individual social, political and commercial circumstances. A few legal systems prevail across groups of countries. Australia, together with most of the English-speaking countries, has the 'common law' system inherited from England. However, although this leads to some similarities, any dispute may receive a different interpretation and have a different outcome depending on which state of Australia the events occurred in. Laws established at international forums have been adopted by many national governments, but these represent only a small part of each country's legislative base.

There is a large body of law called Conflict of Laws which is directed towards identifying which jurisdiction's law is to be applied to any dispute — that is, whether it be the state, national, foreign or international law, and which is the most suitable court (or 'forum') in which the dispute is to be heard.

In order for a court to hear a matter with a trans-border dimension, various tests have to be applied to determine the appropriate **jurisdiction**. A key consideration is that one party to the hearing or the subject matter of the hearing must have some connection with its jurisdiction; for example, that a **contract** was signed within the jurisdiction. However, all manner of complications can occur. The other party may be resident overseas and may decide not to appear to defend the proceedings. In that case, even if the court were to make a judgment in the plaintiff's favour, the plaintiff may not be able to enforce the judgment. It is possible to enforce judgments outside Australia only in a limited number of countries (such as the United Kingdom) under reciprocal arrangements.

Alternatively, the aggrieved party may have to take action in the defendant's jurisdiction by commencing new proceedings. The other party may even initiate counter proceedings in a foreign jurisdiction. Further complications arise when evidence required for the hearing is outside the court's jurisdiction and it may not be possible to compel the evidence to be made available, effectively bringing the action to a halt.

These are the sorts of problems that can occur in the more conventional modes of commercial transactions. They are increasingly likely to occur also with transactions conducted over the Internet because much of the trading is conducted outside the existing legislative framework.

A recent court decision in France will have important implications for the Internet. Through the Yahoo! portal, Nazi memorabilia became accessible to French citizens through Yahoo!'s French subsidiary. Under French law, providing access to such information constitutes a public disturbance. The key questions were whether US content on the Internet should be subject to French law and whether it was technically possible to control the flow of information to certain areas. The court decided that it did have jurisdiction to order Yahoo! to prevent such content from becoming available and did so, appointing a panel of experts to identify means of restricting access by French users.

DEFAMATION

The question of court jurisdiction is particularly important in relation to defamation. The print and broadcasting media are obliged to carefully monitor their outputs to avoid litigation by individuals or companies protecting their interests. It is also necessary for web site owners and bulletin board participants to be careful. Consider, for example, the following situation in the United States.

After making allegations concerning a White House aide on his web site, Matt Drudge was faced with a potentially ruinous **defamation** suit according to a newspaper article 'The Internet has turned anyone with a mouth and a modem into a global publisher'.[23] However, it is important to note in this example that Mr Drudge clearly identified himself and both the parties were resident in the same country, the United States. Therefore, US law could be applied. The situation becomes progressively far more complicated if Mr Drudge:

• resided in another country
• posted the information on a web site located in a third country
• used an ISP in a fourth country
• chose to remain anonymous or used a fictitious name.

All of these scenarios would be quite feasible on the Internet and would make it exceedingly difficult, if not impossible, for the offended party to obtain a legal remedy. An illustration of some of these difficulties is provided by a decision in the 'Macquarie Bank' case in the Supreme Court of NSW.[24]

In this case the Macquarie Bank failed in a bid to shut down an Internet site which it claimed was defaming it. While agreeing that the material was defamatory according to Australian law, the judge ruled that Australian courts had no jurisdiction to restrain the publication of material over the Internet. The judge found that once published on the Internet and transmitted around the world it may be that the defamation laws in other countries allowed an unfettered right to publish the material. In this case 'to make an order interfering with such a right would exceed the proper limits of the use of the injunction power of this court'.

A recent Australian defamation case, *Gutnick v. Dow Jones & Co. Inc.* (2001) VSC 305 could have far-reaching international ramifications and shows the importance of the legal question as to where the material is deemed to be 'published'. A person is defamed where the material is published. Joe Gutnick, a prominent Australian businessman, claimed that he was defamed in an online periodical 'Barrons Online' published by Dow Jones (which also publishes the *Wall Street Journal*).[25] Gutnick chose to sue in Victoria. The judge ruled that the case could be heard in the state of Victoria and the court decided that the information was 'published' when it appeared on the subscriber's computer screen — that is, when it was downloaded.

Dow Jones appealed to the High Court of Australia on the question of place of publication, and claimed that the place of publication was New Jersey, where the company's web servers were located. Dow Jones claimed that if web site operators could be sued in any country where there was access to the Internet, publishers faced an impossible task in ensuring that they complied with every country's laws. The matter is ongoing.

It is important to note that email transmissions can also give rise to defamation proceedings. Anything written in an email or that is included in an attachment that is likely to injure the reputation of another person may be defamatory if it is 'published' to a third party. Publication does not need to be intentional but can arise even if you accidentally forward a copy of defamatory email. If the courts do decide that 'publication' occurs in every jurisdiction in which defamatory email is received, the sender could be the subject of multiple court proceedings!

THE CONTRACT

The issue of jurisdiction is particularly important in relation to contracts for goods or services. There is no international law which completely defines obligations under a contract, although it is open to the parties to decide which jurisdiction's laws will apply.

We will use the example of purchasing a CD from a music store to demonstrate the three main elements of a binding contract, which are:

- offer
- acceptance
- consideration.

When you take the CD to the cashier and pay for it, you are making an 'offer' to purchase. The offer is 'accepted' when the cashier takes the money which represents the 'consideration'. CDs are ideal for Internet commerce, being a low-weight, high-value item.

If, when you arrive home, you find that the CD is faulty, you can take the CD back to the store and demand a replacement or obtain a refund of your money. If the store will do neither, you have an action under the general law of contract to obtain recompense, or, more conveniently — particularly where small sums are involved — consumer protection legislation (in New South Wales, the *Fair Trading Act 1974* will provide the remedy). You need neither know nor care whose fault it was that the CD was damaged or who made the CD. You are able to obtain recompense from the store because you had a contract with it and the store has legal obligations to provide goods of sufficient quality.

In usual circumstances, a store will willingly accommodate you when you return faulty merchandise because your legal remedies would be well known. There would be little point in the store trying to evade its responsibilities as it could not hope to win if you went to court. The store could well reason that you would not bother to go to court for such a small sum. However, because it operates within a local area, it would not want any adverse publicity which could affect consumer confidence and hence sales.

Because a transaction like the one described above was conducted in one place within one state, if you wished to take legal action the local state jurisdiction would provide the remedy.

If the transaction was conducted over the Internet and both parties were resident in the one state, in all probability you would also have the same protection as in the example given above. However, you may not be able to ascertain the identity of the party from whom you made the purchase in order to seek recompense for a faulty CD. Overseas Internet advertisers, content service providers and content creators may be completely outside any jurisdiction which could offer redress. In any event, there is the difficulty of obtaining proof of details of the transaction. Web sites can be created and removed in an instant, and the use of hyperlinks confuses the situation still further.

Our simple example does not begin to explore the complexities of contract formation which can occur, for example, where large sums of money are involved and negotiations take place over weeks or months. In such examples the precise time of formation of a binding contract can be crucial. Since early this century, the 'postal rule' applied: the time of contract acceptance was taken to be when the letter containing the acceptance was slipped into a post box (this says a lot about the perceived reliability of the postal service at that time). The legal system has had to cope with a great many other forms of transmission since then. Acceptance of a contract by fax, for example, is taken to occur when the fax arrives on the destination machine.

However, no such simple rule can be applied in the case of email transmission. Who is to blame for delay or non-delivery of email? Who is liable if a multi-million dollar contract is lost and how can liability be proven? The problem may be due to server failure, network failure, the sender using a wrong email address or the recipient simply not reading their email.

To facilitate the orderly conduct of consumer transactions over the Internet, some form of 'electronic contract' is required. In Australia, the *Electronic Transactions Act 1999* provides some certainty that electronic transactions will receive the same treatment in law as paper-based dealings. It is based on the Model Law for electronic commerce prepared by the United Nations Commission on International Trade Law (UNCITRAL).[26] Subject to certain restrictions, the Act provides that where contract law requires writing or a manual signature, this can be done by electronic communication or electronic signature and provides default rules on when and where an electronic message is sent and received.

With a view to addressing some of the problems of selling over the Internet, the Australian government has produced policies and guidelines on consumer protection to help build consumer confidence in electronic commerce.[27] The OECD has produced extensive material in this area.[28]

The use of credit cards, as 'consideration', for purchases over the Internet does not, of itself, necessarily produce legal issues peculiar to the Internet as the credit card transaction is based on three quite separate contracts: between the issuer and cardholder, the issuer and the merchant, and the cardholder and the merchant. It is more than likely that each one of these contracts was drawn up within one local jurisdiction. Nevertheless, the possibility of fraud is greatly increased when the transaction is conducted over the Internet. In an attempt to address the problems of security and also the fact that the credit card is not appropriate for small transactions due to the relatively high cost of processing, a Secure Electronic Transaction (SET) protocol was developed by the card issuers but it has not proved popular.[29]

ADVERTISING

We return to our example of the CD purchase to illustrate the legal aspects of **advertising** and protection for the consumer. Suppose you bought the CD because you saw an advertisement proclaiming The Stones' 'Greatest Hits' but you found out that some of the tracks were not great at all or that the Stones' 'Greatest Hits' were sung by another group! You have protection and remedies in the various states under legislation which mirrors the *Trade Practices Act 1974* (Cwlth) prohibiting misleading or deceptive conduct in advertising and other areas.

If the store had reproduced the same advertising message on the CD rack, then the consumer protection legislation would give you the same protection under the 'misleading and deceptive' conduct provisions even though the store itself was quite unaware of the misleading nature of the advertisement. Again, the place and identity of the parties are readily ascertainable. Compare this situation with a purchase over the Internet where similar problems could arise as for the case of contracts discussed above.

The key issue here is the possibility of someone – the 'hacker' – gaining access to a communication between two parties which may contain commercial secrets or credit details and deliberately altering the contents of the communication to prejudice the interests of the parties to the communication or using the information for some other illegal use.

Encryption provides the key to providing greater security, and various organisations are considering policies on cryptography. A major problem looming for cryptography as an Internet security measure is the battle by intelligence agencies, particularly in the United States, to ensure that they are able to read any messages sent over the Internet in the interests of national security. Concerns by civil liberties groups and commercial interests are based on the belief that if the intelligence agencies have the facilities to break any given code then sooner or later, and probably sooner, hackers with criminal intent will be able to do the same.

A handwritten signature provides, in law, valuable evidence as to the authenticity of documents and particularly contracts. The digital signature, by the use of encryption, goes further than the traditional signature by setting up links between the signature and content of the electronic message, ensuring that the content has not been altered. This is achieved through the requirement of a Certification Authority to regulate the process.

The European Union (EU) has in place a legal framework for the promotion of electronic commerce within the Union.[30] A collaboration of platform, software and technology vendors is developing a specification to facilitate security within the PC operating system.[31]

Another issue relating to security is the very real danger of viruses being transmitted by communications over the Internet and the question of where the liability attaches if viruses are responsible for losses to a business. It behoves both the sender and receiver of Internet communications to maintain virus control procedures.

The magnitude of the problem can be gauged from recent surveys (the 2002 Australian Computer Crime and Security Survey[32] and, in the United States, the 2002 CSI/FBI Computer Crime and Security Survey[33]). In the United States, 90 per cent of the respondents detected computer security breaches within the last 12 months, with the most serious financial losses occurring through theft of proprietary information and financial **fraud**, and 40 per cent detected system penetration from the outside and denial of service attacks. Total annual losses were estimated at $445 million. However, some commentators estimate the losses are more likely to run into the tens of billions of dollars, pointing out that 86 per cent of the organisations approached refused to participate in the survey. It has been said that most companies report a security lapse only if it becomes public. Reasons why companies are disinclined to report security breaches include the fear of legal liability if customer data is exposed and a backlash from investors.[34]

What is being done to counter such problems? The Australian government is pursuing an e-security policy to increase public confidence in the security of the online environment.[35] It has introduced the Cybercrime Bill 2001 with the aim of providing a strong deterrent to persons engaging in **cybercrime** activities such as hacking, computer virus propagation, denial of service attacks, stalking and fraud. The legislation also allows for enhancement of enforcement powers relating to the search and seizure of electronically stored data. The key offences are consistent with the terms of the draft Cyber Crime Convention being developed by the Council of Europe and other countries, including the United States.

The Computer Emergency Response Team (CERT) was established to research and advise organisations on computer security problems in the United States.[36] AusCERT is the equivalent operation in Australia.[37]

PRIVACY AND EMAIL

Although security measures can provide some protection for information transmitted over the Internet, they do not hide the trail created by each transaction. A web server is able to send a program called a 'cookie' over the Internet to be deposited on a user's hard drive without disclosure or consent.

The cookie was introduced as part of Netscape's web technology. When a web browser requests a page from a web server, the web server sends back to the web browser not just the requested page, but also an instruction to the browser to write a cookie — that is, a record — into the client computer's storage. Once written into the storage, the user can be identified each time they visit the same site thus allowing a profile of the user to be established based on usage patterns.

Potentially, such an arrangement could have advantages for both merchants and online consumers, in that the merchant is able to offer a service tailor-made for the user. However, the main objections to the use of cookies is that they have been introduced to a user's hard drive without disclosure or consent and the information collated could then become accessible to other organisations, including the government. Clearly, the objections could be overcome if the user were to be informed of cookie placement, the uses to which it would be put, and given the choice as to whether the user wished to proceed or not.

However, as we have seen earlier, because of the international nature of the Internet any national regulations may not apply to a foreign company. Furthermore, it may not even be possible to determine in which country the company is located so that enforcement of privacy provisions may be impossible.

Although guidelines have been prepared by such bodies as the United Nations, they carry no legal authority. The most influential provision to date is the European Union Council Personal Data Protection Directive which was formally adopted in July 1995. This establishes a set of legal principles for privacy protection applicable to both public and private sectors and legislation has since been enacted by all EU member states modelled on the directive.[38]

Although these legal principles apply only in the EU, their effect is far reaching. This is because the directive also prohibits the transfer of data from the EU to countries which do not have adequate data protection laws. Conversely, the import of data from such countries may also trigger the requirement of the importer to abide by the EU directive. This is one of the factors putting pressure on countries such as Australia to improve their privacy protection laws.

In Australia, the *Privacy Act 1988* (Cwlth) provides privacy safeguards which federal government departments must observe in collecting, storing and using personal information. The *Privacy Amendment (Private Sector) Act 2000* extended privacy protection to personal data held by the private sector in accordance with the 10 National Privacy Principles (NPPs),[39] a key principle providing a right of access to an individual so that they can check that the information is correct. Companies are given the choice of adopting these principles or adopting their own which, however, must comply with the principles. It remains to be seen whether Australia's privacy legislation is strict enough to meet EU laws.[40]

WC3 has prepared the Platform for Privacy Preferences (P3P) Project[41] to allow users to gain more control over the use of personal information on web sites they visit. The system established a standardised format to enable browsers to read a snapshot of the site's privacy policies and compare it with the customer's own set of privacy preferences.

Spamming — the sending out of unsolicited bulk email — is a growing problem.[42] Recently MonsterHut of Niagra Falls sent hundreds of millions of advertisements through emails, and 750 000 users complained. New York State is suing MonsterHut under traditional deceptive practice and false advertising statutes. Successful court actions have been achieved against spammers in the United States under trespass and computer fraud laws. Several US states now have anti-spam laws which prohibit false messages or headers in email messages.

The EU has just approved an anti-spam and online privacy directive that will significantly affect the practice of email marketing.[43] 'Opt-in' is established as the default rule for commercial email and all email communications in existing customer relationships must have an 'opt-out' feature. Among privacy provisions, web surfers must be told ahead of time about the site's cookie procedures, giving consumers the right to refuse cookie-based data collection. However, there is one very controversial regulation which states that ISPs, while normally allowing only third-party access to consumers' data with their permission, must allow that data to be divulged in the event of criminal investigations or matters of national or public security. This could be seen to be a threat to individual liberty. However, each EU member state has to pass the legislation as part of its own national laws, a process which could take several years.

In Australia, the Australian Communications Authority (ACA)[44] is the regulator for the communications industry and has made recommendations to the government on the Telecommunications Interception Amendment Bill, formalising the processes by which ISPs hand over information to assist law enforcement agencies.

The Privacy Foundation[45] provides useful information on current privacy issues. How much privacy do we have, or are we entitled to, when sending emails to each other – especially when using the Internet in the workplace? The Australian Federal Privacy Commissioner has prepared guidelines on workplace email, web browsing and privacy.[46] The guidelines stress the importance of the company preparing an inhouse policy so that all employees understand what is acceptable use, the extent of logging and monitoring of email communications by management, and what individual privacy limits will be respected by the company. Sales of employee surveillance software is booming around the world.

In terms of email generally, the tragic events of September 2001 in New York have led to governments increasing their powers to monitor email traffic around the world, consequently diluting privacy.

ETHICS

Anyone engaging in business activities should pay regard to the obligations imposed on them by legislation and industry codes of practice. However, in the absence of legislation or codes, which as we have seen may well be the case in Internet business, what should be the guiding principles in establishing and operating the business? It is here that ethical considerations play a part. They may be thought of as the moral dimension to business. Most professional bodies have established codes of **ethics** to regulate their dealings with their employers, members of the public or clients to ensure that their respective interests are safeguarded.[47]

Below are listed the 'Ten Commandments of Computer Ethics' established by the Computer Ethics Institute:

1. Thou shalt not use a computer to harm other people.
2. Thou shalt not interfere with other people's computer work.
3. Thou shalt not snoop around in other people's computer files.
4. Thou shalt not use a computer to steal.
5. Thou shalt not use a computer to bear false witness.
6. Thou shalt not copy or use proprietary software for which you have not paid.
7. Thou shalt not use other people's computer resources without authorisation or proper compensation.
8. Thou shalt not appropriate other people's intellectual output.
9. Thou shalt think about the social consequences of the program you are writing or the system you are designing.
10. Thou shalt always use a computer in ways that insure consideration and respect for your fellow humans.[48]

If you are proposing to conduct business on the Internet, and you are uncertain that what you are proposing is appropriate, you should ask yourselves these questions:

- Are you hiding certain facts because you fear disapproval?
- Are you purposely colouring facts to bias your message?
- If what you were doing was done to you, would you feel upset?
- Could anyone object to your action as unfair?
- Will anyone be harmed by your action?
- Do you feel the need to rationalise your behaviour?
- Could a destructive practice or trend evolve?[49]

If the answer to any of the above questions is 'yes', then you should reconsider your proposed action.

SUMMARY

There are at present very few legislative controls on the Internet although efforts are being made in various countries and internationally to draw up suitable model laws and guidelines.

Current laws and industry self-regulation have some applicability to Internet transactions within the state or nation. Consumer protection laws provide protection against misleading advertising and faulty goods. However, problems arise in trans-border transactions in determining which country's laws apply and which country's courts have jurisdiction. Problems are exacerbated if the parties to a transaction cannot be determined. This is possible due to the anonymity which the Internet can provide, especially through the use of hyperlinks, and the ease of establishing and closing down web sites in a short space of time.

A major hurdle to be overcome is to provide security over Internet communications to prevent fraud. Encryption techniques are being developed to facilitate monetary transfers and ensure that messages are not corrupted, accidentally or deliberately, by third parties. Hand in hand with the question of security is the question of protecting the privacy of the Internet user, who leaves a 'trail' every time he or she uses the Internet which can be followed and recorded.

Lastly, there is the question of who controls the content on the Internet. Countries are adopting different approaches to this issue, depending upon their societal and cultural values.

Key terms

advertising (p. 253)	ethics (p. 257)	legislation (p. 243)
censorship (p. 243)	fraud (p. 254)	meta tagging (p. 247)
contract (p. 249)	intellectual property	patents (p. 246)
copyright (p. 245)	(p. 245)	privacy (p. 243)
cybercrime (p. 255)	jurisdiction (p. 249)	trademarks (p. 247)
defamation (p. 250)	law (p. 243)	

THE ONLINE PRIVACY FRONTIER

By Katina Michael, University of Wollongong © 2002

PERSONALISATION AT A PRICE

Many web sites pride themselves on offering personalised customer service, but that really depends on the amount of information the online shopper is willing to give the online merchant. In most cases, unless a purchase is made or some other form of transaction is enacted, the online shopper will not declare their identity. How personalised can an experience be online if one entity decides to remain anonymous? The online merchant has little, if any, information to go on apart from perhaps a cookie that tells them that the visitor is a repeat visitor to that web site. The seller does not know anything about the background of the online shopper at the time of browsing – where they are geographically located, whether they are male or female, the age of the individual, etc. The geo-demographic statistical information that direct-mail campaigns were once based on is almost impossible to gather online unless the customer willingly provides their personal details. It is for this reason that database marketing strategies and techniques have had to be redefined as more and more customers have sought an online experience.

The question of how many individuals would be voluntarily willing to part with their personal details online is a good one. The first instinctive response would be that very few people would give their details to any online query form in any web site, mostly due to privacy concerns. And why should they, since they are not receiving anything in return? A contract, an agreement, can only be made if both parties involved benefit from the engagement.

Some months ago, I observed the behaviour of students at the local gymnasium. A promotional stall offering free drinks in exchange for a name and address was set up near the exit. One by one, as students came out of the change rooms, they would stop at the stall, collect their drink and provide their details. The disturbing thing was that most of them did not even ask what was going to happen to the details they were providing; they just wanted to know if indeed the drink was free. The drink of course was free, which meant that the students were saving $1.50. It immediately made me think about the value we place on our personal details and how much we really are concerned about privacy when our name and address could be bought for a couple of dollars.

Getting your 'free' web site passport

Web sites that do deliver some value-added service to their existing and prospective customers online have started to demand a fairer exchange. If you want this white-paper, then tell me who you are and where you are from. If you want a free online newsletter, then you will have to give me your email address. If you want to download our latest software update free for a period of 30 days, then you will have to register your company details.

If you want to download this multi-media clip, then please give us your address so we can send you a colour catalogue via post. Companies are now luring prospective buyers, particularly professionals, to their web sites by offering them something 'free'.[50]

The notion of 'free', however, has taken on another guise today — especially over the Internet. 'Free' usually means that some exchange must take place first, just like the example of the free drink samples that were being distributed at the gymnasium. However, company online registration forms make it even clearer which compulsory fields need to be filled out to obtain user access to a particular section(s) of the web site. Failure to fill out all required fields means that access is denied and an ID in the form of a site-pass (also known as a passport[51]) is not granted.

The data usually requested on the online registration form includes the user's name, fixed address, telephone number and email address (at least). Online companies specialising in business-to-business activities also request a company name, position title, facsimile, industry type, and a revenue estimate in some cases. A user need only register once to receive a valid pass code. Thereafter, the same login and pass code is used for subsequent visits allowing the user to download from otherwise protected parts of the site.

Now, while the access to the online content is important to the user, since the individual goes to the effort of filling out an online form, one is still led to question what actually happens to the data once it has been collected.

Most companies would lead us to believe that they are doing us a favour by collecting our personal details because that means they can send us timely and relevant information. Of course, the online merchant would use it for internal market intelligence purposes, but what else? Could the data collected perhaps also be shared with other business partners? Could the data collected be on-sold to other merchants at a premium? And who would have access to that information; would it be securely stored and where?

The online privacy statement

Companies that engage in business-to-business (B2B) activities have always provided legal statements on their web sites. More recently, however, privacy statements have also been added, not only to inform the user of how their information is being used, but also why it is being collected, who is most likely to use it, how cookies are being applied, and how the user can 'opt-out' from future unwanted communications. The hyperlinks to the company's legal, copyright and privacy policies are usually located at the bottom of the home page. Although the hyperlinks are usually so small that they go unnoticed, it is recommended that any individual wishing to register their personal details online should at least read the privacy statement of the company. What you may consider to be a breach of privacy in the future may have been documented on the online privacy statement. As long as the user is informed of how their information will be used, and the company privacy statement complies with jurisdictional privacy acts, where products or services are sold, the company is not in any way liable.

Companies that engage in business-to-consumer (B2C) activities are not exempt from online privacy statements. In most cases, the privacy statements of these companies are more detailed than B2B companies. When one considers the customer base of a company like Amazon[52] and the type of information that is likely to be gathered from customer browsing, repeat purchases, enquiries via email, book reviews, wish lists, discussion boards and chat rooms, the importance of privacy is heightened. Perhaps, however, instead of deterring customer interaction the Amazon approach has actually done the reverse – made customers feel part of an online community, that their unique voice and feedback is valued and that the personalisation is more useful than harmful. In its privacy statement, Amazon even states the individual entities that it may share information with although not to the level of specificity that would be more appropriate. For example, when Amazon states that it may share information with affiliated companies which it has no control over, such as Drugstore.com (its health and beauty merchant), it is not very reassuring for the customer. For instance, how many other affiliates are there? Ten, fifty, hundreds?

One thing is certain: a company, whether B2C or B2B, can use sign-in features to discriminate between customers who are just browsing, and customers who are serious about purchasing or who want to learn more about products and services.

A user who fills out an online form is most likely a customer that a company would want to have in its lead database. They may not purchase anything but chances are they will either return or contact a sales representative by telephone for more information.

Of course, there is nothing to stop an individual from setting up a dummy email account and providing dummy personal details during the whole registration process. But even setting up a dummy email account, perhaps using MSN's 'free' hotmail service,[53] requires you to fill in yet another online form and to enter yet more dummy details. To protect your personal details, it is a lot of trouble to go to. No sooner have you created a fake identity for yourself, you are subsequently trying to remember what those fake attributes were that you defined! Apart from this there is the added requirement that you may have to eventually make a purchase on the site you have been browsing, and a secure purchase online would not allow for such anonymity. Entering credit card details with a name, number and valid expiry date, as well as billing and shipping location information, requires an authorisation process to take place at the time of checkout.

The hidden impact of web server analytics

While the information that customers willingly give company web sites is one form of online data collection, there are more sophisticated means available of collecting data that are more obscure. Web server statistical software[54] can help web hosting companies or individual companies that host their own web sites understand the goals of their customers and their online behaviour.

Basic web server results include the number of hits the web server and particular pages have received, the number of sessions of each individual Internet protocol (IP) address, the session length of each individual shopper, and whether or not the customer is a repeat visitor.

Newer, more sophisticated, Internet analytical software also gathers the type of complex customer data that can be used to target individual users 'on the fly'. Path tracking[55] functionality can even follow the movements of customers once they enter a particular web site. Coupled with secure login, it not only becomes possible to identify the actual customer but also to look at how they specifically browse for products. For example, does a customer's spending capacity lead them to shop for high-end items or low-end items or somewhere in the middle? In the future it is not inconceivable that companies will use the power of extensible markup language (XML) to dynamically show customised web pages that promote particular products at a particular price range, based on the online historical spending and browsing patterns of a given customer.

The responsibility and accountability factors

The issue of privacy is again forthcoming in the virtual world, just as it was and still is in the physical world. The vast majority of companies online do declare how they use information that is willingly given to them by customers – but what about the type of data that is gathered without the knowledge of the user? What happens to that information? How many privacy policies actually address the idea of cyber-surveillance?

Even a technique like cookies, whose purpose is to relate future transactions to past ones using a unique alphanumeric identifier, can be used to track the individual patterns of an online surfer.[56] Whether the online surfer is anonymous or not is beside the point. Cookies have the ability to retrieve information from your computer that was not originally sent in the cookie. Some company web sites demand the use of cookies, others grant the user the option, still others do not even allude to them.

What is, however, becoming more and more obvious is that companies collecting customer information online need to become increasingly responsible by informing their users about what they are actually doing. Users in turn have the equal responsibility of increasingly becoming educated about how their privacy may be infringed by the latest developments in online information-gathering techniques and how they can protect themselves in the cyberworld. Accountability is something that is shared among all the entities entering into an agreement.

QUESTIONS

1. What are the different ways that company web sites can gather personal information about their customers?
2. Discuss the online privacy notice of the largest bookseller in the world, Amazon, by visiting the company's web site (www.amazon.com). What are the specific issues that are covered by the privacy notice?

3. What is a cookie? How and why do companies use cookies on their web sites?
4. What are web server analytics? What type of information can be gathered by a web server? Visit www.123loganalyzer.com/sample/ to view some web analyser results.
5. What is web site user path tracking? What can a company do with path tracking information? Visit www.accrue.com/products/ for assistance.
6. How can companies ensure that the information gathered on their online web site is protected against potential breaches of privacy?

Questions

If you were in the process of establishing a commercial web site in Australia:
1. What issues would you address in order to safeguard your operation from any legal disputation?
2. How would you provide users with some confidence that transactions conducted with your site would protect the privacy of the user?
3. Would you need to investigate the bona fides of linked site(s) if you provided hypertext links to other web sites? Could you protect yourself from legal disputation arising from users who gained access to the linked site through your own? If so, how?
4. Would your answers be any different if you were establishing your site in:
(i) Europe   (ii) the United States?
If so, how?

Suggested | reading

Adam, N. R. 1999, *Electronic Commerce: Technical, Business and Legal Issues*, Prentice Hall PTR, www.phptr.com.

Allen, M. 2002, *E-business, the Law and You*, Prentice Hall, New Jersey.

Fitzgerald, A. and Fitzgerald, B. 2002, *Cyberlaw: Cases and Materials on the Internet, Digital Intellectual Property and Electronic Commerce*, Butterworths, Sydney.

Forder, J. and Quirk, P. 2001, *Electronic Commerce and the Law*, John Wiley & Sons, Brisbane.

Lawson, J. 1999, *The Complete Internet Handbook for Lawyers*, American Bar Association, Chicago.

Lessig, L. 1999, *Code and Other Laws of Cyberspace*, Basic Books, New York.

End | notes

1. For current news on national approaches to this and other Internet issues see Global Internet Liberty Campaign, www.gilc.org.
2. *Reno* v. *American Civil Liberties Union*, 521 US 844 (1997).
3. Alcorn, G. 2002. 'Court strikes down law on "virtual" child porn', *Sydney Morning Herald*, 18 April, p. 8.
4. Internet Content Rating Association, www.icra.org.
5. Telecommunications Industry Ombudsman, www.tio.com.au.
6. Australian Broadcasting Authority, aba.gov.au.
7. Internet Industry Association, www.iia.net.au; Electronic Frontiers Australia, www.efa.org.au; Internet Society of Australia, www.isoc-au.org.au.

8. Dearne, K. 2000, 'Censorship law's joke', *Australian*, 24 October, p. 24, www.australianIT.com.au.

9. Censorship in a Box, cyber-Liberties 1998, American Civil Liberties Union, www.aclu.org/issues/cyber/box.html#blocking.

10. Deital, H. M., Deital P. J. and Nieto, T. R. 2000, *e-Business and e-Commerce; How to Program*, Prentice Hall, New Jersey, p. 174.

11. Thornburgh, D. and Lin, H. S. (eds) 2002, *Youth, Pornography and the Internet*, National Academies Press, Washington, DC.

12. Australian Copyright Council, www.copyright.org.au.

13. www.riaa.com.

14. Adar, E. and Huberman, B. A. 2001, *Free Riding on Gnutella*, Internet Ecologies Area, Xerox Palo Alto Research Centre, Palo Alto, 4304.

15. For further information see www.ipaustralia.gov.au.

16. Anonymous 1999, 'Amazon's one click suit', an article from the *New York Times* reproduced in the *Sydney Morning Herald*, 25 October 1999, p. 41.

17. 149 F3d 1368 (Fed Circ 1998), cert denied 1195 Cr 851 (1999).

18. www.w3.org.

19. For further information see www.ipaustralia.gov.au.

20. For rules and policies on registration see www.internetnamesww.com.au.

21. www.maxamine.com.

22. www.auda.org.au.

23. Kurtz, H. 1997, 'New media, old rules', *Sydney Morning Herald*, 23 August, Icon, p. 14.

24. *Macquarie Bank Limited & Anor v. Berg* 1999 NSWSC 526 (2 June 1999), www.austlii.edu.au/do/disp.pl/au/cases/nsw/supreme_ct/1999/526.html.

25. www.wsj.com.

26. www.uncitral.org/en-index.htm.

27. See www.ecommerce.treasury.gov.au.

28. www1.oecd.org/dsti/sti/it/ec/news/cont-e.htm.

29. Mastercard, Secure Electronic Transaction (SET) Protocol, www.mastercardintl.com/newtechnology/set.

30. The European Commission, 'Commission welcomes final adoption of legal framework directive', europa.eu.int/comm/internal_market/en/commerce/2k-442.htm.

31. Trusted Computing Platform Alliance, www.trustedcomputing.org.

32. www.deloitte.com.au.

33. www.gocsi.com/press/2002040407.html.

34. *Los Angeles Times* 2001, 'Computer crime flourishes behind states of denial', in *Sydney Morning Herald* 20 March, IT, p. 1.

35. Protection of Australia's National Information Infrastructure and E-Security Policy, www.noie.gov.au/Projects/Information_economy/e-security/nat_agenda.htm.

36. www.cert.org.

37. www.auscert.com.au.

38. For an example see the United Kingdom's *Data Protection Act 1998*, www.legislation.hmso.gov.uk/acts/acts1998/19980029.htm.

39. www.privacy.gov.au.

40. *UNSW Law Journal*, 'Valuing privacy: legal protections and exceptions', www.law.unsw.edu.au/unswlj/forum/valuing.

41. www.w3.org.

42. Coalition against Unsolicited Bulk Email, www.caube.org.au.

43. 'EU OK's spam ban, online privacy rules', www.internetnews.com/IAR/article.php/1154391.

44. www.aca.gov.au.

45. Privacy Foundation, www.privacyfoundation.org.

46. www.privacy.gov.au/internet/email.

47. For example, see Australian Computer Society Code of Ethics, www.acs.org.au/national/pospaper/acs131.htm.
48. www.cpsr.org/program/ethics/cei.
49. Based on Parker, C. C. 1996, *Understanding Computers Today and Tomorrow*, Dryden Press, p. SOC 2–22.
50. See www.mapinfo.com/free/index.cfm.
51. See www.siebel.com/common/includes/passport/passport_sign_up.shtm.
52. See www.amazon.com.
53. See www.hotmail.com.
54. See www.123loganalyzer.com/sample/.
55. See www.accrue.com/products/.
56. Whitaker, R. 1999, *The End of Privacy*, The New Press, New York, pp. 103–4.

CHAPTER 11

Future trends

LEARNING outcomes

You will have mastered the material in this chapter when you can:

- understand the concept of the dot.com economy
- identify new forms of intermediation
- define an Internet portal, auction and knowledge exchange
- explain the key aspects of portals and online auction technologies
- describe and explain a virtual private network (VPN)
- understand XML and XQuery and their importance to Internet commerce
- describe the potential impact on Internet commerce of mobile commerce and Bluetooth
- explain the meaning of P2P computing
- identify the major trends in government and Internet commerce
- describe how industry structures are changing through new business models.

'Any sufficiently advanced technology is indistinguishable from magic.'

Arthur C. Clarke, *Profiles of the Future*, Harper & Row, New York, 1973.

INTRODUCTION

In 1996, the chairman of the US Reserve Bank Dr Alan Greenspan depicted investors in the booming US economy as possessing an 'irrational exuberance'.[1] Since that famous speech, the quotation has been used synonymously to describe the turbulent, overheated dot.com environment which existed in the late twentieth century.

The 'great shakedown of 2000' which began in April 2000, saw the death of many dot.com companies along with their innovative business models and the promise of astonishing returns for investors. This rationalisation or consolidation of the Internet landscape forced entrepreneurs and investors alike to rethink their financial and business models. A realisation swept the industry — Internet business is still business — the fundamentals of business still apply to the Internet world.

Despite the 'great shakedown', the Internet phenomenon remains strong and continues to expand at an astonishing rate across the globe.[2] Without doubt, the Internet provides tangible value to businesses and offers unlimited potential for companies to improve the reach to their customers and trading partners.

By now we appreciate that the Internet presents many new opportunities to businesses. With these new opportunities come new challenges, forcing firms to seek new strategies that might work in an ever-changing technological and economic environment. For those firms who wish to succeed in Internet commerce, mastery of the three fundamental Internet characteristics still holds — ubiquity, interactivity and speed.[3]

Everywhere on the Internet is accessible to users on what is essentially an unlimited and equal basis — this is ubiquity. The user can go anywhere on the Internet with a minimum of effort and there is no real technological reason for the user to start at a specific spot or web site. Because the Internet is interactive, exciting new forms of interactivity have developed. Software is distributed and tested online, information is exchanged and modified more easily — data may be stored online and virtual organisations can operate more effectively through interacting on a global basis at any hour of the day or night.

The speed at which businesses can be established on the Internet places a great deal of emphasis on being first in a particular market category, as has been discussed in previous chapters. Further, many Internet-based businesses have been developed as overlays of existing infrastructure, which has reduced start-up costs and time of deployment.

Because the Internet provides an instant, convenient channel for researching, working, communicating, exchanging and choosing information, Internet commerce is now allowing firms to reconsider which functions they should perform in-house and which are best outsourced. In fact, Forrester Research has coined a new word 'exsourced' and defines an exsourcer as a 'help provider that manages multi-company processes and technologies across the Internet'.[4]

New relationships are being formed to streamline and enhance supply-chain processes. Companies such as FedEx and UPS are finding that their roles as logistic intermediaries are expanding, as it is vital that the ordered goods are delivered quickly. American Express, an example of a financial intermediary, now offers an enhanced purchasing card that supports online purchasing by facilitating the process of placing an order, fulfilment, reconciliation, data management and program maintenance. These shifts in process can result in significant cost savings.[5]

The main drivers of business acceptance and uptake of Internet commerce into the future century appear to be:

- continued global expansion, or globalisation
- convergence of media and communications technologies
- increasing awareness and familiarity by consumers and business users of Internet tools
- easier-to-use Internet interfaces (e.g. browsers, directories and search engines)
- new business opportunities in new forms.

There is no doubt that change is the only constant as everything becomes faster and as the rate of change accelerates. Companies failing to join online business communities could be left behind, missing out on the preferred way of doing business in the next millennium. Looking towards the future of e-commerce, we see broad trends emerging:[6]

- *Internet security*: Security and safety of Internet commerce through the application of secure technologies such as smart cards will find increased acceptance.
- *E-metrics*: The measurement and analysis of web activity and web-assisted revenue will continue to be highly important to companies.
- *The 'e' factor*: Companies now realise that Internet business is still business — the fundamental principles of business apply, regardless of the medium. Companies are now dropping the 'e' from their initiatives.
- *The customer*: Much hype has been given to the importance of the Internet customer and yet true, viable customer-focused solutions continue to evade web companies. The Internet customer and their inherent value will become the single priority for companies.
- *P2P commerce*: Peer-to-peer (P2P) technology will continue to converge with B2B technology helping to improve e-commerce solutions and connectivity between supply-chain participants.
- *U-commerce*: Ubiquitous commerce (U-commerce) describes commerce which occurs automatically without disrupting daily life. As technologies converge and become ubiquitous, we will see the rise of automatic transactions and commerce.

In this final chapter we take a look at the emerging new models of digital business, drivers of new trends and technical developments, the concerns and influence of government in the internationalisation of economies, and provide some forward projections for Internet business in general.

DOT.COM INDUSTRY

As we described earlier in the chapter, the dot.com sector has undergone major rationalisation in the last few years. However, this has not stopped the progression and growth of the dot.com industry, as shown in figure 11.1. How do we define a dot.com? Typically, a dot.com company has the following characteristics:

- it does business almost entirely on the Internet, that is, it generally has no physical shopfront or outlets
- it conducts business by trading information, services or products online.

E-commerce snapshot
- As of May 2002, approximately 560 million people across the globe use the Internet.[7]
- B2B spending for 2004 is expected to exceed the US$1 trillion mark.[8]
- Australia has 10.6 million (52 per cent) people online and New Zealand has 1.95 million people online.[9]
- Nearly 10 per cent of the workforce in NSW tele-works.[10]
- E-business transactions in Australia will be worth A$87.1 billion by 2006, up from A$6.2 billion in 2001.[11]

FIGURE 11.1: Snapshot of e-commerce activity

Throughout the world, dot.com companies continue to flourish. Many entrepreneurs are now targeting China, which has a huge untapped cyber-market that is expected to grow substantially in the twenty-first century. Currently, China is second only to the United States in the number of home users who are online.[12] Some developments there include Sina.com, and alibaba.com. Australia has seen listings of dot.com companies in almost every sector, with names such as NineMSN, eChoice, Shopfast, Green-grocer.com, Wishlist and E*Trade becoming household icons.

The Internet revolution continues to influence every industry from banking to selling groceries or cars, from planning weddings and birthday parties to managing farms and web servers, from routing container ships to making steel or selling postage stamps. Companies are combining Internet technology and marketing budgets to compete with companies founded before the Web arrived. Larger older companies may be too slow and too concerned with their histories to compete effectively in the new dot.com economy. The classic example of the above was seen by the slow reaction of Barnes & Noble to Amazon. The founders of these new dot.com companies believe they can use the Internet to create value for customers and wealth for investors before the traditional bigger older companies realise the opportunity.

Larger and more traditionally structured companies have often found it harder to react quickly to the Internet phenomenon. Some have created their own dot.com departments and some have formed smaller companies hoping that they can move quickly enough to catch the cyber start-ups. Some have acquired smaller companies that have taken the lead on the Internet; for example, Harris Technology was bought by the Coles Myer Group. Parent companies often find that the effort required to set up an electronic commerce division in-house is potentially too great to justify the investment. Overcoming the built-in barriers in a more conservative organisational structure and thinking and reacting like a venture-backed start-up may take too long. Shareholder pressures, corporate culture and legacy systems are some of the problems bigger companies confront in activating Internet-based initiatives.[13]

THE INFOMEDIARY

We have considered disintermediation and reintermediation in previous chapters of this book. Early Internet commerce theory proposed that the commercial function of the Internet would be simply to cut out the intermediary – the middle-man – allowing companies such as Dell Computers to put up a web site and sell direct to the masses.[14] In fact, as the Internet community grows, we see a trend towards reintermediation through the birth and evolution of a new entity – the information intermediary (infomediary) – a person or company who acts as an agent to enterprises, providing information, products and services as required.

As we saw in chapter 2, the **infomediary** concept has evolved from the early Internet business models which included online auctions and catalogues through to present-day models such as the exchange and e-marketplace. The evolution of the infomediary is expected to continue and fundamentally alter current Internet business models. Table 11.1 outlines the evolution of the infomediary and suggests how the role of the infomediary will evolve over time.[15]

TABLE 11.1	THE EVOLUTION OF THE INFOMEDIARY	
MODEL	**VALUE PROPOSITION**	**STRATEGY**
Portals and auctions	Commodity exchange	Focus on buying and selling commodified products, information and services.
E-marketplaces and collaborative hubs	Commodity exchange with value-added support services	Provide value-added services to support customers with transactional and customised products and services.
Knowledge exchanges	A collaborative knowledge network	The development of knowledge tools creating the building blocks for global knowledge exchanges and a global knowledge network.
Global value trust exchanges	Value trust networks (VTNs)	VTNs become the integration point for business processes, technology, products and services. VTNs will integrate enterprises, marketplaces, industries and individuals together into global digital workgroups.

SOURCE: Adapted from W. Raisch 2001, *The eMarketplace: Strategies for Success in B2B eCommerce*, McGraw-Hill, New York, p. 3.

Portals

One of the most popular Internet models to emerge in recent years has been the **portal**. Portals have been likened to the front page of a newspaper or magazine; an all-in-one web site used to find other sites. LookSmart, Yahoo!, Excite, Anzwers and NineMSN home pages are typical examples of broadly targeted portals. Portals can include email, search engines, news, sport, weather, e-commerce, entertainment, special interest chat groups and links to myriad other services. Business-to-business portals appear to have essentially emerged from business-based virtual communities. Within the business sector, portals focused on aggregating information relevant to specific interest groups are referred to as online vertical trade communities or **vortals**. Chemdex.com is an example of an industry-specific (or niche) vortal that allows laboratory personnel to search a vast catalogue of chemical supplies from various providers. The Australian Cultural Network web site (see figure 11.2) is an example of a community-focused vortal.

FIGURE 11.2: An example of a community-focused vortal
(www.cultureandrecreation.gov.au)

Web site personalisation

The future of the portal is promising. The aggregation of information and services in a single browser window is both convenient and popular for the consumer. As consumers spend more and more time online, one trend set to continue will be the personalisation or customisation of the web experience. For companies creating portals, as competition in the space grows, so too does the challenge to attract and retain customers. Keeping a web site interesting and compelling will present a major challenge to companies in the B2C and B2B space. Providing a personalisation engine is one mechanism for improving content relevance for customers.

Personalisation is the act of recognising a customer, subscriber or visitor as an individual and modifying actions based upon information known about the customer. Thus, personalisation makes the interaction better for the customer through relevance of information and service, and better for the company through higher margin selling and higher revenue. There are several types of personalisation that may be used:

- *Implicit personalisation (inference tracking)*: The recording and assessment of day-to-day customer actions. Examples include purchase and transaction history, click-streams, and session-specific data such as browser type, access speed and site of origin. This is often referred to as inference tracking.
- *Explicit personalisation*: Information explicitly entered by the customer into the database system. Examples include date of birth, email address and postcode.
- *Profiling*: Profiling involves collecting customer information on a systematic basis so that this information can be used to enable one-to-one marketing efforts.
- *Collaborative filtering*: Recommends products and services to the customer based upon purchases made by customers with similar tastes. Examples include Amazon and Yahoo!

Auctions and reverse auctions

As outlined in chapter 2, **online auctions** have changed the face of electronic commerce. In many cases they are add-on businesses for online retailers, another form of buyer interaction. Sites offering online auctions have redefined business for collectors, resellers, consumers and shipping companies. They can create international markets linking like-minded individuals on different continents in communities of interest.

In May 2001, US Internet users spent US$556 million at auction sites with the giant of the global online auctions, eBay, attracting over 64 per cent of all online auction consumer spending in that time.[16] Using a business model where sellers pay for the site's costs, eBay has been consistently profitable despite the fact that it does not have to handle the goods itself. Anyone auctioning goods must pay eBay a fee, as well as a percentage of the sale.

Priceline.com is a 'name your price' online auction model, referred to as the Reverse Auction model in chapter 2. It allows would-be buyers to name the price for airline tickets, then checks whether major airlines will sell a seat at that price.

The success of consumer-oriented auctions may be emulated or even surpassed by business-to-business auctions. In this model, companies usually sell surplus inventory or commodities in large quantities like electric power or medical equipment generally either to invited dealers or pre-screened partners.

Online auctioneers are expanding their inventory to include a wider range of goods to keep buyers coming back. Real-world farm auctioneers Farmbid (www.farmbid.com) provides a full auction service online for supplies and livestock. Upscale auction houses, often in association with Internet partners, are going online. The second-largest auction house in the world, the 250-year-old Sotheby's Holdings, has signed up 1500 art dealers for its auction site, which was launched in July 1999.

To date, online auctions have faced surprisingly little pressure for regulation, even from consumer advocacy groups, as all parties are reluctant to stifle the boom.[17] This new industry must address many controversial elements before it can become a permanent fixture, including fraud, taxes and the sale of regulated goods ranging from wine to weaponry.

E-marketplaces

Following the proliferation of portals and vortals across the Web, focused trading communities will tend to converge into smaller communities known as **e-marketplaces** or collaborative hubs. The term **hub** comes from the networking world where it is a central device from which everything radiates. In the Web this means that the hub becomes the focus of activities, not just a gateway to pass through.

E-marketplaces have a narrow focus, typically in one industry. To succeed as an e-marketplace, the site must specialise in terms of content, commerce and community, appropriate to the specific audience and provide value-added services. The e-marketplace provides support to trading members at all levels, from supplying the e-commerce technology platform through to managing the buyer and seller relationships within the industry. E-marketplaces are seen to be collaborative because they offer more than just transactional service and the buying and selling of commodities. Business partners can exchange proprietary or confidential information, co-manage projects and cooperate on the design of new products, all via an intermediary web server with simple web browser technology at the client site. This collaborative commerce also has the ability to accelerate the cycle time for trading partners. By sharing pricing information, inventory and credit details for example, trading partners can transact in the online environment at an accelerated pace, thus making their trading cycles more efficient.[18]

In addition to the core transactional and collaborative services, e-marketplaces may also offer second-tier value-added services such as:
- aggregated buying
- business and financial services
- advertising
- trade facilitation – transportation and logistics support.

In Sydney, 15 energy companies have collaborated to implement a new way to trade electricity generated from renewable energy sources. The Green Electricity Market (GEM) project (www.greenelectricitymarket.com) will be an Internet-based e-marketplace that allows members to trade in electricity.[19] Cable & Wireless Optus Australia has used an e-marketplace to streamline its internal procurement operations and has realised a 75 per cent reduction in purchase order time saving thousands of employee hours.[20]

It's possible that cooperative competition will continue indefinitely as the working model for the new economy. Historical versions of this emerging e-marketplace network economy, such as the early European markets or even the modern shopping mall, were successful because they were able to offer the same valuable proposition that is being offered to Internet customers today – it was cheaper and more time-effective to trade within their walls than outside them.

Knowledge exchanges

As we move further into the information age, the need for organisations to effectively collate, store and reference information will be the key to profit-ability and indeed survival. Specifically, the effective creation and understanding of information assets (or knowledge assets) will play a significant part in the building and operation of the future organisation. With the twenty-first century already upon us, the age of the information worker or knowledge worker has come. Organisations of the future will become dependent on the effectiveness of their knowledge workers and the extent to which these workers collaborate with each other.

Competing in the information age will require organisations to rapidly form knowledge worker teams comprising members from both inside and outside the physical boundaries of the organisation. Knowledge teams may network via knowledge exchanges to leverage the skills of experts, best practice technologies and frameworks, and business partners across the globe.[21]

These **knowledge exchanges** (knowledge marketplaces) will be collaboration points for knowledge workers and will provide databases of information either specific to an industry or horizontally across many interests. Through collaboration and networking, the knowledge exchange will bring together the right information and people to assist customers with specific challenges; provide customised solutions; and identify and capitalise on new opportunities.

The knowledge exchange will be structured by collaboration of:

- knowledge workers – inter- and intra-organisational employees working with knowledge
- knowledge networks – interconnected knowledge sources
- production networks – design and production teams digitally connected
- global resource planning (GRP) networks – aimed at optimising business processes and production.[22]

Value trust networks

The **value trust network (VTN)** brings together transactional capability, value-added services and knowledge networks to offer the customer true value both in a physical and digital sense. For the concept of the VTN to work, it must offer a complete solution to the customer while also leveraging the trusted relationships that exist in the supply chain between trading partners.

The VTN is based upon the e-marketplace model whereby the buyer and seller are offered transactional capability or exchange as is present in many exchanges today. However, the VTN will add value by offering additional digital and physical coordination services to enhance the transactional capability. Digital value-add services may include financial services or consulting. The physical services may include logistic and distribution support. Finally, the VTN will also offer extensive knowledge services and trade collaboration services. The VTN will enable organisations to access data warehouses, participate in web workflows and coordinate in integrated business process re-engineering. The offerings of a VTN include:

- information/knowledge services – data warehousing, mining and intelligence reporting
- collaboration services – web workflow, integrated business solutions
- supply-chain services – coordination of logistics and distribution services
- community services – communities of interest for members
- trading services – transactional capabilities – buy/sell, auction, catalogue
- integration services – system and business integration between trading partners.[23]

A VIRTUAL PRIVATE NETWORK

A **virtual private network (VPN)** utilises a public network, such as the Internet, to transmit private data. VPNs are an emerging form of extranet that may become a viable replacement for traditional wide area networks (WANs). It is vital that the data is kept secure, confidential and maintains its integrity when it is being transmitted over the Internet. Creating an extranet over existing Internet infrastructure brings international companies closer to the idea of operating as a virtual enterprise. A VPN could also be thought of as a collection of technologies such as host authentication using Secure Shell (SSH) protocol or protocol tunnelling using encryption (and sometimes compression) to create secure connections or 'tunnels' over regular Internet lines (see figure 11.3).

The virtual private network allows:

- network managers to cost-efficiently increase the span of the corporate network
- remote users to securely and easily access their corporate network
- corporations to securely communicate with business partners
- enterprises to outsource hosting of servers and applications
- service providers to grow business by providing value-added services.[24]

The cost advantages of a virtual private network are generally acknowledged as:

- cheap and easy access rather than using the more expensive traditional remote access solutions (e.g. leased lines)
- reduces infrastructure cost and complexity by utilising a company's existing investment in the Internet
- eliminates access and maintenance costs to support 1800 numbers or banks of modems for direct dialling and long-distance call charges.

For companies with multiple locations, telecommuters, mobile workers or the need to exchange information with trading partners, a VPN offers a viable alternative to such traditional remote access solutions as X.25, leased lines, frame relay, 1800 numbers and long-distance modem dial-in.

The VPN brings the best features of the wide-open Internet to the secure and reliable world of private services such as leased lines or a frame relay service. Although the concept of a VPN has been largely associated with establishing encrypted tunnels across the Internet for the use of 'road warriors' or telecommuters, the majority of IP-VPNs (Internet protocol-based virtual private networks) will be hosted on private networks.

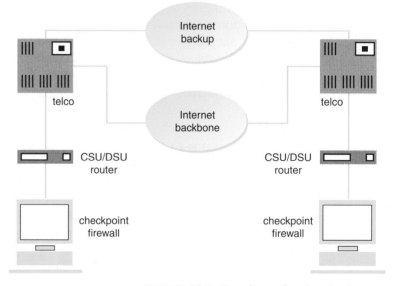

FIGURE 11.3: Flow chart of a virtual private network
SOURCE: FishNet Security 1999, www.kcfishnet.com/vpn.html.

ENTERPRISE INFORMATION PORTALS

One of the major problems in nearly every organisation has been distributing information across different platforms to knowledge workers. With a browser and access to the Internet, every user is able to access the same information at the same time, regardless of platform or organisational department. This means that the myriad of once platform-specific applications are now being used by entire organisations through Intranet technology. This freedom of access, ease of information flow and distribution allows an organisation to operate more effectively by being able to disseminate information and clearly express its vision, strategies and future goals to employees.

Corporate intranets, now being called **enterprise information portals (EIPs)**, are being used to manage this organisational knowledge. Internet users are familiar with a web browser interface (even an operating system such as Windows XP has modelled its appearance on such an interface). As a result, corporate intranets have applied the same model to the distribution of information to their employees.

EIPs afford an effective means of knowledge management within organisations by offering the following:

- bottom-up improvement – the users, not management, drive knowledge management
- intranets encourage knowledge-sharing techniques and virtual learning
- platform-independent software means integration of legacy systems and disparate information sources is straightforward
- three-tiered approach to application implementation means intranet applications are easily modified to accommodate rapid shifts in technical and organisational structure.[25]

The challenge of the EIP is to manage the knowledge within the organisation. An EIP site may include a search engine covering the entire intranet, a categorisation of information on the site, news sources, links to internal sites and popular external web sites, and the ability to personalise the page. The EIP may help to provide a framework for data, turning information into knowledge for employees to use.

The main features of an EIP are as follows:

- an easy-to-understand 'map' of the data (metadata). One such tool is Mindmap, an easy-to-use piece of software that maps the business organisation's web site.
- the ability to publish all types of information – data, word-processing files, spreadsheets, audio, video, images, streaming video, HTML, email, reports, etc. Many companies find it useful to train their staff online using streaming video. The School of Computing Sciences at the University of Technology is a registered Cisco Academy and several staff members are trained as Cisco Certified Network Administrators using online Cisco material.
- management of user profiles – information technology (IT) should be able to administer individual and group profiles alike, and individuals should be able to finetune their own profiles within the boundaries established by IT. The Cisco material, for example, is set up so that instructors see certain materials including teaching tips, while students have their own profile that, obviously, does not show the tips.
- the ability to support triggers or alerts (exception reporting), which is a key component of an EIP.
- both push and pull implementations. An EIP should 'pull' information to publish to the appropriate receiver, based on the profiles, and also 'push' information on a regular basis.[26]

Users should be able to subscribe, design, create, collaborate on, publish and distribute information efficiently and effectively on the business's EIP. EIPs should:

- increase productivity
- be easy to use

- allow users to focus on the content, context and relevance of corporate information
- lead to improved decision making.

Organisations throughout the world are benefiting from the tangible and intangible advantages arising from intranet implementation. Primarily used to increase cost-effectiveness and enhance corporate business practice, companies are discovering that intranet architecture is permitting departments to improve on management processes without incurring costly IT architecture overhauls. Intranets enable organisations to re-engineer their business management processes and increase knowledge sharing without sacrificing the previous investment in legacy applications and database systems.

XML

XML stands for extensible markup language. It is a meta language — that is, it is a language used to describe or define other languages. It is used to define text markup so that the text can be used and interpreted by different applications, including those that present information to people. It resembles HTML (hypertext markup language) which is the markup language used to display data in a web environment. Essentially, whereas HTML describes the layout of information, XML describes what kind of information is being displayed.

The usefulness in XML lies in the fact that new tags such as 'Product-Number', 'ProductName', 'Year' and 'Position' may be defined. XML applications are useful to businesses as they allow non-technical personnel to update web pages easily — it becomes as simple as filling in a form.

XML is a universal representation that can be used to prepare text not only for the Internet and other electronic applications. Other applications include:
- electronic publishing to various media, including paper, the Web, CD-ROM, hand-held devices, audio, even Braille
- electronic data interchange
- defining a single, common data format that could be used for interchange among different applications, such as Microsoft's PowerPoint, Word and Excel
- exchanging consumer financial information among financial institutions (OFX, the new financial data exchange standard, is being translated into XML)
- creating standard patient descriptions for data sharing in the healthcare industry.

Thus, the same XML data could be presented to the consumer on the Web, processed by the consumer's bank, and transferred to a third party for an electronic funds transfer.

A recent development in the XML language was the release of XQuery version 1.0 in April 2002 by the World Wide Web Consortium (W3C) (www.w3c.org). XQuery is an 'SQL-like' query language that uses the structure of XML to express queries across different kinds of XML data sources, whether physically stored in XML or viewed as XML via middleware.[27]

In May 2002, the Australian financial lending industry announced LIXI — the lending industry XML initiative (www.lixi.org.au). LIXI was formed to leverage the powerful capabilities of XML to provide a faster, better service to customers. LIXI intends to achieve this by establishing a platform independent, open language based upon XML to allow the exchange of lending-related data between institutions.

The XML standard promises an open interface for secure business-to-business Internet commerce that will be sure to entice small-to-medium-sized enterprises (SMEs). For i-commerce software vendors and industry groups, XML's universal data interchange format offers a standards-based language to use with other protocols, such as HTTP and TCP/IP. Vendor support has been forthcoming with database vendors Oracle and IBM supporting XML natively; Versions 5.0 and above of the Microsoft and Netscape Web browsers interpret XML; and Sun Microsystems considers the standard to be the portable data language for Java.

The benefits of XML include:

- XML is open standards-based — data and presentation tags are separate; the language is extensible; style sheets can be self-controlled; and XML is flexible enough to be used in both business-to-business e-commerce and application integration.
- XML has industry support — W3C adopted XML in 1998, and other major industry groups such as OASIS, OBI, CommerceNet and BizTalk all have endorsed the use of XML in B2B exchanges.
- XML documents can be transmitted using HTTP — XML is supported by the infrastructure of the Internet.[28]

MOBILE COMMERCE (M-COMMERCE)

M-commerce is set to be the next growth area of electronic commerce. Advances in wireless telecommunications infrastructure and mobile technology have led to major improvements in the applicability of m-commerce technology to real-world scenarios. For example, the Swedish Postal Bank (Postbanken) and Teli's Mobil Smart service allow consumers to make Giro payments from their mobile telephones. In Singapore, Citibank clients can use their mobile telephones to access account balances, pay bills and transfer funds.[29]

Everyday tasks — including making telephone calls, doing banking, trading shares, organising business and personal affairs, and sending email — will be done more efficiently because of the power and convenience of wireless applications combined with the decreasing cost of wireless usage.

Network technologies

The growth of m-commerce, however, will be largely dependent on the development and availability of the core network infrastructure which enables m-commerce to operate. The key network technologies which will contribute to the enablement of m-commerce are described in table 11.2.

TABLE 11.2	NETWORK TECHNOLOGIES
NETWORK TECHNOLOGY	**DESCRIPTION**
GSM (Global System for Mobile Communication)	A digital mobile telephone technology that is the de facto wireless standard for Europe and the prevailing standard in the Asia–Pacific region.
HSCSD (High-Speed-Circuit-Switched Data)	A circuit-switched protocol based upon GSM. HSCSD is able to transmit data up to four times the speed of typical wireless transmission rates of 14.4 Kbps (i.e. 57.6 Kbps) by using four radio channels simultaneously.
GPRS (General Packet-Switched Radio Service)	A packet-based wireless protocol as defined in the GSM standard that offers instant access to networks. GPRS promises data rates from 56 up to 114 Kbps and continuous connection ('always on' connection) to the Internet for mobile phone and computer users.
EDGE (Enhanced Data Rates for Global Evolution)	A faster version of the GPRS wireless service that is designed to deliver data at rates up to 384 Kbps and enable the delivery of multimedia and other broadband applications to mobile phone and computer users.
3G (3rd Generation)	The generic term for the next big step in mobile technology development.
UMTS (Universal Mobile Telecommunications Service)	A 3G technology allowing broadband, packet-based transmission of text, digitised voice, video, and multimedia at data rates up to 2 Mbps that will offer a consistent set of services to mobile computer and phone users no matter where they are located in the world.

SOURCE: Adapted from Durlacher Research 1999, *Mobile Commerce Report*, pp. 19–21, accessed July 2002, www.durlacher.com/downloads/mcomreport.pdf.

⌐ Service technologies

Built on the network or data-link technologies described above are the service technologies which provide communication programs allowing the consumer to interact with the mobile network and the m-commerce community in general. See table 11.3 below.

TABLE 11.3	SERVICE TECHNOLOGIES
SMS (Short Message Service)	Since 1992 the Short Message Service has provided the ability to send and receive text messages to and from mobile phones. Each message may contain up to 160 characters and has seen exponential growth in Europe, Asia and Australia.
WAP (wireless application protocol)	Wireless application protocol (WAP) is an open global standard to facilitate the easy access to information by handset users. Wireless carriers can receive information on a mobile telephone such as banking details, share trading, advertising information, weather reports, traffic reports and news reports. Additional business functions include access to company telephone directories and the ability to check the telecommunications carrier account via the Internet. The devices that deliver these services will vary from mobile telephones to hand-held devices. The wireless markup language (WML) is a language based on XML that allows web page text to be displayed on mobile telephones and personal digital assistants (PDAs) via wireless access — much the same way HTML is used to display information in an Internet browser.
Web clipping	In the United States, the web clipping service has been successful for Palm Computing's PDA known as the Palm Pilot. Web clipping is a Palm proprietary format allowing delivery of web-based information to the Palm Pilot via wireless communication.

SOURCE: Adapted from Durlacher Research 1999, *Mobile Commerce Report*, pp. 21–24, accessed July 2002, www.durlacher.com/downloads/mcomreport.pdf.

M-commerce location technology

The clear strength of m-commerce is the ability for the consumer to be mobile or on the move. The key to the continuing growth of m-commerce will be to provide value-added services based upon the geographic location of the mobile device. Mobile location technology will enable new consumer services to be possible – such as providing directions to a railway station or offering 'sale prices' based on a consumer's proximity to a retail store. The dominant market for this technology is currently the United States where mobile phone operators have been forced to provide location aware services for emergency 911 callers.[30]

The major LFS (Location Fixing Scheme) is GPS (Global Positioning System). GPS is a network of 24 strategically placed satellites circling the Earth that allow consumers with GPS receivers to determine their geographic location. The location accuracy can be between 10 and 100 metres for most civilian equipment; however, accuracy can be up to within one (1) metre with military equipment. GPS receivers are becoming commonplace and are used in sports such as ballooning and sailing. GPS is also becoming very popular in road vehicles to determine location, access road 'hotspots' and weather reports. Other LFS technologies expected to be popular in the twenty-first century are the E-OTD (Enhanced Observed Time Difference) system, which uses the current GSM network to locate a mobile device, and COO (Cell Of Origin), which uses mobile cell technology to determine a mobile device's location.[31]

The future of m-commerce

The ongoing creation of mobile networks, services and applications continues to propel m-commerce forward as a viable and commercial reality for both businesses and consumers alike. The possibilities for m-commerce are unlimited with applications being developed in major sectors including:

- Financial services – consumers will be able to complete their banking and stockbroking via mobile phone and also receive bills and make payments in the mobile environment.
- Shopping – the purchase of goods and services from 'm-tailers' may include books, CDs and groceries from the mobile phone. Mobile purchase and reservation of tickets to events, mobile auctions, and reservations for hotels and restaurants are becoming possible.
- Entertainment – mobile users will be able to receive news on current affairs, and sporting and financial information; participate in mobile gaming; listen to music; and watch videos.
- B2B – the future of B2B m-commerce is exciting with possibilities including supply-chain integration whereby a salesperson in the field could immediately check the availability of a stock item; telemetry or remote control of systems and machines; and application of mobile CRM (m-CRM).[32]

Consumers will no longer have to be confined to their offices, working at their desktops – the age of the mobile worker, equipped with a variety of hand-held, wireless devices offering mobile applications is here. Emerging and developing nations can bypass the wired telephony model and move directly to a wireless infrastructure for basic telephone service. This will create tremendous demand for business applications – and help make wireless technology a ubiquitous global communications medium.[33]

BLUETOOTH

Bluetooth is a low-power radio technology that allows computers, mobile phones, PDAs and other wireless devices to connect and communicate with each other without the need for cables.[34] The Bluetooth specification allows devices to link together within a range of 10 metres and exchange data via a wireless transceiver and be connected to any device able to integrate the Bluetooth chip. Thus, Bluetooth will enable any business or household device to 'go wireless', including computers, printers, microwave ovens and refrigerators. Additionally, communication with point of sale (POS) devices and ticketing machines will be possible, allowing the further convergence of mobile phone, PDA and PC technologies.

Bluetooth has specific application in environments where cables and power cords may become obstructive or dangerous. Within the medical profession, Bluetooth technology is successfully being implemented to remove the need for cords in operating theatres and in hospital wards. Patient vital signs such as heartbeat, ECG channels and respiration may be monitored without the need for expensive and obstructive cabling.[35] Other examples include the Bluetooth mouse and keyboard released by Microsoft in April 2002[36] and Toshiba's Bluetooth server which performs all server duties and allows connectivity between computers, printers and even digital televisions.[37]

PEER-TO-PEER COMPUTING

In chapter 2 we described **peer-to-peer (P2P) computing** as a communications model whereby all parties in the network have the same capabilities and any 'peer' in the network may act as a client or server at any one time. Although this network model has been in existence for many years, the arrival of the Internet and m-commerce has created many new opportunities for this technology.

The collaborative or 'groupware' nature of P2P means that it can be used to build public and private commerce communities and even replace technologies such as VPNs in providing secure communication channels. P2P computing has many tangible benefits:

- the technology does not need central servers to operate – hence delays and security issues associated with current messaging systems such as email servers are avoided
- reduction in costs through reduction of centralised resources such as real estate and physical and digital storage

- flexibility and personal efficiency among P2P members. P2P workers gain a sense of personal freedom and empowerment by communicating where they want and when they want.[38]

The application of P2P computing to m-commerce is wide and varied. In situations where consumers or trading partners need to rapidly collaborate or aggregate and perform transactions in real-time, P2P computing is a perfect solution. Examples of P2P commerce applications include:

- trading
- negotiating
- designing
- planning
- managing projects
- sharing knowledge
- harnessing computer power.[39]

The future of P2P computing is promising and one that will be closely aligned to that of m-commerce in terms of application to the business world. It is anticipated that the technology will develop far beyond the basic system tools of searching, file sharing and instant messaging that are available today. P2P networks will enable integration between systems and more effective customer relationship management through greater emphasis on the context, meaning and purpose of customer information.

THE ROLE OF GOVERNMENT

The role of governments in Internet commerce is being widely debated across the globe. Because of the global nature of e-commerce, there are efforts being made to formulate an international policy.[40] A number of key committees, comprising major government representatives, are considering such issues as the legal framework, taxation, intellectual property protection and the removal of barriers to competition. These committees are from organisations including the OECD, the United Nations, the Global Information Infrastructure, the World Wide Web Consortium, and many more.

The OECD's work program follows the 'OECD Action Plan for Electronic Commerce' endorsed by ministers in Ottawa in 1998, and encompasses the following:

- building trust for users and consumers
- establishing ground rules for the digital marketplace
- enhancing the information infrastructure for electronic commerce
- maximising the benefits of electronic commerce.[41]

The Working Party for the Information Economy (WPIE) is the working group within the OECD that drives economic analysis and associated issues on business-to-business e-commerce. It is responsible for:

- reviewing and evaluating economic and social implications of e-commerce
- submitting to the OECD committees and council an analysis of the factors that encourage the uptake of e-commerce
- analysing the policy frameworks for the information economy.

For the period 2001–2003, the work program for the WPIE approved by the Committee on Fiscal Affairs (CFA) in January 2001 includes the following tasks:

- verification of the declared jurisdiction of residence of the customer in B2C online transactions
- verification of the status of the customer
- technology-based and technology-facilitated collection mechanisms
- simplification options and initiatives
- compliance-related questions
- longer-term strategies for exploiting the potential of technology-based mechanisms.[42]

Internet commerce in government is predominantly concerned with the delivery of services online. Steve Curran, Director of ETC Electronic Trading Concepts in Australia, believes that these trends include:

- increasing amounts of information available online
- development of 'entry points' and other means to improve the ease with which this information can be located
- increasing availability of online transactions and increasing confidence in being able to conduct these transactions securely
- minimising the need for the public and business to repeatedly enter data when conducting interactions and transactions with government
- integrating the government's online services with conventional services to improve the overall efficiency and convenience of service delivery.[43]

The added value these 'entry points' provide includes:

- providing pathways to information that do not rely on the user having a knowledge of the government or departmental structure – that is, without having to know who provides the information
- providing search engines which can locate required information by searching for key words in the documents and other information resources stored (or hosted) on the site
- enhancing this search capability to include information held on other sites and increasing the relevance of search results through the use of consistent 'descriptions' of information by government agencies
- links to related information sites.

The Business Entry Point – An Australian government initiative

The Business Entry Point, managed by the Commonwealth government and developed collaboratively by all levels of government in Australia, provides a world-leading example of these value-adding elements.

The Business Entry Point makes it easier for Australian businesses to deal with the government. Currently through the entry point, businesses can:

- access current information on a wide range of government assistance programs and services, and on topics such as taxation, record-keeping, superannuation, occupational health and safety, customs, intellectual property protection and workplace relations (see figure 11.4)

- gain a better understanding of their obligations – for example, as an employer and for taxation
- tailor their query to suit their business and area of operation
- privately and securely undertake a number of initial business registrations which are tailored to the business's needs.

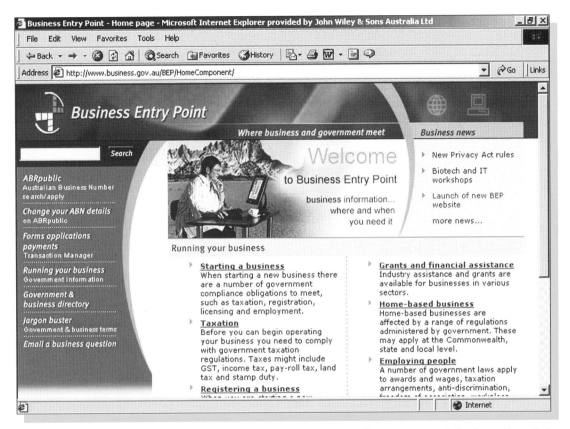

FIGURE 11.4: Home page for the Australian government's Business Entry Point (www.business.gov.au/BEP2002/)

The entry point provides access to resources from approximately 50 Commonwealth government agencies, 100 state and territory government agencies and 125 industry associations.

The United States and e-commerce

The United States government released the report *Emerging Digital Economy IV* in 2002. This report concludes that despite economic slowdown and recession, US industries have continued to build the nation's IT capital stock, add jobs in key IT employment categories, and create as a result the enduring foundation of a stronger economy.[44]

The government is aware of information technology's growing importance to the US economy, the convergence of technology and telecommunications, and the impact of technology on ordinary citizens. Despite economic slowdowns, the information technology and telecommunications industries grow increasingly important to the US economy and e-commerce has become a legislative battleground.[45]

DISINTERMEDIATION AND REINTERMEDIATION

Jobs are both created and destroyed by technology, trade and organisational change. The overall effects of electronic commerce on employment are:

- the creation of direct new jobs (such as security experts, web designers and m-commerce programmers)
- the creation of indirect jobs created by increased demand and productivity (e.g. delivery/fulfilment specialists)
- job losses (due to workers at retailers or other intermediaries being replaced by electronic commerce).

Gains and losses may differ by industry, by geographic area and by skill group. To assess the impact of electronic commerce, it is essential to understand which industries it is generating, which industries will experience new growth and demand because of electronic commerce, which types of job will be destroyed and which created, and what the overall needs are in terms of skills.[46]

A number of industries are affected by electronic commerce:

- the distribution/fulfilment sector is directly affected – physical goods (e.g. groceries) still need to be delivered, whereas movies and music can be delivered electronically
- industries related to ICTs (information, communication and technology – the infrastructure that enables electronic commerce) are affected (e.g. as the Internet grew so did the need for routers such as Cisco)
- content-related industries (information-related goods and services, entertainment, software and digital products) are affected (e.g. TrendMicro sells its virus protection software PC-Cillin over the Internet at www.antivirus.com)
- transactions-related industries (i.e. those affected by the size and type of economic transaction such as the financial sector, the postal sector, advertising, travel and transport) are affected.[47] The United States Postal Service (www.usps.com) sells stamps over the Internet.

Businesses have been affected by the growth in electronic commerce. They have to become flexible organisations and increase their operational efficiencies. Both small businesses and multinationals are having to compete in a global environment. The increased competition, global access and organisational change are impacting labour markets by influencing employment demand, wages and skill requirements.[48]

Electronic commerce is certainly driving the demand for IT professionals but it also requires IT expertise to be coupled with strong business application skills, thereby generating demand for a flexible, multiskilled workforce. The United States Government Department of Commerce predicts that by 2006, almost half the US workforce will be employed by industries that are either major producers or intensive users of information technology products and services. IT workers continue to earn more than non-IT workers. Innovation has:

- caused a surge in demand for highly paid IT personnel such as computing scientists, electrical engineers and telecommunications experts
- created new IT jobs such as web masters and online marketing experts
- changed skill levels for non-IT jobs — for example, motor mechanics now use computers to test engines
- raised minimum skill requirements for many occupations.

Outsourcing

As Internet adoption moves to a 'collaboration' model, there is a growing need for increased integration of Internet front-end applications with enterprise operations, legacy applications and back-end databases. The lack of staff to support ongoing Internet/intranet maintenance and development, coupled with integration problems and cost and time overruns, drives demand for outside services providers to help plan and implement solutions. Some companies are moving their information technology sectors to India where there is a large pool of IT workers and pay rates are lower. Countries such as Australia are losing many of their skilled IT workers to the United States and Europe, where they can earn more money. Activities in demand include security design and firewall implementation, web page design and creation, and Internet/intranet application development.[49]

With the spread of electronic commerce, and the consequent re-engineering of business processes and changes in competitive paradigms, software will increasingly be used to create business value. Electronic commerce will thus sustain a high demand for IT personnel. This is expected to exacerbate what has been called a critical shortage of IT workers.

Disintermediation

The same innovations in computing and telecommunications technologies that are rapidly creating jobs in some industries are causing jobs to be lost in other industries. This is referred to as a 'churning' effect in the US government's *Emerging Digital Economy IV* report. New occupations are being created while others are being redefined and workers must undertake continuing education and worker retraining. Workers of the twenty-first century must be multiskilled and commit to lifelong learning and retraining in order to remain flexible in rapidly changing labour markets.

The demand for skilled labour in the IT industry is being driven by the growth of IT itself as well as attrition among the workforce. Organisational life is also becoming much more fluid and dynamic with almost no 'standard' work day or working pattern. The Internet and intranets make possible 'anytime/anyplace' work. This flexibility is already enabling millions of individuals to work part-time or on a self-employed basis (refer to the idea of the 'business of one' as discussed in chapter 1).

Reintermediation

What we are seeing is a break with the traditional way of organising economies along industrial lines. This new economic model has portals emerging as a central plank and new intermediaries/infomediaries being established. Successful companies in the new economic model will be the ones that know the most about their customers and follow customer relationship principles. They are able to bring together goods and services tailored to the individual customer, and deliver at a single time- and cost-effective point, the 'my' portal.

There is an increasing trend towards the unbundling of organisational functions and in many cases the outsourcing and/or exsourcing of these. The managed funds industry, both in Australia and internationally, is such a case where investment application and redemption processes are outsourced. Often one provider will handle the functions of competing organisations. Such a move would not be possible without electronic commerce.

The electricity industry is another example. E-commerce is an important part of breaking the nexus between distribution and supply, which is at the heart of much restructuring in the electricity industry. One of the key drivers to consolidation in the finance industry is the necessity of integrated e-commerce systems and the cost of developing them and integrating them with legacy systems. This is reinforced by increasing perceptions that customers are demanding bundled or 'wrapped' financial services, and the reality that start-up organisations are seeking to provide these.

E-commerce can move markets towards much better information, and it is widely expected that wider market reach, a greater number of buyers and sellers in a market and improved information is leading to an irreversible shift in the balance of power between producer and consumer. It is possible that cooperative competition ('coopertition' is the buzzword that has been coined) will continue indefinitely as the working model for the new economy. Pfaffenberger speaks of a value constellation where businesses look upon suppliers and customers as allies and consolidate the relationship with them.[50]

INTERNET2

In 1996 a project known as **Internet2** was born in Chicago, involving more than 154 US universities together with representatives from a few high-tech and telecommunications companies. The project is establishing gigabit-per-second points of presence nationwide on a very-high-speed backbone network (VBNS). It will give people more control over how their information is used and, as it will be more secure, it will be of great interest to Internet commerce companies.

In February 1999, Internet2 went live on the Abilene fibre optic network developed by the University Corporation for Advanced Development, Indiana University and corporate partners Cisco Systems, Nortel Networks and Qwest

Communications International. The three companies have invested an estimated US$500 million in this superior Internet. With speeds up to 2.4 Gigabits per second, Abilene is potentially 85 000 times faster than a standard 28 Kbps connection.[51]

In May 2002, in collaboration with VBrick Systems, the University of California connected five of its medical centres to the San Diego campus via Internet2 and MPEG-2 video technology. The network will enable the university to provide video-quality medical education to rural clinics via UCTV, the university's broadcast channel.[52]

EMERGING TECHNOLOGIES

The authors of this book have undertaken substantial research to bring to you the theory and ideas presented in this chapter. We think it appropriate to provide you with a brief overview of other technologies which we think may help shape the future. Table 11.4 provides a summary of emerging technologies.

TABLE 11.4	EMERGING TECHNOLOGIES
TECHNOLOGY	**DESCRIPTION**
Bionics	Bionics is the science of using mechanical parts to help humans regain lost faculties such as mobility, vision or hearing. Cochlear implants and artificial hearts are examples of bionic technology available today. In the future as the science of bionics advances, brain implants which react to electrical impulses from the brain will be able to control bionic limbs, thus, for example, enabling people with disabilities to use their arms and legs once again (see www.medoto.unimelb.edu.au/bei/).
Nanotechnology	Nanotechnology (otherwise known as molecular manufacturing) refers to the design and manufacture of extremely small electronic circuits and mechanical devices built at the molecular level of matter. These molecular devices, known as nanobots, are nanometre-scale (one one-billionth of a metre) robots that use tiny arms to pick up and move atoms and possess tiny electronic brains to direct the process (see www.nanotechplanet.com/, www.nanotech-now.com/).
Superconductivity	Superconductivity is defined as the ability of materials to conduct an electric current while exhibiting almost zero electrical resistance. This lack of resistance enables superconductors to be used in a variety of applications such as ultra high speed computer chips, magnetic trains, and magnetic resonance imaging (MRI) equipment (see www.csr.umd.edu/).
Tele-immersion	Tele-immersion enables users at geographically distributed sites to collaborate in real-time in a shared, simulated, hybrid environment as if they were in the same physical room (see www.advanced.org/teleimmersion.html).
Wearable computer devices	In the future, computers that sit on our desks may become obsolete. Laptops which have provided us with mobility have become an accepted part of our daily lives — wearable computer devices will take this one step further. The science of wearable computing suggests that a computer should be worn, much as glasses or shoes are worn, and interact with the user based on the context of the situation. With heads-up displays, unobtrusive input devices, personal wireless local area networks, and a host of other context sensing and communication tools, the wearable computer will act as an intelligent assistant (see www.media.mit.edu/wearables/).

SUMMARY

Internet commerce is still in its infancy. Building the infrastructure to do business on the Web and through mobile devices will ultimately give way to a more mature, methodical approach to exploiting this new medium while continuing to nurture and develop existing ones. The successful companies will create web-based efficiencies customers will embrace, although power will be transferred to those customers in the process.[53]

Technological innovation and the global expansion of commerce are the forces combining to contribute to the further growth of Internet commerce, particularly among the developing nations.

It is clear that the most important change that Internet commerce brings is the way businesses and people interact with one another and the way products and services will be offered. Aggregators, e-auctions and online exchanges will become the new electronic marketplaces of the future, running on broadband or on wireless or mobile appliances.

Differentiated and customised products will offer more choices than mass-produced goods, for which firms with sufficient economies of scale will have the cost advantage.

In this book we have considered digital models for both consumer and business-to-business Internet commerce, we have explored the issues that in some ways are perceived to be obstacles to the further development of web commerce – issues such as security, taxation, and legal and ethical considerations – and we have speculated on future trends and the overall changing global marketplace.

Internet commerce will provide countless opportunities and challenges to our economies and societies. Traditional institutions – such as banks, universities, established business intermediaries, the media and publishing houses – are now finding it necessary to redefine their roles in the new global commercial environment.

Key terms

corporate intranets (p. 276)

disintermediation (p. 287)

e-marketplaces (p. 273)

enterprise information portals (EIPs) (p. 276)

hub (p. 273)

infomediary (p. 270)

Internet2 (p. 288)

knowledge exchanges (p. 274)

online auctions (p. 272)

peer-to-peer (P2P) computing (p. 282)

personalisation (p. 272)

portal (p. 271)

value trust network (VTN) (p. 274)

virtual private network (VPN) (p. 275)

vortals (p. 271)

Case study

CS

By Katina Michael, University of Wollongong © 2002

THE MOBILE REVOLUTION

The introduction of the mobile phone revolutionised the way people traditionally communicated with one another. People suddenly became accessible independent of their location, at any time of the day or week. A salesperson in business for instance, who was always on the road could now be reached and could in turn make phone calls conveniently between customer meetings.

Bundled with the basic mobile voice service was messaging in the form of voice or text. The latter has especially proven to be a useful and cost-effective method for conveying a short message. Collectively residential and business mobile subscribers use the short message service (SMS) to send millions of text messages per day (each not more than 160 characters in length). Information 'push and pull' services in the form of SMS, such as the latest sports results or betting odds, are now commonplace value-added features offered by second-generation (2G) mobile service providers.

One of the shortcomings of 2G networks is the limited bandwidth data transmission rate that is only 9.6 kilobits per second (Kbps) per user. Most 2G handsets contain modem adaptors that allow users to plug their laptops in and send fax or email transmissions but that is as far as the capabilities will stretch. The majority of users never utilise this modem feature (save for emergency situations) because on-air tariffs are timed and it becomes too expensive and cumbersomely slow due to the speed of transmission. Sending one megabyte (1024 Kb) of information using a 2G mobile phone would make for a very expensive call. And why? The GSM network was never built with a data world in mind.

Mobile meets Internet

Only a few years after mobile telephony was launched in Europe, the Internet browser also made its way into the fore. At the time no one predicted that the World Wide Web would become so popular and there were more than a few sceptics who doubted the impact of mobile telephony. However, what was to follow was rapid growth in household and business adoption of information technology (IT). Mobile telephony became a vital part of how people communicated, and the Web, among many other capabilities, gave people the opportunity to conduct commerce online. As mobile handsets became smaller and broadband access was offered to Internet users, a vision of third-generation (3G) mobile networks began to formulate. Two of the most influential technologies of the late twentieth century were set to converge. The wireless Internet concept was embraced by network equipment vendors like Nortel Networks,[54] handset providers like Nokia[55] and many other software vendors like SignalSoft[56] who spent hundreds of millions of research and development dollars to ensure the theory would soon become practice.

Towards 3G mobile networks

While the third-generation (3G) mobile spectrum has been auctioned off in most parts of the world, service providers have hesitated to act on their initial investments concerned with the unpredictable state of the market. However, a number of Asian countries like Japan and South Korea are committed to having fully functional 3G systems in operation by the end of the year.

NTT DoCoMo's i-Mode and c-Mode

Japan's NTT DoCoMo launched i-Mode[57] in 1999 to trial a packet-switched mode of transmission over the current 2G mobile environment. Some three thousand companies are now offering transaction capabilities over i-Mode officially linked to DoCoMo's mobile commerce billing system. The results speak for themselves; more than 25 per cent of the Japanese population use i-Mode and some 40 000 new subscribers are joining the network each day (see figure C11.1).[58] The phenomenal growth is attributed to satisfying consumer and business demand via i-Mode application offerings, and the added convenience of centralising subscriber messages and providing a single bill.

Current i-Mode applications allow the user to do almost anything that the 'fixed' Internet offers, such as book airline tickets, buy and sell shares on the stock market, play their favourite games, check the latest weather forecasts, shop and browse for products, play government-approved lotteries, download images and even use the company's intranet. Currently, movies cannot be downloaded using i-Mode due to the limited bandwidth but as soon as 3G is launched, this too will be possible.

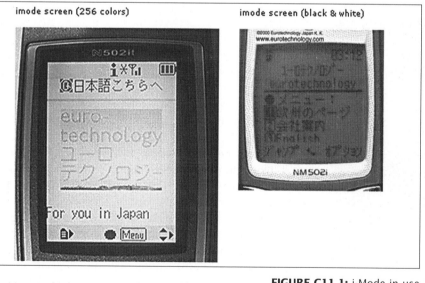

FIGURE C11.1: i-Mode in use
SOURCE: www.eurotechnology.com/imode/faq-use.html.

DoCoMo's newly marketed c-Mode is also set to challenge the way in which consumers make purchases. Using their wireless handset, they will be able to purchase items from vending machines and be billed accordingly on their i-Mode bill. In the future it is not inconceivable that the wireless personal digital assistant (PDA) or e-wallet will become the future mechanism by which all purchases, even government transactions, are made. In this manner, it is not difficult to see why analysts forecast that the value of mobile commerce transactions will exceed that of electronic commerce by 2010.

The future of mobile data

Among the plethora of mobile commerce applications that are expected to do very well are location-based services (LBS). The types of remote queries that LBS applications may answer include: Where is the nearest restaurant? How do I get from here to there? How far away is the next petrol station? In terms of emergency services, 3G applications will give authorities opportunities to locate exactly the position of a wireless caller who is in need of urgent assistance. LBS applications have the potential to save lives, whether used by the police, ambulance or fire department.

4G mobile and beyond

And if 3G is not pioneering enough, fourth-generation (4G) intelligent communications based on software solutions are already on the drawing board. 4G will use location-based and scheduling information to intelligently allocate or re-allocate resources according to a set of generically defined rules for a variety of applications. 4G can only work in smart environments where real-time data is collected, filtered and updated regularly. A typical 4G example could be as follows. An employee who works for a multinational company is travelling from Sydney to China and making a stopover in Singapore. While on his way to Sydney airport, the employee encounters a major traffic accident on the Harbour Bridge. Traffic comes to a standstill while police and ambulance treat people at the scene. A camera on the bridge tracks all delays, alerting the roads and traffic authority (RTA). The RTA (with additional police information) estimates that the delay will be in excess of two hours and sends this information to the central information bureau. The employee is alerted by the wireless service provider that he will most likely miss his flight and will have to stay at Sydney's Airport Hilton overnight waiting for the next available flight which is scheduled to depart in the morning. The employee replies to the message and updates are made to his itinerary as detailed on his reply message. The panic of having to reorganise everything is removed from the traveller. Though he will end up missing the first meeting in Singapore, he is relieved with the almost instantaneous knowledge that he will be leaving Sydney in time for subsequent meetings.

All the essential signs for a future where mobility is the key driving force in communications are already present. The most vital attribute of mobile commerce is ubiquity. Future applications will utilise both the time-critical and location-based factors to enhance the way we work and live.

QUESTIONS

1. How have mobile communications changed the way people communicate? What are some of the key attributes of mobile communications?
2. Define mobile commerce. How does electronic commerce differ? Give examples.
3. Visit NTT DoCoMo's web site (www.nttdocomo.com/top.html). What mobile commerce services are currently being offered via i-Mode and c-Mode?
4. What are location-based services (LBS)? Give some examples of the LBS solutions offered by SignalSoft (www.signalsoftcorp.com/).
5. Visiti Nokia's web site (www.nokia.com) and describe the wireless PDA handsets that are being marketed and sold today.

Questions

1. What do you believe are the main inhibitors of Australian companies taking up m-commerce in the near future?
2. Will broadband infrastructure be capable of delivering the Internet-based commercial transactions and business information we demand in the future?
3. Are there some aspects of business which do not lend themselves to online delivery? Explain.
4. Will some countries' economies be disadvantaged because of the Internet? Explain.
5. Will 'e-business' just be 'business' in the near future? Explain.
6. Make five predictions for future trends in Internet commerce in the next decade.
7. If usage costs dramatically increase, will Internet users continue to use the Internet?
8. Will the global marketplace diminish?
9. What are the other possibilities for next generation devices?

Suggested | reading

Aldrich, D. F. 1999, *Mastering the Digital Marketplace: Practical Strategies for Competitiveness in the New Economy*, John Wiley & Sons, New York.

Davydov, M. 2001, *Corporate Portals and eBusiness Integration*, McGraw-Hill, New York.

Hagel, J. and Singer, M. 1999, *Net Worth*, Harvard Business School Press, Boston.

Holmes, D. 2001, *EGov: eBusiness Strategies for Government*, Nicholas Brealey, United States.

Kalakota, R. and Robinson, M. 1999, *E-Business: Roadmap for Success*, Addison-Wesley Longman, United States.

Sawhney, M. et al. 2001, *The Seven Steps to Nirvana: Strategic Insights into eBusiness Transformation*, McGraw-Hill, New York.

Seybold, P. B. and Marshak, R. 1998, *Customers.Com: How to Create a Profitable Business Strategy for the Internet and Beyond*, Times Books, United States.

Siebel, T. 2001, *Taking care of eBusiness*, Doubleday, United States.

Tapscott, D., Lowy, A. and Ticoll, D. 1998, *Blueprint to the Digital Economy: Wealth Creation in the Era of E-Business*, McGraw-Hill, New York.

Ware, J., Gebauer, J., Hartman, A. and Roldan, M. 1998, *The Search for Digital Excellence*, McGraw-Hill, New York.

End | notes

1. Greenspan, A. 1996, 'Remarks by Greenspan', www.federalreserve.gov/BOARDDOCS/SPEECHES/19961205.htm.
2. Nua Surveys 2002, 'Internet grows 10% from April 2001 to April 2002', May, www.nua.com/surveys/index.cgi?f=VS&art_id=905357952&rel=true.
3. Kenney, M. and Curry, J. 1999, *E-Commerce: Implications for Firm Strategy and Industry Configuration*, July, E-conomy Project working paper, Berkeley Roundtable on the International Economy (BRIE), brie.berkeley.edu/~briewww/pubs/wp/ewp2.html.
4. E-Commerce Today 2000, 'Security "exsourcing" emerges in Australia', issue 79, 24 February, www.ecommercetoday.com.au.
5. United States Department of Commerce 1999, Emerging Digital Economy II, 22 June, United States Government, www.ecommerce.gov/ede/report.html.
6. ECNow 2002, *Ten Top Trends for eCommerce*, ecnow.com/top10trends2002.htm.
7. Global Reach Statistics 2002, www.global-reach.biz/globstats.
8. Nua Surveys 2002, 'Bouncing Back', April, www.nua.ie/surveys/analysis/weekly–editorial/archives/issue1no224.html.
9. Australian Internet Industry 2002, Telecommunications Performance Report 2000–2001; *Chapter 13*, www.aca.gov.au/publications/reports/performance/2000–01/chap13.pdf.
10. Nua Surveys 2002, Teleworking proves popular in Australian State, www.nua.ie/surveys/index.cgi?f=VS&art_id=905357848&rel=true.
11. Nua Surveys 2002, 'B2B ecommerce booming in Australia', March, www.nua.ie/surveys/index.cgi?f=VS&art_id=905357738&rel=true.
12. Nua Surveys 2002, 'China number two in home net usage', April, www.nua.ie/surveys/index.cgi?f=VS&art_id=905357873&rel=true.
13. Duvall, M. 1999, 'To spin off or not to spin off', *Inter@ctive Week*, 18 October, www.zdnet.com.
14. Davidson, J. 1999, 'Evolving e-economy shifts the balance of power', *Australian Financial Review*, 12 March.
15. Raisch, W. 2001, *The eMarketplace: Strategies for Success in B2B eCommerce*, McGraw-Hill, New York, p. 3.
16. Nua Surveys 2001, 'Auction sites ever more popular', July, www.nua.com/surveys/index.cgi?f=VS&art_id=905356927&rel=true.
17. Clark, T. 1999, 'Sites redefine buying online', CNET News.com, 24 February, www.cnet.com.
18. Raisch, W. 2001, op. cit., p. 142.
19. Wired.com 2000, 'Aussies to trade green power', July, www.wired.com/news/technology/0,1282,37914,00.html.
20. Raisch, W. 2001, op. cit., p. 157.
21. Ibid., p. 165.
22. Ibid., p. 173.
23. Ibid., p. 236.
24. VPnet 2000, 'A virtual private networking primer', p. 1, www.firstvpn.com/papers/vpnet/VPNet%20VPNprimer1.pdf.
25. Newton, S. 1999, *Electronic Business – Factors for Success*, UTS, Sydney, p. 100.
26. Atre, S. 1999, 'Enterprise information portals, the right way', *PlanetIT*, 18 May, www.planetit.com.
27. W3C 2002, April, www.w3.org/TR/xquery/.
28. Lawrence, E. et al. 2001, *Technology of Internet Business*, John Wiley & Sons, Brisbane, p. 154.
29. Birch, D. 1999, 'Mobile financial services: The Internet is not the only new digital channel', Electronic Markets, Business Briefing: Electronic Commerce: An Analysis of

Electronic Commerce and Perspectives on the Future, World Markets Research Centre, England, p. 97.

30. Durlacher Research 1999, *Mobile Commerce Report*, p. 32, accessed July 2002, www.durlacher.com/downloads/mcomreport.pdf.

31. Ibid., p. 33.

32. Durlacher Research 2001, *UMTS – An Investment Perspective*, pp. 80–107, www.durlacher.com/downloads/mcomreport.pdf.

33. *Red Herring Magazine* 1998, 'Ten trends for the post-PC world', December, www.redherring.com/mag/issue61/trends.html.

34. Bluetooth 2002, www.bluetooth.com/tech/works.asp.

35. Bluetooth 2002, www.bluetooth.com/news/news.asp?A=2&PID=141&ARC=1.

36. Bluetooth 2002, www.bluetooth.com/news/news.asp?A=2&PID=127&ARC=1.

37. Bluetooth 2002, www.bluetooth.com/news/news.asp?A=2&PID=137&ARC=1.

38. Fingar, P. et al., 2001, *The Death of 'e' and the Birth of the Real New Economy*, Meghan-Kiffer Press, p. 113.

39. Ibid., p. 112.

40. Alliance for Global Business 1999, *Trade-Related Aspects of Electronic Commerce*, World Trade Organisation, April, www.wto.org.

41. Organisation for Economic Cooperation and Development 2002, 'How does the OECD contribute to policy analysis and debate on electronic commerce?', www.oecd.org/EN/document/0,,EN-document-29-nodirectorate-no-14-6560-29,00.html.

42. Organisation for Economic Cooperation and Development 2002, 'Working Group Plan', www.oecd.org/EN/document/0,,EN-document-101-nodirectorate-no-4-25844-29,00.html.

43. Curran, S. 1999, 'Regional summit tool kit – Practical leadership strategies', Online Australia Conference, April, www.onlineaustralia.net.au.

44. United States Department of Commerce 2002, *Emerging Digital Economy IV – Fourth Annual Report*, www.stat-usa.gov/pub.nsf/vwAbsInt/dig2002?OpenDocument.

45. Ibid.

46. Organisation for Economic Cooperation and Development 1999, *The Economic and Social Impacts of Electronic Commerce: Preliminary Findings and Research Agenda*, February.

47. Ibid.

48. United States Department of Commerce 2002, op. cit.

49. Organisation for Economic Cooperation and Development 2002, op. cit.

50. Pfaffenberger, B. 1998, *Building a Strategic Extranet*, IDG Books, United States, p. 6.

51. Wilcox, J. 1999, 'Expanding the information highway', *TechWeb*, 6 July.

52. Internet2.com 2002, archives.internet2.edu/guest/archives/I2-NEWS/log200205/msg00000.html.

53. Kindel, S. 1999, 'Reassessing e-commerce', *Executive Edge*, GartnerGroup, February–March, www.ee-online.

54. www.nortelnetworks.com.

55. www.nokia.com.

56. www.signalsoftcorp.com/.

57. www.nttdocomo.co.jp/english/index.shtml.

58. www.eurotechnology.com/imode/faq-use.html.

appendix

APPENDIX 1

Web sites listed by chapter

CHAPTER 01

INTRODUCTION TO INTERNET COMMERCE

www.ssw.com.au
SSW Database and Internet Consultants, Sydney

www.davidjones.com.au
David Jones

www.cyberconsult.com.au
Cyber.Consult

www.setco.org
Secure Electronic Transaction

www.aptstrategies.com.au
APT Strategies

www.noie.gov.au
National Office for the Information Economy

www.internic.net
Internet Network Information Centre

www.ina.com.au
Internet Names Australia

www.netregistry.com.au
NetRegistry

www.hills.com.au
Hills Industries

www.learnthenet.com
LearntheNet.com

www.britannica.com
Encyclopaedia Britannica

www.docspace.com
docSpace

www.maxi.com.au
NEC

www.vgpb.vic.gov.au
Victorian Government Purchasing Board

www.stuff.com.au
Stuff Marketplace

www.ato.gov.au
Australian Taxation Office

www.infringements.nsw.gov.au
NSW Infringement Processing Bureau

www.telstra.com.au
Telstra

www3.optus.com.au
Optus

www.sold.com.au
Sold.com.au

www.priceline.com
Priceline.com

www.ebay.com
eBay

www.ebusinessforum.com
ebusinessforum.com

www.registrypro.com
RegistryPro Ltd

www.nic.aero
.aero

www.nic.coop
.coop

www.nic.museum
Museum Domain Management Association

www.nic.name
Global Name Registry

www.nic.info
Afilias Ltd

www.nic.biz
NeuLevel, Inc.

CHAPTER 02

BUSINESS MODELS FOR INTERNET COMMERCE

www.anzwers.com.au
ANZWERS search engine

www.rpdata.net.au
RP Equipment

www.ninemsn.com.au
ninemsn

www.yellowpages.com.au
Yellow Pages

www.woolworths.com.au
Woolworths

www.sold.com.au
Sold.com.au

www.priceline.com
Priceline.com

www.ebay.com
eBay

www.respond.com
Respond.com

www.lowestbid.com.au
Lowestbid Group

www.line56.com
Line56

www.retailtrade.net
TradeConnection

www.b2btoday.com
B2Btoday.com

www.amazon.com
Amazon.com

www.dell.com
Dell

www.shopfast.com.au
Shopfast.com

www.corprocure.com.au
corProcure

www.covisint.com
Covisint

www.yieldbroker.com
YieldBroker.com

www.commerceone.net
Commerce One

www.tradehub.net
Tradehub

www.napster.com
Napster

www.mycompany.com
MyCompany.com

www.store.yahoo.com
Yahoo!Store

www.royalsunalliance.com
Royal & SunAlliance

www.musiccity.com
Morpheus

www.aimster.com
Aimster

http://home.netscape.com
Net Search

www.netscape.com/netcenter/index.html
Netscape

www.microsoft.com
Microsoft

www.public.iastate.edu/~PremCourses/dutchauc.html
Competition in the Dutch Flower Markets

www.isworld.org/isworld/ecourse
Site for e-commerce resources

www.time.com
Time's Pathfinder web site

www.tradegate.org.au
Tradegate ECA

www.ninemsn.com.au
ninemsn

www.violet.com
Gift service

www.ibook.com
iBook — online publisher

www.infocus.com
InFocus — online publisher

www.napster.com
Napster for MP3

www.business2.com
Business 2.0

www.bankone.com
BankOne

www.corba.org
Corba

www.bizsite.com.au
ANZ BizSite

www.choicemall.com
Choice Mall

CHAPTER 03

TECHNOLOGY BASICS

www.blackwell-science.com/products/journals/isj.htm
MISQ *and* **Information Systems Journal**

www.autobytel.com
Autobytel

www.asx.com.au
Australian Stock Exchange

www-cec.buseco.monash.edu.au
Centre for Electronic Commerce at Monash University

CHAPTER 04

WORLD WIDE WEB COMMERCE

www.abc.net.au
ABC Online

www.greengrocer.com.au
Greengrocer.com.au

www.libragirl.com.au
Sancella (Libra products)

www.cyberhorse.com.au
Everything to do with Horses

www.shark.com
Greg Norman site

www.netcraft.co.hk.survey
Netcraft web server survey

www.cart32.com
Cart 32 Shopping cart

www.interworld.com
Interworld

www.economist.com
Economist

www.vetshoponline.com
VetShopOnline

www.treasury.gov.au
Queensland Treasury

www.hostcompare.com
HostCompare.com

www.ibm.com
IBM

www.noie.gov.au
National Office for the Information Economy

www.cynosure.com.au
Cynosure

CHAPTER 05

ELECTRONIC PAYMENT SYSTEM

www.unece.org/trade/untdid/texts/d422_d.htm
Electronic Data Interchange for Administration, Commerce and Transport

www.cs.newcastle.edu.au/Research/pabolins/mseg.html
University of Newcastle

www1.worldcom.com
WorldCom

www.expedia.co.uk
Expedia.co.uk

www.xamax.com.au
Xamax Consultancy Pty Ltd

www.trintech.com
Trintech

www.howstuffworks.com
HowStuffWorks

www.woolworths.com.au
Woolworths

www2.discovercard.com
Discover Financial Services

www.echeck.com
eCheck

www.ecml.org
Ecml.org

www.paydirect.yahoo.com
Yahoo! PayDirect

www.commerce.net
CommerceNet

www.setco.org
Set

www.paypal.com
PayPal

www.egold.com
E-Gold

www.telecab.com.sg
TeleCab

www.library.upenn.edu
University of Pennsylvania library

www.news.bbc.co.uk
BBC

CHAPTER 06

SECURITY AND INTERNET COMMERCE

www.genome.wi.mit.edu/WWW/faqs/wwwsf1.html
World Wide Web Consortium

www.cert.org
Computer Emergency Response Team

www.ihug.com.au
iHug

CHAPTER 07

THE INTERNET CUSTOMER

www.doubleclick.com.au
DoubleClick

www.qantas.com.au
Qantas

CHAPTER 08

ORGANISATIONAL COMMUNICATION

www.woolworths.com.au/vendorguide/index.stm
Woolworths

www.employment.com.au
Commonwealth Government Employment site

www.macromedia.com
Macromedia

www.econ-icom.hku.hk
University of Hong Kong

www3.forddirect.fordvehicles.com
FordDirect.com

www.sap.com
SAP

www.peoplesoft.com
People Soft

www.jdedwards.com
JD Edwards

www.baan.com
BAAN

www.siebel.com
Siebel Systems

www.onyx.com
Onyx Software

www.frontrange.com
FrontRange Solutions

www.oracle.com
Oracle Corporation

www.interactcommerce.com
Interact Commerce

CHAPTER 09

TAXATION OF INTERNET COMMERCE

www.oecd.org/dsti/sti/it/ec/index.htm
Organisation for Economic Cooperation and Development

www.revenue.irlgov.ie
Irish government paper on eCommerce and the Irish Tax system

www.offshore.com.ai
Vince Cate site

www.ato.gov.au
Australian Taxation Office

www.zdnet.com.au
ZDNet News

http://ntrg.cs.tcd.ie
Network and Communications Research Group

www.standards.com.au
Standards Australia

www.customs.gov.au
Australian Customs Service

www.dcita.gov.au
Department of Communication, Information Technology and the Arts

www.aph.gov.au
Parliament of Australia

www.skm.dk
Danish Ministry of Taxation

www.visa.com
VISA

www.accc.gov.au
Australian Competition and Consumer Commission

CHAPTER 10

LEGAL AND ETHICAL ISSUES

www.netnanny.com
Net Nanny

www.fastcompany.com
Fast Company

www.cybersitter.com
Cybersitter

www.surfwatch.com
Surfwatch

www.siebel.com
Siebel Systems

www.amazon.com
Amazon

www.123loganalyzer.com
123LogAnalyzer

www.accrue.com
Accure Software, Inc.

CHAPTER 11

FUTURE TRENDS

www.kcfishnet.com
FishNet Securities

www.usps.com
United States Postal Service

www.business.gov.au
Commonwealth Government Business site

www.cultureandrecreation.gov.au
Australian Cultural Network

www.farmbid.com
Farmbid

www.w3c.org
World Wide Web Consortium

www.lixi.org.au
Lixi

www.durlacher.com
Durlacher Research

www.antivirus.com
TrendMicro

www.medoto.unimelb.edu.au
East Melbourne Hearing Research Group

www.nanotechplanet.com
NanoelectronicsPlanet.com

www.csr.umd.edu
Center for Superconductivity Research

www.advanced.org
Advanced Network and Services, Inc.

www.media.mit.edu
MIT Media Lab

www.eurotechnology.com
eurotechnology.com

www.signalsoftcorp.com
SignalSoft

www.nokia.com
Nokia

appendix

2

APPENDIX 2

Web sites
listed by
industry sector

BANKING/FINANCE

www.anz.com.au
ANZ Bank

www.amp.com.au
AMP Society

www.afr.com.au
Australian Financial Review

www.asx.com.au
Australian Stock Exchange

www.axa.com.au
AXA Australia

www.colonialfirststate.com.au
Colonial First State Investments

www.citicorp.com.au
Citicorp Bank

www.commbank.com.au
Commonwealth Bank

www.eyonline.com.au
Ernst and Young Online

www.macquarie.com.au
Macquarie Bank

www.mastercard.com
MasterCard

www.national.com.au
National Australia Bank

www.pricewaterhousecoopers.com
PricewaterhouseCoopers

www.stgeorge.com.au
St George Bank

www.westpac.com.au
Westpac Bank

COMPUTER INDUSTRY

www.adobe.com
Adobe Systems Inc.

www.allaire.com
Allaire Grap

www.apple.com
Apple Computers

www.aiia.com.au
Australian Information Industry Association

www.brother.com
Brother Corporation

www.compaq.com.au
Compaq

www.dell.com.au
Dell Computer

www.estrategies.com.au
eStrategies — e-commerce consulting

www.firmware.com.au
Firmware

www.hotwired.com/synapse
Synapse: technology, culture and society

www.ibm.com
IBM Corporation

www.interworld.com
InterWorld

www.macromedia.com
Macromedia

www.microsoft.com
Microsoft Corporation

www.netscape.com
Netscape

www.oracle.com
Oracle Corporation

www.ozemail.com.au
Ozemail

www.sap.com
SAP

www.sausage.com.au
Sausage Software

www.sun.com
Sun Systems

www.ssw.com.au
Superior Software

www.tpis.com.au
TP Information Systems

www.unisys.com
Unisys

www.wired.com
Wired News

www.yahoo.com
Yahoo!

INDIGENOUS ORGANISATIONS

www.atsic.gov.au
Aboriginal and Torres Strait Islander Commission (ATSIC)

www.aiatsis.gov.au/index.htm
Australian Institute of Aboriginal and Torres Strait Islander Studies

www.alga.com.ai/indig.htm
Australian Local Government Association – Indigenous Issues

www.austlii.edu.au/car/
Council for Aboriginal Reconciliation

www.indiginet.com.au
Jumbonna – UTS, Centre for Australian Indigenous Studies

www.koori.usyd.edu.au
Koori Centre, University of Sydney

www.nntt.gov.au
National Native Title Tribunal

INSURANCE

www.ampgeneral.com.au
AMP General

www.aii.com.au
Australian Insurance Institute

www.axa.com.au
AXA Australia

www.fai.com.au
FAI Insurance

www.hannangroup.com.au
Hannan Group Global Insurance Solutions

www.ica.com.au
Insurance Council of Australia

www.iinz.org.nz
Insurance Institute of New Zealand

www.lawcover.com.au
Lawcover – Professional Indemnity Insurance

www.legalandgeneral.com.au
Legal and General Australia

www.qbe.com.au
QBE Insurance Group

LAW

www.auslii.edu.au
Australian Legal Information Institute

www.copyright.org.au
Australian Copyright Council Home Page

www.butterworths.com.au
Butterworths: Legal Publishers

www.cch.com.au
CCH Australia

www.fitzroy-legal.org.au
Fitzroy Legal Service Online

www.lawfoundation.net.au
Foundation Law

www.lawcouncil.asn.au
Law Council of Australia

www.aph.gov.au
Parliament of Australia

www.phillipsfox.com.au
Phillips Fox Lawyers

www.house.gov
US House of Representatives

MINING AND MANUFACTURING

www.amcor.com.au
AMCOR

www.bhp.com.au
BHP

www.boeing.com
Boeing

www.csr.com.au
CSR

www.ford.com.au
Ford Australia

www.gec.com
General Electric

www.hills.com.au
Hills Industries

www.johnsonjohnson.com
Johnson & Johnson

www.kelloggs.co.uk
Kelloggs, UK

www.mim.com.au
MIM Holdings

www.motorola.com
Motorola

www.riotinto.com
Rio Tinto

www.samsung.com
Samsung Electronics

www.toyota.com.au
Toyota

www.wmc.com.au
WMC Ltd

POPULAR CULTURE

www.theaustralian.news.com.au
The Australian Online

www.abc.net.au
Australian Broadcasting Corporation

www.cdnow.com
CDNow

www.eonline.com
eOnline

www.sofcom.com.au/TV/
Australian TV Guide

www.foxtel.com.au
Foxtel

www.mtv.com
MTV

www.mca.com.au
Museum of Contemporary Art

www.nme.com
New Musical Express

www.theonion.com
The Onion

www.rollingstone.com
Rolling Stone Magazine

www.sanity.com.au
Sanity

www.sony.com
Sony

www.wired.com
Wired News

RETAIL

www.amazon.com
Amazon

www.the-body-shop.com
The Body Shop

www.dstore.com.au
DStore

www.esprit.com
Esprit

www.gleebooks.com.au
Gleebooks

www.greengrocer.com.au
Greengrocer Online

www.interflora.com.au
Interflora, Australian Unit

www.myerdirect.com.au
Myer Direct Online

www.plusone.com.au
*Plus One Marketing: Australian Business Bookshop
(can pay with e-cash)*

www.radiorentals.com.au
Radio Rentals

www.realestate.com.au
Real Estate.com

www.travel.com
Travel.com

www.virtual-showroom.co.uk
Virtual Showroom — Vehicles

www.woolworths.com.au
Woolworths

SPORT

www.arl.org.au
Australian Rugby League

www.ausport.gov.au
Australian Sports Commission

www.bathurst100.com.au
Bathurst 100

www.aus.cricket.org
CricInfo — The Home of Cricket on the Internet

www.foxsports.com.au
Fox Sports

www.golf.com.au
Australian golf site

www.ninemsn.com.au
Wide World of Sports

www.ozsports.com.au
Links to Australian sports sites

www.pgatour.com
PGA Tour site

www.scrum.com
Rugby Union

www.s2h.tas.gov.au
Sydney-to-Hobart Yacht Race

www.olympic.org/games/sydney
Sydney 2000 — Games of the XXVII Olympiad

www.tennisaustralia.com.au
Tennis Australia

TOURISM/HOTELS

www.australia.com
Australian Tourist Commission

www.biztravel.com
Biztravel.com: the Internet company for business travellers

www.thetrip.com
Business Travel Information/Services

www.industry.gov.au
Department of Industry, Tourism and Resources

www.fodors.com
Fodors Travel Online

www.frommers.com
Frommer's Encyclopedia of Travel

www.itn.com
Internet Travel Network

www.lonelyplanet.com.au
Lonely Planet *Travel Guide*

www.expedia.msn.com
Microsoft Expedia

www.peppers.com.au
Peppers Hotel Group Australia

www.flightcentre.com.au
Flight Centre

www.rydges.com.au
Rydges Hotels and Resorts

www.statravel.com.au
STA Travel

UNIVERSITIES — AUSTRALIA

www.acu.edu.au
Australian Catholic University

www.adfa.oz.au
Australian Defence Force Academy

www.anu.edu.au
Australian National University

www.bond.edu.au
Bond University

www.cqu.edu.au
Central Queensland University

www.csu.edu.au
Charles Sturt University

www.curtin.edu.au
Curtin University of Technology

www.deakin.edu.au
Deakin University

www.cowan.edu.au
Edith Cowan University

www.flinders.edu.au
Flinders University

www.gu.edu.au
Griffith University

www.jcu.edu.au
James Cook University

www.latrobe.edu.au
Latrobe University

www.mq.edu.au
Macquarie University

www.monash.edu.au
Monash University

www.murdoch.edu.au
Murdoch University

www.ntu.edu.au
Northern Territory University

www.qut.edu.au
Queensland University of Technology

www.rmit.edu.au
Royal Melbourne Institute of Technology

www.scu.edu.au
Southern Cross University

www.swin.edu.au
Swinburne University of Technology

www.adelaide.edu.au
University of Adelaide

www.ballarat.edu.au
University of Ballarat

www.canberra.edu.au
University of Canberra

www.unimelb.edu.au
University of Melbourne

www.une.edu.au
University of New England

www.newcastle.edu.au
University of Newcastle

www.nd.edu.au
University of Notre Dame

www.unsw.edu.au
University of New South Wales

www.uq.edu.au
University of Queensland

www.usyd.edu.au
University of Sydney

www.unisa.edu.au
University of South Australia

www.usq.edu.au
University of Southern Queensland

www.utas.edu.au
University of Tasmania

www.uts.edu.eu
University of Technology, Sydney

www.uwa.edu.au
University of Western Australia

www.hawkesbury.uws.edu.au
University of Western Sydney, Hawkesbury

www.macarthur.uws.edu.au
University of Western Sydney, Macarthur

www.nepean.uws.edu.au
University of Western Sydney, Nepean

www.uow.edu.au
University of Wollongong

www.vut.edu.au
Victoria Institute of Technology

UNIVERSITIES — NEW ZEALAND

www.aut.ac.nz
Auckland Institute of Technology

www.canterbury.ac.nz
Canterbury University

www.lincoln.ac.nz
Lincoln University

www.massey.ac.nz
Massey University

www.otago.ac.nz
Otago University

www.auckland.ac.nz
Auckland University

www.waikato.ac.nz
Waikato University

www.vuw.ac.nz
Victoria University of Wellington

UNIVERSITIES — OTHER

www.bath.ac.uk
University of Bath

www.cam.ac.uk
University of Cambridge

www.harvard.edu
Harvard University

www.hku.hk
University of Hong Kong

www.nus.edu.sg
National University of Singapore

www.ox.ac.uk
University of Oxford

www.stanford.edu
Stanford University

www.taylors.edu.my
Taylors College, Malaysia

www.temple.edu
Temple University

active server pages: HTML pages that include one or more scripts (small embedded programs) that are processed on a Microsoft web server before the pages are sent to the user. (p. 60)

advertising: the act or practice of bringing anything, such as a business activity, to the attention of the public. (pp. 166, 253)

Advertising model: a business model based on offering advertising space on web pages to obtain revenue (*see also* banner advertisements). (p. 31)

Affiliation model: a business model that encourages web site owners to sign up under what is known as an associate or affiliate program. For example, Amazon invites web site owners to sign up to sell the bookseller's inventory. Once approved, the affiliate is sent an email with instructions on how to set up links and banner ads. These affiliates do not directly sell but merely direct web surfers to the online store, which takes and fills the order. The merchant then pays the affiliate a small set fee for playing the rainmaker. (p. 33)

agents: electronic shopping software tools that assist users to search the Internet for product items. Users interact with a shopping agent by submitting agent requests. The agent then searches relevant online shops for items matching the search criteria. One example is the web site at www.mysimon.com. (p. 96)

application service provider (ASP): software providers who rent out rather than sell their software or part of their software to consumers. (p. 93)

AS 4269: the Australian Standard for complaint resolution, which establishes the minimal conditions for resolving disputes. (p. 173)

attachments: files, such as word-processed or spreadsheet files, that are sent along with an email. Most email packages support several common standards for sending attachments across the Internet, such as UUencoding and MIME (multipurpose Internet mail extensions). Receivers of an attachment are then able to either save the attachment to their disk or launch the appropriate program to read the file (*see also* multipurpose Internet mail extensions). (p. 190)

Auction model: a business model that uses real-time or live auction bidding on the Internet. (p. 33)

AusCERT (Australian Computer Emergency Response Team): a single, trusted point of contact in Australia for the Internet community to deal with computer security incidents and their prevention (www.auscert.org). (p. 152)

authentication: a means of countering the threat of masquerade – online data and information transmission in electronic form requires that the message sent reaches the intended recipient and only that recipient. (p. 146)

availability: a requirement so that the communications infrastructure and the network systems in place can receive and send information and data and enable electronic transactions in business. (p. 143)

banner advertisements: passive advertisements that are encountered by simply visiting a web page. They usually appear across the top or bottom of web pages. (p. 167)

Bluetooth: Bluetooth wireless technology is a de facto standard, as well as a specification for small-form factor, low-cost, short-range radio links between mobile PCs, mobile phones and other portable devices. (p. 10)

bookmarking: a means of creating a list, stored in a browser, of the title and URL of favourite pages or sites on the Web. It assists users to return quickly to the web page in a future session. It is sometimes called a 'hotlist'. (p. 38)

browser: a software application used on the Web that allows the user to navigate and view various Internet resources, move to other documents via hypertext, view images, listen to audio files, etc. (p. 5)

business-to-business (B2B): refers to companies doing business with other companies on public networks like the Internet and its derivations, extranets and intranets. Organisations benefit from having a common standard for information sharing and exchange. The outcome will mean shifting the business model from a supply chain to a supply web. (p. 29)

business-to-consumer (B2C): companies doing business with consumers (retail customers) on the Internet. (p. 29)

Buy-Side model: *see* eProcurement model. (p. 35)

censorship: the suppression of material in media, such as books, films, etc., that is deemed to be objectionable on moral, political, military or other grounds. (p. 243)

CERT (Computer Emergency Response Team): an overarching trusted point of contact for the Internet community to deal with computer security incidents and their prevention. (p. 152)

'click-through' advertising: advertising on a web page that takes an Internet user to the site of the advertiser. By clicking on the advertisement, the user is routed to the advertiser's URL. (p. 168)

COM (Component Object Model): Microsoft's building block approach to developing software applications. (p. 42)

common gateway interface (CGI): specifies a standard mechanism for a web server to communicate with a script or program running on the same server in order to pass data between them. (p. 62)

complaint resolution: the process by which businesses receive and process customer complaints (*see also* AS 4269). (p. 173)

compliance: ensuring that the population complies with a country's laws, such as those on taxation. (p. 217)

conference: using the Internet so that a group of people in different locations can hold interactive meetings. Cheap software, such as NetMeeting, enables people to see one another on screen and even collaborate using interactive electronic whiteboard software. (p. 16)

confidentiality: concerned with the notion that there is protection from intrusion, that no one can access the contents of data or information being sent and that no one can identify who is sending or receiving a message. (p. 138)

contract: an agreement between two or more parties creating obligations that are enforceable or otherwise recognisable at law. (p. 249)

cookies: files that a web server stores on a user's computer when a web site is visited. A cookie gathers information about the user. (p. 15)

copyright: the exclusive right, created by law, to make copies of, or otherwise control, a literary, musical, dramatic or artistic work for a certain number of years. Copyright is included in the all-embracing term 'intellectual property', which extends to industrial property providing protection to patents, inventions, trademarks and industrial designs. (p. 245)

corporate intranet: a business intelligence portal (BIP) or enterprise information portal (EIP). An EIP site may include a search engine covering the entire intranet, a taxonomy showing clearly what's available on the site, news sources, links to internal sites and popular external web sites and the ability to personalise the page. The EIP may help to provide a structure for data, turning information into knowledge for employees to use. (p. 276)

CPM (cost per thousand presentations model) advertising: the method of counting the number of clicks per thousand on any given advertisement. It is used to help establish advertising rates. (p. 168)

Cryptolope: IBM's trademark for its *crypto*graphic enve*lope* technology. Cryptolope objects are used for secure, protected delivery of digital content and can be compared to secure servers. Both use encryption to prevent eavesdroppers from stealing or interfering with content. Both use digital signatures to offer the end user a guarantee that the content is genuine. (p. 149)

customer: any recipient of information or products. For example, a customer can be a purchaser of a CD, the reader of a report or any other recipient of a product. (p. 164)

customer relations: occur when a supplier interacts with and seeks to enhance the relationship with a customer. (p. 170)

customer security: the integrity of the consumer's data transmission; for example, somebody stealing a customer's credit card details from the Internet. Customer security concerns differ from those of business proprietors. (p. 174)

CyberCash: a company (www.cybercash.com) that offers payment services for credit card, micropayment and Internet cheque transactions. CyberCash services credit cards securely over the Internet by linking storefronts with credit-card processors providing authorisations in real-time at the time of purchase. They also offer the CyberCoin® Service, which provides special tools to deliver information to the user, which can either be the content for which the user is paying or an electronic receipt that provides access for the user to get to the content elsewhere. This system is particularly useful for 'pay-per-view' areas, selling small programs and utilities online, and selling one-day passes to sites that otherwise require monthly subscriptions or 'pay-per-play' games. (p. 114)

cybercommunity: a virtual place where a group of individuals engaged in computer-mediated communication moves beyond the basic exchange of information into the formation of a community structure based on the exchange of shared goods of value. (p. 170)

cybercrime: an act, a failure to act or other conduct that is prejudicial to the community, rendering the person responsible liable to a fine or other punishment. (p. 255)

data integrity: refers to protection of data at all levels, from the operator (the human element) to the systems being used (browsers, networks, servers and communications infrastructure). (p. 142)

DCOM (Distributed Component Object Model): a Microsoft protocol that enables distributed software components to communicate over a network in a reliable and secure manner. DCOM serves a similar purpose to CORBA, but is restricted to Windows-based systems. (p. 42)

defamation: the publication of a false or derogatory statement about another person without lawful justification. (p. 250)

DigiCash: the company that markets eCash™, the Internet implementation of David Chaum's anonymous electronic cash system. The eCash™ system uses electronic tokens to exchange goods and services in an online environment. Banks are used to verify the value of the token. (p. 114)

disintermediation: the connecting of producers and consumers directly, cutting out the intermediaries such as wholesalers, distributors and retailers. (p. 287)

domain name: the part of the URL following the two forward slashes that identifies an Internet host site. (p. 7)

dot.com: dot.com companies (dot.coms) are those companies specifically formed to do business almost entirely on the Internet – i.e. they generally have no physical shop front or outlets, and they conduct business by trading information, services or products online. (p. 2)

e-Cash™**:** digital cash. (p. 114)

e-marketplace: industry-focused hub where buyers and sellers may communicate, collaborate and participate in all trade-related activities. (p. 273)

EDIFACT (Electronic Data Interchange for Administration, Commerce and Transport): a standard for EDI transactions. (p. 128)

electronic data interchange (EDI): computer-to-computer exchange of business information, such as orders and invoices, between customers and vendors. (pp. 57, 106)

electronic funds transfer (EFT): the exchange of money electronically, such as the electronic transfer of funds from one bank account to an account in another bank. (p. 123)

electronic funds transfer at point of sale (EFTPOS): the transfer of value electronically at the checkout in a shop or supermarket. (p. 111)

electronic payment system (EPS): information system designed to record, transfer, store and process data about goods and services purchased. (p. 106)

electronic purchasing: the use of any electronic technology to transact or buy goods, services or information. (p. 106)

email: an application that allows messages to be transmitted via data communications to electronic mailboxes. The text or multimedia messages are transmitted asynchronously. (p. 5)

encryption: the process of enabling information/data/knowledge to be coded in such a way that it cannot be read without a decoding system or key. (p. 146)

enterprise information portal (EIP): *see* corporate intranet. (p. 276)

enterprise resource planning (ERP) systems: business management systems that contain many diverse modules. The modules are integrated and work together to manage information that supports a business's daily activities. The common modules for an ERP system are accounting, human resources, financial, production and marketing. (p. 196)

eProcurement model (Buy-Side model): the use of the Internet to enable large-scale purchasing by organisations and the electronification of information such as that found in catalogues. (p. 35)

ethernet: a communications standard commonly used in local area networks for transmitting data among computers on a network. (p. 56)

ethics: a system of moral principles by which human actions or proposals may be judged good or bad or right or wrong. (p. 257)

extensible markup language (XML): a meta language – a language for defining other languages. It is used to define text markup so the text can be used and interpreted by different applications, including those that present information to people. XML allows developers to develop custom tags such as product-number, product-name, etc. XML will allow for rich searches and allow transaction-processing tasks to be implemented by browser and web server. XML, derived from SGML, retains SGML's power while reducing its complexity. Unlike HTML, XML allows the developer to create new tags that describe the data, and optionally create a set of rules called Document Type Definitions (DTDs). Any standard XML parser can read, decode and validate this text-based, self-describing document, extracting the data elements in a platform-independent way so that applications can access the data objects through yet another standard called Document Object Model (DOM). (pp. 5, 60)

extranet: a collaborative network that uses Internet technology to link businesses with their suppliers, customers or other businesses that share common goals. (pp. 12, 52)

extra-organisational communication: communication that occurs between members of an organisation and some external person. (p. 193)

fat client system: fully configured desktop computers with local storage, operating systems and peripherals. In these systems, data is most commonly centralised. However, applications are located on the desktop. (p. 72)

file transfer protocol (FTP): a communication protocol that is used to transmit files over the Internet. (pp. 5, 60)

firewalls: refers to both the software and hardware that stands between the Internet and a corporate network for security access control. (pp. 38, 152)

flat-fee advertising: occurs when a single set rate is billed for advertising (e.g. selling an advertisement at $100, regardless of how many times it is viewed). (p. 167)

flow state: the state of mind where interaction with the Internet becomes a unified movement from one site or event to the next with little or no awareness of distraction, outside influences or irrelevant thoughts. (p. 170)

fraud: obtaining material advantage by unfair or wrongful means. It involves the making of a false representation knowingly, without belief in its truth or recklessness. (p. 254)

fringe benefits tax: a tax on a non-salary component of a person's income. Some taxpayers seek to minimise their taxation burden by using flexible salary packages, sometimes known as 'salary sacrifice'. In such a case, a person might have their children's school fees paid directly to the school or their parking fees paid directly to the parking station. This money therefore does not appear as salary and lowers the taxpayer's tax burden. (p. 217)

global software team: a team that actively collaborates on a common software/systems project but that is separated by national or geological boundaries. (p. 185)

goods and services tax (GST): a tax on goods and services at a fixed rate; for example, adding 10–15 per cent to every meal served at a restaurant to raise revenue for the government. (p. 217)

Gopher: a menu-type program that helps users to locate and retrieve files on the Internet. (p. 30)

groupware: an application that allows many people to interact together. This software is often used to run virtual meetings. (p. 16)

hacker: someone who accesses a computer system without permission. (p. 138)

Horizontal Marketplace: hub providing products and services across a range of industries and streamlining e-commerce across the supply chain. (p. 36)

hotlink: a word, picture or feature highlighted within a document that triggers a link to another document, which may be located on another computer in some other location in the world. (p. 59)

hub: a central position from which everything radiates — it becomes the focus of activities, not just a gateway to pass through. (p. 273)

hypertext: software technology that allows for fast and flexible access to information. Users browse and retrieve information by following hotlinks rather than following a linear structure. (p. 5)

hypertext markup language (HTML): a page description language used to compose and format most of the content found on the Web. It defines hypertext links between documents. It is a subset of standardised general markup language (*see* standardised general markup language). (p. 5)

hypertext transfer protocol (HTTP): a multimedia transport protocol used in communications between browser clients and web host computers. (p. 5)

income tax: an aggregate tax, whereby the liability is arrived at by considering the aggregate result after adding up all items of assessable income and subtracting all allowable deductions. Income tax imposes a personal liability on the person who derives the income. Thus, personal identity is extremely important. In cases of a taxpayer defaulting on payment of income tax, the identity, whereabouts and financial position of the taxpayer are all relevant. (p. 216)

infomediary: a person or company who acts as an agent providing information, products and services. (p. 270)

intellectual property: an all-embracing term covering copyright, patents and trademarks. The term describes those rights that protect the product of a person's or corporation's work by hand or brain against unauthorised use or exploitation by others. (p. 245)

interactive mail access protocol (IMAP): allows for better control over the way messages are delivered. When a user connects to a mail host, the user is able to see a one-line summary of each message. This allows the user to selectively download the messages that the user wishes to receive. Selective deletion of email is also possible. (p. 190)

Internet: a network of computer networks. It allows public access to information on a huge number of subjects and allows users to send messages and obtain products and services. It works because there are agreed rules or protocols about how information is exchanged. (p. 2)

Internet2: a project to establish gigabit-per-second points of presence nationwide. Internet2 went live in late February 1999. (p. 288)

Internet protocol (IP): a set of traffic rules, procedures and standards designed to allow transmission of data and information. (p. 57)

Internet protocol television (IP/TV): a protocol that allows the delivery of full motion video to desktop PCs via existing Internet protocol data networks, instead of requiring dedicated video cable, monitors and viewing rooms (*see* www.precept.com). (p. 16)

Internet shopping mall: a collection of virtual businesses, each of which may pay some fee to the mall proprietor, who then markets the entire mall. The Internet shopping mall simply develops an economy of scale in marketing and other services. (p. 166)

intranet: a locally operated hypertext environment generally using TCP/IP architecture and services that is delivered to browser software on networked PCs and desktop workstations. It is just like the Internet, but can usually be accessed only from within an organisation. It is privately developed and operated within a business or organisation. (pp. 7, 52)

intra-organisational communication: communication that occurs within an organisation. (p. 188)

IT (information technology) audit: the systematic checking of all IT components in a business system. (p. 138)

Java: a programming language used as a software development tool for the Internet. (p. 72)

Java applets: programs written in the programming language, Java. The applets are downloaded to client machines. These applets then execute on a user's machine. (p. 38)

JavaBeans: a portable, platform-independent component model written in the Java programming language. JavaBeans's components are reusable software components that can be manipulated visually in a builder tool. (p. 72)

JavaScript: a scripting language originally developed by Netscape and now available on most browsers. Designed to coexist and interact with HTML source code, thus facilitating client-side tasks such as interactivity and validation of user-entered data. (p. 61)

joint application development (JAD): a process in which a group of users and/or team members interact, learn from one another and discuss problems for resolution. A structured workshop can be used to define requirements and design system externals. (p. 93)

jurisdiction: the power of a court or judge to hear an action, petition or other proceeding, and the district or limits within which the judgement or orders of a court can be enforced. (p. 249)

just-in-time (JIT): systematic management process for the delivery of component parts just in time for their use in a production process. (p. 106)

just-in-time (JIT) information: information that is timely and relevant. It is produced when it is needed, with little lead time. (p. 186)

knowledge exchange: information hub where knowledge workers may network and leverage the skills of experts and best-practice frameworks to deliver the best solution to their customers. (p. 274)

law: the body of rules which a state or community recognises as binding on its members or subjects. (p. 243)

legislation: the body of laws enacted by the legislature. (p. 243)

load-balancing techniques: allow an application to scale effectively by running across a number of processors and machines. (p. 41)

local area network (LAN): a networked group of computers, usually within an organisation, contained in a small geographic area such as a building. (p. 56)

meta tagging: refers to the technique whereby a word or words are incorporated into a site to increase the chances of a search engine returning the site. This tag, <META> part of the HEAD of an HTML document, provides information that describes the document in various ways. It contains valuable information for search robots to use in adding pages to their search indexes. It can also be used to search locally for similar files or files that need reviewing or updating. Information in each <META> tag is expressed as a NAME= and value= pair. The NAME can be used to distinguish one type of <META> statement from another. (p. 247)

middleware: software that operates between an application, such as a database or email program, and the transport layer that performs the services and hides the details of that layer. For example, in a database situation, a client program might send a request message, and the database middleware program passes the request to the database middleware on the server machine. This then puts the request in whatever format is needed to get the desired data. These programs are useful for linking database servers to traditional legacy database programs (e.g. written in COBOL). (p. 71)

money: unit of value used in exchange. (p. 106)

money laundering: the placing of money, gained by illegal means, such as from selling illicit drugs, into general circulation so that its origin cannot be traced. In Internet commerce, there is concern that it might be possible to launder money from criminal activities by shifting it electronically between different accounts and countries. (p. 211)

multipurpose Internet mail extensions (MIME): a TCP/IP standard used on the Internet to allow electronic mail headers and mail bodies to contain information other than plain text. It enables mail transfer in complex organisations. (p. 60)

Netscape: a computer software company that markets Internet and web software, such as Netscape Navigator and Netscape Communicator. (p. 16)

non-repudiation: a requirement that the sender and recipient of a message can validate their role in the transmission of data. (p. 149)

online auction: real-time or live auction bidding on the Internet. (p. 272)

Online Yellow Pages model: a web business model using menu systems to point to other sources and information. (p. 30)

open buying on the Internet (OBI): a standard and open, flexible design for B2B Internet commerce. It is intended for high-volume, low-dollar transactions that account for 80 per cent of most organisations' purchasing activities (*see* www.openbuy.org). (p. 129)

paradigm: the third new P of marketing. It is a pattern example or a model way of doing things. (p. 86)

paradox: the first new P of marketing. It is a statement or proposition which, on the face of it, seems self-contradictory, absurd and at variance with common sense, but which upon investigation may prove to be well founded or essentially true. (p. 84)

passion: the fifth new P of marketing. Cybermarketers must be passionate about their Internet commerce site. The Internet is an exciting communication channel and the web site business needs to persuade the consumer to visit the web site. (p. 87)

patents: refers to government grants to inventors granting them the sole right to make use of and sell such inventions for a limited time. (p. 246)

peer-to-peer (P2P) computing: communication model whereby all parties in the network have the same capabilities and a 'peer' in the network may act as a client or server at any one time. (p. 282)

peer-to-peer (P2P) networks: on the Internet, a peer-to-peer (P2P) network is a type of transient Internet network that allows a group of computer users with the same networking program to connect with each other and directly access files from one another's hard drives. (p. 11)

Peer-to-Peer (P2P) Networking model: model whereby all parties in the network have the same capabilities and 'peer' in the network may act as a client or server at any one time. (p. 37)

Performance and Assessment Results 4 (PAR4): software that maintains a record of key performance indicators and is used by managers in conducting performance appraisals of employees. (p. 191)

personalisation: the act of recognising a customer or visitor to a web site and modifying content and behaviour to make the experience relevant to that individual. (p. 272)

personal digital assistants (PDAs): hand-held computers, often supporting personal information management (PIM) applications. (p. 10)

perspective: the second new P of marketing. It is vital to view the products from the consumer's perspective. The cyberbusiness must determine those consumer requirements the product or service satisfies and how it satisfies those requirements differently and better than its competitors. (p. 86)

persuasion: the fourth new P of marketing. All businesses try to persuade people to buy their product or service. As Internet commerce is a new medium, companies are attempting different ways to persuade people to their site and get them to buy. To master persuasion, it is essential to concentrate on credibility, content and involvement of the listener. (p. 87)

point-to-point protocol (PPP): a protocol that provides a method for transmitting packets over serial point-to-point links. It is a standard for telephone modem communication between a user's personal computer and an Internet service provider (ISP). (p. 57)

portals: web sites designed to offer a variety of Internet services from a single convenient location. The goal of the portal is to be designated as your browser's start-up page. Most portals offer certain free services such as: a search engine; local, national and worldwide news, sports and weather; references such as *Yellow Pages* and maps; shopping malls; email and chat rooms. (pp. 68, 271)

Portal model: a business model where a web site is designed to offer a variety of Internet services from a single convenient location (*see also* portals). (p. 34)

post office protocol (POP): a TCP/IP protocol used in electronic mail that allows users working on intelligent devices such as personal computers to do a lot of work on local devices. POP may also refer to 'point of presence', which is a site with a collection of telecommunications equipment, usually digital-leased lines and multi-protocol routers. (p. 57)

privacy: the right to not have one's private life intruded upon or unjustifiably brought into the public arena. The issue of privacy is imperfectly recognised in many legal systems. (p. 243)

Procurement Marketplace model: marketplace allowing many buyers and suppliers to form relationships and trade online. (p. 35)

protocol: a set of traffic rules, procedures and standards designed to allow transmission of data and information. (p. 52)

prototype: working model of proposed system. (p. 93)

proxy: a small program that is able to read messages on both sides of a firewall. (p. 154)

publish–subscribe system: enables information producers (publishers) to disseminate relevant, high-value information to consumers (subscribers) via a P2P network. This is a communication infrastructure that enables data access and sharing over disparate systems and among inconsistent data models. (p. 74)

rapid application development (RAD): development of software throughout the system development process. A common approach in RAD is prototyping, which is the development of a working model of the proposed system. (p. 93)

Reverse Auction model: a business model whereby bidders set their price for items such as airline tickets or hotel rooms and sellers decide whether to supply the items. This model was originally set up by Priceline.com (*see* www.priceline.com). (p. 33)

sales tax: an example of transaction tax, whereby liability results from an imposed tax on particular types of transactions. For example, a consumer buying a car is subject to a sales tax on that car and the advantage for the government is that the car dealer collects the tax. (p. 216)

search engine: a program that gathers and sorts through information on the Web. (p. 65)

Secure Electronic Transaction (SET): encrypted data transmission, which allows financial transactions to occur. SET is used by banks to engage in financial transactions with customers via the Internet. (p. 175)

security: protection of information systems and operating systems from illegal or unauthorised interference. (p. 138)

Sell-Side model: *see* Virtual Storefront model. (p. 34)

server: a special purpose device within a LAN that performs a specific function. For example, the file server will provide access to the shared files for all LAN users. The file server is usually a computer that has no other function in the network. (p. 5)

server security: refers to keeping network servers safe from attack. The servers normally store various software packages that enable mail, FTP, news groups, network operating systems, the Web, CGI scripts and Telnet. Security checks must be done on a network's server and regular tests made on its operation and on the security of each of the component software packages it operates. This involves not only implementation of a security policy and security audit, but also the use of additional features to ensure screening and repetitive testing. (p. 152)

simple mail transfer protocol (SMTP): a TCP/IP protocol used on the Internet to deliver messages between electronic mail hosts and to specify message structure. (p. 60)

smart card: a credit-sized card containing a computer chip that is capable of receiving, processing, storing and transmitting monetary information. (p. 108)

standard generalised markup language (SGML): a protocol that defines documents in a plain text using tags that are embedded in the text to specify the definition. (p. 59)

stored value card (SVC): a card that stores information about value and can be used in exchange for goods and services. (p. 118)

structured query language (SQL): a standard fourth-generation language for relational database systems. (p. 71)

Subscription model: an Internet commerce business model that has been borrowed from publishing. Just as a consumer might subscribe to a monthly or weekly magazine, so too a consumer is able to subscribe to an online version of such a magazine or any product with updated versions offered on an ongoing basis. (p. 31)

supply chain: description of the structure and/or process used in bringing together components in a production process. It is simply the staged process of sourcing, producing and distributing goods and services. (p. 193)

target advertisement: an advertisement that users can click on and be automatically directed to the web page belonging to the advertiser. For example, by clicking on an advertisement of IBM e-commerce on the Web Wombat site, the Internet user would be redirected automatically to IBM's web site. (p. 167)

tax avoidance: refers to schemes to lower the taxation burden, such as moving money offshore. In Internet commerce, the key issue will be the extent to which the Internet will allow business activities to be undetectable or anonymous, so that the taxing and auditing requirements of the existence and identity of persons or transactions cannot be determined. The migration of businesses to the Internet may be partially driven by the tax avoidance and evasion opportunities it presents. (p. 211)

tax evasion: refers to activities, generally illegal, aimed at ensuring that tax is not paid. A high level of non-detection could lead to tax evasion in a highly competitive global business environment where businesses may be forced to adopt non-compliance facilities to compete with other businesses, thus exacerbating non-compliance (*see* tax avoidance). (p. 211)

tax neutrality: a concept that rejects the imposition of new or additional taxes on electronic transactions. Neutrality requires that the tax system treat similar income equally, regardless of whether it is earned through electronic or existing means. (p. 210)

teleworking: refers to an employment situation where employees are able to work from home rather than at the usual workplace. The use of information technology and improved telecommunications make this a feasible option for employees. It is sometimes called telecommuting. (p. 185)

templates: style sheets containing such information as font, style, spacing, formatting information and possibly text that might always be used such as headings and titles. Such templates may be useful in defining the layout of a commercial web page. (p. 90)

thin client system: a user interface where most of the computing is done on a powerful back-end server. (p. 72)

3.5.7 model: an Internet commerce business model that lays the foundation for commercial success by focusing on using the Internet as a business communication tool. It advocates three steps to a better focus, a five-dimensional strategy and a seven-point tactical guide for doing business on the Internet. (p. 32)

TRADACOMS: a protocol or standard for EDI transactions. (p. 128)

trademarks: refers to signs used, or intended to be used, to distinguish goods or services provided in the course of trade by a person from goods or services provided by any other person. These signs could be letters, words, names, signatures, numbers, devices, brands and even a smell or scent. (p. 247)

transmission control protocol/Internet protocol (TCP/IP): a set of commands and communication protocols used by the Internet to connect dissimilar systems and control the flow of information. This protocol allows users of the Internet to find information, use email, interact with other businesses, find personal details of people who have developed their own home pages, exchange business information and data, or download software from the Internet. (p. 54)

uniform resource locator (URL): the defining terminology that identifies other web sites and specific web pages. A URL is a means of specifying a resource by incorporating the protocol, machine address, path and filename. (p. 6)

unified modelling language (UML): a standard notation for the modelling of real-world objects as a first step in developing an object-oriented design methodology. Its notation is derived from and unifies the notations of three object-oriented design and analysis methodologies. (p. 93)

value-added network (VAN): an online service that provides proprietary software to communicate with firms registered with the service. (p. 125)

value trust network (VTN): provides the complete solution to a customer by combining transactional capability, value-added services and knowledge exchange. (p. 274)

Vertical Marketplace: brings industry-specific buyers and sellers together to trade. (p. 35)

very-high-speed backbone network service (VBNS): a spine or backbone that allows very-high-speed interaction for the next-generation Internet. (p. 63)

virtual private network (VPN): utilises a public network, such as the Internet, to transmit private data. VPNs are an emerging form of extranet implementation that may become a viable replacement for traditional wide area networks (WANs). (p. 275)

virtual reality modelling language (VRML): a language that allows graphical representations and models generated by computers to be broken into smaller components and transmitted across the Internet. (p. 73)

Virtual Storefront model (Sell-Side model): a full information service designed to include the marketing of a business's services, products, online purchasing and customer support on the Internet. (p. 34)

virtual wallet software: an electronic storage of 'virtual cash' or financial credit. A user places an amount of money or credit in their virtual wallet, and deducts specified amounts in financial transactions. (p. 175)

virus: a program written with malicious intent that is loaded into the computer system of an unsuspecting victim. It normally tries to destroy or interfere with the running of other programs or applications on the host computer and aims to spread through multiple computer systems. (p. 143)

vortal: a vertical portal, providing information and services relevant to a specific target audience. (p. 271)

wireless application protocol (WAP): an industry open standard to facilitate the easy access to information by handset users. It was engineered with the low bandwidth of current mobile technology, which uses small monochrome screens. WAP is a specification for a set of communication protocols to standardise the way that wireless devices, such as cellular telephones and radio transceivers, can be used for Internet access, including email, the Web, newsgroups and Internet Relay Chat (IRC). While Internet access has been possible in the past, different manufacturers have used different technologies. In the future, devices and service systems that use WAP will be able to interoperate. The WAP layers are: wireless application environment (WAE), wireless session layer (WSL), wireless transport layer security (WTLS) and wireless transport layer (WTP). The WAP was conceived by four companies: Ericsson, Motorola, Nokia and Unwired Planet (now Phone.com). IEEE 802.11 is emerging as the standard for wireless LANs. Bluetooth technology will enable many different devices to share information seamlessly. (p. 10)

wizards: specialised applications that reduce the complexity of using an application. For example, Sofcom has wizards that enable novices to design commercial web pages. (p. 39)

World Wide Web (the Web): a graphical hypertext environment that operates within the Internet. It contains a collection of distributed documents, referred to as 'pages', located on computers all over the world. (p. 5)

worm: a malicious program designed to corrupt an information system or operating system. The worm propagates and exists independently. It does not have to attach to another program or part of the operating system to propagate, unlike a virus. (p. 143)

X.25 protocol: an international standard for connecting devices to a packet-switching network. (p. 127)

X.400 protocol: a family of open systems interconnection (OSI) protocols used to deliver messages between electronic mail hosts and to specify message structure. (p. 128)

X.500 protocol: a standard that describes how to create a directory containing all the electronic mail users' names and their addresses. (p. 128)

INDEX

e-business leaders   2, 3
e-commerce *see* Internet commerce
e-commerce software overview   95–6
e-commerce web sites
  developmental methodologies   93–5
  steps in building   94–5
e-marketplace design success factors   41–2
e-marketplace models   35–6
e-marketplaces   273–4
e-metrics   268
e-readiness rankings of countries   2–4
e-tax for Australian individuals lodging income
    tax returns, case study   235–8
eCash™   114
EDIFACT   128
EFTPOS   111–12, 123
electronic cheques   112–13
electronic commerce *see* Internet commerce
electronic data interchange (EDI)   7, 57, 106,
    123–9
  communication channels   124–7
  Internet   129–30
  standards   127–8
  traditional   124
    benefits of   128
    shortcomings of   129
electronic funds transfer (EFT)   123
electronic funds transfer at point of sale
    (EFTPOS)   111–12, 123
electronic payment systems (EPS)   106
  B2B   123–9
  B2C   108–23
  transition from traditional payment methods
      106–8
electronic purchasing   106
electronic shopping agents   96
electronic tax pack   231
Electronic Transactions Act 1999   253
electronic wallets   113
email   5, 188–90
  and privacy   255–7
emerging technologies   289
employment
  disintermediation   287
  e-commerce effects   286–8
  outsourcing   287
  reintermediation   288
encryption   146
  and codes to restrict access   148
  and security writing   147

enterprise information portals (EIP)   276–8
enterprise resource planning (ERP) systems
    196–7
  customer relationship management   197–8
eProcurement model   35
ethernet   56
ethics   257–8
European Union, tax implications of Internet
    commerce   225–7
explicit personalisation   272
extensible markup language (XML)   5–6, 60,
    278–9
extra-organisational communication   193–6
  recruiting employees   195–6
  supply chain   193–5
extranets   12, 52, 53–4, 187

F

fat client system   72
file transfer protocol (FTP)   5, 60
firewalls   38, 70, 152–4
flat-fee advertising   167
flow state   170
four T's of database marketing   174
fraud   254
fringe benefits tax   217
fundamental models   30–4

G

gambling   220–2
global access   169
global communication issues   199–201
global hypertext publishing with HTML and
    HTTP   59–61
Global Positioning System (GPS)   281
global software teams   185–6
glossary   308–24
goods and services tax (GST)   14, 217
Gopher   30
government role in Internet commerce   283–4
  Business Entry Point   284–5
  United States and e-commerce   285–6
government-to-business (G2B)   14
government-to-consumer (G2C)   14
government-to-government (G2G)   13–14
graphical browsers as front-end interfaces
    192–3
groupware   16

self-representation 170
Sell-Side model 34–5
SEPP 115
server 5
server security 152–3
service-selling sites 97
service technologies 280
SGML 59
shopping experience issues 17
simple mail transfer protocol (SMTP) 60
smart cards 108, 118–23
software filters 244–5
spamming 256
specifying access 147
specifying user names and passwords 147–8
stakeholders in Internet commerce 19
standard generalised markup language (SGML) 59
standards issues 17
stored value cards (SVCs) 108, 118–23
 advantages and risks in business 122–3
 types of 121–2
strategic competitive advantage 14
strategic planning, implementing the business models 37–8
structured query language (SQL) 71
STT 115
Subscription model 31
superconductivity 289
supply chain 193–5

T

tailoring 174
tapping 174
target advertisements 167
targeting 174
tax avoidance 211
tax evasion 211
tax implications of Internet commerce 216–17
 international cooperation 229–30
 international response 222–9
 role of cypherpunks 230
tax neutrality 210
taxation
 and Australia 216
 and online banking 231
 and the Internet 210–11
 e-tax for Australian individuals lodging income tax returns, case study 235–8

taxes on Internet purchases and income generated by Internet purchases
 businesses 217–18
 consumers 218–19
 digitised goods 220
 Internet gambling 220–2
TCP/IP 54, 60
telecommunication infrastructure of Internet 55
Telecommunications Industry Ombudsman 244
tele-immersion 289
teleworking 185–6, 198–9
templates 90
theory of creative destruction 8–9
thin client system 72
3.5.7 model 32–3
TRADACOMS 128
Trade Practices Act 1974 (Cwlth) 253
trademarks 247–8
translation check 151
transmission control protocol/Internet protocol (TCP/IP) 54, 60
transmitting voice traffic 74
trojans 70
tying 174

U

U-commerce 268
ubiquity 9–10, 267, 268
unified modelling language (UML) 93
uniform resource locators (URLs) 6, 61
United States, tax implications of Internet commerce 223–5
United States government, and e-commerce 285–6
US National Tax Associations Electronic Commerce Taxation Project 224–5
user-friendly interface (to Web) 65
user names and password specification 147–8
utility 169

V

value-added networks (VANs) 125–7
value trust networks (VTNs) 274–5
Vertical Marketplace model 35–6
 using 40–2
very-high-speed backbone network service (VBNS) 63
virtual credit cards 111
virtual private network (VPN) 275–6